OUTLINES OF INDIAN PHILOSOPHY

BY THE SAME AUTHOR

ESSENTIALS OF INDIAN PHILOSOPHY

OUTLINES OF INDIAN PHILOSOPHY

by

M. HIRIYANNA, M.A.

Formerly Professor of Sanskrit, Maharaja's College, Mysore

London

GEORGE ALLEN & UNWIN LTD

RUSKIN HOUSE . MUSEUM STREET

First published in 1932

Tenth impression 1975

ISBN 0 04 181008 2

Printed in Great Britain
by Lewis Reprints Ltd.
member of Brown Knight & Truscott Group
London and Tonbridge

PREFACE

THIS work is based upon the lectures which I delivered for many years at the Mysore University and is published with the intention that it may serve as a text-book for use in colleges where Indian philosophy is taught. Though primarily intended for students, it is hoped that the book may also be of use to others who are interested in the Indian solutions of familiar philosophical problems. Its foremost aim has been to give a connected and, so far as possible within the limits of a single volume, a comprehensive account of the subject; but interpretation and criticism, it will be seen, are not excluded. After an introductory chapter summarizing its distinctive features, Indian thought is considered in detail in three Parts dealing respectively with the Vedic period, the early post-Vedic period and the age of the systems; and the account given of the several doctrines in each Part generally includes a brief historical survey in addition to an exposition of its theory of knowledge, ontology and practical teaching. Of these, the problem of knowledge is as a rule treated in two sections, one devoted to its psychological and the other to its logical aspect. In the preparation of the book, I have made use of the standard works on the subject published in recent times; but, except in two or three chapters (e.g. that on early Buddhism), the views expressed are almost entirely based upon an independent study of the original sources. My indebtedness to the works consulted is, I trust, adequately indicated in the footnotes. It was not possible to leave out Sanskrit terms from the text altogether; but they have been sparingly used and will present no difficulty if the book is read from the beginning and their explanations noted as they are given. To facilitate reference, the number of the page on which a technical expression or an unfamiliar idea is first mentioned is added within brackets whenever it is alluded to in a later portion of the book.

There are two points to which it is necessary to draw attention in order to avoid misapprehension. The view taken here of the Mādhyamika school of Buddhism is that it is pure nihilism, but some are of opinion that it implies a positive conception of reality. The determination of this question from Buddhistic sources is difficult, the more so as philosophic considerations become mixed with historical ones. Whatever the fact, the negative character of its teaching is vouched for by the entire body of Hindu and Jaina works stretching back to times when Buddhism was still a power in the land of its birth. The natural conclusion to be drawn from such a consensus of opinion is that, in at least one important stage of its development in India, the Mādhyamika doctrine *was* nihilistic; and it was not considered inappropriate in a book on Indian philosophy to give prominence to this aspect of it. The second point is the absence of any account of the Dvaita school of Vedāntic philosophy. The Vedānta is twofold. It is either absolutistic or theistic, each of which again exhibits many forms. Anything like a complete treatment of its many-sided teaching being out of the question here, only two examples have been chosen—one, the Advaita of Śaṁkara, to illustrate Vedāntic absolutism, and the other, the Viśiṣṭādvaita of Rāmānuja, to illustrate Vedāntic theism.

I have, in conclusion, to express my deep gratitude to Sir S. Radhakrishnan, Vice-Chancellor of the Andhra University, who has throughout taken a very kindly and helpful interest in this work, and to Mr. D. Venkataramiah of Bangalore, who has read the whole book and suggested various improvements.

M. H.

August 1932

CONTENTS

ABBREVIATIONS

ADS. Āpastamba-dharma-sūtra (Mysore Oriental Library Edn.).
AV. Atharva-veda.
BG. Bhagavadgītā.
BP. Buddhistic Philosophy by Prof. A. B. Keith (Camb. Univ. Press).
Bṛ.Up. Bṛhadāraṇyaka Upaniṣad.
BUV. Bṛhadāraṇyakopaniṣad-vārtika by Sureśvara.
Ch.Up. Chāndogya Upaniṣad.
EI. Ethics of India by Prof. E. W. Hopkins.
ERE. Encyclopaedia of Religion and Ethics.
GDS. Gautama-dharma-sūtra (Mysore Oriental Library Edn.).
IP. Indian Philosophy by Prof. S. Radhakrishnan: 2 vols.
JAOS. Journal of the American Oriental Society.
Mbh. Mahābhārata.
NM. Nyāya-mañjarī by Jayanta Bhaṭṭa (Vizianagaram Sans. Series).
NS. Nyāya-sūtra of Gautama (Vizianagaram Sans. Series).
NSB. Nyāya-sūtra-bhāṣya by Vātsyāyana (Vizianagaram Sans. Series).
NV. Nyāya-vārtika by Uddyotakara (Chowkhamba Series).
OJ. Outlines of Jainism by J. Jaini (Camb. Univ. Press).
OST. Original Sanskrit Texts by J. Muir. 5 vols.
PB. Vaiśeṣika-sūtra-bhāṣya by Praśastapāda (Vizianagaram Sans. Series).
PP. Prakaraṇa-pañcikā by Śalikanātha (Chowkhamba Series).
PU. Philosophy of the Upaniṣads by P. Deussen: Translated into English by A. S. Geden.
Rel.V. Religion of the Veda by Maurice Bloomfield.
RV. Ṛgveda.
SAS. Sarvārtha-siddhi with Tattva-muktā-kalāpa by Vedānta Deśika (Chowkhamba Series).
SB. Śrī-bhāṣya by Rāmānuja with Śruta-prakāśikā: Sūtras 1–4. (Nirṇaya Sāg. Pr.).
SBE. Sacred Books of the East.

SD. Śāstra-dīpikā by Pārthasārathi Miśra with Yukti-sneha-prapūraṇī (Nirṇaya Sāg. Pr.).

SDS. Sarva-darśana-saṁgraha by Mādhava (Calcutta), 1889.

SK. Sāṅkhya-kārikā by Īśvarakṛṣṇa.

SLS. Siddhānta-leśa-saṁgraha by Appaya Dīkṣita (Kumbhakonam Edn.).

SM. Siddhānta-muktāvalī with Kārikāvalī by Viśvanātha: (Nirṇaya Sāg. Pr.), 1916.

SP. Sāṅkhya-pravacana-sūtra.

SPB. Sāṅkhya-pravacana-bhāṣya by Vijñāna Bhikṣu.

SS. Six Systems of Indian Philosophy by F. Max Müller (Collected Works, vol. XIX).

STK. Sāṅkhya-tattva-kaumudī by Vācaspati Miśra.

SV. Śloka-vārtika by Kumārila Bhaṭṭa (Chowkhamba Series).

TS. Tarka-saṁgraha by Annaṁbhaṭṭa (Bombay Sanskrit Series).

TSD. Tarka-saṁgraha-dīpikā (Bombay Sanskrit Series).

VAS. Vedārtha-saṁgraha by Rāmānuja with Tātparya-dīpikā. (Chowkhamba Series), 1894.

VP. Vedānta-paribhāṣā by Dharmarāja Adhvarīndra (Veṅkateśvara Press, Bombay).

VS. Vedānta-sūtra by Bādarāyaṇa.

YS. Yoga-sūtra by Patañjali.

YSB. Yoga-sūtra-bhāṣya by Vyāsa.

INTRODUCTION

The beginnings of Indian philosophy take us very far back indeed, for we can clearly trace them in the hymns of the Ṛgveda which were composed by the Aryans not long after they had settled in their new home about the middle of the second millennium before Christ. The speculative activity begun so early was continued till a century or two ago, so that the history that we have to narrate in the following pages covers a period of over thirty centuries. During this long period, Indian thought developed practically unaffected by outside influence; and the extent as well as the importance of its achievements will be evident when we mention that it has evolved several systems of philosophy, besides creating a great national religion—Brahminism, and a great world religion—Buddhism. The history of so unique a development, if it could be written in full, would be of immense value; but our knowledge at present of early India, in spite of the remarkable results achieved by modern research, is too meagre and imperfect for it. Not only can we not trace the growth of single philosophic ideas step by step; we are sometimes unable to determine the relation even between one system and another. Thus it remains a moot question to this day whether the Sāṅkhya represents an original doctrine or is only derived from some other. This deficiency is due as much to our ignorance of significant details as to an almost total lack of exact chronology in early Indian history. The only date that can be claimed to have been settled in the first one thousand years of it, for example, is that of the death of Buddha, which occurred in 487 B.C. Even the dates we know in the subsequent portion of it are for the most part conjectural, so that the very limits of the periods under which we propose to treat of our subject are to be regarded as tentative. Accordingly our account, it will be seen, is characterized by a certain looseness of perspective. In this connection we may also perhaps refer to another of its drawbacks which is sure to strike a student who is familiar with *Histories* of European philosophy. Our account will for the most part be devoid of references to the lives or character of the great thinkers with whose teaching it is concerned, for very little of them is now known. Speaking of Udayana, an eminent Nyāya thinker, Cowell wrote:[1] 'He shines like one of the fixed stars in India's literary firmament, but no telescope can discover any appreciable diameter; his name is a *point* of light, but we can detect therein nothing that belongs to our earth or material existence.' That description applies virtually to all who were responsible for the development of Indian thought; and even a great teacher like Śaṁkara is to us now hardly more than a name. It has been suggested[2] that this indifference on the part of the ancient Indians towards the personal histories of their great men was due to a realization by them that individuals are but the product of their times—'that they grow from a soil that is ready-made for them and breathe an intellectual atmosphere which is not of their own making.' It was perhaps not less the result of the humble sense which those great men had of themselves. But whatever the reason, we shall miss in our account the biographical background and all the added interest which it signifies.

If we take the date given above as a landmark, we may divide the history of Indian thought into two stages. It marks the close of the Vedic period[3] and the beginning of what is known as the Sanskrit or classical period. To the former belong the numerous works that are regarded by the Hindus as revealed. These works, which in extent have been compared to 'what survives of the writings of ancient Greece,' were collected in the latter part of the period. If we overlook the changes that should have crept into them before they were thus brought together, they have been

[1] Introduction to *Kusumāñjali* (Eng. Translation), pp. v and vi.

[2] SS. p. 2.

[3] It is usual to state the lower limit of the Vedic period as 200 B.C., including within it works which, though not regarded as 'revealed' (śruti), are yet exclusively concerned with the elucidation of revealed texts. We are here confining the term strictly to the period in which Vedic works appeared.

preserved, owing mainly to the fact that they were held sacred, with remarkable accuracy; and they are consequently far more authentic than any work of such antiquity can be expected to be. But the collection, because it was made chiefly, as we shall see, for ritualistic purposes, is incomplete and therefore fails to give us a full insight into the character of the thoughts and beliefs that existed then. The works appear in it arranged in a way, but the arrangement is not such as would be of use to us here; and the collection is from our present standpoint to be viewed as lacking in system. As regards the second period, we possess a yet more extensive literature; and, since new manuscripts continue to be discovered, additions to it are still being made. The information it furnishes is accordingly fuller and more diverse. Much of this material also appears in a systematized form. But this literature cannot always be considered quite as authentic as the earlier one, for in the course of long oral transmission, which was once the recognized mode of handing down knowledge, many of the old treatises have received additions or been amended while they have retained their original titles. The systematic treatises among them even in their original form, do not carry us back to the beginning of the period. Some of them are undoubtedly very old, but even they are not as old as 500 B.C., to state that limit in round numbers. It means that the post-Vedic period is itself to be split up into two stages. If for the purpose of this book we designate the later of them as 'the age of the systems,' we are left with an intervening period which for want of a better title may be described as 'the early post-Vedic period.' Its duration is not precisely determinable, but it lasted sufficiently long—from 500 B.C. to about the beginning of the Christian era—to be viewed as a distinct stage in the growth of Indian thought. It marks a transition and its literature, as may be expected, partakes of the character of the literatures of the preceding and of the succeeding periods. While it is many-sided and not fully authentic like its successor, it is unsystematized like its predecessor.

Leaving the details of our subject, so far as they fall within the scope of this work, to be recounted in the following chapters, we may devote the present to a general survey of it. A striking characteristic of Indian thought is its richness and variety. There is practically no shade of speculation which it does not include. This is a matter that is often lost sight of by its present-day critic who is fond of applying to it sweeping epithets like 'negative' and 'pessimistic' which, though not incorrect so far as some of its phases are concerned, are altogether misleading as descriptions of it as a whole. There is, as will become clear when we study our subject in its several stages of growth, no lack of emphasis on the reality of the external world or on the optimistic view of life understood in its larger sense. The misconception is largely due to the partial knowledge of Indian thought which hitherto prevailed; for it was not till recently that works on Indian philosophy, which deal with it in anything like a comprehensive manner, were published. The schools of thought familiarly known till then were only a few; and even in their case, it was forgotten that they do not stand for a uniform doctrine throughout their history, but exhibit important modifications rendering such wholesale descriptions of them inaccurate. The fact is that Indian thought exhibits such a diversity of development that it does not admit of a rough-and-ready characterization. Underlying this varied development, there are two divergent currents clearly discernible—one having its source in the Veda and the other, independent of it. We might describe them as orthodox and heterodox respectively, provided we remember that these terms are only relative and that either school may designate the other as heterodox, claiming for itself the 'halo of orthodoxy.' The second of these currents is the later, for it commences as a reaction against the first; but it is not much later since it manifests itself quite early as shown by references to it even in the Vedic hymns. It appears originally as critical and negative; but it begins before long to develop a constructive side which is of great consequence in the history of Indian philosophy. Broadly speaking, it is pessimistic and realistic. The other doctrine cannot be described thus briefly, for even in its earliest recorded phase it presents a very complex character. While for example the prevailing spirit of the songs included in the Ṛgveda is optimistic, there is sometimes a note of sadness in them as in those addressed to the goddess of Dawn (Uṣas), which pointedly refer to the way in which she cuts short the little lives of men. 'Obeying the behests of the gods, but wasting away the lives of mortals, Uṣas has shone forth—the last of many former dawns and the first of those that are yet to come.'[1] The characteristic marks of the two currents are, however, now largely obliterated owing to the assimilation or appropriation of the doctrines of each by the other during a long period of contact; but the distinction itself has not disappeared and can be seen in the Vedānta and Jainism, both of which are still living creeds.

These two types of thought, though distinct in their origin and general spirit, exhibit certain common features. We shall dwell at some length upon them, as they form the basic principles of Indian philosophy considered as a whole:—

(i) The first of them has in recent times become the subject of a somewhat commonplace observation, viz. that religion and philosophy do not stand sundered in India. They indeed begin as one everywhere, for their purpose is in the last resort the same, viz. a seeking for the central meaning of existence. But soon they separate and develop on more or less different lines. In India also the differentiation takes place, but only it does not mean divorce. This result has in all probability been helped by the isolated development of Indian thought already referred to,[2] and has generally been recognized as a striking excellence of it. But owing to the vagueness of the word 'religion,' we may easily miss the exact significance of the observation. This word, as it is well known, may stand for anything ranging from what has been described as 'a sum of scruples which impede

[1] Cf. RV. I. 124. 2.

[2] We may perhaps instance as a contrast the course which thought has taken in Europe, where the tradition of classical culture, which is essentially Indo-European, has mingled with a Semitic creed. Mrs. Rhys Davids speaks of science, philosophy and religion as being 'in an armed truce' in the West. See *Buddhism* (Home University Library), p. 100.

the free use of our faculties' to a yearning of the human spirit for union with God. It is no praise to any philosophy to be associated with religion in the former sense. Besides, some Indian doctrines are not religion at all in the commonly accepted sense. For example, early Buddhism was avowedly atheistic and it did not recognize any permanent spirit. Yet the statement that religion and philosophy have been one in India is apparently intended to be applicable to all the doctrines. So it is necessary to find out in what sense of the word the observation in question is true. Whatever else a religion may or may not be, it is essentially a reaching forward to an ideal, without resting in mere belief or outward observances. Its distinctive mark is that it serves to further right living; and it is only in this sense that we can speak of religion as one with philosophy in India.[1] The ancient Indian did not stop short at the discovery of truth, but strove to realize it in his own experience. He followed up tattva-jñāna, as it is termed, by a strenuous effort to attain mokṣa or liberation,[2] which therefore, and not merely an intellectual conviction, was in his view the real goal of philosophy. In the words of Max Muller, philosophy was recommended in India 'not for the sake of knowledge, but for the highest purpose that man can strive after in this life.'[3] The conception of mokṣa varies from system to system; but it marks, according to all, the culmination of philosophic culture. In other words, Indian philosophy aims beyond Logic. This peculiarity of the view-point is to be ascribed to the fact that philosophy in India did not take its rise in wonder or curiosity as it seems to have done in the West; rather it originated under the pressure of a practical need arising from the presence of moral and physical evil in life. It is the problem of how to remove this evil that troubled the ancient Indian most, and mokṣa in all the systems represents a state in which it is, in one sense or another, taken to have been overcome. Philosophic endeavour was directed primarily

[1] Indian philosophy may show alliance with religion in other senses also, but such alliance does not form a common characteristic of *all* the doctrines.

[2] Cf. NS. I. i. 1.

[3] SS. p. 370.

to find a remedy for the ills of life, and the consideration of metaphysical questions came in as a matter of course. This is clearly indicated for instance by the designation —sometimes applied to the founders of the several schools —of 'Tīrtha-kara' or 'Tīrthaṁ-kara,' which literally means 'ford-maker' and signifies one that has discovered the way to the other shore across the troubled ocean of saṁsāra.

But it may be thought that the idea of mokṣa, being eschatological, rests on mere speculation and that, though it may be regarded as the goal of faith, it can hardly be represented as that of philosophy. Really, however, there is no ground for thinking so, for, thanks to the constant presence in the Indian mind of a positivistic standard, the mokṣa ideal, even in those schools in which it was not so from the outset, speedily came to be conceived as realizable in this life, and described as jīvan-mukti, or emancipation while yet alive. It still remained, no doubt, a distant ideal; but what is important to note is that it ceased to be regarded as something to be reached in a life beyond. Man's aim was no longer represented as the attainment of perfection in a hypothetical hereafter, but as a continual progress towards it within the limits of the present life. Even in the case of doctrines like the Nyāya-Vaiśeṣika[1] or the Viśiṣṭādvaita[2] which do not formally accept the jīvan-mukti ideal, there is clearly recognized the possibility of man reaching here a state of enlightenment which may justifiably be so described because it completely transforms his outlook upon the world and fills with an altogether new significance the life he thereafter leads in it. Such an ideal was already part and parcel of a very influential doctrine in the latter part of the Vedic period, for it is found in the Upaniṣads. One of these ancient treatises says; 'When all the desires the heart harbours are gone, man becomes immortal and reaches Brahman *here*.'[3] It points beyond intellectual satisfaction, which is often mistaken to be the aim of philosophy, and yet by keeping within the bounds of possible human experience avoids the dogma of mokṣa in the

[1] See NSB. IV. ii. 2; NV. I. i. 1. *ad finem*.

[2] See SB. IV. i. 13.

[3] *Kaṭha Up*. II. iii. 14.

eschatological sense. The latter view also, known as videha-mukti, has survived, but it is a relic from earlier times when it was believed that the consequences of a good or bad life led here were to be reaped elsewhere in a state beyond death; and the retention of it by any school does not really affect its philosophic standpoint.

(ii) A necessary corollary to such a view of the goal of philosophy is the laying down of a suitable course of practical discipline for its attainment. Philosophy thereby becomes a way of life, not merely a way of thought. It has been remarked with reference to Jainism that its fundamental maxim is 'Do not live to know, but know to live'[1] and the same may well be said of the other Indian schools also.[2] The discipline naturally varies in the two traditions; but there is underlying it in both an ascetic spirit whose inculcation is another common characteristic of all Indian doctrines.[3] Sureśvara, a famous disciple of Śaṁkara, remarks[4] that, though systems of thought including heretical ones like Buddhism may differ in the substance of their theories, they are all at one in teaching renunciation. It means that while agreeing with one another in regard to the necessity of renunciation, they assign different reasons for it. That the heretical systems which in general were pessimistic should have commended absolute detachment is quite intelligible, for they were pervaded by a belief in the vanity and nothingness of life. What is specially noteworthy here is that the orthodox schools also, some of which at least were optimistic, should have done the same. But there is a very important difference between asceticism as taught in the two schools. The heterodox held that man should once for all turn away from the world whatever his circumstances might be. But the orthodox regarded the ascetic ideal as only to be

[1] OJ. p. 112.

[2] Compare in this connection Professor Whitehead's characterization of Buddhism as 'the most colossal example in history of applied metaphysics': *Religion in the Making*, p. 39.

[3] The Cārvāka view is an exception; but it is hardly a system of philosophy in the form in which it is now known. See Ch. VIII.

[4] BUV. pp. 513–15. st. 405–411.

progressively realized. As Dr. Winternitz observes,[1] it is in their opinion to be approached 'only from the point of view of the āśrama theory according to which the Aryan has first to pass the state of Brahmacārin, the student of the Veda, and of the householder (gṛhastha) who founds a family, offers sacrifices and honours the Brāhmaṇas, before he is allowed to retire from this world as a hermit or an ascetic.' The contrast between the two ideals is set forth in a striking manner in a chapter of the Mahābhārata known as the 'Dialogue between Father and Son.'[2] Here the father, who represents the orthodox view, maintains that renunciation should come at the end of the āśrama discipline, but is won over to his side by the son, who holds the view that it is the height of unwisdom to follow amidst the many uncertainties of life such dilatory discipline and pleads for an immediate breaking away from all worldly ties.[3] That is, detachment according to the former cannot be acquired without a suitable preliminary training undergone in the midst of society; but, according to the latter, it can be achieved at once, any moment of disillusionment about the world sufficing for it. The one believes social training to be indispensable[4] for the perfection of character; the other looks upon it as more a hindrance than a help to it. But the social factor, it should be added, is disregarded by the heterodox only as a means of self-culture, and their attitude towards it is neither one of revulsion nor one of neglect. For we know as a matter of fact that they attached the greatest value to society in itself and laid particular stress upon the need for

[1] 'Ascetic Literature in Ancient India': *Calcutta University Review* for October 1923, p. 3.

[2] xii. 277.

[3] This does not mean that there is no place for the laity in heterodox society, but only that lay training is not viewed as obligatory before one becomes a monk.

[4] The rule relating to the discipline of the āśramas was, as we shall see in a subsequent chapter, much relaxed in later times by the orthodox; but even thus the option to become an ascetic is to be exercised only after one has passed through the first stage of brahma-carya. It should also be stated that the relaxation, to judge from current practice, is mostly in theory and that early renunciation is the exception, not the rule.

sympathy and kindness for fellow-men. There are other differences as well such as the pursuit of ascetic morality by the heterodox, as the sole mode of practical discipline, and by the orthodox as only a preparation for a fresh course of training which may itself be different in different schools. But whatever the differences in matters of detail, asceticism as such serves as a bond of union between the two traditions. Even systems which do not at first appear to countenance it are, as a little reflection will show, really favourable to it. Thus ritualism with its promise of prosperity in a world to come actually results in complete self-denial so far as this world is concerned, because the fruit of the deeds it prescribes is to be reaped not here, but elsewhere and amidst conditions totally different from those of the present life. The principle of detachment implicit in such doctrines was, as we shall see, rendered explicit, and even the ulterior motive of self-love which is involved in striving for reward hereafter was eliminated by the Gītā with its teaching of disinterested action.

Owing to the spirit of renunciation that runs through them all, the way of life which the Indian doctrines prescribe may be characterized as aiming at transcending morality as commonly understood. In other words, the goal of Indian philosophy lies as much beyond Ethics as it does beyond Logic. As however the *rationale* of the ascetic ideal is explained in two different ways by Indian thinkers, the supermoral attitude bears a somewhat different significance in the several schools; but this distinction does not, like the previous one, correspond to the division into orthodox and heterodox traditions. Some schools admit the ultimacy of the individual self while others deny it in one sense or another. Buddhism for example altogether repudiates the individual self as a permanent entity, while Absolutism takes it as eventually merging in the true or universal self so that its individuality is only provisional. Theism on the other hand like that of Rāmānuja and pluralistic systems like Jainism or the Nyāya-Vaiśeṣika recognize the individual self to be ultimate, but point out that the way to deliverance lies only through the annihilation of egoism (ahaṁ-kāra). Now according to the systems which deny the individual self in one form or another, the very notion of obligation ceases to be significant finally, the contrast between the individual and society upon which that notion is based being entirely negated in it. Referring to a person that has attained to such a super-individual outlook, the *Taittirīya Upaniṣad* says[1]: 'He is not troubled by thoughts like these: Have I not done the right? Have I done the wrong?' In the other systems which admit the ultimacy of the individual self but teach the necessity for absolute self-suppression, the consciousness of obligation continues, but the disciple devotes himself to its fulfilment with no thought whatsoever of his rights. That is, though the contrast between the individual and society is felt, that between rights and duties disappears; and so far, the motive is lifted above that of common morality. According to both the views, the essential duality of the moral world is transcended on account of the total renunciation of personal interest; in neither is it merely an adjustment, however difficult or delicate, of rights and duties between the individual and his social environment.

There is a sense, we may add, in which the practical training, even in its preliminary stages, may be said to aim at transcending morality as ordinarily conceived. The individual's obligations, according to the Indian view, are not confined to human society, but extend to virtually the whole of sentient creation. To the common precept 'Love thy neighbour as thyself,' it adds, as has been observed by one than whom nobody now is better fitted to interpret the Indian ideal of life, 'And every living being is thy neighbour.'[2] Such an extension of the world of moral action accords well with the spirit of Indian ethics whose watchword is devotion to duties rather than assertion of rights. Beings that are not characterized by moral consciousness may have no duties to fulfil, but it does not mean that there is none to be fulfilled towards them. This ideal of the fellowship of all living beings is best illustrated by the principle of non-injury (ahiṁsā), which forms an integral part of every one of the higher Indian

[1] ii. 9. [2] See Romain Rolland: *Mahatma Gandhi*, p. 33.

faiths and was practised not only by saints and sages, but also by emperors like Aśoka. It may minimize the importance of human society. That is because the ideal has not less regard for it but more for the wider whole which comprehends all animate being. It does not thereby ignore the spirit of human unity. Only it conceives of that spirit as consisting not in striving for human well-being alone, but also in discharging towards all living creatures the obligation corresponding to the position of privilege which mankind occupies in the scheme of the universe. Social morality, however much it may widen our outlook from the individual's standpoint, really keeps us isolated from the rest of creation. In addition to personal egoism, there is what may be called the egoism of the species which leads inevitably to the belief that the sub-human world may be exploited for the benefit of man. That also must be got rid of, if man is to become truly free; and he will do so only when he has risen above the anthropocentric view and can look upon everything as equally sacred—whether it be, in the words of the Gītā,[1] 'a cow or elephant or dog, the cultured Brahmin or the outcaste that feeds on dogs.'

These are the two elements common to all Indian thought—the pursuit of mokṣa as the final ideal and the ascetic spirit of the discipline recommended for its attainment. They signify that philosophy as understood in India is neither mere intellectualism nor mere moralism, but includes and transcends them both. In other words it aims, as already stated, at achieving more than what Logic and Ethics can. But it must not be forgotten that, though not themselves constituting the end, these are the *sole* means of approach to it. They have been represented as the two wings that help the soul in its spiritual flight. The goal that is reached through their aid is characterized on the one hand by jñāna or illumination which is intellectual conviction that has ripened into an immediate experience and, on the other, by vairāgya or self-renunciation which is secure by reason of the discovery of the metaphysical ground for it. It is pre-eminently an attitude of peace which does not

[1] v. 18.

necessarily imply passivity. But the emphasis is on the attitude itself or on the inward experience that gives rise to it, rather than on the outward behaviour which is looked upon as its expression and therefore more or less secondary. The value of philosophic training lies as little in inducing a person to do what otherwise he would not have done, as in instructing him in what otherwise he would not have known; it consists essentially in making him what he was not before. Heaven, it has been remarked, is first a temperament and then anything else.

We have so far spoken about the main divisions of Indian tradition, which, though exhibiting certain common features, are fundamentally different. The history of Indian philosophy is the history of the ways in which the two traditions have acted and reacted upon each other, giving rise to divergent schools of thought. Their mutual influence, however much desirable as the means of broadening the basis of thought, has led to a considerable overlapping of the two sets of doctrines, rendering it difficult to discover what elements each has incorporated from the other. It is impossible, for instance, to say for certain to which of the two traditions we owe the ideal of jīvan-mukti to whose importance we have drawn attention. In the course of this progressive movement, now one school and now another was in the ascendant. The ascendancy at one stage belonged conspicuously to Buddhism, and it seemed as if it had once for all gained the upper hand. But finally the Vedānta triumphed. It has naturally been transformed much in the process, although its inner character remains as it was already foreshadowed in the Upaniṣads. We may indeed regard the several phases in the history of the heretical tradition as only so many steps leading to this final development. The Vedānta may accordingly be taken to represent the consummation of Indian thought, and in it we may truly look for the highest type of the Indian ideal. On the theoretical side, it stands for the triumph of Absolutism and Theism, for whatever differences may characterize the various Vedāntic schools, they are classifiable under these two heads. The former is monistic and the latter, though avowedly pluralistic, may also be said to be governed by the spirit of monism owing to the emphasis it places on the entire dependence of everything on God. On the practical side, the triumph of the Vedānta has meant the triumph of the positive ideal of life. This is shown not only by the social basis of the ethical discipline which the Vedānta as an orthodox doctrine commends, but also by its conception of the highest good which consists, as we shall see when we come to consider the several systems in detail, not in isolating the self from its environment as it does for the heterodox schools but in overcoming the opposition between the two by identifying the interests of the self with those of the whole. Both ideals alike involve the cultivation of complete detachment; but the detachment in the case of the Vedānta is of a higher and finer type. Kālidāsa, who, as the greatest of Indian poets, may be expected to have given the truest expression to the ideal of practical life known to the Indians, describes it[1] as 'owning the whole world while disowning oneself.' The Vedāntic idea of the highest good also implies the recognition of a cosmic purpose, whether that purpose be conceived as ordained by God or as inherent in the nature of Reality itself, towards whose fulfilment everything consciously or unconsciously moves. The heretical schools, except in so far as they have been influenced by the other ideal, do not see any such purpose in the world as a whole, though they admit the possibility of the individual freeing himself from evil.

[1] *Mālavikāgnimitra*, i. 1.

PART I

VEDIC PERIOD

CHAPTER I

PRE-UPANIṢADIC THOUGHT

OUR source of information for this chapter is two-fold: (i) the Mantras or metrical hymns composed by the Aryans after they had settled in their new Indian home, and (ii) the Brāhmaṇas, a certain other class of works which generally speaking belong to an age subsequent to that of the Mantras and may be broadly described as liturgical in character. The former have been preserved to us chiefly in what are known as the *Rk*- and the *Atharva-saṁhitās*. The first in its present form dates from 600 B.C. and the second from somewhat later. They are religious songs in praise of one or more deities and were intended generally to be sung at the time of offering worship to them. These songs, especially the earlier ones among them, are written in very old Sanskrit; and it is for that reason not infrequently difficult to determine what precisely their import is. The difficulty of interpretation arising from the archaic character of the language is increased by the break in tradition which seems to have occurred quite early—even before the composition of the Brāhmaṇas.[1] To give only a simple instance: Nothing is more natural for a poet than to speak of the sun as 'golden-handed'; yet this poetic epithet appearing in a hymn is taken literally and explained in a Brāhmaṇa by a story that the sun lost his hand which was afterwards replaced by one made of gold. To these factors contributing to the difficulty of understanding aright the views of this early period, we should add the fragmentary nature of the Mantra material that has come down to us. The very fact that the hymns had been, for so many generations before they were brought together, in what may be described as a floating condition, shows that some of them must have been lost. When at last they were collected, not all of them were included in the collection, but only such as had a more or less direct bearing upon ritual,

[1] See Max Müller: *Ancient Sanskrit Literature*, pp. 432–34.

which had by that time come to occupy the centre of real interest. The result is that the information that can be gathered from them is incomplete and one-sided. Unlike the Mantras, the Brāhmaṇas are written in prose. They profess to elucidate the earlier literature of the Mantras, but, as already stated, they misread it at times. Their chief aim, to judge from their present form, should have been the affording of practical aid in the performance of rites by getting together the sacrificial lore as known at the time when they were compiled. They indicate the prevalence then of a complicated ritual and their lucubrations have generally little bearing upon philosophy. But while explaining the nature of rites, the authors of the Brāhmaṇas sometimes indulge in speculative digressions which give us a glimpse of the philosophic thought of the age. As handed down traditionally, the Brāhmaṇas include the Upaniṣads, which usually form their final sections. But in their thoughts and sentiments they are essentially different. Moreover, the Upaniṣads are of very great importance, so much so that they have been viewed by some as the fountain-head of all Indian philosophy. For these reasons they require a separate treatment and we shall deal with them in the next chapter, confining our attention here to the Mantras and the Brāhmaṇas strictly so termed.

I

The origin of religion is shrouded in mystery and has given rise to much difference of opinion. We may take for granted that its earliest form consists in the worship of natural powers. Man, when he first emerges from mere animal consciousness, realizes that he is almost entirely dependent upon the powerful forces of nature amidst which he is placed; and, accustomed as he is in his own experience to associate all power with voluntary effort, he ascribes those forces to sentient beings working behind them unseen. In other words, early man personifies the powers of nature which in virtue of their great strength become his gods. He cultivates a spirit of awe and reverence towards them, sings their praises and offers worship or sacrifice to them with a view either to propitiate them or to secure their favour. These deities, however, are divine only in a qualified sense, for, though called 'gods,' they are necessarily conceived in a human mould and are regarded as being actuated by the same motives and passions as the person that conceives them. They are in reality glorified human beings and are therefore neither wholly natural nor wholly supernatural. Though this faith looks simple and childlike, it is not altogether without a philosophic basis. It signifies a conviction that the visible world is not in itself final and that there is a reality lying hidden in it. It is also at bottom a seeking after an explanation of observed facts, implying a belief that every event has a cause; and to believe in the universality of causation is perforce to believe in the uniformity of nature. Unless primitive man had noticed the regularity with which natural phenomena recur and unless he were inwardly convinced that every event has a cause to account for it, he would not have resorted to the creation of such deities in explanation of them. It is true that he merely ascribed those phenomena to certain agencies supposed to be working behind them, and was therefore very far from explaining them in the proper sense of the term. Besides he was for the most part unaware that he was explaining at all. Nevertheless, there is clearly implied here a search for the causes of observed facts, however unsuccessful or unconscious it may be. Acquiescence in any kind of accidentalism is inconsistent with the spirit of such speculation.

We are not, however, directly concerned here with this early form of belief, for Aryan religion when it appears in India has already a history behind it. As an American scholar has paradoxically put it, 'Indian religion begins before its arrival in India.'[1] It is a continuation of the primitive faith of the Indo-Europeans to which the Aryans that came to India belonged. There are to be found even now in Sanskrit old words which serve as clear indications of this fact. The word 'deva' (*div*, 'to shine') for instance, which means 'god' in Sanskrit, is cognate with

[1] Rel.V. p. 16.

Latin 'deus,' and points to a period when the Indo-European in his original home associated his conception of godhead with the luminous powers of nature. The spirit of veneration with which he regarded such deified powers is equally well indicated by the root *yaj*, 'to worship,' which is common to more than one Indo-European language. Again we have for example in the Vedic god Mitra the Indian counterpart of Iranian Mithra, whose cult was once in great vogue in Western Asia and Europe. These instances are sufficient to indicate what the antecedents of early Indian religion were. It had passed through the Indo-European stage as well as the Indo-Iranian in which the ancestors of the future Indians and Persians lived together and shared a common belief. The Vedic pantheon includes not only the old gods belonging to the two pre-Indian periods, but also several others whose conceptions the Aryan settlers formed in their new home, e.g. the river-deities like Sarasvatī. The number of these gods—old and new—is indefinite. Sometimes they are reckoned at thirty-three and classified into three groups of eleven each according to their abode, viz.: (i) gods of the sky, like Mitra and Varuṇa; (ii) gods of mid-air, like Indra and Maruts; and (iii) gods of the earth, like Agni and Soma—a classification which, by the way, indicates a desire to discover the interrelations of the gods and arrange them systematically. They are all of co-ordinate power and no supreme God as such is recognized, although some of them are more imposing than others—particularly Indra and Varuṇa, the gods respectively of the warrior and of the pious devotee.

It is not necessary to dwell here at length upon the details of Vedic mythology. We may note only such of its characteristics as have a philosophic bearing. The first point to attract our attention in it is how surprisingly close to nature the Vedic gods are. There is for instance absolutely no doubt in regard to what constitutes the basis in nature of Agni and Parjanya. They are gods and at the same time natural objects, viz. 'fire' and 'cloud.' There are other gods, it is true, like the Aśvins and Indra, whose identity is not so transparent; but what we have to remember is that, unlike

Greek mythology for example, the prevailing type of Vedic gods is one of incomplete personalization. This is a remarkable feature seeing how far removed, comparatively speaking, Vedic religion is from its source. It is commonly described as 'arrested anthropomorphism'; but the expression is apt to suggest that the Vedic conception of divinity lacks a desirable feature, viz. complete personification, while in reality it points to an excellence—a frame of mind in the Vedic Aryan highly favourable to philosophic speculation. It may be that the particularly impressive features of nature in India, as has been suggested,[1] explain this 'unforgetting adherence' to it; but it is at least as much the result of the philosophic bent of the Indian mind. The fact is that the Vedic Indian did not allow his conceptions to crystallize too quickly. His interest in speculation was so deep and his sense of the mystery hiding the Ultimate was so keen that he kept before him unobscured the natural phenomena which he was trying to understand until he arrived at a satisfying solution.[2] This characteristic signifies a passion for truth and accounts not only for the profundity of Indian philosophic investigation, but also for the great variety of the solutions it offers of philosophical problems.

Another feature of early Indian religion equally remarkable is furnished by the conception of ṛta which finds a conspicuous place in the Mantras.[3] Expressions like 'guardians of ṛta' (gopā ṛtasya) and 'practisers of ṛta' (ṛtāyu) occur frequently in the description of the gods. This word, which is pre-Indian in origin, originally meant uniformity of nature or the ordered course of things such as is indicated by the regular alternation of day and night, while in the Mantras it not only bears this significance but also the additional one of 'moral order.'[4] The Vedic gods are accordingly to be viewed not only as the maintainers of cosmic order but also as upholders of moral law. They are friendly to the good and inimical to the evil-minded, so that, if man is not to incur their displeasure, he should strive to

[1] Rel.V. p. 82. [2] Cf. *Id*. pp. 85, 151. [3] See *Id*. p. 12.

[4] Contrast anṛta, which means 'untrue' or 'false.' This extension of meaning belongs to the Indo-Iranian period.

be righteous. This equal responsibility of divinity for the maintenance of cosmic as well as moral order is particularly clear in the conception of Varuṇa. He represents the sky and is the god of heavenly light. He is described as having fixed the laws of the physical universe which no one can violate. Through his power for instance, it is said, the rivers flow into the ocean without over-filling it. But his sway is not restricted to the physical sphere; it extends beyond to the moral, where his laws are equally eternal and inviolable. He is omniscient so that the least sin even will not escape detection by him. To indicate the all-searching nature of his vigilant sight, the sun is sometimes poetically described as his eye. The conception of Varuṇa was soon superseded in Vedic mythology by that of Indra who, as we have stated above, is a god of battles rather than of righteousness. This has led some modern scholars to the conclusion that there was a corresponding lapse in the moral standard of the Indian.[1] But they forget the peculiar circumstances in which the conception of Indra came into prominence. The immigrant Aryans had to subdue the numerous indigenous tribes; and it was in the process of this subjugation in which Varuna—essentially a god of peace—could not well be invoked that the idea of this warrior-god as known to the Ṛgveda was developed. 'Nations are never coarser,' it has been said,[2] 'than when they put their own nationality into antagonism against another nation.' We may grant that during the period of Indra's supremacy the self-assertion and violence which distinguish him were reflected in the character of his worshippers. But it was only a passing phase. Indra did not finally become the supreme God of the Indians, but had to yield place to others ethically more lofty so that it does not seem justifiable to conclude that in the Indian view might once for all replaced right. Indra besides is not altogether bereft of moral traits; nor is Varuṇa the only support of ṛta, all the sun-gods of whom he is one being regarded as equally so.[3] Further, Varuṇa stands only for a certain type of theistic conception—the Hebraic, as it

[1] See e.g. *Cambridge History of India*, vol. i. pp. 103, 108.
[2] Rel. V. p. 175. [3] See Macdonell: *Vedic Mythology*, pp. 18, 65.

has been said. But the development of religious thought in Vedic India, as we shall presently see, proceeded on altogether different lines rendering the idea of divinity generally speaking more and more impersonal. The neglect into which the Varuṇa ideal fell in the course of the period may therefore be taken as indicating the gradual rejection then of that idea of godhead and it need not necessarily mean a fading away from the Aryan mind of the moral idea itself. That question has to be settled on independent considerations. Without entering into the details of this discussion, we may cite the opinion of Rudolph Roth, one of the deepest Vedic scholars of modern times, who in considering this question,[1] reviews the fundamental conceptions of the Veda such as those touching the relation of man to god and the future state of departed souls, and concludes that it is impossible not to allow a positive moral value to them and 'esteem a literature in which such ideas are expressed.'

II

Early Vedic ritual was quite simple in its form as well as in the motive which inspired it. The gods worshipped were the familiar powers of nature, and the material offered to them was such as milk, grain and ghee. The motive was to secure the objects of ordinary desire—children, cattle, etc., or to get one's enemy out of the way. Occasionally the sacrifice seems to have served as thanksgiving to the gods for favours already won from them. The idea of sacrament also was perhaps present in some measure, the worshipper believing that he was under a sacred influence or in communion with the divine when he partook of the sacrificial meal. This simplicity soon disappeared; and, even in some of the early Mantras, we find instead of this childlike worship an organized sacrificial cult which is already hieratic. Yet the ritual in the early Vedic period cannot be said to have outgrown its due proportions. But it did so and became highly wrought in the age of the later Mantras and the Brāhmaṇas. As however the direct bearing of this development on Indian

[1] JAOS. vol. iii. pp. 331–47. See also EI. pp. 44, 61–62.

philosophy is not great, a detailed consideration of it is not called for here. It will suffice to indicate some only of its general features: One such feature is the great change that takes place in the character of the gods to whom offerings are made. In addition to the old ones, drawn chiefly from some sphere or other of natural phenomena, we now see honoured at the sacrifice several artificial deities. Thus the clay-pot used in a certain rite is made 'the object of fervid adoration as though it were a veritable deity of well-nigh paramount power.'[1] The poet-priest, we sometimes find, chooses to glorify any insignificant thing, if it only happens to be connected in some way with a sacrifice. There is for example an entire poem devoted to the sacrificial post,[2] and we have another which seriously institutes a comparison between the ornamental paint on it and the splendour of Uṣas or the goddess of Dawn.[3] Symbolism also comes to prevail on a large scale. According to an old myth, Agni was the offspring of water. So a lotus leaf, betokening water, is placed at the bottom of the sacrificial altar on which fire is installed.[4] More striking still is the change which comes over the spirit with which offerings are made. In the place of conciliation and communion as the motive, we now have the view that the sacrifice is the means not of persuading the gods, but of compelling them to grant to the sacrificer what he wants. Not only can the gods be compelled by the sacrificer to do what he likes; the gods themselves, it is thought, are gods and are able to discharge their function of maintaining the world-order by virtue of the offerings presented to them. In other words, the sacrifice is now exalted above the gods—a position the logical consequence of which is their total denial later in the Pūrva-mīmāṁsā system. It is now commonly held that in this new turn in the efforts of the Vedic Indian to accomplish his desire, we discover a distinctly magical element introduced into the ritual; and that priest and prayer henceforward become transformed into magician and spell. The relation of religion

[1] See Eggeling: *Śata-patha Brāhmaṇa,* (SBE.) Part V. p. xlvi.

[2] RV. III. viii.

[3] RV. I. 92, 5.

[4] See Eggeling: *op. cit.* Part IV. pp. xix–xxi.

to magic and the extent to which magical elements enter into the Vedic ritual are matters of controversy; but we need not stop to discuss them as they are of little consequence to us here.

It should not be thought that ritualism in this extreme form was in any sense the creed of the people at large. The Mantras of the Ṛgveda and the Brāhmaṇas which have so far been the basis of our conclusions were the compositions of poet-priests who had developed a cult of their own, and unfold but an aristocratic religion.[1] Even in the aristocratic circles, we may remark in passing, the excessive development of ritualism does not seem to have wholly superseded the older idea of sacrifice as what man *owes* to the gods, for we find that idea also persisting along with the other in later Vedic literature. Thus sacrifice is sometimes pictured in the Brāhmaṇas as a ṛna or 'debt' due to the gods.[2] The creed of the common people continued to be simple and consisted, in addition to the more primitive forms of nature-worship alluded to above, in various practices such as incantations and charms intended to ward off evil and appease the dark spirits of the air and of the earth. We get an idea of these folk-practices from the Atharva-veda, which, though somewhat later than the Ṛgveda, records in certain respects a more ancient phase of religious belief.

III

The emphasis on rites which appears in the literature that has come down to us from this ancient period is due in part to its selective character, to which we have already referred, and therefore indicates more of the spirit of the age in which the selection was made than of the one in which that literature was produced. Yet there is no doubt that ritualism, with its implications of excess and symbolism, marks one characteristic development of early Vedic religion. There are other developments of it as well which also are attested by the same literature, though their features appear there rather faintly. We cannot, with the records at our disposal,

[1] Cf. Rel.V. pp. 22, 210. [2] See e.g. *Taittirīya-saṁhitā*, VI. iii. 10. 5.

describe them as anything more than tendencies of thought showing themselves in the period in question. It is difficult to trace these tendencies to their proper source, because they appear in very close association with the sacrifice with the spirit of which they seem to be essentially in conflict. They may be due to speculative activity outside the circle of priests, or more probably[1] they are the result of a reaction among the priests themselves against ritual which had become artificial and over-elaborate. Whatever their origin, they are of great importance to the student of philosophy, for in them are to be found the germs of much of the later thought of India. We shall now give a brief description of them.

(i) *Monotheism.*—The belief in a plurality of gods, which was a characteristic feature of early Vedic religion, loses its attraction gradually; and the Vedic Indian, dissatisfied with the old mythology and impelled by that longing for simplicity of explanation so natural to man, starts upon seeking after not the causes of natural phenomena, but their first or ultimate cause. He is no longer content to refer observed phenomena to a multiplicity of gods, but strives to discover the one God that controls and rules over them all. The conception of a unitary godhead which becomes explicit now may be said to lie implicit already in the thought of the earlier period. For, owing to the incomplete individualization of deities and the innate connection or mutual resemblance of one natural phenomenon with another (e.g. the Sun, Fire and Dawn), there is in Vedic mythology what may be described as an overlapping of divinities. One god is very much like another. Different deities thus come to be portrayed in the same manner; and, but for the name in it, it would often be difficult to determine which god is intended to be praised in a hymn. There is also to be mentioned in this connection the well-known habit of the Vedic seers of magnifying the importance of the particular deity they are praising and representing it as supreme, ignoring for the time being the other deities altogether. To this phase of religious belief Max Müller gave the name of 'henotheism,'

[1] Cf. Rel.V. pp. 35, 212–220.

i.e. belief in *one* God as distinguished from monotheism or belief in *one only* God; and, regarding it as the instinct for unity asserting itself unconsciously, he represented it as a definite stage in the advance from polytheistic to monotheistic belief.[1] This view has not commended itself to many. Such overdrawing, it is thought, is natural to all religious poetry and does not consequently involve any necessary implication of progress from the thought of the many to the thought of the one. But yet this 'opportunist monotheism,' as the henotheistic tendency has been called, may be taken to have on the whole conduced to the formulation of a belief in a single God in place of the multiple deities of an earlier time.

To reduce the many gods of early mythology to one, the easiest course, we might suppose, is to elevate the most imposing of them to the rank of the Supreme. That was not the course followed in Vedic India. Varuṇa indeed at one time and Indra at another were on the point of fulfilling the conditions of a monotheistic creed in this sense; but neither did in fact become the supreme God conceived definitely as a personality. So we may say that monotheism in the ordinary sense of the term proved abortive in the Vedic period. The unity of godhead came to be sought after in a different manner then, and attempts were made to discover not one god above other gods but rather the common power that works behind them all. The basis of even this 'philosophic monotheism,' as it may be termed, can be noticed in the early Mantras, for the Vedic poets couple the names of two deities like Mitra and Varuṇa for example—sometimes of even more—and address them as if they were one. It is the outcome of this tendency that we find expressed in passages of a relatively later date like the following: 'What is but one, wise people call by different names—as Agni, Yama and Mātariśvan.'[2] The same is the significance also, no doubt, of the refrain of another hymn of the Ṛgveda: Mahat devānām asuratvam ekam: 'The worshipful divinity of the gods is one.'[3] Though thus con-

[1] SS. p. 40. [2] RV. I. 164. 46.
[3] III. 55. Cf. OST. vol. v. p. 354.

vinced that there is but one ultimate cause which accounts for the diverse phenomena of nature, the Vedic Indian felt perplexed for long as regards what its exact nature might be. He tried one solution after another, but could not rest content with any. One of the earliest ways of arriving at a unitary conception of divinity was by taking a collective view of the gods, designating them Viśve-devas—an expression equivalent to 'all-gods.' Such a mode of unity may appear to be quite mechanical; but it is not really so, for it implies a consciousness of the harmony of purpose underlying the workings of nature. A more abstract way of arriving at unity was to select some one distinguishing feature of divinity—'a predicate of several gods'—to personify it and regard it as the supreme God. Thus the word viśva-karman, which means 'maker of everything,' originally appears as a descriptive epithet of Indra and the Sun. But later it ceases to be used as an adjective and becomes installed as God above all gods.[1] A mere logical abstraction thus grows into a concrete god. The same thing happens in the case of several other predicative epithets. What is remarkable about these supreme gods is that none of them retains his supremacy long. 'The god that takes hold of the sceptre lays it down soon.' One conception is felt as inadequate and there quickly springs up another in its place, so that Vedic monotheism even of the philosophic type may be described as unstable and as continually shifting its ground. It is with the broken idols of this period, some one has observed, that in later times the temple of Purāṇic mythology was adorned.

There is no need to mention here all the gods that successively became pre-eminent during this long period. It will suffice to refer to only one of them—Prajā-pati, 'Father god,' the most important of them all, who is the personification of the creative power of nature. The origin of this god is similar to that of Viśva-karman. His name signifies 'lord of living beings' and is first applied as an epithet to gods like Savitṛ, 'the vivifier.' But later it assumes the character of an independent deity which is responsible for the creation and

[1] RV. x. 81, 82.

governance of the universe. This god occupies the first place in the Brāhmaṇas. There are, one Brāhmaṇa says, thirty-three gods and Prajā-pati is the thirty-fourth including them all.[1] Even in the Ṛgveda, where the references to him are not many, there is quite a sublime description.[2] One feels that such a deity should have satisfied the yearning of any people after a supreme God, and that Prajā-pati might well have constituted the goal in the Indian search after unity in godhead. But even he ceases to appeal to the philosophically fastidious Vedic Aryan and yields place in course of time to other principles like Prāṇa[3] or 'deified breath,' the cosmic counterpart of individual life and Time,[4] the maker and destroyer of all. To some of them we shall recur later.

(ii.) *Monism.*—The conceptions thus far described as monotheistic are often found mixed with monistic ones; and it is difficult to separate them. But yet in particular passages, the one or the other view is seen to prevail. That is our justification for speaking of them as two tendencies. Of them, the monotheistic conception, regarded purely as such, is bound to involve dualism. What it aims at is only unity of godhead—the reduction of the many gods to one who is above and apart from the world which he makes and guides. It regards nature as set over against God and can therefore satisfy the longing for unity only in a qualified sense. There is a higher conception of unity, viz. monism, which traces the whole of existence to a single source. It is fully worked out in the Upaniṣads, but is foreshadowed more than once in the literature of the period we are now considering. There are in it at least two distinct shades of such monistic thought. To begin with, there is the pantheistic view which identifies nature with God. One of its most notable expressions is found in a passage of the Ṛgveda where goddess Aditi (the 'Boundless') is identified with all gods and all men, with the sky and air—in fact with 'whatever has been or whatever shall be.'[5] The central point of the pantheistic doctrine is to deny the difference between God and nature which as we have shown is the necessary

[1] *Śata-patha Brāhmaṇa,* V. i. 2. 10 and 13. [2] X. 121.
[3] AV. XI. iv. [4] AV. XIX. liii and liv. [5] I. 89. 10.

implication of monotheism. God is conceived here not as transcending nature but as immanent in it.[1] The world does not proceed from God, but is itself God. Although the object of this view is to postulate unity, it retains, somewhat inconsistently as it seems, both the notions of God and nature and so far fails to satisfy the mind in its search after true unity. Such a consideration may be regarded as having been at the root of another conception of unity which we come across in the literature of the period—for example, in the 'Song of Creation'[2] which has been extolled as containing 'the flower of Indian thought.' It is in parts obscure and almost baffles translation. Yet there are several renderings of it into English and the following metrical one by J. Muir is one of the best[3]:

'Then there was neither Aught nor Nought, no air nor sky beyond.
What covered all? Where rested all? In watery gulf profound?
Nor death was then, nor deathlessness, nor change of night and day.
That One breathed calmly, self-sustained; nought else beyond it lay.
Gloom hid in gloom existed first—one sea, eluding view.
That One, a void in chaos wrapt, by inward fervour grew.
Within it first arose desire, the primal germ of mind,
Which nothing with existence links, as sages searching find.
The kindling ray that shot across the dark and drear abyss—
Was it beneath? or high aloft? What bard can answer this?
There fecundating powers were found, and mighty forces strove—
A self-supporting mass beneath, and energy above.
Who knows, who ever told, from whence this vast creation rose?
No gods had then been born—who then can e'er the truth disclose?
Whence sprang this world, and whether framed by hand divine or no—
Its Lord in heaven alone can tell, if even he can show.'

In this hymn, which may be said to have passed over into world-literature, we have the quintessence of monistic thought. Here the poet-philosopher recognizing, unlike the pantheist, the principle of causality, not only traces the

[1] For this reason it is not right to adduce the Puruṣa-sūkta (RV.X.90), as it is the common practice to do, as an illustration of pantheism. The sūkta starts by emphasizing the transcendent character of the ultimate Reality: 'Having enveloped the earth on every side, he stood out beyond it the length of ten fingers.'

[2] RV. X. 129.

[3] OST. vol. v. p. 356.

whole universe to a single source but also tackles the problem of what its nature may be. All opposites like being and non-being, death and life, good and evil, are viewed as developing within and therefore as ultimately reconcilable in this fundamental principle. In regard to the origin of the universe, we have here, instead of the view of creation by an external agency, the view that the sensible world is the spontaneous unfolding of the supra-sensible First Cause. The conception is wholly impersonal and free from all mythological elements. Even the theistic colouring discernible in pantheism is absent here. It is denoted in this song by two most cautiously chosen epithets—'That One' (Tad Ekam), which suggest nothing beyond the positive and unitary character of the ultimate principle. We are here on the threshold of Upaniṣadic monism.

IV

Yet another tendency has to be noted which may comprehensively be described as 'Vedic free-thinking.'[1] But it must be remembered that it does not form part of the teaching of the Veda. There are only allusions to it there which, though occasional, are quite clear. Those that indulged in it are denounced as 'haters of the Veda' (brahma-dviṣ), 'maligners of gods' (deva-nid), 'men of no principle' (apavrata). That such heterodox views were not unknown in ancient India may also be gathered from the tradition of Jainism. It reckons several prophets who preceded Mahāvīra. Of them at least one, Pārśvanātha, is now generally taken to have been an historical personage and assigned to the eighth century B.C., which according to the accepted chronology takes us back to the period[2] when the Brāhmaṇas were composed. This tendency manifests itself sometimes as doubt and sometimes as disbelief. But under whatever form it may appear, it sets itself against the orthodox teaching of the Veda. There is a whole hymn[3] in the Ṛgveda addressed to Faith which concludes with the prayer: 'O Faith, make us

[1] See Rel.V. p. 187.
[2] See *Cambridge History of India*, Vol. i. p. 153.
[3] X. 151.

faithful.' Such an invocation, as Deussen has observed,[1] would be unintelligible if we did not assume a certain lack of faith as prevalent in the age in which the hymn was composed. As other instances of unbelief we may mention two hymns, also found in the Ṛgveda—one[2] which pointedly refers to current disbelief in the existence and supremacy of Indra and endeavours by recounting his great deeds to convince the unbelievers of his majesty and power, and the other[3] which ridicules the votaries of the Veda by describing them as 'selfish prattling priests that go about self-deluded.' It was this tendency that in course of time gave rise to the heretical schools (p. 16) whose importance in the history of Indian philosophy has already been noticed.

V

We shall conclude this chapter with a brief description of the general outlook on life and things in the period. Nature and man alike form the subject-matter of speculation. The external world, whose reality is never questioned, is looked upon as an ordered whole, divided into the three realms of earth, the atmospheric region and heaven, each guided and illumined by its own specific deities. In fact, it is to account for its cosmic character that the several nature-gods are invented. The gods may be many, but the world they govern is one. This idea of unity naturally comes to be emphasized with the growth of monotheistic and monistic beliefs. Notions of creation and evolution both appear. Where the universe is spoken of as created, only one creation is mentioned; and the belief, so well known to a later age, in a series of creations, each being followed by dissolution, is absent.[4] Various accounts of the order of creation are found—one of the commonest being that water was first created and that everything else sprang from it afterwards. Sometimes we

[1] *Indian Antiquary* for 1900, p. 367. [2] II. 12. [3] X. 82.

[4] There seems to be a stray reference to it in RV. X. 190. 3: Dhātā yathā-pūrvam akalpayat. But it may be interpreted differently. See PU. p. 221.

meet with the idea that the world was built by the gods, much in the manner of building a house. One poet who pictures Varuṇa as the cosmic architect describes the moving sun as his measuring-rod.[1] Another expresses wonder as to wherefrom the material might have come: 'What indeed was the wood? What too that tree from which they fashioned heaven and earth?'[2] Sometimes the world is stated to have been generated, Heaven and Earth being its parents. There is still another view which, under the influence of ritualism, traces the world to a sacrificial act. This conceit occurs in more than one place in the Veda and particularly in the hymn known as the Puruṣa-sūkta, where the cosmic man, who is himself described as emerging from a transcendental Being, is taken to have furnished, when sacrificed, the material for the entire variety of the universe. 'The moon was born from his mind; from his eye, the sun; from his mouth, Indra and Agni; and from his breath, Vāyu. From his navel came into being the mid-region; from his head, the sky; from his feet, the earth; from his ear, the quarters.' It is really the breaking up of the seen whole into its parts—a process which is the reverse of the one we sometimes find in the Upaniṣads,[3] viz. reconstructing the whole out of its several parts as given in common experience. We have already spoken of the more philosophical view of evolution in connection with the Song of Creation.

Naturally a prominent place is given in the plan of life to the performance of sacrifices whose efficacy in securing for man what he wants is never doubted. Indeed sacrifice, as we have seen, is sometimes regarded as a ṛna. It is the first of what is described as the 'triad of obligations' (ṛna-traya)—a description which implies a clear conception of duty. The second is indebtedness to the sages of old for the heritage of culture which they have left behind. It is to be discharged by receiving that tradition and handing it on to the coming generation. The last obligation is what is due to the race, which is to be met by becoming a householder and begetting sons. The ideal thus does not stop with the performance of sacrifices but comprehends the preservation of the race and

[1] RV. V. 85. 5. [2] RV. X. 31. 7. [3] Cf. *Ch. Up.* V. xi–xviii.

the conservation of the culture for which it stands. It also includes the practice of virtues like adherence to truth, self-restraint and kindness to fellow-beings. Benevolence to neighbour and friend is particularly praised and niggardliness censured in the Ṛgveda,[1] which for instance states: Kevalāgho bhavati kevalādī: 'He that eats by himself will keep his sin to himself.' The tendency to asceticism also appears in the period, the Ṛgveda alluding[2] to the muni with long hair and coloured garments. We have already considered the place of morality in the earlier part of the period. As regards the later, some are of opinion that the excessive importance attached to the sacrifice in it led to a neglect of ethical ideas and gave rise to the practice of judging goodness by the standard of ritualistic correctness. But in view of the fact to which attention has been drawn that ritualism was only one of the lines of development of early Vedic thought, it would be more correct to hold that, though in circles where the sacrifice was dominant it might have caused some confusion between ethical and ritualistic values, the idea of morality itself did not disappear. Thus Prajā-pati, the principal deity of the Brāhmaṇa period, is represented not merely as the lord of creation, but also as an ethical authority[3] reminding us of the still earlier view that the gods were responsible for upholding moral as well as cosmic order.

This ancient belief is more than a system of rewards and punishments on this side of death. Both the pious and the impious are believed to be born in another world; but except perhaps in a single passage in a Brāhmaṇa,[4] there is no allusion to transmigration. The reward of virtue and piety is enjoyment of happiness in heaven in the company of the gods. Later this blessed existence is represented as being led in the company of the virtuous dead and under the control of Yama, who appears as the ruler of heaven and not yet of the dread abode of hell. The punishment for sin and vice is eternal damnation. The reference to hell is not explicit in the Ṛgveda, but is clear in the Atharva-veda and the Brāhmaṇas. It is described as a place of eternal darkness

[1] X. 117. 6. [2] X. 136. 2.
[3] Cf. EI. p. 50. [4] See Macdonell: *Vedic Mythology*, p. 166.

below, in contrast to heaven, which is one of light above; and those that go there, it is stated, can never escape from it. All this points to a belief in the immortality of the soul. Death does not mean destruction, but only the continuance of existence elsewhere where happiness or misery results according to one's deserts.

CHAPTER II

THE UPANIṢADS

WE now take up the study of the Upaniṣads which stand by themselves although tradition associates them closely with the Brāhmaṇas (p. 30). Primarily they represent a spirit different from and even hostile to ritual and embody a theory of the universe quite distinct from the one that underlies the sacrificial teaching of the Brāhmaṇas. All the earlier Upaniṣads in some form or other indicate this antagonism while in a few it becomes quite explicit.[1] Thus in the *Muṇḍaka Upaniṣad*[2] we have one of the clearest onslaughts against the sacrificial ceremonial, in the course of which it is stated that whosoever hopes for real good to accrue from these rites is a fool and is sure to be overtaken again and again by death and decrepitude. This opposition more often appears indirectly in the substitution of an allegorical for a literal interpretation of the rites.[3] An illustration will show how this is done The aśva-medha is a well-known sacrifice whose celebration signifies overlordship of the world. It is to be performed by a Kshattriya and the chief animal to be sacrificed in it is a horse. The *Bṛhadāraṇyaka Upaniṣad*[4] gives a subjective turn to this sacrifice, and transforms it into a meditative act in which the contemplative is to offer up the whole universe in place of the horse and by thus renouncing everything attain to true autonomy—a result analogous to the overlordship associated with the performance of the regular aśva-medha. The antagonism between the two teachings gradually disappears or at least is considerably softened, indicating

[1] See PU. pp. 61–2, 396; Macdonell: *India's Past*, p. 46.

[2] I. ii. 7.

[3] Such interpretations are common in the Āraṇyakas or 'forest-books,' which in the several Vedas serve as a connecting link between the Brāhmaṇas proper and the Upaniṣads. The Āraṇyakas were so called because their teaching was to be imparted in the seclusion of the forest (araṇya). See PU. pp. 2–3.

[4] I. i. and ii. See Deussen: *System of the Vedānta*, p. 8.

that as the Upaniṣadic doctrine more and more triumphed, an attempt was made to reconcile them. The reconciliation is clearly traceable in the later Upaniṣads. The *Śvetāśvatara Upaniṣad* for example alludes approvingly to Agni and Soma, the chief sacrificial deities, and commends a return to the old ritualistic worship.[1]

The divergence between the two views as embodied in the Brāhmaṇas and the Upaniṣads respectively is now explained by some scholars as due to the divergence in ideals between the Brahmins and the Kshattriyas—the priests and princes of ancient India. There is indeed some ground for such a view, because the Upaniṣads ascribe more than one of their characteristic doctrines to royal personages and represent Brahmins as seeking instruction of them in respect of those doctrines. But it does not afford, as some modern scholars themselves recognize, sufficient warrant for connecting this difference in ideals with a social distinction. The prominence given to the Kshattriyas in the Upaniṣads may after all mean nothing more than that kings were patrons of Brahmins and that the doctrines, though originating among the latter, were first welcomed by the former rather than by the ritual-ridden section of the Brahmins themselves.[2] It also implies that Brahma-knowledge (Brahma-vidyā) was not confined to the priests as the knowledge of the sacrifice, for the most part, was. But we need not further consider this question for, being a purely historical one, it does not directly concern us.

The word 'upaniṣad' has been variously explained by old Indian commentators, but their explanations cannot be regarded as historically or philologically accurate, for what the commentators have done is merely to read into the word the meaning which, as the result of long use, it had come to possess by their time. Moreover, the same commentator often derives the word in alternative ways showing thereby that he was speaking not of a certainty, but only of what he considered a mere possibility.[3] While thus the commentators

[1] ii. 6 and 7. See PU. pp. 64–5.
[2] See PU. p. 396; Rel.V. pp. 220 ff.
[3] Cf. Śaṁkara on *Kaṭha Up.* Introduction.

give us no help, we fortunately find the word used in the Upaniṣads themselves, and there it generally appears as synonymous with rahasya or secret. That should accordingly have been its original meaning. Etymologically the word is equivalent to 'sitting (sad) near by (upa) devotedly (ni),' and in course of time it came to signify the secret instruction imparted at such private sittings.[1] That the teaching of these works was regarded as a mystery and that much care and anxiety were bestowed upon keeping it from the unworthy lest it should be misunderstood or misapplied, come out clearly in several Upaniṣads. According to the *Praśna Upaniṣad*, for example, six pupils go to a great teacher seeking instruction of him in respect of the highest reality; but he asks them to live with him for a year before instructing them, obviously with the purpose of watching them and satisfying himself of their fitness to be taught by him. Again, when Naciketas, according to the *Kaṭha Upaniṣad*, desires to know whether or not the soul survives after death, Yama does not reply until he has tested the sincerity and strength of mind of the young inquirer. The reluctance to impart the highest truth to every one without discrimination, we may observe in passing, was not peculiar to India, but was common to all ancient peoples. Heraclitus in early Greece, for example, is reported to have stated, 'If men care for gold, they must dig for it; otherwise they must be content with straw.'

The origin of Upaniṣadic literature as it has been handed down to us is somewhat hard to trace. Hindu tradition places it on the same footing as the other species of Vedic literature —the Mantras and the Brāhmaṇas—regarding them all alike as śruti or 'revelation,' i.e. as works not ascribable to human authors. In the absence of any help from this source, we are left to mere conjecture. In the Upaniṣads we now and then come across short and pithy statements which bear the impress of set formulas, and the literary material in which they are found imbedded seems merely to amplify and illustrate the truth enshrined in them. Further, these sayings are not infrequently styled there as 'upaniṣad.' From this

[1] PU. pp. 10–15.

it has been concluded, with much probability, that the term was in the beginning applied only to these formulas which contain in a nutshell some important truth of Upaniṣadic philosophy.[1] As an example of them we may instance *Tat tvam asi*, 'That thou art,'[2] which teaches the ultimate identity of the individual and the cosmic souls. It was these philosophic formulas alone that were once communicated by teacher to pupil, the communication being preceded or followed by expository discourses. The discourses, it is surmised, assumed in course of time a definite shape though not committed to writing yet, giving rise to the Upaniṣads as we now have them. To judge from the way in which these texts have grown, they contain not the thoughts of a single teacher, but of a series of teachers, and thus represent a growth in which new ideas have mingled with the old. Such a view explains the heterogeneity sometimes seen in the teaching of even one and the same Upaniṣad. At a later time, when all the ancient lore of the Hindus was brought together and arranged, the Upaniṣads in this form were appended to the Brāhmaṇas. The significance of such close association of the Upaniṣads with the Brāhmaṇas is that when this grouping was effected the two were regarded as equally old—so old that neither of them could be referred to any specific authors. Standing thus at the end of the Veda, the Upaniṣads came to be known as 'Vedānta' or 'end of the Veda'—much as the Metaphysics of Aristotle owed its designation to its being placed after Physics in his writings. A word which at first only indicated the position of the Upaniṣads in the collection developed later the significance of the aim or fulfilment of Vedic teaching, it being permissible to use *anta* in Sanskrit, like its equivalent 'end' in English, in both these senses.

The number of Upaniṣads that have come down to us is very large—over two hundred being reckoned, but all are not equally old. The great majority of them in fact belong to comparatively recent times and hardly more than a dozen are of the period we are now considering. Even among these classical Upaniṣads, chronological differences are trace-

[1] PU. p. 20.

[2] *Ch. Up.* VI. viii. 7.

able; but generally speaking they all exhibit a family likeness both in their thoughts and in the language in which those thoughts are clothed. Hence all of them may be referred to practically the same stage in the evolution of Indian thought. We shall take into account here only the older or canonical Upaniṣads. Their date cannot be exactly determined, but they may all be regarded as pre-Buddhistic. They represent the earliest efforts of man at giving a philosophic explanation of the world, and are as such invaluable in the history of human thought. They are the admitted basis of at least one of the most important systems of Indian philosophy, viz. the Vedānta, 'which controls at the present time nearly all the higher thought of Brahminical India.' Their importance is much more than historical, for their unique spiritual power and the elements of universal appeal which they contain may exercise a considerable influence on the re-construction of thought and realignment of life in the future.

A word may now be added as regards the manner of these works. They are generally in the form of dialogues, especially the larger ones among them. Their method is more poetic than philosophic. They have been described as philosophical poems and indicate truths generally through metaphor and allegory. The language, although never bereft of the charm peculiar to the Upaniṣads, is sometimes symbolic. The style is highly elliptical and shows that the works were intended to be expounded orally by one that could readily supply whatever was lacking in their presentation of the subject. These peculiarities render the interpretation of many passages not a little difficult and account for the varied explanations given of them in the past as well as in the present. But the indefiniteness is only in regard to details, the general tenor of the teaching being quite unmistakable. Among the works comprising Vedic literature, the Upaniṣads were the first to attract the attention of foreigners. Several of these works were translated into Persian in Moghul times and were thence rendered into Latin about the beginning of the last century. It was through this Latin translation that they came to be known for the first time in Europe; and it was through it that Schopenhauer, for instance, learnt to admire them.[1] In recent times, numerous translations of them, direct from the Sanskrit, have appeared in Western languages. The subject-matter of Upaniṣadic teaching also has repeatedly engaged the attention of foreign scholars; and, among the many works published, should be mentioned Deussen's masterly work on the philosophy of the Upaniṣads, particularly for the wealth of information it contains and for the care and thoroughness of its analysis.

I

The first point that has to be considered is whether all the Upaniṣads—even the genuine ones—teach the same doctrine or not. Indian commentators have all along held the view that they do[2]; and it is inconceivable that they should have thought otherwise, for they believed that these works were *revealed* in the literal sense of that word. The agreement of the commentators, however, does not extend beyond the general recognition of the unity of Upaniṣadic teaching. As to what the exact nature of that teaching is, they differ widely from one another. This diversity of opinion should be a long-standing one, for we have references to it even in the earliest extant work systematizing the teaching of the Upaniṣads, viz. the *Vedānta-sūtra* of Bādarāyaṇa.[3] Such wide divergence in interpretation naturally suggests a doubt that, in spite of the traditional insistence to the contrary, the Upaniṣads do not embody a single doctrine; and the doubt is confirmed by an independent study of these ancient works. A modern student, not committed beforehand to follow any particular school of Vedāntic thought, will be forced to think that there are not two or three discordant views in the Upaniṣads, but several. Nor is there anything surprising in this, for the

[1] 'Schopenhauer used to have the Oupnekhat lie open upon his table, and was in the habit, before going to bed, of performing his devotions from its pages'—Rel.V. p. 55.

[2] Cf. VS. I. i. 4.

[3] See e.g. VS. I. ii. 28–31.

problem dealt with in them lends itself to such a variety of solutions and these works were moulded into their present form in a more or less casual way. All the doctrines presented in them do not, however, stand out equally prominent. Some are merely flashes of thought, others are only slightly developed and still others are but survivals from the older period. The most prominent and the best developed teaching may, if we overlook for the moment minor details, be described as monistic and idealistic. Statements like 'There is no variety here,' 'All this is Brahman,' which insist on the unity of everything that exists, are neither few nor far between in the Upaniṣads. This monistic view may be described as idealistic for, according to an equally striking number of Upaniṣadic sayings, there is nothing in the universe which, if it is not itself mental, does not presuppose mind. 'Not there the sun shines, nor the moon or the stars, not these lightnings either. Where then could this fire be? Everything shines only after the shining spirit; through its light all this shines.'[1]

Before giving an account of this doctrine we should explain the Upaniṣadic terms for the ultimate reality. These terms are two—'Brahman' and 'ātman,' which have been described as 'the two pillars on which rests nearly the whole edifice of Indian philosophy.' Their origin is somewhat obscure. The word 'Brahman' seems at first to have meant 'prayer,' being derived from a root (*bṛh*) meaning 'to grow' or 'to burst forth.' Brahman as prayer is what manifests itself in audible speech. From this should have been derived later the philosophic significance which it bears in the Upaniṣads, viz. the primary cause of the universe—what *bursts forth* spontaneously in the form of nature as a whole and not as mere speech only.[2] The explanation of the other word is more uncertain. In all probability 'ātman' originally meant 'breath' and then came to be applied to whatever constitutes the essential part of anything, more particularly

[1] *Kaṭha Up*. II. ii. 15.

[2] This derivation is what Max Müller gives, following Indian commentators. See SS. pp. 52–5. Others have seen in it other meanings such as 'magical spell.' See article on 'Brahman' in ERE.

of man, i.e. his self or soul.[1] Thus each of these terms has its own independent significance: the distinctive meaning of 'Brahman' is the ultimate source of the outer world while that of 'atman' is the inner self of man. What is remarkable about these terms is that, though entirely different in their original connotation and though occasionally bearing it still in Upaniṣadic passages, they come to be prevailingly used as synonymous—each signifying alike the eternal source of the universe including nature as well as man. The development of the same significance by these two distinct terms means that the Indian, in the course of his speculation, identified the outer reality with the inner; and by such a happy identification at last reached the goal of his long quest after unity—a goal which left all mythology far behind and was truly philosophical.

It is necessary to dwell at some length on how this identification was brought about and what its full significance is. We have stated that the word ātman developed in course of time the meaning of soul or self. That was the result of a search for the central essence of the individual as distinguished from the physical frame with which he is associated. The method here was subjective and the result was arrived at through introspection. In place of the body, breath, etc., which may easily be mistaken for the individual, we find here a deeper principle, which is psychical, finally regarded as the essence of man. Now there was from the time of the later Mantras and Brāhmaṇas the habit of seeking for a correspondence between the individual and the world and trying to discover for every important feature of the one, an appropriate counterpart in the other. It represented an effort to express the world in terms of the individual. Such an attempt at rising from the known particular to a knowledge of the unknown universal is clearly seen in the Puruṣa-sūkta for example, where parts of the universe are described as parts of Puruṣa or a giant man (p. 45). It is equally clear from one of the funeral hymns[2] which, addressing the departed, says: 'Let thine eye go to the sun; thy breath, to the wind, etc.' And we have it again

[1] SS. pp. 70–2.

[2] RV. X. 16.

when prāṇa, which as vital breath stands for an important aspect of the individual, is universalized and, as cosmic Prāṇa, is represented as the life of the world (p. 41). This notion of parallelism between the individual and the world runs throughout the literature of the later Vedic period and is found in the Upaniṣads as well.[1] The practice of viewing the whole world as a cosmic individual naturally had its influence on the conception of ātman and transformed what was but a psychical principle into a world-principle. Ātman, which as the soul or self is the inmost truth of man, became as the cosmic soul or self the inmost truth of the world. When the universe came once to be conceived in this manner, its self became the only self, the other selves being regarded as in some way identical with it.

Though this process secures the unity of the self, it does not take us as far as the unity of all Being. For the self in the case of the individual is distinguishable from the not-self such as the body; and the world-self similarly has to be distinguished from its physical embodiment, viz. the material universe. Now there was all along another movement of thought just complementary to the one we have so far sketched. It traced the visible universe to a single source named Brahman. The method there was objective, for it proceeded by analysing the outer world and not by looking inward as in the line of speculation of which ātman was the goal. In accordance with the general spirit of Indian speculation, several conceptions were evolved here also[2]—each more satisfying than the previous one to account for the universe, and Brahman was the last of the series of solutions. At some stage in the evolution of thought, this primal source of the universe, viz. Brahman, was identified with its inmost essence, viz. ātman. Thus two independent currents of thought—one resulting from the desire to understand the true nature of man and the other, that of the objective world—became blended and the blending led at once to the discovery of the unity for which there had been such a prolonged search. The physical world, which according to the ātman doctrine is only the not-self, now becomes

[1] See e.g. *Aitareya Up.* i.

[2] Cf. *Taittirīya Up.* iii.

reducible to the self. The fusing of two such outwardly different but inwardly similar conceptions into one is the chief point of Upaniṣadic teaching and is expressed in the 'great-sayings' (mahāvākya) like 'That thou art,' 'I am Brahman' or by the equation Brahman = ātman. The individual as well as the world is the manifestation of the same Reality and both are therefore at bottom one. There is, in other words, no break between nature and man or between either of them and God.

Such a synthesis, besides showing that Reality is one, carries with it an important implication. The conception of Brahman, being objective, can at best stand only for a hypothetical something—carrying no certainty necessarily with it. It is also likely for that very reason to be taken as non-spiritual in its nature. The conception of ātman on the other hand has neither of these defects; but in the sense in which we commonly understand it, it is finite and cannot represent the whole of Reality. Even as the cosmic self, it is set over against the physical world and is therefore limited by it. When, however, the two conceptions of Brahman and ātman are combined, then by a process of dialectic a third is reached which is without the flaws of either taken by itself. Like ātman it is spiritual and at the same time it is infinite unlike it. It is also indubitable, since it is conceived as fundamentally one with our own immediate self. So long as we look upon the ultimate as something not ourselves—as mere Brahman—it remains more or less an assumption and a dogma; but the moment we recognize it as one with our own self, it becomes transformed into a positive certainty, we being under an intuitive obligation to admit the reality of our own existence, however much we may be in the dark in regard to its precise nature. It is this higher reality that is described for instance as satyam jñānam anantam,[1] where satyam points to its immediate certainty, jñānam to its spiritual nature and anantam to its all-inclusive or infinite character. That is the Upaniṣadic Absolute—neither Brahman nor ātman in one sense, but both in another. It manifests itself better in the human self—though not fully

[1] Cf. *Taittirīya Up*. ii. 1.

even there—than in the outer world which inhibits still more of its nature, because it appears there as mere insentient matter.[1] The enunciation of this doctrine marked the most important advance in the whole history of India's thought. It introduced almost a revolution in the point of view from which speculation had proceeded till then. The following illustration may perhaps be of use in comprehending the nature of this change. Let us suppose that some people know Venus as only appearing in the East, and others know it as appearing only in the West—each set of people regarding the planet they observe as distinct from what the others do. If then the discovery is made by some one that the two are but the same and that the Eastern star is the Western star, the resulting transformation in the view of Venus would correspond to the change in the present case. The true conception of unity was reached in India only at this stage.[2]

All this is very beautifully brought out in a celebrated section of the *Chāndogya Upaniṣad*.[3] It is in the form of a dialogue between a father and his son. The name of the father is Uddālaka and that of his son, Śvetaketu. Śvetaketu has been to a *guru* and has just returned home after completing his education in the conventional sense. The father, who notices a lack of humility in Śvetaketu, fears that he might not after all have learnt from his teacher the true meaning of life. Inquiry only confirms him in this view; and he himself therefore undertakes to instruct his son. The teaching that is imparted, as is clear from these preliminaries, should be of the highest value. Uddālaka begins by postulating an ultimate entity which is to be regarded as mental or spiritual because it is stated to have *thought*

[1] See *Aitareya Āraṇyaka*, II. iii. 2.

[2] Even this synthesis is not quite unknown to literature anterior to the Upaniṣads (See AV. X. viii. 44); but it appears there only faintly and may therefore be justifiably described as Upaniṣadic. Compare in this connection the remark of Deussen (*System of the Vedānta*, p. 18) that 'the sparks of philosophic light appearing in the Rigveda shine out brighter and brighter until at last in the Upanishads they burst out in that bright flame which is able to light and warm us to-day.'

[3] *Ch. Up.* VI

(aikṣata) and which he terms Sat or Being. He then proceeds to describe how the whole universe is a manifestation of it. 'In the beginning Sat alone was, without a second. It thought "May I be many."' Its diversification—first into the three elements, viz. tejas or 'fire,' ap or 'water' and pṛthivī or 'earth' and then into others until organic bodies, including those of human beings, have emerged—is afterwards explained. What is made out by this is that the spiritual entity postulated in the beginning is all-comprehensive and that whatever is, has sprung from it. Then 'suddenly and with dramatic swiftness' the original Sat is identified with the self of Śvetaketu: Tat tvam asi, Svetaketo. The purpose of the identification is obviously to bring home to the mind of Śvetaketu the undoubted reality of the postulated source of the universe. However splendid the account of Sat and its transformations which Uddālaka gives at first, it is objective and therefore lacks a most essential feature, viz. certitude. It is merely to be taken for granted. Uddālaka puts it forward as a hypothesis and, though convincing to Uddālaka himself because he has realized the truth, it can be nothing more than a probability for Śvetaketu. But this probable source of the universe becomes a positive certainty to him the moment he realizes that it is identical with his own self, which he knows to be real even without being taught. This teaching of course does not leave Śvetaketu's view of his own self unchanged, for it is not his individual self that he can regard as the source of the world, but rather the universal self that is immanent in it. It is true that the world has emerged from the one and that that one is Śvetaketu's self; yet it is not his private self that can explain the universe, but his self only in so far as it is one with Sat or the universal self. 'I live; yet not I, but God liveth in me.'

When we come to consider in detail this doctrine of idealistic monism, we find it appear in two forms between which there is rather an important difference. In some passages the Absolute is presented as cosmic or all-comprehensive in its nature (saprapañca); in some others again, as acosmic or all-exclusive (niṣprapañca). There are many passages and even whole sections in the Upaniṣads treating of either. To illustrate their character, we shall refer here to one of each type:—

(1) *Cosmic Ideal.*—One of the best-known descriptions of this ideal is found in a section of the *Chāndogya Upaniṣad*[1] designated Śāṇḍilya-vidyā. After defining Brahman cryptically as tajjalān—as that (tat) which gives rise (ja) to the world, reabsorbs (li) it and supports (an) it—the section proceeds to describe it as 'comprehending all activities, all desires, all odours, all tastes, reaching all, and so self-complete as ever to be speechless and calm.' Then follows its identification with the individual self: 'This is my self within the heart, smaller than rice, or barley corn, or mustard seed or grain of millet or the kernel of a grain of millet; this is my self within the heart, greater than the earth, greater than the mid-region, greater than heaven, greater than all these worlds. This is Brahman. May I become it when I depart hence.'

(2) *Acosmic Ideal.*—For this we shall select a passage from another Upaniṣad[2]' Here a learned lady, Gārgī by name, asks Yājñavalkya, the greatest thinker of the age and probably the first idealist of the world, to tell her what the basis of the universe is. Yājñavalkya, tracing it to its penultimate source, answers that it is space (ākāśa) Further asked to explain what constitutes the basis of space itself, Yājñavalkya mentions a principle which he describes only in a negative way, implying thereby that the ultimate reality is beyond the grasp of human experience. The negative description given is as follows: 'This is the imperishable, O Gārgī, which wise people adore—not gross, not subtle, not short, not long, not red, not adhesive, without shadow, without darkness; without air, without space; unattached, without taste, without smell, without sight, without ears, without speech, without mind, without light, without breath, without mouth, without form, and without either inside or outside. Not that does anything eat; nor that does eat anything.' Lest the description should be taken to mean 'pure nothing,' Yājñavalkya adds immediately after it that whatever is, owes its being to this tran-

[1] III. xiv.

[2] *Bṛ. Up.* III. viii.

scendental reality, suggesting that if the Ultimate was a sheer blank or non-entity, it could not have given rise to the world of appearance.

It is not difficult to discover the basis for this two-fold teaching in pre-Upaniṣadic tradition. The first or saprapañca ideal resembles the doctrine underlying the 'Song of Creation' (p. 42). Only the First Principle here, unlike Ṭad Ekam there, is not conceived objectively, but as Brahman—ātman in the sense explained at the beginning of this section. As regards the second or niṣprapañca ideal, we have already drawn attention (p. 41) to the prevalence of the pantheistic tendency in the later Mantras and the Brahmaṇas and described it as somewhat inconsistent, since it aims at unity and yet clings to the double notion of God and nature. To arrive at true unity, one only of these two should be retained. If it is the notion of nature that is retained, there will be no God apart from the world. This outcome of the pantheistic tendency, viz. viewing the unity of the world as itself the Absolute, does not figure very much in the Upaniṣads, probably because it tends towards naturalism, which, though not wholly unfamiliar to them, is widely removed from their prevailing spirit.[1] If, on the other hand, it is the notion of God that is selected for retention in preference to that of nature, the world of common experience with all its variety will cease to exist apart from God. That is precisely the acosmic conception; only the theistic term is here replaced by the philosophic one of Brahman.

The determination of the relative position and importance of these two conceptions is one of the most difficult problems connected with the Upaniṣads and has occupied the attention of thinkers for a very long time. According to Śaṁkara, this problem is discussed by Bādarāyaṇa in the *Vedānta-sūtra*[2]; and it is not improbable that at one stage it engaged the attention of the Upaniṣadic sages themselves.[3] The two views as they appear here have been explained by Śaṁkara as really the same, and the apparent distinction between them as due to a difference in the standpoint from which

[1] We have an example of this in *Ch. Up*. V. xi–xviii. See p. 45, *ante*.

[2] III. ii. 11 ff.

[3] See e.g. *Praśna Up*. i. 1; v. 2.

the Absolute is looked at—cosmic from the empirical standpoint, but acosmic from the transcendental. This view is supported by the juxtaposition sometimes of the two conceptions in one and the same passage, as for example in the *Muṇḍaka Upaniṣad*[1] where we have 'What is invisible, intangible, colourless, nameless, eyeless and earless, devoid of hands and of feet—that is what is coeval with time and space, is all-pervading, subtle and changeless, which the wise know to be the source of beings.' The saprapañca conception must in that case be understood negatively as signifying that the world is not outside Brahman and the niṣprapañca conception positively as signifying that Brahman is more than the world. There is no world apart from Brahman, but it is not therefore unreal for it has its basis in Brahman. Brahman again is not nothing for it furnishes the explanation of the world, though it is not identical with it or exhausted in it. The former view would emphasize the immanence of Brahman and the latter, its transcendence, the Upaniṣadic view being that it is both immanent and transcendent. Or probably we have here two different views as the result of a difference in interpreting the result of the synthesis of the conceptions of Brahman and ātman alluded to above. The Upaniṣadic Absolute which represents this result is not, as we have seen, something objective; nor is it the subject as such, though neither is unrelated to it. Such an Absolute may be understood as being both. That would be saprapañca Brahman. In this view, the manifold things of experience have a real place in the Absolute. They actually emerge from it and are re-absorbed into it. It is Brahma-pariṇāma-vāda or the doctrine which maintains that Brahman evolves into the world. Or the Absolute may be regarded as the mere ground of both the subject and the object, in which case we would have the niṣprapañca ideal. The things of common experience are then to be regarded as only phenomena, Brahman being the noumenon. That would be Brahma-vivarta-vāda[2] or the doctrine which maintains that

[1] I. i. 6.

[2] 'Brahma-pariṇāma-vāda' and 'Brahma-vivarta-vāda' are later Vedāntic terms. See Ch. XIII.

Brahman does not change into, but merely appears as, the world. Whatever the truth may be, the distinction has given rise to a good deal of controversy. We shall have to consider this question when treating of the Vedānta system. Meanwhile we shall proceed on the basis that, though idealistic monism is the prevalent teaching of the Upaniṣads, that doctrine is presented in them in two somewhat distinct forms.

The second of these forms necessarily involves the notion of Māyā, it being understood as the principle which shows the niṣprapañca Brahman as saprapañca. It is not, therefore, right to maintain, as some have tried to do, that the doctrine of Māyā is unknown to the Upaniṣads. It is already there, but naturally it does not yet exhibit all the various features which, as the result of later elaboration and development, are associated with it in Śaṁkara's Advaita. The word 'Māyā' again, it is true, occurs only rarely in the earlier Upaniṣads; but it is found in literature still older though its meaning there may not always be clearly determinable, and also in the Upaniṣads which are not very late.[1] Even in the earliest Upaniṣads where we do not find 'Māyā,' we have its equivalent 'avidyā.'[2] There are also statements in them like the following: 'Where there is duality *as it were* (iva) one sees another'[3] which, as recognized by scholars like Deussen,[4] clearly point to the existence in the Upaniṣads of the idea that the world is an appearance.

In whichever of these two forms they may present Brahman, the Upaniṣads distinguish from it the common things constituting the universe as known to us by pointing out that they are merely nāma and rūpa. By rūpa is here meant the specific form or nature of a thing; and by nāma, the name or word that serves as its sign. By the two terms together we have to understand, in the case of any object, its particularity or determinate character; and the emergence of the world from Brahman is conceived as the differentiation of names and forms. Whether we regard these particular things as actual modes or as only appear-

1 See *Śvetāśvatara Up.* iv. 10.
2 Cf. *Kaṭha Up.* I. ii. 5.
3 *Bṛ. Up.* IV. v. 15.
4 PU. pp. 228 ff. See also Macdonell: *India's Past*, p. 47.

ances of Brahman, they are not real apart from it, which according to the monism of the Upaniṣads is the sole reality. It is not easy to discover the necessity for nāma in this characterization, as rūpa by itself seems sufficient for particularization. It probably has reference to a belief, current at the time, in the existence of a speech-world answering to the world of things and to the need there generally is for names as much as for things in practical life.[1] Sometimes the description of empirical objects is made more complete by introducing a third term, karma or 'movement,'[2] and thus explicitly referring to the dynamic factor, an important aspect of the world of experience.

As regards the details of the things derived from Brahman which are characterized by nāma and rūpa, there is to be made at the outset a distinction between the inorganic and the organic. While the latter are the abode of transmigrating souls or jīvas, the former are not. They serve only as 'the stage erected by Brahman on which the souls have to play their part.' In the inorganic realm, the Upaniṣads recognize five fundamental elements (bhūtas) termed pṛthivī (earth), ap (water), tejas (fire), vāyu (air) and ākāśa (ether). All the five were not known from the beginning. 'Water' seems to have been the sole element thought of at first (p. 44). The next stage of advance is marked by the recognition of three elements, earth, water and fire, as in the *Chāndogya Upaniṣad*, which are stated to emerge from Brahman in the reverse order. They correspond roughly to the solid, fluid and gaseous phases of the material universe. The last stage in the evolution of this thought, which was final and was accepted by practically all the later philosophers of India, was reached when the number of the so-called elements was raised to five by the addition of air and ether.[3] It is clear that in this its last form the classification is connected with the five-fold character of the sensory organs, whose distinctive objects, viz. odour, flavour, colour, temperature and sound, are respectively the distinctive features of earth,

[1] Cf. BP. p. 101, where its association is referred to a primitive period when the name was treated as 'a possession and part of the individual.'

[2] *Bṛ. Up.* I. vi. 1.

[3] *Taittirīya Up.* II. i.

water, fire, air and ether. But these elements, it should be remembered, are subtle or rudimentary (sūkṣma-bhūta). Out of these are made the gross ones (sthūla-bhūta), each of which contains an admixture of the other four, but gets its name as a compound from the element predominating in it.[1] The gross elements are what we find in nature; and strictly it is they that are to be understood by the terms pṛthivī, ap, etc., the corresponding subtle elements being known as pṛthvī-mātra, āpo-mātra, etc.[2] The organic bodies are divided into three classes 'born from the egg' (aṇḍa-ja), 'born from the germ' (jīva-ja) and 'bursting through the soil' (udbhijja).[3] To these is afterwards added[4] a fourth variety 'born from sweat' (śveda-ja), thus making four classes altogether. When organic bodies disintegrate, they are reduced to the form of the five gross elements out of which other similar bodies may be built up. Their dissolution into their constituent subtle elements does not take place until the whole universe breaks up. Regarding the time when such breaking up takes place, there is some vagueness. As in the earlier literature (p. 44), the theory of kalpa or the eternal recurrence of creation and dissolution is not explicit in the Upaniṣads. We have not, however, to wait long for its appearance. The *Śvetāśvatara Upaniṣad*, which, though one of the classical Upaniṣads, is among the latest of them and is so rich in suggestions helpful in tracing the history of early Indian thought, points to it in more than one place. Thus the Highest is there stated to have 'got angry at the end of time and retracted all the worlds' and to repeat that act many a time.[5] The theory is closely connected with the doctrine of karma to which we shall refer in a subsequent section.

[1] Strictly the mode of deriving the gross from the subtle elements (tri-vṛtkaraṇa) is explained in the Upaniṣads only with reference to three elements (see *Ch. Up*. VI. ii. 3–4). The Vedānta extended it to the five elements (pañcī-karaṇa). See VS. II. iv. 22.

[2] *Praśna Up*. iv. 8.

[3] *Ch. Up*. VI. iii. 1.

[4] *Aitareya Up*. v. 3.

[5] iii. 2; v. 3.

II

When the word 'psychology' is used in Indian philosophy, it should be understood in its original sense as the science or doctrine of the soul ('psyche'), for its teaching, except in one or two cases, is based upon the supposition that the soul exists. This study in India never branched off from philosophy and every system has therefore its own psychology. The various psychologies have, of course, a common body of doctrine; but each has its own special features as well, which are adapted to the particular school of thought to which it is affiliated. To the Upaniṣadic seers the existence of the soul is a necessary presupposition of all experience. It is the basis of all proof and itself therefore stands in need of none. 'By which, one knows all this—whereby could one know that? Lo, by what means could the knower be known'?[1] Although for this reason the Upaniṣads do not attempt to adduce any direct proof of the existence of the soul, they contain various suggestions touching the point. For example, the soul or jīva is often described as puruṣa, which is explained as puri-śaya or 'what lies in the citadel of the body.' It means that the existence of the physical body, with its diverse but co-operating parts, implies the existence of something whose end it serves. That something, apart from which the mechanism of the body would be meaningless,[2] is the soul. Another suggestion, which is based upon the karma theory, is sometimes found. In the narrow span of a single life, we cannot possibly reap the fruits of all that we do. Nor can we, so long as we confine our attention to this life alone, fully account for all the good or evil that may come to us. A single birth being thus inadequate to render intelligible all the observed facts of life, we must, if the common belief in moral requital be well founded, admit a transmigrating soul to whose actions in past lives we must look for an explanation of whatever is inexplicable in its present condition and in whose continuance after death we must find redress of any seeming injustice in this life.[3]

1 *Bṛ. Up.* II. iv. 14.
2 *Kaṭha Up.* II. ii. 1, 3 and 5.
3 *Kaṭha Up.* II. ii. 7.

The relation of the soul to the ultimate reality or of the jīva to Brahman is somewhat differently conceived in the two views of the Absolute found in the Upaniṣads. According to the cosmic view it is an actual, though only a provisional, transformation of Brahman and is as such both identical with and different from it. According to the acosmic view, it is Brahman itself appearing as the jīva and therefore not at all different from it. Whether the jīva is an actual transformation or not, its jīva-hood consists in the forgetting of its essential identity with Brahman. Though ordinarily believing that it is finite and therefore distinct from the Absolute, the soul sometimes—whenever, for any reason, desire is absent—rises above such belief and ceases to be conscious of its individuality. Such self-transcendence suggests, according to the Upaniṣads, that the jīva is not in reality the limited entity it generally takes itself to be. The question is dealt with in what is known as 'the doctrine of kośas' in the *Taittirīya Upaniṣad.*[1] The unique experience characterizing this self-transcendent state is represented there as higher than the experience of the conscious (manomaya) and the self-conscious (vijñānamaya) levels of life, because the conflicts and confusions typical of them are overcome in it; and it is described as ānandamaya[2] to indicate that its essential mark is peace. Yet it is not identifiable with mokṣa,[3] for it is only a passing phase and those who rise to it quickly fall away from it. The peace and self-forgetfulness that distinguish it show that the attitude induced by the contemplation of Art is its best illustration.[4] It stands midway between common experience and mokṣa, where the soul's true nature is fully revealed; and if it points in one direction to the empirical self

[1] ii. 1–5.

[2] The corresponding adjuncts constitute three of the five kośas or 'sheaths' regarded as enfolding the soul. The remaining two are termed annamaya and prāṇamaya—the first, which is the outermost of the kosas, being the body or material covering of the jīva and standing for the physical side of individual existence; the second, representing its vital or organic side.

[3] Cf. Brahma puccham pratiṣṭhā.

[4] Compare in this connection the use of the term rasa, 'aesthetic pleasure,' for Brahman: Raso vai saḥ (*Taittirīya Up.* ii. 7).

with its many struggles and imperfections, it does so equally definitely in the other to its oneness with Brahman, which is beyond all strife and contradiction.

The word 'jīva' is derived from the root *jīv*, which means 'to continue breathing.' The name gives prominence to one of the two aspects of life's activity, viz. the biological or unconscious such as breathing, which goes on even when the mind is quiescent as in deep sleep. The Upaniṣads use two other terms for the soul, viz. bhoktā, 'experient' and kartā,[1] 'agent,' which together emphasize the other, viz. the psychological or conscious aspect of the activity. The principle of unconscious activity is termed prāṇa; and that of conscious activity, manas. Every soul is conditioned by these two principles throughout its empirical existence. To these comparatively permanent adjuncts of it should be added the material body, which alone is replaced at every birth. These three together—the body, prāṇa and manas,[2] form a sort of 'empirical home' for the soul. The conscious side of the soul's activity is carried on by manas with the aid of the ten indriyas—five of knowledge, viz. cakṣus, śrotra, tvak, ghrāṇa and rasanā, which are respectively the organs of sight, hearing, touch, smell and flavour; and five of action—vāk, pāṇi, pāda, pāyu and upastha, which are respectively the organs of speech, holding, moving, excretion and generation. Various faculties of manas like vijñāna and ahaṁ-kāra are mentioned; but the Upaniṣads, at the same time, are careful to emphasize its unity. The *Bṛhadāraṇyaka Upaniṣad*,[3] after giving a list of several such faculties, avers 'All these are manas only.' As the central organ of consciousness, it is one, however widely its functions may differ. It controls both the sensory and motor organs. It co-ordinates the impressions received from outside through the former and also resolves, when necessary, upon acting with the aid of one or other of the five organs of action. The relation of

[1] Cf. *Praśna Up*. iv. 9; *Kaṭha Up*. I. iii. 4.

[2] If we reckon manas as three-fold with its conscious, self-conscious and self-transcendent phases, we have here the five 'sheaths' of the doctrine of kośas. See Note 2 on the previous page.

[3] I. v. 3.

manas to these two sets of organs has been compared[1] to the relation of brain to the sensory and motor nerves.

The theory of cognition according to the Upaniṣads is not easy to find out. Yet there are a few hints which we may put together here: The usual Upaniṣadic expression for the things of experience, we know, is nāma-rūpa, which signifies that whatever is thought of or spoken about is the particular. The mind and the organs of sense function only within the realm of names and forms. That is, empirical knowledge is inevitably of the finite. But this does not mean that Brahman, the infinite, is unknowable. The very purpose of the Upaniṣads is to make it known. So Brahman also is knowable; only its knowledge is of a higher type than empirical knowledge. The *Muṇḍaka Upaniṣad*[2] classifies all knowledge into two—the higher (parā vidyā) and the lower (aparā vidyā), which are respectively the knowledge of Brahman and of empirical things. The higher knowledge may not enlighten us about the details concerning particular things, but it gives us an insight into the principle of their being, as the knowledge of a lump of clay for example may be said to do in regard to everything made of clay.[3] In this sense it may be described as complete knowledge, and, as such, different from the lower knowledge, which even at its best is fragmentary. But there is no conflict between them. That is, however, only according to the cosmic conception of Brahman. There is another view equally prominent in the Upaniṣads, which harmonises with the acosmic conception. Brahman, according to it, transcends the very conditions of knowledge and consequently cannot be known. 'Speech and thought recoil from it, failing to find it.'[4] The Upaniṣads bring out this unknowability of Brahman in itself in various ways. The *Īśa Upaniṣad*, for example, does so by predicating contradictory features of Brahman: 'It moves; it moves not. It is far; it is near. It is within all this and also without all this.'[5] But the best instance of it seems to have been found in an Upaniṣad, no longer extant, to which Śaṁkara refers in his commentary on the *Vedānta-sūtra*.[6]

[1] PU. p. 263. [2] I. i. 4–5. [3] Cf. *Ch. Up*. VI. i. 3–4.
[4] *Taittirīya Up*. ii. 4. [5] Mantra 5. [6] III. ii. 17.

Bādhva, asked by Bāṣkali to expound the nature of Brahman, did so, it is stated, by keeping silent. He prayed: 'Teach me, Sir.' The other was silent, and, when addressed a second and a third time, he replied: 'I am teaching, but you do not follow. The self is silence: Upaśāntoyam ātmā.' This view denies the name of vidyā to empirical knowledge, which, from the ultimate standpoint, is not knowledge at all, but only a sort of ignorance or avidyā. It may be asked whether such a view, by denying the possibility of knowing Brahman, does not make the teaching agnostic. The answer is that though we cannot *know* Brahman, we can *be* it. 'He who "knows" Brahman will be Brahman.'[1] It is to the means leading to such a consummation that the name vidyā is confined here. Even before this result is reached we may realize *that* Brahman is though not *what* it is, for Brahman being fundamentally the same as our self, its existence, as already pointed out, is an immediate certainty. We cannot think of the Absolute, but all the same we are always in immediate contact with it in our own selves. Indeed we can never miss it.

We have so far had in view only the waking state. The Upaniṣads take a wider view of life and study the self under three other heads, viz. dream, dreamless sleep and what is termed the turīya state. Of these, dreaming like waking falls under psychology proper, for in it the mind functions; but the other two are supra-mental and are considered with a view to discover the real nature of the soul. It is noteworthy that at so early a period Indian thinkers should have thought of studying phenomena under varying conditions, which by eliminating or introducing one or more factors aid the discovery of their true character. Out of these four states only two seem to have been known at first, viz. waking and dream.[2] Later, not only is a distinction made between dream and dreamless sleep, but a *fourth* or the turīya state is added whose very name implies a precedent stage when only three states were recognized. We shall now briefly characterize these three states:

(1) *Dreams.*—The references to dreams in the Upaniṣads

[1] *Muṇḍaka Up.* III. ii. 9.

[2] PU. p. 298.

are frequent, implying that they attracted a good deal of attention at the time. The dream-state is intermediate between waking and deep sleep. Its physical condition is that the organs of sense should become wholly quiescent; and the senses then are stated to unite with the manas. The essential difference therefore between waking and dreams is that while the manas in the former receives from outside impressions which it builds up into ideas, in the latter it fashions a world of forms unaided and by itself. For this purpose it uses the material of waking hours—generally visual and auditory. Although the stuff of which dreams are made is thus revived impressions, the experience of a dream is quite unlike reminiscence. It is felt as real for the time being—as real as perceptual experience, for as everybody knows the things dreamt of are apprehended as present and not as belonging to the past. For this reason, dreams have been described as 'perception without sensation.'

(2) *Dreamless sleep.*—In this state, described as suṣupti, the manas as well as the senses is quiescent and there is consequently a cessation of normal or empirical consciousness. There is no longer any contrasting of one object with another or even of the subject with the object, and the embodied self is then said to attain a temporary union with the Absolute. As however suṣupti is not identified with the state of release, this statement has to be understood negatively—as only signifying that the consciousness of individuality is absent at the time though the individual himself continues to be, as shown by the sense of personal identity connecting the states before and after sleep. It is not a state of consciousness in the ordinary sense; but it is not a state of blank or absolute unconsciousness either, for some sort of awareness is associated with it. It is not, however, the 'objectless knowing subject' that endures in it, as it is sometimes stated[1]; for along with the object, the subject also as such disappears then. It is rather a state of non-reflective awareness, if we may so term it. This state is above all desire and is therefore described as one of unalloyed bliss. 'Sleep makes us all *pashas*.' In a dream-state

[1] See e.g. PU. p. 306.

the interests of the waking state may be absent, but it can by no means be called disinterested. It has its own pains and pleasures and lacks that complete calm which characterizes deep sleep. The perfect peace or happiness of sleep we even recollect after waking, for then our feeling is not merely that we have slept but that we have slept soundly.

(3) *Turīya state.*—This is a state which, as its improvised name suggests, is not within the experience of ordinary man. It may therefore be regarded as lying outside the strict limits of any empirical investigation. It is brought about voluntarily by the elimination of discursive thought, and resembles dreamless sleep in all respects but one. There is in it the same withdrawal of normal consciousness, the same absence of desires and the manifestation of almost the same bliss. But while the self fully reveals itself in the fourth state, the experience of dreamless sleep is extremely dim. The turīya is a mystic state to be testified to only by the person that is gifted with yogic power. But the truth he vouches for is not wholly beyond us. For we have on the one hand the negative evidence of suṣupti and on the other the positive one of the ānandamaya phase of experience, which together enable us to get a 'conjectural insight' into the nature of the knower's experience. The attainment of this state is regarded as the culmination of spiritual training.

III

The diversity of views noticed in connection with the theoretical teaching of the Upaniṣads has its reflex in their practical teaching—both in regard to the ideal to be achieved and the means of achieving it. To take the latter as an example: We find one Upaniṣad[1] mentioning three such different means for the attainment of immortality—devotion to truth, penance and Vedic study—and ascribing them to three specific teachers. There is sometimes also an attempt made to reconcile two opposing views current at the time, each of which was probably pursued independently. The *Īśa Upaniṣad*, whose main feature seems to be this spirit of

[1] *Taittirīya Up.* i. 9.

synthesis, tries to harmonize two such views in regard to attaining salvation. In the first of its eighteen verses it inculcates renunciation, but in the next verse qualifies it by adding that incessant exertion also is necessary. The Upaniṣad means thereby that one should not renounce activity and withdraw from the world, but give up only all thought of reaping any personal benefit from it—thus anticipating the well-known teaching of the Bhagavadgītā. We cannot consider all this diversity of views here, but shall refer only to the more prevalent among them.

The basis of Upaniṣadic ethics is to be found in the conception of evil, not as offending against the will of the gods or swerving from sacrificial rectitude as in the earlier period, but as the result of a metaphysical error which sees variety alone where there is also the unity of Brahman.[1] Empirical thought, failing to grasp the ultimate reality, distorts it or cuts it up into parts and presents them as distinct from one another. Evil is due on the practical side to this mistaken view of Reality as finiteness is on the theoretical side. It is thus contingent and has no place in the Absolute rightly understood. This misleading presentation of Reality is seen in the case not only of the objective world, but also of the self. It is because each of us regards himself as distinct from others that he strives to guard or aggrandize himself. 'When unity is realized and every being becomes our very self—how can there be any delusion or sorrow then?'[2] In other words, all evil is traceable to ahaṁ-kāra, the affirmation of the finite self, and the consequent tendency to live not in harmony with the rest of the world, but in opposition or at best in indifference to it. The impulse behind this ahaṁ-kāra is not in itself bad and does not need to be wholly suppressed. The instinct to live or to strive to be,

[1] According to the acosmic ideal, no doubt, both the unity and diversity are equally unreal. Yet even in that view evil disappears the moment unity is realized. In other words, there is no difference between the two teachings so far as the problem of ethics is concerned. Evil originates, according to both alike, in the consciousness that diversity *alone* is true and it is overcome by the knowledge that unity underlies it, whatever explanation may eventually be given of that unity-in-diversity itself.

[2] *Īśa Up.* 7.

which is what aham-kāra signifies, is a common feature of all animate existence and is only a manifestation of the desire for self-realization. But, being really a desire to transcend finite being, it will remain unsatisfied until it is rationalized through a knowledge of the ultimate truth and the wider self is averred in place of the narrower one. That is the meaning of Aham Brahma asmi,[1] which represents the realization of Brahman in one's own self as the highest ideal of life.

There are two well-defined descriptions of the ideal in the Upaniṣads. What is sought after in the Mantras and the Brāhmaṇas is the continuance after death of individual existence in some exalted form (p. 46). This ideal of reaching life's goal after death survives in the Upaniṣads; and Brahma-realization is represented as taking place after dissociation from the physical body, as for instance in the passage quoted in a previous section to illustrate the cosmic ideal.[2] This eschatological ideal, however, appears here very much modified for, in accordance with the prevalent view of the Upanisads, what is to be reached is represented not as other than but as identical with what reaches it. 'This is Brahman. May I become it when I depart hence.' The significance of such a view is that mokṣa is a state of eternal bliss (ānanda), for it transcends duality which is the source of all strife.[3] Along with this is found another ideal[4] which regards mokṣa as a condition, not to be attained after death, but to be realized here and now, if one so wills. A person that has reached this state continues to see variety, but he is not deluded by it because he has realized in his own experience the unity of all. We have already drawn attention (p. 19) to the significance of this ideal in the history of Indian thought. What is most noteworthy about it is its recognition of the adequacy of the present life to perfect oneself. Unlike the

[1] *Bṛ. Up.* I. iv. 10.

[2] Deussen regards this as the mokṣa doctrine appearing in an empirical form and therefore as derived from the other. See PU. pp. 358–9.

[3] Cf. *Bṛ. Up.* I. iv. 2: 'Fear springs from a second.'

[4] These two views were described later as krama-mukti and jīvan mukti respectively.

former, it signifies that mokṣa or release does not consist in a *becoming* something. It only means the discovery of what has always been a fact, and is compared to the discovery of a treasure which was all along lying hidden under the floor of one's house, but which one had so far failed to find, though passing to and from over it constantly.[1] It is the view that accords with the acosmic conception of Brahman with its implication of the phenomenality of the universe.

The practical teaching of the Upaniṣads is devised to bring about Brahma-realization in the above sense. It aims, as all such teaching should do, at the rectification of our thoughts and of our deeds. Broadly speaking, the course of discipline prescribed comprises two states:—

(1) *Cultivation of detachment* (*vairāgya*).—The prime object of Upaniṣadic discipline is the removal of ahaṁ-kāra, which is the basis of all evil; and vairagya is the name given to that attitude towards the world which results from the successful eradication of the narrow selfish impulses for which it stands. Its accomplishment necessarily presupposes a long course of training through the three āśramas or disciplinary stages—those of the religious student (brahma-carya), the householder (gārhasthya) and the anchorite (vāna-prastha)—so far as they were understood at the time. As the very word āśrama ('toil') means, they are stages of strife when selfishness is slowly but steadily rooted out. 'The good is one thing, the pleasant, another; and he that wishes to live the life of the spirit must leave the sensual life far behind.'[2] This training leads to saṁnyāsa; but we should remember that the term does not yet bear in the Upaniṣads its present significance of a formal stage in the spiritual ascent of man. It there means only the transcending of the triple mode of āśrama life, and is regarded as a consequence of Brahma-knowledge rather than a means of attaining it. In the latter sense, saṁnyāsa appears comparatively late.[3] The Upaniṣads, while fully recognizing the value of this preparatory training, do not ordinarily dwell at length upon it. They rather take it for granted and address themselves

[1] *Ch. Up.* VIII. iii. 2.

[2] *Kaṭha Up.* I. ii. 1 and 2.

[3] See PU. p. 374.

to such as have already successfully undergone that training and have acquired vairāgya.[1] That is the implication, for example, of the efforts made to keep the Upaniṣadic truth as a secret which we have already mentioned. The preliminary discipline, however, should not be viewed as wholly implicit in the Upaniṣads, for occasionally direct references to it in one or other of its various aspects are found, as for instance in a very short but most interesting section of the *Bṛhadāraṇyaka Upaniṣad.*[2] Here the inmates of the world are classified as gods (deva), men (manuṣya) and demons (asura), and are all described as the children of Prajā-pati. They approach their father seeking instruction from him as to how they should conduct themselves. The answer is brief, but it clearly indicates the necessity for grades in moral discipline according to the capacity and temperament of the persons in question. To the asuras, the commandment given is 'Have compassion on man' (dayadhvam); to the manuṣyas, 'Be generous' (datta); and to the devas, 'Learn self-control' (dāmyata). The first two of these prescribe regard for others as the chief principle of action. The third is unlike them and may appear to be purely individualistic; but, being addressed to the best, it should be taken to presuppose the training of the other two stages. The same Upaniṣad in another of its sections represents the gods as unwilling to allow man to withdraw from the sphere of social or relative morality, which is merely a rhetorical way of expressing that man ought not to break away from society (p. 21) until he has discharged his duty towards it and gained its goodwill, so to speak.[3]

(2) *Acquisition of knowledge (jñāna).*—Evil being due to a misconception of the nature of Reality, its removal can be

[1] The failure to recognize this fact has been the source of some incorrect views regarding the place of morality in the Upaniṣadic scheme of life. Thus one of the common criticisms levelled against it is that it cares little or nothing for social morality and concerns itself solely with pointing out the way for individual perfection. Deussen e.g. has stated (PU. pp. 364–5) that among the ancient Indians 'the consciousness of human solidarity, of common needs and interests was but slightly developed.'

[2] V. ii.

[3] I. iv. 10. Cf. Śaṁkara's commentary.

only through right knowledge; and if the cultivation of detachment is also laid down as necessary, it is only to render the acquisition of such knowledge possible. Detachment is a pre-condition of right knowledge. 'Having become calm, subdued, quiet, patiently enduring and collected, one should see the self in the self' says the *Bṛhadāraṇyaka Upaniṣad*.[1] The training of this second stage is threefold: śravaṇa, manana and nididhyāsana.[2] The first stands for the study of the Upaniṣads under a proper guru: 'He that has a teacher knows.'[3] It defines the place of precept and tradition in the training. It also means that the influence of an ideal is never so great on us as when we are brought into personal contact with one who is a living embodiment of that ideal. Though necessary, śravaṇa is not enough; so it is supplemented by manana or continued reflection upon what has thus been learnt with a view to get an intellectual conviction regarding it. This training is to be further supplemented by nididhyāsana or meditation, which assists directly in the realization within oneself of the unity underlying the multiplicity of the universe. The necessity for this part of the training arises as follows: Our belief in the reality of diversity as such is the result of perception and is therefore immediate. So nothing but an equally immediate apprehension of unity can effectively remove it. If variety, in the reality of which we almost instinctively believe, is not to delude us, we must *see* the unity underlying it, not merely know it. Seeing is believing. That is why the Upaniṣads speak of darśana or 'spiritual perception' in respect of the ātman or Brahman.[4] A mere reasoned conviction is not enough, though it is necessary to give us the mark, as it were, at which to shoot.[5] A successful pursuit of this course of training will result in right knowledge, which, according to the eschatological view, will lead to mokṣa later, but which, according to the other, secures it at once.

Nididhyāsana in this sense is the highest form of medita-

[1] *Bṛ. Up.* IV. iv. 23.
[2] *Id.* II. iv. 5.
[3] Ācāryavān puruṣo veda: *Ch. Up.* VI. xiv. 2.
[4] Cf. Ātmā vā are draṣṭavyaḥ: *Bṛ. Up.* II. iv. 5.
[5] Cf. *Muṇḍaka Up.* II. ii. 2–4.

tion and is possible only after considerable practice in concentration of thought. Hence the Upaniṣads prescribe several meditative exercises of a preliminary character. They are usually called upāsanas, and the prominence given to them in the Upaniṣads is comparable to that given to rites in the Brāhmaṇas. We need notice only one or two points about them. In upāsanas, the thought may be directed wholly outwards and two selected objects, both external, may be mentally identified as in the meditation of the universe as a 'horse' alluded to above; or only one external object may be chosen and it may be thought of as identical with the contemplative's own self. There is an important difference between the two forms of meditation. While the former affords exercise only in concentration, the latter gives scope, in addition, to the cultivation of sympathetic imagination—the power to place oneself in the position of another. It accordingly serves as a more direct aid to Brahma-realization, wherein also what is contemplated, viz. Brahman, is to be identified with the contemplative's self. Again the objects of contemplation may be real objects or only symbols. Among real objects which the disciple is asked to think of as one with Brahman, we often find conceptions which were once taken for ultimate reality itself, but which in course of time, as philosophic thought progressed, were superseded by higher conceptions. Such for instance is the case with Prāṇa[1] which marked an actual stage in the evolution of the conception of the Absolute. Among the symbols used for Brahman may be mentioned the famous Om, the mystic syllable, which finds a very important place in the Upaniṣads.[2] Whatever form these meditations may take, they prepare the disciple for the final mode of contemplation as Aham Brahma asmi. When a person that has morally purified himself and has after formal study and reflection convinced himself intellectually of the truth of unity, succeeds through nididhyāsana in transforming what was heretofore known only mediately into an immediate certainty, he attains the spiritual goal.

It is, however, only a very few that can achieve this goal.

[1] See e.g. *Bṛ. Up.* I. iii.

[2] Cf. *Praśna Up.* v.

The Upaniṣads themselves refer to a knower of Brahman as a rarity. 'What is hard for many even to hear, what many fail to understand even though they hear: a marvel is he that can teach it and lucky is its obtainer—a marvel is he that knows it, when taught by the wise.'[1] The many fail, the one succeeds. The majority, according to the Upaniṣads, are born again after death.[2] The constant stream of births and deaths until mokṣa is attained is what is known as saṁsāra or transmigration. It is the lot not only of those that are not virtuous, but also of those that restrict their activity to works of piety and lack right knowledge. The law which governs the kind of birth which such a jīva gets every time it dies, is known as the law of karma. It signifies that nothing can happen without a sufficient cause in the moral as in the physical world—that each life with all its pains and pleasures is the necessary result of the actions of past lives and becomes in its turn the cause, through its own activities, of future births. It traces all suffering eventually to ourselves and thus removes bitterness against God or our neighbour. What we have been makes us what we are. According to it the future, as we shall see in a later chapter, lies entirely in our own hands so that belief in this law serves as a perpetual incentive to right conduct. The principle underlying it is thus essentially different from the notion of good as a gift of the gods which we found prevailing in an earlier period.[3] It may appear to substitute fate for the gods of old, but it is a fate of which man himself is the master. The doctrine, however, cannot be regarded as embodying a demonstrable truth. Nevertheless, its value as a hypothesis for rationally explaining the observed iniquities of life is clear.

There is some difference of opinion as regards the origin of this doctrine. Some have stated that it was borrowed by the Aryans from the primitive people of their new home, among whom a belief in the passing of the soul after death into trees, etc., was found. But the view ignores that that belief was a superstition and therefore essentially

[1] *Kaṭha Up.* I. ii. 7. [2] See *Ch. Up.* V. x. 8.

[3] It is more akin to the view that sacrifices properly performed automatically yield their result.

irrational, while the doctrine of transmigration aims at satisfying man's logical as well as his moral consciousness. On account of this important difference, the doctrine should be regarded as not connected with any primitive belief, but as gradually evolved by the Indians themselves. It is true that it is not distinctly mentioned before the age of the Upaniṣads and, even among them, not all lay equal emphasis on it. All that can be said with certainty is that it had fully developed and belief in it had widely spread by the time of Buddha. But it is not difficult to trace its gradual development from earlier times.[1] The Mantras indicate a belief in the immortality of the soul; and there is also prevalent in them the idea of ṛta or moral order. But these notions, though underlying the doctrine of transmigration, do not constitute its distinctive features. The survival of the soul after death and the determination of its condition then by the moral worth of its deeds in this life are assumed by practically all religions. A true link with the doctrine is found in the notion of iṣṭāpūrta, which indeed has been described as a 'distant precursor' of karma[2]; and it already occurs in the Ṛgveda. Iṣṭa stands for the sacrifice offered to the gods and the word pūrta[3] means the gifts given to the priests. The main point about it for us to note is that the merit resulting from these acts cannot strictly be termed ethical and that it was yet believed to precede the person to the other world and there to await his arrival like a guardian angel, to secure bliss for him. In a funeral hymn the dead man is asked to join his iṣṭāpūrta. If we dissociate this belief from its exclusively sacrificial reference and widen it so as to include all deeds—good and bad, religious and secular—we see its closeness to the belief in karma. Again a gradation of rewards and punishments corresponding to the good and evil deeds of this life appears in the Brāhmaṇas and among the serious punishments meted out to the sinful is 'repeated dying' (punar-mṛtyu), which is represented as taking place in another world. The notion of repeated birth is not mentioned; but it is clear that it is implicit in that of repeated death. What the Upaniṣads

[1] See PU. pp. 313 ff.

[2] Prof. Keith: *Religion and Philosophy of the Veda*, pp. 250, 478.

[3] The word in classical Sanskrit means 'charitable deeds.'

did was to render this idea explicit and transfer the whole circle of births and deaths to this world from a hypothetical region. The soul according to this belief passes at death into another body whose character is determined by its former deeds. In its initial form, as enunciated by Yājñavalkya,[1] there is no interval between the end of one life and the beginning of the next. The belief did not, however, long remain unmodified, because it got mixed up with the earlier belief in recompense in another world. In this modified form the doctrine teaches a two-fold reward or punishment, first in the world beyond and then in a life here.[2] But that is a detail of Hindu faith which need not be further dwelt upon here.

IV

We have described how the theism of the Mantras decayed in later times under the ritualistic preoccupation of the priests. So far as it survived, it was transformed by the general philosophic bias of Indian thinking and resulted in the monotheistic conception of Prajā-pati—a god who does not represent any of the old Vedic deities, but is one above and beyond them (p. 40). The old nature-gods do not regain their position in the Upaniṣads. They are not indeed abandoned, but find mention in one connection or another. Some of them even continue to be cosmic powers which is not different from their original character; but they pale before the single reality that has now been discovered and are invariably represented as subordinate to it. Asked how many gods there are, Yājñavalkya makes light of the number thirty-three fixed in an earlier period (p. 32) and replies that there is but one, viz. Brahman.[3] All the other gods, being only its manifestations, are necessarily dependent upon it. The *Kena Upaniṣad* speaks of Agni, Vāyu and even Indra as worsted by the might of Brahman and represents them as unable to meddle even with a blade of grass without its aid.[4] Elsewhere the sun and the other gods are described

[1] *Bṛ. Up.* III. ii. 13.
[2] See *Bṛ. Up.* VI. ii; *Ch. Up.* V. iii–x.
[3] *Bṛ. Up.* III. ix. 1.
[4] iii; iv. 1–3.

as discharging their functions through its fear.[1] This is the case not merely with the ancient gods of the Mantras; even Prajā-pati, the supreme god of the Brāhmaṇas, becomes thus subordinated. The *Kauṣītakī Upaniṣad* portrays him and Indra as the door-keepers of the abode of the Highest[2]; and in the *Chāndogya Upaniṣad* he figures as but a preceptor.[3] The fact is that we cannot properly look for any theistic view in the Upanisads whose main concern is with the philosophic Absolute, except where that Absolute itself is personified and spoken of as God. Such a theistic rendering of the doctrine of the Absolute is sometimes found. Of the two forms of this doctrine, it is the cosmic that lends itself easily to such transformation. But a God so derived, being identical with the ātman, cannot ultimately be differentiated from the jīva. He can stand only for an inner principle and not for an object of adoration distinct from him that adores. The Upaniṣads explicitly repudiate such an objective conception of God. 'Whoever worships a deity thinking that to be one and himself another—he does not know.'[4] The idea of God in the Upaniṣads therefore differs fundamentally from the old Vedic view of deva—a luminous something presented as external to us (p. 32)—or even from that of the later Prajā-pati and can be described as theistic only by courtesy. The Upaniṣadic God is described as the 'inner ruler immortal' (antaryāmyamṛtaḥ) or the 'thread' (sūtra) that runs through all things and holds them together.[5] He is the central truth of both animate and inanimate existence and is accordingly not merely a transcendent but also an immanent principle. He is the creator of the universe, but he brings it into being out of himself as 'the spider does its web' and retracts it again into himself, so that creation really becomes another word for evolution here. In the terminology of the later Vedānta he is the efficient and, at the same time, the material cause of the universe (abhinna-nimittopādāna).[6]

[1] Cf. *Kaṭha Up*. II. iii. 3. [2] i. 5. [3] VIII. vii–xii.
[4] *Bṛ. Up*. I. iv. 10. Cf. *Kena Up*. i. 4–8. [5] See *Bṛ. Up*. III. vii.
[6] Such a conception, being the personalized form of Brahman, may well have been designated Brahmā. It does not, however, seem to be

Though theism in the ordinary sense thus really is incompatible with the general spirit of the Upaniṣads, we occasionally come across it in them. In the *Kaṭha Upaniṣad*[1] references are made to a God who appears to be differentiated from the individual soul. A clearer indication of it is seen in the *Śvetāśvatara Upaniṣad*, where we find all the requirements of theism—belief in God, soul and the world and the conviction that devotion to the Lord is the true means of salvation.[2] But even here the personal conception more than once gets assimilated to the impersonal or all-comprehensive Absolute; and it is difficult to believe that we have here anything more than monotheism in the making, though some scholars like Bhandarkar are of a different opinion and take it as distinctly personal.[3]

the case anywhere in the Upaniṣads or in the literature of the earlier period. Where the word Brahmā occurs as in the *Muṇḍaka Upaniṣad* (I. i. 1), it is not the name of the Highest but represents Prajā-pati regarded as a secondary deity or the 'first embodied' (prathama-ja). See SS. p. 281.

[1] I. ii. 23.

[2] i. 10 and 12.

[3] *Vaiṣṇavism, Śaivism*, etc. p. 110.

PART II

EARLY POST-VEDIC PERIOD

CHAPTER III

GENERAL TENDENCIES

So far we have dealt with the religion and philosophy of the Vedic period. We have now to give an account of the growth of Indian thought between the close of that period and the beginning of the age of the systems. These limits are not easily determinable; but, as stated in the Introduction (p. 15), it is certain that they were separated by a long interval when speculation made great strides. The diversity of doctrines which we found characterizing the previous period becomes more pronounced now, and the views that we have to deal with here include not only those whose development we have thus far described, but also those that are the result of a secession from them. This schismatic tendency, no doubt, existed in earlier times also, the Upaniṣadic doctrine itself in some of its chief aspects being a departure from the earlier teaching of the Brāhmaṇas (p. 48). But these earlier differences were either such as could in course of time be somehow composed or such as did not attain to sufficient prominence in the period to find a conspicuous place in its literature. It was otherwise in the period we are now to consider when definite heterodox schools of thought emerged, the breach between which and the old faith has never since been wholly repaired. In addition to Hindu thought, we shall consider in this Part two such prominent schools—Buddhism and Jainism. The doctrines of this period, whether orthodox or heterodox, exhibit certain common features which it is instructive to note. First, they are not intended, broadly speaking, for any specific sections of the community, but are for all, without distinction of caste or sex. It is not only Buddhism and Jainism that manifest this liberal spirit; Hinduism also does the same, as is clear from the view entertained to this day that the Mahābhārata—a very important source of information for this period—is designed chiefly for the instruction of such as have no direct access to the sacred scriptures, viz. women, śūdras and degenerate Brahmins.[1] This extended appeal should have started with the teachers of heterodox schools; but soon, and probably as a consequence of it, the orthodox also threw open their teaching in substance, if not also in form, to a wider public. Secondly, the thought of this period is predominantly realistic. Buddhism and Jainism are avowedly so. Hinduism, so far as it is the outcome of Upaniṣadic influence, no doubt still retains the old idealistic background; but it also manifests a certain concern to emphasize the reality of the external world as such and prefers to dwell on the idea of the cosmic Absolute rather than the acosmic, remodelling it into well-defined theism. Characteristics like these unmistakably point to a general awakening of the common people at the time, but it is not necessary for us to enter into the details of this popular movement, which is a matter for history rather than for philosophy.

Our authorities for the period in respect of heterodox views are, in addition to Sanskrit sources, a vast literature written in one or other of the Prākṛitic languages such as Pāli in which the teachings of early Buddhism appear. As regards orthodox thought, we have for our source of information, some out of the many remaining Upaniṣads and a species of literature consisting of concise aphorisms and known as Kalpa with its triple division into the Śrouta, Gṛhya and Dharma Sūtras.[2] The Upaniṣads, though setting forth the doctrine of the Absolute, exhibit a development particularly on theistic and realistic lines. The classical Upaniṣads all alike deal with practically the same doctrine; but the later ones fall into groups, each dealing predominantly, if not exclusively, with a special topic which is either new or is but briefly touched on in the earlier ones. Thus there are Upaniṣads treating of contemplation (yoga) or renunciation (saṁnyāsa) as means of salvation or glorifying Śiva or Viṣṇu conceived as God supreme. But we

[1] *Bhāgavata* I. iv. 25–26; Mbh. xii. 327, st. 44 and 49 (Bombay Edn.).
[2] Much of the material in the smṛtis like that of Manu relates to this period, though the version in which it now appears is generally late.

cannot take them all into consideration here, as there is considerable doubt regarding the date of many of them. We shall select as a representative of the class but one, viz. the *Maitrī Upaniṣad,* about whose assignment to this period there is a more general agreement, though even that Upaniṣad is not free from portions appended later. Of the latter, viz. the Kalpa, the Śrouta-sūtras profess to systematize the sacrificial lore of the Brāhmaṇas, but doubtless include much later material. The Gṛhya-sūtras portray the ideal of life from the standpoint of the family and describe ceremonies such as marriage and upanayanam or the initiation by the teacher of the pupil into the study of the Veda. The Dharma-sūtras, dealing as they do with customary law and morals, present the norm of life from the standpoint of the state or society. All these aphoristic codes, like the Mantras and the Brāhmaṇas, are concerned chiefly with priestly life; and whatever advance they indicate or whatever further amplification they contain is ritualistic in character so that their interest for philosophy is but indirect. A much more valuable source of information for us here than either the Upaniṣads or the Kalpa-sūtras is to be found in the older sections of the epics, especially of the Mahābhārata, which has been described as a great store-house of post-Vedic mythology and doctrine, and whose comprehensive character is well indicated by a statement occurring in the last of its eighteen sections—'Whatever is worthy to be known in matters relating to the welfare of man is here; and what is not here is nowhere else to be found.' Strangely, however, it contains orthodox and heterodox views side by side and often mixes up one doctrine with another 'without any apparent sense of their congruity.' This is accounted for by the fact that it is not the work of a single author or of a single age, but represents the growth of many generations —even of centuries. Though it contains a good deal bearing upon the period we are now considering, it includes much that is undoubtedly subsequent to it; but it is very difficult to distinguish the old from the new in it. This cause, combined with the vastness of the work and the uncritical character of its editions so far published, prevents us from entering into details. We can indicate only the broad tendencies of thought discoverable in it so far as the period we are now considering is concerned.[1] We shall take up the Sanskrit works in the present chapter, postponing to the last two chapters of this Part the consideration of Buddhism and Jainism whose early teachings have come down to us through the medium of Prākṛt. We shall also in dealing with the Mahābhārata reserve the Bhagavadgītā for separate treatment on account of its great importance.

I

All the four currents of thought alluded to in the previous Part are represented here—Ritualism, Absolutism, Theism and what, following Bloomfield, we have described as 'Vedic free-thinking.' But each exhibits more or less important modifications which we shall now briefly indicate:

(1) *Ritualism.*—This is the teaching of the Kalpa-sūtras, whose aim is to elaborate and systematize the ritualistic teaching of the Veda. For this purpose they attempt to consolidate the literature in which that teaching is contained. They define its limits and lay down strict rules for its study and preservation, speaking of the very recitation of the Veda (svādhyāya) as a 'sacrifice' and as the highest form of self-discipline (tapas).[2] In this connection they further regulate the institution of the four āśramas (p. 75)—particularly that of the religious student by whom the Veda is to be studied and that of the householder to whom most of its behests are addressed. The Sūtras are thus essentially retrospective in their attitude and represent the conservative element in the thought of the period. Ritualism as a creed is not of much consequence for us now; and whatever further observations on it are necessary will be postponed to the chapter on the Mīmāṁsā system in the next Part. The

[1] We shall take as the chief basis for our conclusions the *Mokṣa-dharma* of the *Śānti-parva*, which is the biggest philosophical section of the epic and which in importance stands next only to the Bhagavadgītā.

[2] ADS. I. xii. 1 and 3.

only point that may be noticed is that we are here almost entirely in the realm of tradition regarded as an inviolable authority. Respect for tradition can be traced in the Brāhmaṇas also, which now and then, by way of supporting their views, cite an earlier text or mention an old teacher. But it is only implicit there, and is not formally recognized as here. The tradition itself is two-fold; it is either that of the Veda or of samaya, as it is termed, which means the habitual observances of the cultured Aryans (śiṣṭas). But the Kalpa-sūtras try to make out that such observances also are based upon the authority of the Veda, if not in its extant form in some other which, as it is naïvely declared, has since been lost.[1] The diligent attention paid to the codification of old laws and customs implies a consciousness of inferiority in its authors as compared with their forefathers.[2] It also signifies a fear that their social and religious institutions might become corrupt by outside influence—a fear justified by the fact that the heretical sections were then growing in strength and had begun to exhibit constructive power and formulate their own rival doctrines.

In the later Upaniṣads, as we have already had occasion to notice (p. 49), there is a tendency to revert to sacrificial worship as taught in the Brāhmaṇas. In the *Maitrī Upaniṣad*, which we have chosen as our specimen for the period, the tendency reaches its climax, for there we find adherence to Vedic ceremonial represented as indispensable to a knowledge of the self. After defining duty as 'what is taught in the Veda,' the Upaniṣad adds that no one that transgresses it can be said to lead a disciplined life.[3] But these Upaniṣads at the same time contemplate a state when the obligation to perform Vedic rites is transcended so that their attitude towards ritualism, though not unfavourable, is not the same as that of the Kalpa-sūtras which subordinate everything else to it. Thus the same Upaniṣad,[4] speaking of a knower, says: 'He

[1] All rules for guidance, it is stated, are given in the Brāhmaṇas, but where there is no quotable text to support a current practice, its existence once is to be inferred from such practice. See ADS. I. xii. 10. There were also other ways of justifying samaya. See com. on GDS. i. 6. [2] Cf. ADS. I. v. 4. [3] iv. 3. [4] vi. 9.

meditates only on himself; he sacrifices only in himself'—a statement which, in the light of the view the Upaniṣad takes of Vedic ceremonial in general, should be understood not as suggesting any hostility towards it, but only as denying the need for it in the case of one that has passed the stage of preparatory discipline. Here we find a new conception of ritual which becomes quite prominent later. It is neither a seeking of material favours from the gods nor a mere magical device, but a 'cure for sin' (durita-kṣaya)—a means of purifying the heart and thereby qualifying for a successful pursuit of the knowledge that brings salvation.[1] 'Discipline leads to purity; and purity, to discrimination. Discrimination wins the self, winning which one does not return to this life.[2]

The attitude of the Mahābhārata towards Vedic ritual is quite indefinite. Passages can be cited from it which glorify sacrifice; but there are others in it whose general spirit is unfavourable or even antagonistic to ritualism. Thus in one of the chapters,[3] significantly styled 'Reviling of Sacrifice' (Yajña-nindā), is narrated the story of a pious Brahmin dwelling in a forest who, desiring to perform a sacrifice, but unwilling to injure any living being, presents only grains to the gods. Observing this, an antelope living there, which in reality is only Dharma or the god of righteousness in disguise, addresses him on the futility of such a rite and offers itself to be sacrificed. The Brahmin at first declines the offer, but when the animal reminds him of the good that will result to itself thereby, he assents—a turn in the story obviously to bring out the sophistry of those that were justifying animal sacrifice on the ground that the victim like the sacrificer stood to gain by it. But the story adds that the moment the antelope was immolated the Brahmin lost all the merit that he had acquired by his previous pious life, and that the animal, reassuming its original divine form, taught him the principle of non-injury (ahiṁsā), describing it as 'virtue entire' (sakalo dharmaḥ).[4]

[1] This idea is already found in the *Śvetāśvatara Up.* (ii. 7). Cf. EI. p. 53. [2] *Maitrī Up.* iv. 3. [3] xii. 272.

[4] Ahiṁsā is an integral part of heterodox thought as we now know it from Buddhism and Jainism. But it should not be taken as

(2) *Absolutism.*[1]—While it is evident that monism is the prevalent teaching of the later Upaniṣads, there is, as in the case of the earlier ones, an ambiguity sometimes as to what particular form of it they inculcate. Passages can easily be found in them which taken by themselves support either the cosmic or the acosmic view. But the general tendency is to lay stress upon the realistic side—to look upon the physical world as an actual emanation from Brahman—and to dwell upon the distinction between the soul and Brahman as well as that between one soul and another. The latter, for instance, is very well brought out in the *Maitrī Upaniṣad*, where the empirical self or jīva is termed bhūtātman—the self as enmeshed in the body constituted out of the five elements, and is described as another (anya) and as different (apara)[2] from Brahman. 'Overcome by nature's qualities, it feels deluded and therefore fails to perceive the almighty Lord dwelling within itself.' The distinction no doubt is not intrinsic, being entirely due to the association of the jīva with the physical body, as signified by the name bhūtātman; and it can be overcome and oneness (sāyujya) with Brahman[3] attained by the jīva when it realizes that truth. But yet the recognition of its provisional separateness from Brahman here is clear and its implication is that the physical universe, springing into being from Brahman, is real. Such views already appear in the older Upaniṣads, but the point to be noted is the elaboration and the emphasis they receive here.

As regards the epic, the influence of the Upaniṣads is

unknown to the orthodox. The Kalpa-sūtras like that of Gautama give quite a prominent place to it in their teaching (ii. 19, 23; ix. 70); and it is also found taught in the *Ch. Up.*, for instance, in III. xvii. 4. The fact is that it was originally part and parcel of the vānaprastha ideal of austere life to which the objection commonly urged against this virtue being Vedic, viz. that it is incompatible with the sacrificing of animals, is not applicable. See EI. pp. 165–6 and Prof. Jacobi. SBE. vol. XXII. pp. xxii. ff.

[1] The Kalpa-sūtras refer to 'self-realization' (ātma-lābha) and 'oneness with Brahman' (brahmaṇaḥ sāyujyam) as the highest end of man. But the reference is quite incidental, their foremost aim being to expound ritual. We shall recur to the former aspect of their teaching in the chapter on the Mīmāṁsā system in the next Part. See ADS. I. xxii. 2 ff.; GDS. viii. 22–3; iii. 9. [2] iii. 2. [3] iv. 4.

distinctly traceable both in its thought and in its expression, and monism is a prominent feature of its teaching. But owing to the general uncertainty attaching to such accounts found in the work, it is not easy to determine what particular shade of it we have in any section of it. Both the cosmic and acosmic conceptions appear, and often an account which begins with the one easily drifts on to the other. It is equally hard to say which of these two conceptions is the older there. To judge from the popular character of the original epic, the cosmic conception should be the earlier. Though the same as the Upaniṣadic account, it is set forth with added detail, for, like other epic accounts, it also appears in a mythological setting reminding us of early Vedic thought. Thus in a long section[1] professing to reproduce the conversation between sage Vyāsa and his son Śuka, the Creator is described as having his own 'day' and 'night'—each of which, speaking from the human standpoint, is of almost infinite duration. Creation takes place each day at dawn, and at its close what was created is withdrawn. Brahman is described here[2] as the sole reality existing before creation—'without beginning and without end, unborn, resplendent, above decay, constant, imperishable, difficult to be thought of or known.' It is said to evolve (vikurute)[3] into the universe so that the view is what we have described as Brahma-pariṇāma-vāda (p. 62). There emerge from it first 'intellect' (mahat) and 'mind' (manas); then in order, the five elements beginning with ākāśa, each with its own unique property.[4] In other words, the undifferentiated primal Being becomes differentiated or the timeless comes to be in time. But these seven principles—psychical and physical—each standing apart from the rest, cannot help on the process of evolution. So they combine together to produce an organic body (śarīra). Spirit as embodied in it, the 'first-embodied' (prathama-ja)[5] as it is sometimes styled, is Prajā-pati and he creates individual beings—both animate and inanimate—constituting the world as we know it. Dissolution takes place

[1] xii. 231–255.
[2] xii. 231. 11.
[3] xii. 231. 32.
[4] xii. 232. 2–7.
[5] See Note 6 on p. 82 *ante*.

in the reverse order when Brahman retracts the whole universe into itself. The processes of evolution and dissolution go on successively as implied by the terms 'day' and 'night' in the above account. The points of special interest here are (1) that Māyā has no place in the scheme of creation[1]; (2) that evolution takes place in two stages—the first proceeding from Brahman and giving rise to what may be described as 'cosmic factors' or physical and psychical elements in the aggregate, and the second proceeding from Prajā-pati and bringing into being individual things[2]; and (3) that creation takes place periodically, involving the idea of kalpa which, though not unknown to the earlier literature (p. 65), is by no means conspicuous there.

(3) *Theism.*[3]—We have indicated the place of Theism in Vedic literature. The transformation of the impersonal Brahman or the Absolute into a personal God which was still in progress in the older Upaniṣads is now complete, the earliest of the monotheistic conceptions to appear in the post-Vedic period being Brahmā.[4] According to the evidence of early Buddhistic literature, this conception occupied the highest rank already in Buddha's time.[5] It is to be met with in the earlier portions of the epic; but owing to an old confusion between Prajā-pati and Brahman, who are alike deemed the source of all, Brahmā, whose conception is derived from the latter, is frequently identified with Prajā-pati. To illustrate his supremacy, we may cite the section known as the 'Dialogue between Mṛtyu and Prajā-pati,'[6] which propounds in the form of a legend an

[1] There is indeed a reference to avidyā in one of the two accounts here (Ch. 232, 2); but, as observed by Prof. Hopkins (*The Great Epic of India*; p. 141), it is an after-thought.

[2] Respectively known as samaṣṭi-sṛṣṭi and vyaṣṭi-sṛṣṭi.

[3] We restrict ourselves here to the epic, as theism has but a small place in the Kalpa-sūtras or even in the later Upaniṣads, if we leave out those that glorify Viṣṇu or Śiva specifically.

[4] Macdonell: *History of Sanskrit Literature*, p. 285; and *India's Past*, p. 34.

[5] Cf. Mrs. Rhys Davids: *Buddhism*, p. 57.

[6] Mbh. xii. 256–8. It is not suggested that these sections, in the form in which we now have them, necessarily belong to the period under consideration. They only contain an allusion to what is recognized on all hands now to be the earliest form of post-Vedic monotheism.

answer to the important problem of death. As set forth here, Prajā-pati, who is the same as Brahmā,[1] creates living beings; and when, after the lapse of some time, he finds the three worlds dense with them—'oppressed as it were for want of breath'—he gives vent to his wrath in order to bring about total destruction. All 'movable and immovable things' begin to be consumed by the fire of his anger. Thereupon god Śiva, filled with compassion, approaches Brahmā offering prayer to him. Moved by that prayer, Brahmā substitutes for total destruction individual death, the implication being that death in some form is necessary, in order that life—universal life—may continue and that the disappearance of the particular, so far from being an evil, is imperative for the preservation of the world as a whole. He appoints for the purpose of determining who should die and when, one that is figured, strangely enough, as a lovely maiden sprung from his own wrath. The maiden shows great reluctance to play this doleful part, especially as she is to put an end to the lives of the young as well as the old,[2] but is pacified by Brahmā, who assures her that no sin or blame will attach to her for assisting in the work of destruction, since she acts according to law. The goddess of Death is the goddess of justice (dharma). The underlying thought is what has so long characterized the Indian view of life and is the essence of the belief in karma that neither death nor any other form of punishment is inflicted by an external agency, but is merely the recoil of the deed upon its doer. The wicked suffer in consequence of their sin. Brahmā is here termed the supreme God (paramo devaḥ). He controls all the affairs of this world being its creator, preserver and destroyer. He is depicted as subject to the emotions of anger, love and pity, indicating that the conception is fully personal. He is higher than all the gods and goddesses for even Śiva admits his inferiority by saying that he has been employed by Brahmā to look after the welfare of the world,[3] and goddess Death thinks of nobody else to pray to for escaping from the terrific work that has fallen to her lot.

The shifting character of Vedic monotheism is to some

[1] 258. 13. [2] 258. 4. [3] 257. 11.

extent repeated here and Brahmā's place comes to be taken by Śiva. The conception of Śiva seems to have attained to this position of eminence by the time of the Greek invasion.[1] It occupies that rank in certain comparatively late portions of the epic. The elevation, however, is merely ascribing supremacy to an old Vedic god, for Śiva or Rudra, as he usually appears there, is not only older than Brahmā, but also Prajā-pati, whose conception is not found till the later Vedic period. Being a nature-god, he also represents a different type of divinity. It is interesting to trace the history of this conception from the very beginning. Amongst the powers worshipped by early man there would naturally be benignant as well as malignant ones. Rudra was one of the latter—the 'howling' god that went about spreading devastation with the assistance of Maruts or storm-gods represented as his sons. But in course of time he came to be designated Śiva or 'the auspicious.' A truly divine power cannot in itself be malignant; and whatever dread it may inspire should be ascribed to a sense of sin in man. It is the recognition of this truth that in all probability explains the change in the title of the deity.[2] In this double form of Rudra-Śiva, he was the object of love as well as of fear[3]; and, as his importance gradually grew, he became the supreme God. In the Atharva-veda[4] and at least once in the Ṛgveda,[5] where there is a reference to his 'universal dominion' (sāmrājya), Śiva seems to assume that role already; but taking all things into consideration, his pre-eminence there should be explained as due to the henotheistic tendency to which we have alluded (p. 38). The *Śvetāśvatara Upaniṣad*[6] alludes more than once to this god and there he does more definitely stand for the Highest; but the con-

[1] Macdonell: *History of Sanskrit Literature*, p. 286.

[2] See Bhandarkar: *Vaiṛṇavism, Śaivism*, etc. p. 102. Compare also what Nīlakaṇṭha says in his commentary on Mbh. xii. 284. According to others, the new name is only euphemistic—due to the habit of referring to the dreadful by a gentle name (Macdonell: *India's Past*, p. 30).

[3] To this duality of nature is doubtless due the conception of Śiva as half man and half woman (ardha-nārīśvara).

[4] IV. 28. 1. [5] VII. 46. 2. [6] See e.g. iii. 4.

ception appears in it assimilated to the philosophic Absolute (p. 83), and is hardly that of a people's god as it generally is in the epic. As an instance of his supremacy in the Mahābhārata, or rather as that of a stage in his attaining to it, we may refer to the section[1] where the well-known story is narrated[2] of the destruction of Dakṣa's sacrifice by the emissaries of Rudra because their chief had not been invited to it, and where he is described as the highest of the gods and as both creator and preserver of the world.

About the same period and probably in a different part of the country[3] Viṣṇu, another god, came to prominence. He also, like Śiva and unlike Prajā-pati, is an old Vedic god and appears in the Ṛgveda as a minor deity or at best only on a footing of equality with the others. He is there intimately associated with Indra and is even in later mythology known as 'the younger brother of Indra' (Indrāvaraja). In the Brāhmaṇas, his position is more exalted[4]; and he is repeatedly identified with the sacrifice—an honour which he shares with Prajā-pati and which foreshadows his coming supremacy. He gradually supersedes the other gods and becomes supreme. His elevation, especially above Prajā-pati, can be distinctly traced, for the achievements once ascribed to the latter are gradually transferred to him. Thus according to the *Śata-patha Brāhmaṇa*,[5] Prajā-pati assumes the forms of a tortoise and of a boar; but they later come to be represented as the avatārs or incarnations of Viṣṇu. The desire to manifest himself in this way for saving mankind is indeed regarded now as a mark of Viṣṇu, showing his special characteristic of benevolence. The word *avatār,* we may state by the way, means 'descent,' i.e. a coming down of God to earth and the thought contained in it is that of a deity that intervenes when man, forgetting the divine within him, shows a tendency to lapse into the state of a mere natural being. 'When righteousness wanes and unrighteousness

[1] xii. 284.
[2] The antagonism to the sacrificial cult implied here may be noted.
[3] See Macdonell: *History of Sanskrit Literature*, p. 411.
[4] Prof. Keith: *Religion and Philosophy of the Veda*, pp. 110–12.
[5] VII. iv. 3, 5; XIV. i. 2, 11.

begins to flourish, then I become incarnate.'[1] Assuming a mortal form then, he re-establishes dharma; and in doing so serves as an embodiment of the ideal for man which he should ever keep before himself. There is evidence to show that, like the conception of Śiva, that of Viṣṇu also had reached pre-eminence by the time of the Greek invasion. There was also another conception, viz. that of Nārāyaṇa, gradually evolving in the later Vedic period. The word 'Nārāyaṇa' means 'descendant of Nara or the primeval male,' i.e. Puruṣa from whom the whole universe springs into existence (p. 45), according to the Puruṣa-sūkta. He appears as supreme in certain passages of the Brāhmaṇas,[2] and later is identified with Viṣṇu giving rise to the conception of Viṣṇu-Nārāyaṇa, parallel to that of Rudra-Śiva. Thenceforward these two conceptions dominate the religious thought of India.[3] Brahmā 'has his origin and basis in speculation rather than in popular cult and therefore he did not appeal, in spite of his sublime character, to the religious feelings of the masses.'[4]

The supremacy of the Viṣṇu-Nārāyaṇa conception appears oftenest in the Mahābhārata. But it is generally found blended there with another, whose origin and general features we must now indicate. This second current of theistic thought is what is described as theism of the Bhāgavata type. It recognized only a transcendent God while Vedic theism, as may be expected from its kinship with the Upaniṣads, tended to view him as both immanent and transcendent. The Bhāgavata creed seems to have been non-Brahminic in its origin, though not non-Aryan. It probably originated in that part of the country which lies west of the classic Madhya-deśa between the Ganges and the Jumna, where most of the early Upaniṣads were composed. The creed was founded long before Buddha's time by Śrī Kṛṣṇa, a hero of

1 BG. iv. 7.
2 *Śata-patha Brāhmaṇa*, XIII. vi. 1. 1.
3 But neither, like Brahmā prior to them, is a sectarian deity. That phase of Indian belief is still later and belongs to a period subsequent to the one we are now considering.
4 ERE. vol. ii. pp. 810–811.

the Aryan tribes dwelling there.[1] Its essential features were belief in a single personal God, Vāsudeva, and in salvation as resulting from an unswerving devotion to him. Briefly we may say that it resembles the Hebraic type of godhead which we found in Varuṇa (p. 34) in the Ṛgveda. In fact the influence of Christianity has been traced in it by some like Weber, the German orientalist; but, since the existence of the creed long before the Christian era is indubitable, the theory has not commended itself to scholars in general.[2] Later, as it so often happens, the hero who preached this creed was himself deified and identified with the Supreme. In Śrī Kṛṣṇa's time, the designation of the supreme God was probably 'Bhagavat'[3] or 'the worshipful,' whence the name Bhāgavata or 'worshipper of Bhagavat.' The name 'Bhagavadgītā' ('Lord's song') given to the well-known work, which appears as an inset in the epic, suggests that when it was composed Śrī Kṛṣṇa had come to be worshipped as the Supreme. This religion in still later times was amalgamated with the theistic teaching of the Madhya-deśa, probably as a set-off against the secessions that were gaining strength in the East; and then Śrī Kṛṣṇa was identified with Viṣṇu-Nārāyaṇa, who had by that time come to be looked upon there as the Highest. In this final form the doctrine is very elaborately treated of in the sections of the Mahābhārata known as the *Nārāyaṇīya*[4]; but it there indicates a development which almost certainly is in advance of the period with which we are now concerned. An earlier phase of the same is seen in the Bhagavadgītā where, for instance, the identification of Śrī Kṛṣṇa with Viṣṇu-Nārāyaṇa does not yet appear.[5] It may be assigned to the period under consideration

[1] 'The worship of Krishna seems to have been popular during the first centuries of the development of the Jaina creed'—Prof. Jacobi: SBE. vol. XXII. p. xxxi. n.

[2] See e.g. Prof. Winternitz: *History of Indian Literature* (Eng. Tr.), vol. i. p. 431 n.

[3] It could not, however, have been the exclusive title of this god, since it is used of Śiva in *Śvetāśvatara Up.* (iii. 11). Compare also the term *śiva-bhāgavata* used in the *Mahābhāṣya* under V. ii. 76.

[4] xii. 334–51.

[5] Cf. Bhandarkar: *op. cit.* p. 13.

now, and we shall consider it in some detail in the next chapter.

(4) *Heretical Views.*—It is perhaps necessary to remind the reader that by 'heretical' we mean nothing more than antagonism to the Vedas (p. 16), particularly to their sacrificial teaching and the customs and institutions directly connected with it. We know (p. 43) that the opposition to Vedic religion is very old and that allusions to unbelievers are found so early as the hymns of the Ṛgveda. There is plenty of evidence to show that it was continued in the period under consideration and was further strengthened under the influence of the general reawakening of the people already mentioned. Buddhistic and Jaina works refer to numerous philosophical schools[1] other than the Vedic, as having existed when Gotama and Mahāvīra taught. Hindu tradition also, reaching back to about the same time, refers to the courts of ancient kings, teeming with teachers expounding separate doctrines including heretical ones.[2] Yāska again, the well-known Vedic exegete who flourished about 500 B.C., mentions in his *Nirukta* one Kautsa, who seems to have criticized the Veda as either meaningless or self-contradictory, and controverts at length his anti-Vedic opinions.[3] The Kalpa-sūtras also occasionally refer to infidels (nāstika) classing them with sinners and criminals.[4] It is this heretical thought, almost as ancient as the doctrine of the priests and now become prominent, that gives rise to the distinction between the ideals of the Brāhmaṇas and the Śramaṇas or non-priestly ascetics, frequently mentioned in the records of the period and noticed even by foreigners like Megasthenes.[5]

These views from their very nature must have originated outside the hieratic circles, but it does not mean that Brahmins were not connected with them. We know that there were Brahmins that dwelt in the forest who were not

[1] *Cambridge History of India*, vol. i. p. 150.

[2] See e.g. Mbh. xii. 218. 4–5. [3] I. xv–xvi. [4] Cf. GDS. xv. 15.

[5] *Cambridge History of India*, vol. i. pp. 419 ff. Compare also Prof. Winternitz: *Ascetic Literature in Ancient India*, already mentioned pp. 1–2.

priests by profession.[1] It is most likely that they contributed not a little towards the development of such doctrines. This is also corroborated by tradition. Thus while Vidura, who is of 'low origin,' appears as the spokesman of this type of doctrine often in the epic, there are others like Ajagara[2] who expound the same, but are Brahmins. According to the evidence of early Buddhistic literature also, there were Brahmins as well as Śramaṇas who denied a surviving soul and refused to believe in transmigration.[3] In fact, we have here an exact parallel to what happened in the case of the Indian language.[4] As in the history of the Indian language we have an epic phase distinguished from the language of the priests (śiṣṭas), so we have in the history of Indian philosophy a creed, with ramifications of its own, of the upper reflective classes other than the professional priests.[5] The influence of the heterodox doctrine is transparent in more than one sphere of Indian thought, as we now know it. It has given rise directly or indirectly to religious systems like Jainism and Buddhism[6] and in later scholastic philosophy it is represented, however inadequately, by the Cārvāka system. On the other schools also like the Sāṅkhya it has, as we shall see, left its indelible mark. But it is sometimes very difficult to say in the case of a tenet whether it owed its origin to the priests or to the others; for, as in the case of language whose evolution serves as a pattern for us here, the secular creed, as we may term it, has influenced the orthodox

[1] *Cambridge History of India*, vol. i. pp. 421–2. Cf. Prof. Jacobi: SBE. vol. XXII. p. xxxii.

[2] xii. 179.

[3] See e.g. passage quoted from the *Saṁyuttaka-nikāya* in Oldenberg's *Buddha* (pp. 272–3).

[4] Cf. Keith: *Classical Sanskrit Literature*, pp. 11–12.

[5] To complete the parallel, we have to mention the existence of popular faiths corresponding to the many Prākṛts spoken by the common folk.

[6] 'The similarity between some of those 'heretical' doctrines on the one side, and Jaina or Buddhist ideas on the other, is very suggestive, and favours the assumption that the Buddha, as well as Mahavira, owed some of his conceptions to these very heretics and formulated others under the influence of the controversies which were continually going on with them.' SBE. vol. XLV. p. xxvii. Cf. also Prof. Winternitz: *op. cit.* pp. 1 and 18.

belief and has in turn been influenced by it leading to the obliteration in great part of the distinction between the two sets of tenets (p. 25). The very early alliance with Vedic teaching of the Upaniṣadic doctrine, which should have initiated many a 'heretical' view, is also largely responsible for this result.

Though the heretical doctrine represents so important a stream of thought and incidental references to it in philosophical works are far from scanty, no detailed exposition of it is to be found in any part of early Sanskrit literature. It no doubt appears now and then in the Mahābhārata; but owing to the revision which the epic has undergone at the hands of its later editors, it appears re-touched or largely mixed up with the tenets of other faiths. That the doctrine as now found set forth in that work has also come under the review of unsympathetic thinkers and has possibly suffered distortion is clear from its being traced there often to such objectionable sources as demons (asuras).[1] Though thus modified, the Mahābhārata account is the only considerable one from which we have to draw our information about it for the present period. The doctrine seems to have had its own divergences. The *Śvetāśvatara Upaniṣad* already mentions nearly half a dozen[2] views of the kind, and the epic accounts also suggest a similar diversity in its teaching; but we cannot state the exact scope of any of them. Two of them, however, may here be distinguished for their knowledge will be of service to us in understanding certain aspects of the later history of Indian thought. They are 'accidentalism,' described as Yadṛcchā-vāda or Animitta-vāda, and 'naturalism' or Svabhāva-vāda. Both are found separately mentioned in the *Śvetāśvatara Upaniśad* and later works also make that distinction.[3] While the one maintains that the world is a chaos and ascribes whatever order is seen in it to mere chance, the other recognizes that 'things are as their nature makes them.'[4] While the former denies causation altogether,

[1] For example, Bali and Prahrāda appearing respectively in xii. 224 and 222 are asuras.

[2] i. 2.

[3] Cf. *Kusumāñjali*, i. 5. There is a reference to Animitta-vāda in NS. IV. i. 22–24.

[4] Svabhāva-bhāvino bhāvān. Mbh. xii. 222, 27. See also st. 15 ff.

the latter acknowledges its universality, but only traces all changes to the thing itself to which they belong. Everything is unique and its entire history is predetermined by that uniqueness. Hence according to the Svabhāva-vāda, it is not a lawless world in which we live; only there is no external principle governing it. It is self-determined, not undetermined. So this doctrine, unlike the other, recognizes necessity as governing all phenomena; but it is a necessity that is inherent in the very nature of a thing, not imposed upon it by any external agency. It is because we are blind to this fact that we imagine that things obey no law or that we can intervene with success in the course of events. Both the doctrines are at one in rejecting the idea that nature reveals a divine power working behind it or indeed any transcendental being which controls it or is implicated in it. Nor does either school seek for its views any supernatural sanction. In the former of these, we have to look for the main source of the later sensualist doctrine of the Cārvāka, which also ascribes the events of life to mere accident. It is the latter that is of real philosophic importance and we shall therefore say a few words more about it.

The Svabhāva-vāda should once have been well known, for we come across references to it in old philosophical works[1] like those of Śaṁkara. In the Mahābhārata, there are allusions to it in more than one place.[2] What needs to be noticed about it first is its positivistic character which is implied by the contrast that is sometimes drawn between it and the Adṛṣṭa-vāda[3] or 'belief in the supernatural.' In this it differs from the supernaturalism of the Mantras and the Brāhmaṇas on the one hand, and, on the other, from the metaphysical view of the Upaniṣads. This positivistic character of the teaching—its 'mundane metaphysics'—seems to have been the original significance of the term lokāyata ('restricted to the experienced world'), more generally applied to the doctrine in later literature. Another

[1] See e.g. Śaṁkara on VS. I. i. 2; BUV. I. iv. 1487.

[2] E.g. xii. 179, 222 and 224.

[3] Nīlakaṇṭha makes this distinction in his com. on the Mbh. xii. 213. 11.

point of importance regarding it is its denial of a transmigrating soul, although it might have admitted a self lasting as long as life does.[1] In this respect the doctrine may be contrasted with what is described as Adhyātma-vāda, which took for granted an immortal soul. One of the Mahābhārata sections, on which our account is based, states 'Death is the end of beings.'[2] In fact the repudiation of such transcendental entities is the very aim of this doctrine. As a necessary corollary to the rejection of a permanent soul, the Svabhāva-vāda, it seems, did not believe in the law of karma[3] as commonly understood. As regards the ultimate source of the material universe, we have no means of deciding whether it was conceived as one or many. There is evidence in support of both in the epic accounts. Thus in one of them, the animal organism is finally traced to the five elements[4]; and the epic elsewhere[5] explicitly associates the Svabhāva-vāda with belief in the ultimacy of the elements. Another account seems to favour a unitary source, describing the infinite phenomena of existence as its modifications.[6]

Before we leave this part of our subject, it is necessary to mention another tendency of thought noticeable in the epic which seems to be a modification, particularly under the influence of the Svābhāva-vāda, of the Absolutism of the Upaniṣads—more especially that aspect of it which is described as Brahma-pariṇāma-vāda. Its aim is realistic and pluralistic. It tends to do away with the conception of the Absolute and to set soul or puruṣa against matter or prakṛti

[1] See BP. p. 135 for the prevalence of such a view in the period. Cf. also *Kaṭha Up.* (I. i. 20 ff.), where the point raised is not the general one whether there is a soul or not, but only whether it survives the body (prete). See also SAS. p. 175.

[2] Bhūtānām nidhanam niṣṭhā śrotasāmiva sāgaraḥ: 224. 9. cf. NM. p. 467.

[3] Compare the following statement of Guṇaratna in his com. on the *Ṣaddarśana-samuccaya* (st. 50): Anye punarāhuḥ: Mūlatah karmaiva nāsti; svabhāva-siddhaḥ sarvopyayam jagat-prapañca iti. 'Others again say: All the variety of this world is explained by its own nature and there is no karma whatever serving as its basis.' Cf. also SV. p. 166.

[4] 224. 17.

[5] 232. 19. Svabhāvam bhūta-cintakāḥ. The *Śvetāsvatara Up.*, however, distinguishes between the two.

[6] 222. 26 and 31.

as mutually independent entities, conceiving the former at the same time as many. But this result has not been completely effected. The notion of the Absolute as the supreme—or sometimes that of God—is retained, with puruṣa and prakṛti regarded as subordinate to, though distinct from, it. The relation between the Absolute and prakṛti is not further defined; but it is clear that the latter is taken to be the source from which the whole of the physical universe emerges. Puruṣa and prakṛti are sharply distinguished. The one is the subject in experience; and the other, or rather its products, the object—each with characteristics which, generally speaking, are not predicable of the other. It is a knowledge of the distinction between them which is commonly hidden from man that is believed in this new doctrine to qualify for release from saṁsāra. The noteworthy point here is the conception of the Absolute as passive and the transfer of creative activity almost entirely to prakṛti.[1] In the recognition of permanent souls, the doctrine differs from the Svābhāva-vada as we have sketched it above. But it resembles that doctrine in endowing matter with practically all the power necessary to unfold the whole universe out of itself. Similarly the view, though resembling Absolutism in finding a place for a cosmic spirit conceived as pre-eminent and eternal, differs from it in being dualistic, admitting matter as virtually a second entity by the side of spirit. These characteristics look much like those of the Sāṅkhya doctrine; and some like Garbe are of opinion that it is the fully fledged Sāṅkhya itself appearing in the epic in a popular form.[2] But it seems preferable to regard it, as we shall point out in the next Part, as only proto-Sāṅkhya or Sāṅkhya in the making. It occupies in the epic a very prominent place, comparable only to that of Theism in it. Its importance in the history of Indian thought is great, but for an adequate consideration of it we have to wait till the Sāṅkhya system is taken up. We may observe in passing that this alliance of a heretical doctrine with orthodoxy gave rise to a new stream of tradition in ancient India which

[1] Cf. Mbh. xii. 314, 12; BG. iii. 27, ix. 10, xiii. 19, 20 and 29.

[2] Prof. Keith: *The Sāṁkhya System*, pp. 46 ff.

can be described as neither quite orthodox nor as quite heterodox. The old heterodoxy, like the old orthodoxy, continued to develop on its own lines. That may be represented as the 'extreme left,' while the new became a middling doctrine with leanings more towards orthodoxy than towards heterodoxy. Accordingly orthodox belief itself henceforward may be said to run in two channels, the distinction between which often leads to important controversies.[1] There is indirect reference to this extension of the sphere of orthodoxy in the literature of the early classical period as, for example, in the *Vedānta-sūtra* of Bādarāyaṇa.[2]

II

So much about the theoretical teaching of the period. It will be useful to bring together in the same way the various modes of discipline commended then for reaching the goal of life. Broadly speaking, this disciplinary teaching is threefold, viz. (1) karma, (2) yoga and (3) bhakti, which are respectively to be associated, though only predominantly, with the first three of the four schools of thought briefly sketched above:

(1) *Karma.*—By the term karma, as used here, is to be understood the sacrificial rites and acts allied to them as first taught in the Brāhmaṇas and later systematized in the Kalpa-sūtras, as well as certain duties and practices which, though not explicitly set forth in the Veda, had become sanctified by tradition. But it must not be thought that ordinary virtues—whether social or self-regarding—were ignored,[3] for ethical purity was made the necessary condition

[1] Such, for example, as the one relating to the question whether the Veda is pauruṣeya or not, See Ch. X.

[2] See e.g. II. i. 1, where two classes of smṛtis are distinguished—one like that of Manu based upon the Veda and therefore fully authoritative, and the other like that of Kapila, which, though recognized by some śiṣṭas, are not so, because they do not go back to the Veda.

[3] The emphasis on moral merit which the word dharma in its popular, as distinguished from its technical, use often signifies is to be traced to this insistence on the initial condition of purity of character.

for entering upon the path of karma as shown by statements like the following from Vaśiṣṭha: 'Neither the Veda, nor sacrifice, nor liberality can save him whose conduct is base, who has departed from the right path.'[1] The nature of virtues insisted upon can be gathered for instance from the following characterization by Āpastamba of the religious student: 'He is gentle and serene. He exercises the highest self-control. He is modest and courageous. He has cast off all lassitude and is free from anger.'[2] Gautama not only prescribes, in addition to religious rites, what he calls 'the virtues of the soul' (ātma-guṇa) or the inner ethical virtues, viz. kindness towards all, forbearance, absence of envy, purity, perseverance, cheerfulness, dignity and contentment but also places them on a higher plane than mere ceremonial.[3] Karmas in the above sense are either (i) 'permitted' or 'optional' (kāmya) which aim at specific results such as the attainment of heaven, (ii) 'prohibited' (pratiṣiddha), indulgence in which will lead to sin and to its unwelcome consequences, or (iii) 'obligatory' or 'unconditional' (nitya) which comprehend the duties appropriate to the four varṇas or classes of society and to what we described in the last chapter as the four āśramas (p. 75). It is not necessary to enter into the details of these varieties of karma. We shall merely draw attention to one or two principles underlying this view of discipline which are of interest to us here.

The whole code of conduct presupposes the survival of the self after death and takes for granted that the present life is essentially a preparation for the coming one.[4] Whatever we may think of the metaphysical basis of such a view, its disciplinary value is apparent. By emphasizing the enduring character of the self, it discountenances present indulgence

[1] *Dharma-sūtra*, vi. 2 and 6. See EI. p. 90.

[2] ADS. I. iii. 17–24.

[3] GDS. viii. 20–23.

[4] 'The chief subject on which the Brāhmaṇas talk is death; for this present life, they hold, is like the season passed in the womb, and death for those who have cultivated philosophy is the birth into the real, the happy life. For this reason they follow an extensive discipline to make them ready for death'—Megasthenes. See *Cambridge History of India*, vol. I. p. 419.

in all its forms and leads to the cultivation of self-restraint in whose train so many virtues follow. The rule for the disciple here is, as Vaśiṣṭha says, 'Look far; not near. Look toward the highest, not toward that which is less than the highest.'[1] In the result, an austere life replaces a life of instincts and passions. The discipline does not indeed aim at abolishing desire altogether as in some other schools of thought, for it holds out the prospect of one's own welfare in a future life and may therefore be characterized as 'self-seeking beyond the grave.' But it does dissuade a man from pursuing the goods of this world for their own sake. The true ideal of life is well indicated by the formulation in this period in a definite way of what are called the puruṣārthas or human values—literally, 'the aims of man.' They are three[2] (tri-varga), viz. dharma, artha and kāma, if we leave out mokṣa, which, though not wholly excluded from the Kalpa-sūtras, occupies by no means a prominent place there. Artha and kāma stand respectively for the acquisition of wealth and the enjoyment of the present life, while dharma represents religious merit. The first two also are accepted as legitimate so that worldly aims are not despised. In fact the Sūtras sometimes speak of succeeding in this world as well as in the next,[3] thus linking up, as it has been so well put, 'the realm of desires with the perspective of the eternal.'[4] But dharma is under all circumstances to be preferred.[5] He that adheres to dharma, says Āpastamba, reaps worldly benefits also; but if he does not, it matters little for the attainment of dharma is the supreme aim.[6] The idea of dharma is accordingly of great importance here, as indeed it is in understanding the Hindu view of life as a whole. The word, which may be compared to the earlier ṛta, means literally 'what supports or upholds,' i.e. the final governing principle or law of the universe. In the present period it stands for all established ways of living—secular, moral and religious. This all-embracing significance of the term explains

[1] *Dharma-sūtra*, x. 30; xxx. 1. See EI. pp. 91–2.
[2] GDS. ix. 48.
[3] Cf. ADS. II. xx. 22–23.
[4] Prof. Radhakrishnan: *The Hindu View of Life* p. 79.
[5] Cf. GDS. ix. 49; ADS. I. xxiv. 23.
[6] ADS. I. xx. 3–4.

the vagueness sometimes met with in its use. But, however diverse the significance, dharma is essentially what bears fruit in a future life and implies moral purity as a necessary condition of earning it. So persistent is this idea that in popular mythology it comes to be identified with Yama or the god of death, who allots rewards and punishments to men in another life according to their deserts. The authority for deciding what is dharma or adharma is the Veda and tradition traceable to it. This is the significance of the term vidhi which about this time comes to be used,[1] and stands for a behest from above. That is, dharma in its technical sense is extra-empirical and can be known only through a channel other than common experience, viz. a divine or traditional code. Āpastamba explicitly says that the principles underlying the conventions and observances of the Aryas are not knowable in the ordinary way: 'Dharma and adharma do not hover about us saying—"We are so and so."'[2] Where empirical considerations alone sufficiently explain conduct, there is no need for such a code. The cultivation of worldly prudence is all that is needed.

(2) *Yoga.*—This term is cognate with English 'yoke' and means 'harnessing.' It is essentially a process of self-conquest and was not unoften resorted to in ancient India for the acquisition of supernatural or occult powers.[3] But we are at present concerned with yogic practice as the means of securing release. In this sense it is practically the same as upāsana taught in the Upaniṣads (p. 78), and is predominantly associated with Absolutism. We should remember that yogic meditation is to follow intellectual conviction regarding the unity to be realized and is therefore very far from being an artificial process of self-hypnosis or anything of the kind. It has, on the other hand, been compared to 'the entirely healthy and joyous phenomenon of aesthetic contemplation.'[4] Yoga is thus really a joint aid

[1] Cf. ADS. I. xxiii. 6. [2] ADS. I. xx. 6.

[3] Cf. ADS. II. xxvi. 14, which implies a distinction between two kinds of ascetics—one described as dharma-para and the other, as abhicāra-para, which may respectively be rendered as 'benevolent' and 'malevolent.' [4] See PU. p. 383.

with jñāna or right knowledge, the need for which in one form or another is admitted by nearly all the schools of thought.[1] This means of attaining oneness with the Absolute was known to the early Upaniṣads and, since we have already alluded to it under the name of nididhyāsana, nothing more need be said about it here. It undergoes systematization in this period, but it will be convenient to refer to its details in the chapter treating of the Sāṅkhya-Yoga system in the next Part. We have, however, to observe, before passing on to the next mode of discipline, that the path of yoga in this form, like that of karma, does not neglect the discipline of common morality, whatever may be said of its other forms, which were also in vogue then and aimed at securing various supernatural powers or worldly ends. The *Kaṭha Upaniṣad* for example—to mention an old authority—in referring to concentration of mind as an indispensable aid to Brahma-realization expressly couples it with ethical purity.[2]

(3) *Bhakti.*—This is 'loving devotion' and is the disciplinary means specially appropriate to theism, with belief in a single personal God. Speaking generally, it represents a social attitude[3] while yoga does the reverse. The bhaktas meet together and they find spiritual exaltation in the company of others that are similarly devoted. The yogins, on the other hand, are apt to seek God or the Absolute singly. Their aim is to be alone with the Alone. Bhakti again is predominantly emotional while yoga is predominantly intellectual, for it adds an element of love to devotion. There has been in modern times a good deal of discussion on the origin of the bhakti cult in India.[4] Some have traced it to Christian sources; but, as in the case of the Bhāgavata religion, the hypothesis of a foreign origin has not commanded the assent of scholars in general. The word bhakti derived

[1] The necessity for this element appears least in ritualism; but even there a distinction is made between a blind performance of Vedic rites and a knowing pursuit of them. The latter is spoken of as fetching a greater good, showing thereby that the value of jñāna was not overlooked. See GDS. xv. 28. Cf. also *Ch. Up.* I. i. 10.

[2] I. ii. 24.

[3] Cf. BG. x. 9.

[4] See Bhandarkar: *Vaiṣṇavism, Śaivism,* etc., pp. 28–30.

from a root meaning 'resorting to,' signifies an attitude of mind towards the godhead which was not unfamiliar to the Vedic Indian. Varuṇa, for instance, inspired it to a conspicuous degree. Again in the Mantras, we often come across epithets like 'father' prefixed to the names of gods which indicate that a certain intimacy of relation was felt by the worshipper between himself and the deity which he thus addressed. The very first hymn of the Ṛgveda gives expression to such a feeling: 'O Agni, be easy of access to us, as a father is to his son.' The same idea of love towards what was held to be the Highest can be traced in the Upaniṣads. The *Kaṭha Upaniṣad*[1] possibly alludes once to the need for divine help, the reward of bhakti, before one can be saved. The *Śvetāśvatara Upaniṣad* uses the very word and speaks of the necessity for the highest devotion not only to God but also the *guru*,[2] who is the channel through which a knowledge of God comes to us. Finally, the grammarian Pāṇini (350 B.C.) has a separate aphorism to explain the word, though only as meaning 'the object of loving devotion.'[3] Thus the ideas of devotion to God and of his grace (prasāda), the reward for it, were well known to the Indians long before the Christian era; and there is no need to seek for their source outside India. Of the three Gods whose supremacy belongs to this period, Viṣṇu-Kṛṣṇa is most prominently connected with this idea of bhakti; but it is found mentioned in respect of the others also, as, for instance, Śiva, who is described as 'kind to the devotee' (bhaktānukampin).[4]

Of these modes of discipline, yoga alone can be associated with the heretical views, and even that only as a way of withdrawal from the world and not as a means of attaining union with the Ultimate. It seems to have been so prominent a form of discipline amongst the heterodox that their ideal man, it is stated,[5] was not the half-divine ṛṣi as among the orthodox, but the world-renouncing yogin. As in the case of the other doctrines, the need for moral purity is not ignored here also. Prahrāda, who appears as a heretic in the Mahābhārata, is described as 'adhering to principle'

[1] I. ii. 20 and 23. [2] vi. 23. [3] IV. iii. 95.
[4] Mbh. xii. 284. 167. [5] Prof. Winternitz: *op. cit.* p. 3.

(samaye ratam).[1] But, as may be expected, the heretical teachers, unlike the orthodox, did not believe in the cleansing effect of Vedic karma; and the course of preliminary training which they prescribed was exclusively ethical. Our knowledge of the different heretical schools in the early part of this period is so imperfect that we cannot speak in detail of the moral training prescribed in them. As a general characteristic, we may note its stoic severity. It is a discipline of denial and is intended to free man entirely from personal desires, which are regarded as the prime source of all the ills of existence. Such a view, no doubt, has a pessimistic basis; but, to judge from the generality of accounts found in the epic,[2] it is as far removed from cynicism as it is from hedonism.

Over and above these modes of discipline, we find saṁnyāsa or formal renunciation of the world also recognized in this period, particularly in the heretical schools. Ajagara for instance, to whom reference has already been made is described as a muni[3] and he dwells in the forest. Similarly Samaṅga, who has achieved complete equanimity of mind, says: 'Having given up artha and kāma, having given up desire and delusion, I traverse the earth without pain and without torment.'[4] Though an outstanding feature of the practical teaching of this period, saṁnyāsa was by no means universal, at least among the orthodox. Some of them refused to include it in the normal scheme of life. The only legitimate āśrama other than studentship, according to them, was that of the householder; and the two remaining āśramas of the anchorite and of the monk were explained as intended only for such as were for some reason or other disqualified for performing the karmas appropriate to a householder. This is probably the oldest view, for it is here that full significance attaches to the numerous rites that are with so much elaboration taught in the Brāhmaṇas.[5] Even according to those among the orthodox who accepted saṁnyāsa as a normal stage of life, it could be assumed

[1] xii. 222. 4. [2] Cf. xii. 179. 18 ff. [3] xii. 179. 2.
[4] Mbh. xii. 292. 19. [5] GDS. iii. 36.

only last.[1] From this standpoint, then, the modes of discipline prevalent in the period admit of a fresh division into the positive and the negative. The former is described as the path of pravṛtti or active life, because it insists on strict adherence to Vedic ritual and the discharge of the manifold duties taught in the Kalpa-sūtras; and the latter, as that of nivṛtti or quietism, because it demands an escape from the absorptions of social and sacrificial life in order that one may devote oneself entirely to contemplation. The distinction, we shall find to be of value in following the later development of Indian thought.

What is the nature of the condition that is to be reached by such discipline? According to those that follow the ideal of the three-fold aim of man (tri-varga), the goal of life is the attainment of heaven after death by means of earning religious merit (dharma) in this life. Those on the other hand that recognize mokṣa as the highest ideal, conceive of it in more than one way. It may be union with the Ultimate as in Absolutism, or reaching the presence of God as in Theism, or the merely negative one of escape from the trammels of saṁsāra as in some heretical schools. In the last sense, it is more often styled nirvāṇa (literally 'blowing out'), which brings out clearly its negative character. But however it is conceived, the ideal of jīvan-mukti continues and, we may say, receives greater emphasis in this period. In a series of verses in the Dialogue between Sagara and Ariṣṭanemi ending with the burden 'He indeed is free,' the Mahābhārata[2] proclaims an attitude of passionless serenity attainable in this life as itself mokṣa. This ideal, though adhered to by many of the orthodox schools like the Advaita, may have originated in heretical circles with the general world-view of some of which it so well agrees. The conception of mokṣa

[1] Cf. *Manu-smṛti*, vi. 35. It was only later that restrictions ceased to be placed on the freedom of the individual to select, after studentship, the course of life he preferred. The only criterion thereafter is detachment; Whoever has it is entitled to renounce the world. Cf. Yadahareva virajet tadahareva pravrajet: *Jābāla Up*. 4. See Note 3 on p. 21.

[2] xii. 288, st. 25 ff.

as a condition to be attained after death is incompatible, for instance, with the Svabhāva-vāda, which did not look forward to a future life; and it should naturally have represented the ideal as achievable within the limits of the present one. But on account of the early mixing up of doctrines, already mentioned, it is difficult to be sure about it.[1]

[1] Compare in this connection ADS. II. xxi. 14–16.

CHAPTER IV

BHAGAVADGĪTĀ

In point of popularity the Gītā is second to no work in the world of Indian thought. It has always commanded great admiration and its popularity now, if anything, is on the increase. This unique position it owes to a variety of causes. It forms a portion of an epic whose study has enraptured generations of men and women. The two characters that figure in it are most fascinating; and the occasion which calls forth its teaching is one of extreme seriousness when the fate not only of the country but of righteousness (dharma) itself is at stake. The work is written in a simple and charming style, and is in the form of a dialogue which imparts to it a dramatic interest. But such formal excellences alone are not adequate to account for its great attractiveness. It has, as we shall see, a specific message to give. For the present, it will suffice to refer to one or two other points in its teaching which invest it with special value. The work breathes throughout a spirit of toleration which is an outstanding characteristic of Hindu thought. 'Whoever with true devotion worships any deity, in him I deepen that devotion; and through it he fulfils his desire.' 'Those that devotedly worship other gods, they also worship me though only imperfectly.'[1] The thought here is not, as it sometimes unfortunately is, that 'one man's God is another's devil,' but that every conception of God, however crude or defective in itself, still has its own divine side and that it is not so much the nature of the object worshipped as the spirit in which the worshipper turns to it that counts. To this feature, which entitles the poem to the first place in Hindu scriptures as bringing out best their governing spirit, it adds another which explains why it has been reckoned as part of the world's literature ever since it came to be known outside India. Its author, as may be expected from one whom tradition reckons as the inspirer

[1] vii. 21–22; ix. 23. See also iv. 11.

of practically all the Sanskrit poets, does not discuss here the subtle and recondite details of ethics or metaphysics, but deals only with the broad principles underlying them, relating them at the same time to the most fundamental aspirations of man. And this he does not by means of any abstract disquisition, but by selecting a specific situation involving a moral dilemma and pointing out how it is overcome. This concrete mode of treatment, with the suggestiveness natural to it, very much widens the scope of the teaching and makes its appeal almost universal.

All this, however, does not mean that the work is easy of understanding. Far from it. It is one of the hardest books to interpret, which accounts for the numerous commentaries on it—each differing from the rest in some essential point or other. Part of this diversity in interpretation is due to the assumption that the Gītā not only concerns itself with the problem of conduct whose solution is a pressing need for man if he is to live without that inner discord which arises from consciousness of the ideal unaccompanied by mastery over self, but also is a treatise on metaphysics. Dealing as it does with a moral problem, the work necessarily touches upon metaphysical questions now and again; but they form only the background to the ethical teaching. To regard a consideration of ultimate philosophical questions as falling within the main aim of the Gītā, appears to us to misjudge its character. Though the features characteristic of the background are only vaguely seen and explain the divergent accounts given of them by interpreters, what is in the focus of the picture, viz. its practical teaching, is quite distinct. Another cause of difference among the interpreters of the work is the forgetting of the occasion that evoked the teaching and expecting to find in it a complete theory of morals. The occasion is a particular one and Śrī Kṛṣṇa, in enunciating a course of conduct suited to it, naturally draws attention only to *some* of the principles on which right living should be based. The theme of the work is not accordingly the whole of moral philosophy; and there are, as will become clear later, omissions of importance in it. Our aim will be to explain the nature of the central moral truth inculcated in the work and point out its importance in the history of Indian thought. We shall also try to indicate the general features of the theory which underlies that teaching, but we shall not attempt a complete exposition of the work, by taking into account all the other teachings that may be found interspersed here and there in it. The Gītā in that respect resembles the Mahābhārata, whose heterogeneous character has already been described. Since the *motif* of the poem is in its practical teaching, we shall take it up first. As regards the age to which the work belongs, there has been a great deal of controversy; but scholars are now mostly agreed that in its essential portions at least, it is not later than 200 B.C.—a date which falls within the period at present under consideration.

I

We have stated that so far as the practical teaching is concerned, there is no ambiguity. The reason for this is the setting of the poem. In the beginning, we find Arjuna despondent and declining to fight; but, as a result of Śrī Kṛṣṇa's persuasion, he makes up his mind to take part in the contest. This important element in the conception of the poem would lose its entire significance if we did not regard action as its essential lesson. We may accordingly conclude that the central point of the teaching is activism, or, to use the expression of the Gītā, karma-yoga. To understand what exactly is meant by this expression, it is necessary to consider separately the two terms constituting it. *Karma* literally means 'what is done,' 'a deed'; and the word of course appears with this general meaning sometimes in the work.[1] But by the time of the Gītā it had also come to signify that particular form of activity which is taught in the liturgical portion of Vedic literature, viz. sacrifice. Though we cannot say that the word does not at all bear this special sense in the poem,[2] it by no means represents its prevailing use. What it usually signifies here is duties that, in accord-

[1] Cf. iii. 5; v. 8–9.

[2] See iii. 14–15; xviii. 3.

ance with custom and tradition, were found associated at the time with particular sections or classes of the people,[1] the varṇa-dharmas as they are described.[2] The word is also sometimes used in a fourth sense in the work, viz. divine worship and devotional acts connected with it such as prayer.[3] Of these several meanings, we should, when thinking of karma-yoga as taught in the Gītā, ordinarily take the third, viz. social obligations which in one form or another are acknowledged in all organized society. The word *yoga* means 'harnessing' (p. 110) or 'applying oneself to' so that karma-yoga may be rendered as 'devotion to the discharge of social obligations.' A characteristic of all voluntary deeds is that they are preceded by a desire for something, which is described as their motive or phala. Whenever we knowingly act, we aim at achieving some end or other. In the present case, for instance, Arjuna is actuated by a desire for sovereignty over his ancestral kingdom; and he has undertaken to fight for regaining, if possible, that sovereignty which through the force of circumstances has passed on to his wily cousins. Such an undertaking, however, would not be devotion to karma. It is devotion to its phala, because the karma here, viz. fighting, but serves as a means to bring about a preconceived end. For karma-yoga, the act should be viewed not as a means but as an end in itself. That is, the idea of the result, which is to ensue from the action, must be dismissed altogether from the mind before as well as during the act. The term signifies, as Śrī Kṛṣṇa is never tired of repeating, the doing of a deed without any the least thought of reaping its fruit. 'Your concern is solely with action—never with its fruit.'[4] There follows, no doubt, a result from the deed that is done, but in the case of the karma-yogin, it ceases to be his *end* for this simple reason that it is not desired and that there can be no end conceivable apart from relation to desire. An important consequence of following this principle of action is that one can act with complete

[1] Cf. iv. 15 (pūrvaiḥ pūrva-taram kṛtaṁ) and xviii. 41, where the four castes are mentioned.

[2] There is not much reference in the work to the āśrama-dharma, the twin companion of varṇa-dharma.

[3] Cf. xii. 10.

[4] ii. 47.

equanimity. Desire or self-interest when allowed to have its sway over us may blind us to what is right; and even when we succeed in choosing to do the right deed, undue eagerness to secure its fruit may induce us to swerve from the path of rectitude. The term yoga is in one place[1] explained as signifying just such equanimity or 'balance of mind' (samatvam). This teaching that we ought to engage ourselves in our work as members of a social order in the usual way and yet banish from our mind all thought of deriving any personal benefit therefrom is the meaning of karma-yoga and constitutes the specific message of the Gītā.

The importance of this teaching will become clear if we refer to the two ideals of life that were prevalent at the time among the orthodox—the negative ideal of renunciation and the positive one of active life (p. 114). The first deal of nivṛtti, as it is called, advocated the giving up of all karma and withdrawing from the work-a-day world entirely. The second one of pravṛtti, no doubt, recommended living in the midst of society undertaking all the obligations implied thereby; but it did not exclude the element of selfishness altogether. This is clear in the case of ritualistic activities. Those that engaged themselves in such activities, because they realized the enduring character of the self, did not, it is true, yield to the impulse of the moment, but strove for a good which was attainable in another life. Yet it was their own good they sought. Though their belief in a future life saved them from rating too high the value of worldly good, what they worked for was similar in character and their efforts cannot therefore escape being characterized as at bottom selfish. And in the case of activities which are not other-worldly, they directed their thoughts as much towards rights as towards duties. They regarded themselves as not only bound to discharge their indebtedness to others, but also as having a claim upon those others for what was due to themselves; and so far they fell short of a truly spiritual conception of life (p. 23). The object of the Gītā is to discover the golden mean between the two ideals of pravṛtti and nivṛtti or of action and contemplation, as we might term

[1] ii. 48.

them, preserving the excellence of both. Karma-yoga is such a mean. While it does not abandon activity, it preserves the spirit of renunciation. It commends a strenuous life, and yet gives no room for the play of selfish impulses. Thus it discards neither ideal, but by combining them refines and ennobles both. That particular attitude of the soul which renunciation signifies still remains; only it ceases to look askance at action. In other words the Gītā teaching stands not for renunciation *of* action, but for renunciation *in* action.

Arjuna who at the outset undertook to fight under the influence of one of these old ideals has, as we see him portrayed at the beginning of the work, come to be influenced by the other. He has resolved on a sudden to renounce the world and withdraw from the contest. But he forgets that the advocates of that ideal require, as a condition of adopting it, real detachment in the would-be disciple. Arjuna is but slenderly equipped for it, and yet he thinks of giving up the world. That he has not really risen above the common level in this respect is clear from the fact that his vairāgya does not spring from true enlightenment, but from narrow-mindedness, viz. the love of kith and kin.[1] He continues to make a distinction between his own people and others; and his excuse for inaction, as set forth in the beginning of the poem, leaves the impression that his interest even in his subjects, as distinguished from his kinsmen, is after all secondary.[2] His detachment, or rather his disinclination to fight, is in a large measure due to the uncommon situation in which he finds himself somewhat suddenly. It is not, therefore, his considered view of the universe or of the life that he has to lead in it which prompts him to this indifference. It is the result of weakness—surrendering to the power of the moment. Arjuna's vairāgya is also in a subtle and unconscious manner due to the diffidence and fear that he might not after all win the battle, so that it is at bottom faint-heartedness (hṛdaya-daurbalyam) as Śrī Kṛṣṇa characterizes it and eventually rāga, not virāga.[3] He is still worldly-minded; and it is on empirical, not on ultimate, grounds that he adopts an attitude of inaction. He fails to realize that

[1] Cf. i. 31; ii. 6. [2] Cf. i. 33. [3] ii. 3.

he is not fighting for himself or for his family or clan (kula), but for king and country—that the interests of righteousness are in jeopardy and that, like every right-minded person, he is bound to do his best to set the situation right. The final test that Arjuna is not actuated by genuine detachment is the sadness and despondency (viṣāda) that pervade his speech. Not only is he sad, he is also in doubt.[1] Neither doubt nor sadness is a sign of true spirituality which would result in a feeling of triumphant freedom. Śrī Kṛṣṇa's teaching is that the narrow selfish impulses of which sadness and doubt are the sign should first be overcome; and the way to do it is not to resort to the loneliness of the forest, but to live in the midst of the storm and stress of social life, doing one's duty without any thought of recompense.

This teaching has been traced by some to earlier sources.[2] It is no doubt mentioned in the *Īśa Upaniṣad* (p. 73), but without any elaboration whatsoever. Even granting that the ideal of karma-yoga is not altogether new, there is no doubt that its general acceptance is due to its impressive enunciation in the Gītā. None of the orthodox creeds or systems of thought that were evolved afterwards discarded it. Detached action became the starting-point of life's discipline according to all, superseding virtually the earlier view of activity pursued for its fruit. In this transformation of the ideal of pravṛtti consists one of the chief contributions of the Gītā to Hindu thought. We may add that though the particular circumstances that called forth the teaching have changed, it has not been rendered obsolete. For good or ill, the monastic ideal has all but disappeared now. Ours is an age of self-assertion, not of self-suppression. Men are not now likely to give up their duty to become recluses, as Arjuna wanted to do. The danger comes from the other side. In our eagerness to claim our rights and exercise them, we may ignore our duties. Hence the need for the teaching of the Gītā now is as great as ever. Its value has not lessened through lapse of time; and that is a mark of its greatness.

The propriety of selecting the battle-field for imparting the

[1] ii. 1. and 7.

[2] See Bhandarkar: *Vaiṣṇavism, Śaivism*, etc., p. 27.

teaching is that nowhere else is the subordination of individual aim to the general good so complete. The soldier may know the cause for which he is fighting, but he can hardly say how that fight is going to end. Even supposing that it is to end favourably to his cause, he, for aught he knows, will not be there at the time to share its beneficial results. Yet this uncertainty does not in the least reduce his responsibility as a fighter. He has to do his best and should therefore realize to the utmost his value and importance as an agent, but at the same time forget altogether that he is to participate in whatever good may accrue from the discharge of his duty.[1] It is the cause of a wider entity than himself that he is serving; and his thought should not go beyond realizing that his individual responsibility as an actor in the scene remains at the maximum. That represents the highest form of self-sacrifice—to work for no profit to oneself, but yet to exert oneself to the utmost; and the finest exhibition of this spirit in the world is to be seen on a battle-field. We should, however, remember that Śrī Kṛṣṇa is really addressing all men through his devotee, Arjuna; and the teaching, as already observed, is not restricted in its application to the particular situation that gave rise to it. Its appeal is to all men that find themselves placed in a similar dilemma in life. In this wider sense, it takes as its essential basis the principle that activity is natural to man and that no view of life which overlooks that feature or minimizes its importance can be right. More than once is it stated in the course of the work that no man can abjure activity altogether[2]; but this natural activity needs to be properly directed, for otherwise it is apt to be utilized for selfish or material ends and thus become the means of obscuring from man the higher end for which he exists.

What is the direction in which the activity should be exercised? In answer to this question, the Gītā enjoins on all the performance of their respective duties. 'One should never abandon one's specific work, whether it be high or

[1] To use Sanskrit words, this means that while one should realize to the full that he is a kartā, he should altogether forget that he is a bhoktā.

[2] Cf. iii. 5; xviii. 11.

low.'[1] It attaches little or no value to the intrinsic worth of the deed that is done by any person, so long as it is his own dharma (sva-dharma). The word sva-dharma may bear a wide significance but, as required by the particular context and as specified more than once in the course of the book, it means chiefly, though not solely, the duties incumbent upon the main classes into which society is divided. In other words, it is social obligations mainly that are asked here to be discharged—such as are calculated to secure and preserve the solidarity of society. It is a proof of the severely practical character of the teaching contained in the book that it does not attempt to describe these duties any further. It realizes the impossibility of detailing the acts appropriate to every station in life, and leaves their determination to the good sense or immediate judgment of the individual. There is an attempt made in one or two places[2] to indicate *what* these obligations are, but only in a general way. It may be thought that the mere injunction that one should do one's dharma leaves the matter vague. But we must remember that in the relatively simple organization of the society when the teaching was formulated, the duties of the several classes were known fairly clearly. In the present case at any rate, there is no doubt as to what the sva-dharma of Arjuna is. The prominence given to relative duties, such as depend upon the position in society of the individual, shows by the way that the treatment which the problem of conduct receives here is, as we remarked before, only partial. There is, for example, no allusion to what may be described as 'right in itself' except incidentally, as in distinguishing the worthy from the wicked—the two broad classes into which the book in one of its sections divides the whole of mankind.[3] It emphasizes the social character of man, and, generally speaking, declines to look upon him apart from the community of which he is a member.

From what we have stated so far, it appears that a karma-yogin works without a purpose in view. No voluntary activity, however, seems conceivable without some motive or other. Will without desire, it has been said, is a fiction.

[1] xviii. 47–8. [2] ii. 31–8; xviii. 41–4. [3] Ch. xvi.

What then is the motive for exertion here? There are two answers to this question furnished in the book: (1) ātma-śuddhi,[1] which means 'purifying the self' or 'cleansing the heart,' and (2) subserving the purposes of God (Īśvara)[2]—a fact which, by the way, implies a mixture of teaching here. The spirit in which one engages oneself in activity is different according to the two aims. What is done is done in the one case for the sake of the social whole of which the doer is a member; but in the other it is done for the sake of God, resigning its fruit to him. What in the one appears as duty to others appears in the other as service to God. The former type of agent is directly conscious of his relation to his environment and realizes it as a factor demanding his fealty; the latter is conscious only of God conceived as a personality in constant touch with the world, and whatever he does he regards as God's work, which has therefore to be done. But whether we look upon the work done as duty or as divine service, it is not 'disinterested' in every sense of the term. The first keeps self-conquest or subjective purification as the aim; the second looks forward to the security that has been guaranteed by God—that no godly man will perish: Na me bhaktaḥ praṇaśyati.[3] But if karma-yoga is thus motived by desire, it may be asked, in what sense it has been described as detached. In replying to this question, we should recall what we have stated before—that the activity which is natural to man if not properly guided, will become the means of obscuring from him the higher end for which he exists. By such an end the Gītā understands something more than moral rectitude. It aims at the elimination of worldly desire—even of the type commonly regarded as legitimate. Or as we night otherwise put it, it does not rest satisfied with rationalizing our impulses; it means to spiritualize them. It teaches that an active life led without any thought of securing the worldly results it may yield, sets free the springs of that inner life whose development is the one aim of man. And karma-yoga is disinterested only so far as it turns our mind from these results and sets it on the path leading to the true goal—not that it has no end at all. It does

[1] v. 11. [2] iii. 30; ix. 27. [3] ix. 31.

not thus do away with motives altogether; only it furnishes *one and the same* motive for whatever we may do,[1] viz. the betterment of our spiritual nature. Thus though the teaching, by insisting upon the discharge of social obligations at all costs, seems to ignore the individual, it does not really do so since it provides at the same time for his advancement on a higher plane of life.

The goal to be reached on this plane is conceived in two ways, according to the double motive that is set before the karma-yogin. If the motive is 'cleansing the heart,' the goal is self-realization; if, on the other hand, it is subserving the purposes of God, the end is God-realization. Of these, the first is to be understood here much as in the Upaniṣads. It is becoming Brahman (brahma-bhūyam)[2] or absorption in the Absolute. The second is reaching the presence of God,[3] though it sometimes appears, evidently under the influence of the first, as merging in him: 'He who departs from here, thinking of me alone, will enter my being.'[4] The important point here is whether individuality persists in the final condition—whether the finite as finite can attain perfection. The absolutist view decides against persistence; the purely theistic view, in favour of it. Even though the latter does not recognize the union of the individual with God, it admits the merging of the individual's will in the divine will. Whichever be the goal—becoming Brahman or attaining God's presence—saṁsāra or the realm of good and evil is transcended. Although there are statements in the work which indicate that the goal—particularly the second one—is to be reached after death,[5] the prevalent idea is that it is realizable within the limits of this life.[6] There is more than one beautiful description of the man[7] that has perfected himself; and in the eleventh chapter we find a thrilling account of a direct perception of God by the devotee.[8] The distinctive feature of the perfected state, which is variously termed as

[1] Cf. Śaṁkara on *Bṛ. Up.* (Ānandāśrama Edn.), pp. 57–58.
[2] xviii. 53.
[3] iv. 9; ix. 25.
[4] viii. 5.
[5] viii. 5.
[6] Cf. v. 19 and 26.
[7] ii. 55–58; xiv. 22–25.
[8] Note the expression 'I give you the eye divine'—divyam dadāmi te cakṣuḥ—in xi. 8.

'the life absolute' and 'dwelling in God,'[1] is peace. Only the attitude is predominantly one of jñāna in the case of a person that sets before himself the ideal of self-realization, and one of bhakti or passionate devotion to God in the case of the other. Karma-yoga in the former fulfils itself in enlightenment which enables one 'to see oneself in all beings and all beings in oneself'[2]; in the latter, it finds its consummation when a loving communion is established with God. If we describe the one as the ideal of enlightenment, the other represents the ideal of love; only it is love of God, and through him, of his creatures. But whether we look upon the Gītā as the gospel of enlightenment or of love, it is equally the gospel of action.

The point to which it is necessary to draw special attention in this connection is that the Gītā requires man to continue to work even in this perfected state, there being nothing in outer activity which is incompatible with inner peace. Here we see the exalted position assigned to work by the Gītā. It contemplates no period, when activity may be wholly renounced. Passivity, in its view, is almost as reprehensible as wrong activity. Janaka, king of Videha, renowned in the Upaniṣads, and Śrī Kṛṣṇa are our examples here. The one has become perfect and the other has always been so; and both[3] alike are active. Such a view totally transforms the notion of saṁnyāsa by dissociating it from all inaction; and in this transformation of the ideal of nivṛtti consists another important contribution of the Gītā to Hindu thought. Karma-yoga is accordingly to be understood in a double sense—one having reference to an earlier stage of strife when the disciple, with a steady resolve, is continually weaning himself from selfish activity; and the other, to a later stage when, at the dawn of truth, the strife is over and right conduct becomes quite spontaneous—the outward expression of an inner conviction that has been attained. It is karma-yoga in the first sense, which is ancillary,[4] that forms the essential theme of the Gītā; the second appears

[1] Cf. ii. 72; xii. 8.
[2] vi. 29. Cf. iv. 33.
[3] iii. 20–28.
[4] Cf. v. 6; vi. 3.

now and then as but a characteristic of the goal to be kept in view by the spiritual aspirant.

Before leaving this topic we must refer to an important question discussed, though but briefly, in the work.[1] The teaching so far set forth presupposes that man is free to choose the path he likes in the conduct of life. But it appears that he can only follow the bent of his nature (prakṛti); and when that is predominantly evil, it may be said, persuasion to adopt the right path will be of little avail. In meeting this objection the Gītā first points out how the disposition to act in an evil way operates. 'In respect of every object of sense, there is always love or hatred. One should not come under the sway of either, for they are one's foes.' That is, an evil disposition operates not automatically, but invariably by appealing to our lower or what, in the light of the description given in this connection, may be styled the sensuous self. 'The senses and the mind are its habitation; and through them it deludes man. Do thou subjugate them first in order that you may bring down the ruinous foe.' We are not accordingly driven to do evil against our desire, as Arjuna wrongly assumes (anicchan). No responsibility attaches to man for mere impulsive reaction, except in so far as he is accountable for that impulse itself. In the case of actions on the other hand, which evoke moral judgment, they are always 'willed' by the doer, so that the opportunity to have acted differently after appropriate reflection was presented to him. He should not let go the opportunity by thoughtlessly yielding to the promptings of the sensuous self. But the question still remains whether we can ignore that self. The reply is that we can, if we only will; for we are conscious of the presence in us of a self higher than it. It may remain half-concealed, 'as fire does when enveloped in smoke'; but it is still there giving rise to that inner conflict between wish and will with which we, as human beings, are necessarily familiar. It is in the consciousness of this conflict that the possibility of a right choice lies. For the nature of the higher self is such that it will not allow itself to be subordinated to the other unless we have once for all sunk back into the life of the

[1] See iii. 33–43.

mere animal. The Gītā takes its stand upon this fact, that man cannot ignore the still small voice within, when it asks us to 'steady the self by the self'[1] and commends activity without any reference to the ends which the lower of the two selves may like to pursue. The replacement of the lower aim by the higher, we must remember, is not to be made when or as often as a selfish motive presents itself. That might prove impracticable. We are asked to be forearmed by accepting the true ideal once for all, and to see that our actions become the expression of a single coherent purpose as implied by its acceptance. That is the meaning of telling us to substitute a uniform aim, viz. the betterment of our spiritual nature, for the necessarily divergent ends of the many actions which we have to do in life. Progress in this course may be difficult and protracted, requiring continual self-training. But the Gītā heartens us to put forth our best effort by assuring us that nothing of what we do for self-development really runs to waste. 'No such effort is lost; nor is there any obstacle in the way of its coming to fruition. Even the little that we may do will help to take us nearer the goal'[2]; and again, 'The doer of good, O dear one, never comes to grief.'[3] It is here that precept is of service. It clarifies our notion of the true self and encourages us to persevere in our course. The question discussed here is the familiar one of freedom of will; only the Gītā, as in other matters, restricts the scope of the discussion to the point arising from the context, viz. whether a man can choose the path to the higher life.

As belief in the karma doctrine characterizes the teaching of the Gītā, we may also briefly refer here to the allied question: how freedom is consistent with the necessity implied in this doctrine. If everything we do is the inevitable consequence of what we have done in the past, all moral responsibility should cease and self-effort should become meaningless. In considering this point, it is necessary to remember that every deed that we do leads to a double result. It not only produces what may be termed its direct result—the pain or pleasure following from it according to the karma theory, but it also

[1] iii. 43. [2] ii. 40. [3] vi. 40.

establishes in us a tendency to repeat the same deed in the future. This tendency is termed saṁskāra; and the direct fruit of the karma is known as its phala. Every deed is bound to yield its phala; even the gods cannot prevent it from doing so. But that is all the necessity involved in the karma theory. As regards the saṁskāras, on the other hand, we have within us the full power of control, so that we may regulate them as they tend to express themselves in action. There is thus nothing in the doctrine which either eliminates responsibility or invalidates self-effort. The necessity that governs the incidence of the direct fruit or phala and renders escape from it impossible, so far from unnerving us, should stimulate us to exertion. It must enable us to work for the future with confidence, unmindful of what may happen in the present as the result of our past actions over which we have no longer any control. The important point about the karma doctrine then is that, paradoxical though it may seem, it inspires us both with hope and resignation at once—hope for the future and resignation towards what may occur in the present. That is not fatalism, but the very reverse of it.

II

Coming now to the theoretical teaching we find that, as already stated, it occupies the background and as such its details are not clearly determinable. But it is manifest that there is a mixture of doctrines. All will recognize in the work a current of Upaniṣadic thought which stresses the cosmic conception of the Absolute rather than the acosmic. Expressions drawn from the Upaniṣads occur throughout the work, and even what may be regarded as quotations from them are sometimes found.[1] These references to the Upaniṣads, both direct and indirect, may lead one to think that the work is entirely Vedāntic. That is indeed the traditional view as shown by the familiar verse which, evidently as suggested by Śrī Kṛṣṇa's cow-herd upbringing,

[1] Cf. ii. 29 and vi. 11 with *Kaṭha Up*. ii. 7 and *Śvetāśvatara Up*. ii. 10 respectively.

pictures him as drawing the milk of the Gītā from the Upaniṣads, figured as a cow, for Arjuna, the calf. But, though the Gītā owes much to the Upaniṣads, it would be wrong to take them to be its only source; for there is, as we know, another stream of thought mingling with it, viz. theism of the Bhāgavata type.[1] The theoretical teaching of the Gītā, like its practical one, is a blend of these two distinct creeds whose chief features were set forth in the previous chapters. In fact the distinction on the practical side is the natural counterpart of that on the theoretical. Some have held that the Upaniṣadic doctrine is the older in the work, and that it was later modified in the interests of the Bhāgavata creed; others, that precisely the reverse has taken place. Either way there is no intentional mixing of the doctrines here. In the words of Senart it is 'spontaneous syncretism.' A deliberate blending of them would have eliminated the contradictions which now remain side by side in the poem.[2]

Some scholars have seen in the work the influence of a third current of thought, viz. the Sāṅkhya, and it is maintained by them that that system is very old—in fact as old as the Upaniṣads—and that the Bhāgavata creed, quite early in its history, made use of it to furnish itself with an appropriate metaphysical basis. The creed, as it appears in the Gītā, is according to these authorities already thus 'philosophically equipped'[3]; and that is the reason, they say, why Sāṅkhya elements find a place in the work. The third view as found here, it is admitted, is not fully identifiable with the Sāṅkhya, for there are some vital differences between the two. For instance, it recognizes a super-soul (uttama-puruṣa)[4] which is unknown to the Sāṅkhya. Again there is no reference whatever in the work to the well-known Sāṅkhya ideal of kaivalya or spiritual aloofness, the goal of life, as represented here, being different—'becoming Brahman' or 'reaching the presence of God.' The idea of severance from prakṛti may be implicit in the latter, for

1 Cf. references to 'Vāsudeva' in vii. 19 and xi. 50.
2 See e.g. ix. 29; xvi. 19.
3 See Garbe: *Indian Antiquary* (1918).
4 xv. 17–18.

without wresting itself from the clutches of matter, the soul has no chance of being restored to its original abode. But what we should remember is that the separation from prakṛti is not conceived here as the ultimate ideal. It is only a means to an end, which is positive unlike the negative one of classical Sāṅkhya. Such differences are explained as due to the circumstance that the Sāṅkhya, as it appears here, has been adjusted to the requirements of the Bhāgavata creed. There is, no doubt, some reason to speak of an additional current of thought in the work, for the Upaniṣadic doctrine, as contained in the Gītā, does not throughout retain all its old features, but shows here and there an advance towards realism and dualism. In the Upaniṣads, the single Absolute is sometimes viewed under the triple aspect of Brahman, ātman and the world, though no distinction in fact between them is intended. The Gītā exhibits a tendency to separate them and conceive of them as coeval, although the two latter, viz. ātman and the physical world, are still held to be dependent upon Brahman—the highest principle.[1] The physical universe is no longer traced to Brahman as in the Upaniṣads, but to another source named prakṛti or matter; and it is represented as standing over against ātman or the individual soul which is designated puruṣa. Attention has already been drawn (p. 106) to the prevalence of such a view in the epic taken as a whole, and to its partial resemblance to the Sāṅkhya. But, instead of taking it as the Sāṅkhya doctrine modified to suit the needs of a theistic creed, it seems preferable, for the reasons we shall mention when treating of the topic in the next Part, to regard it as a step in the movement of Upaniṣadic thought towards the Sāṅkhya in its classical form. What particular stage in the growth of the Sāṅkhya is represented in the Gītā it is difficult to say, for the history of that doctrine still remains obscure.

[1] Cf. ix. 10.

CHAPTER V

EARLY BUDDHISM

EARLY Buddhism has to be distinguished from the later, which grew up together with the Brahminical systems long after Buddha had taught. We shall defer the consideration of the latter to the next Part dealing with the systems, and shall confine ourselves to the former, which is now variously styled as 'Pāli Buddhism,' 'Canonical Buddhism,' 'Southern Buddhism' and Theravāda (i.e. Sthavira-vāda, 'the doctrine of the elders'). The founder of this great creed was born about the middle of the sixth century B.C. His name was Siddhārtha and he belonged to the ancient family of Gotama or Gautama. The title of 'Buddha,' which means the 'awakened one,' came to be applied to him afterwards, as a sign of the enlightenment which he had succeeded in acquiring and by which he woke to a sense of fact from the dream of life. As the details of his life are well known, they need not be recounted here. It is enough to say that he was born in an aristocratic family at or near Kapilavastu on the lower slopes of the Himalayas and was a young man of about thirty years when he renounced the world and left the palace for the forest in quest of truth. The immediate cause of the renunciation was the thought of suffering which he saw afflicted mankind as a whole. In conformity with the spirit of the times in which asceticism was the rule of serious life,[1] Buddha betook himself at first to severe penance; but, not meeting with success in that direction, he began a fresh course of self-discipline characterized by less rigour. In this second endeavour, truth at last flashed upon him in regard to the nature of suffering and the means of eradicating it; and, true lover of mankind that he was, he did not spend the rest of his life in the forest in a mood of self-sufficiency, but quickly returned to the abodes of men and

[1] It is recorded of one Ajita Keśa-kambalin, an ascetic teacher of the period, that he used to wear a garment of human hair—'the worst of all garments, being cold in winter and warm in summer.'

began the long and noble work of spreading among the people a knowledge of the truth which had brought him illumination and freedom. The feeling which prompted him to such active beneficence is very well indicated by a saying which tradition ascribes to him, that he would willingly bear the burden of everybody's suffering if he could thereby bring relief to the world.[1] In this work he met with many difficulties for there were at the time several rival doctrines contending for supremacy; but he persevered in his attempt and in the end achieved extraordinary success. His teaching spread widely in course of time and eventually grew into a world religion. It is, on the whole, one of the most remarkable developments of Indian thought. Its followers are now found in the remotest parts of the Asian continent, and it has been truly remarked that 'for a great portion of the Orient, Buddhism was not less a vehicle of culture than Christianity has been for the Occident.' Buddha died at a ripe old age. He is one of the greatest figures in the spiritual history of mankind and his life one of the most inspiring in its lessons to humanity.

Buddha wrote no books; and there is a certain amount of vagueness about his teaching, because it has to be gathered from works that were compiled a long time after his death and cannot therefore be regarded as exactly representing what he taught. That the account which these works give is not completely authentic is implied by the following story related in one of them.[2] After the death of Buddha, Purāṇa, an old disciple, came to Rājagṛha and was invited to accept the canon which the other disciples gathering together had meanwhile fixed; but he declined to do so saying that he preferred to hold fast to what he had learnt from the lips of the exalted Master himself. What we say in this chapter, being necessarily based upon such relatively late compilations, should be taken as describing Buddhism in the early stages of its history, and not as setting forth in every particular what Buddha himself taught. There are elements in it which are certainly the result of later thought and

[1] See Kumārila: *Tantra-vārtika*, I. iii. 4.

[2] See Oldenberg: *Buddha* (Eng. Tr.), p. 344.

possibly also elements older than Buddha, which, though not included by him in the teaching, were afterwards incorporated in it by his followers responsible for the canon. These old works which serve as the basis for our knowledge of early Buddhism are written in Pāli, a literary dialect like Sanskrit, connected in all probability with the spoken language of Magadha. They are often in the form of dialogues and there is no methodical discussion in them of any topic in the modern sense of that expression. Thoughts are couched in metaphor and allegory, and to this circumstance also must in some part be attributed the indefiniteness of our knowledge of Buddha's doctrines. The works, if we exclude the large body of commentaries upon them, are three-fold and are described as the Tri-piṭaka, the 'Three Baskets of Tradition,' i.e. the three-fold canon or 'Bible of sacred documents.' They are Suttas or 'utterances of Buddha himself,' Vinaya or 'rules of discipline' and Abhidhamma or 'philosophic discussions.' Though the doctrine of these works is in essential matters different from and even opposed to that of the Upaniṣads, there is a general resemblance between the two. Indeed it could not have been otherwise, for each of them is equally an expression of the same Indian mind[1] Upaniṣadic speculation may in a sense be regarded as having prepared the way for the peculiar teaching of Buddhism[2]; and often Buddha simply carried to their logical conclusions tendencies which we discover already in the Upaniṣads. Thus the whole tenor of the early Upaniṣads is against belief in a personal God; Buddha dismisses that conception altogether. Again according to many statements in them, the self is to be negatively conceived—as devoid of all attributes; Buddha eliminates the conception of self altogether. There are also other points of resemblance between the two, but the belief in the karma doctrine found in Buddhism serves as the clearest proof of its connection with Upaniṣadic thought. However much transformed in its new application, this belief finds a place in Buddha's

[1] See Rel. V. pp. 2–3; Oldenberg: *op. cit.*, p. 53.

[2] See Bhandarkar: *Peep into the Early History of India*, p. 361; Prof. Stcherbatsky: *Central Conception of Buddhism*, pp. 68–69.

teaching; and it appears, we know, already as an important element in the doctrine of the Upaniṣads.

There are some general features characterizing Buddhistic thought which we may note before speaking of its details:—

(1) It is pessimistic. The burden of its teaching is that all is suffering (sarvam duḥkham). 'All the waters of all the seas are not to be compared with the flood of tears which has flowed since the universe first was.'[1] Evil or the misery of saṁsāra is most real and the foremost aim of man is to effect an escape from it. When we describe Buddha's teaching as pessimistic, it must not be taken to be a creed of despair. It does not indeed promise joy on earth or in a world to come as some other doctrines do. But it admits the possibility of attaining peace here and now, whereby man instead of being the victim of misery will become its victor. It no doubt emphasizes the dark side of life; but the emphasis merely shows that life as it is commonly led is marred by sorrow and suffering and not that they are its inalienable features. If Buddha in his discourses dwells upon the fact of evil, he also points to the way out of it. 'Just this have I taught and do I teach,' he is recorded to have stated, 'ill and the ending of ill.'[2]

(2) It is positivistic. Speculation was almost rampant in the period just preceding the time of Buddha and an excessive discussion of theoretical questions was leading to anarchy in thought. His teaching represents a reaction, and in it we meet with a constant effort to return to the hard facts of life. Following the traditional belief of his time, Buddha frequently referred in his discourses to worlds other than ours and to the beings supposed to inhabit them. That was partly a mode of popular expression which it would have been impossible to avoid for anybody using the language of the day. It was also partly due to his belief in the karma doctrine with its definite eschatological reference. Yet his teaching in its essence may be described as excluding whatever was not *positively* known. The authority of Vedic tradition, especially as regards ritual, he wholly repudiated.

[1] Cf. Oldenberg: *op. cit.*, pp. 216–17.
[2] Mrs. Rhys Davids: *Buddhism*, p. 159.

According to some modern scholars belief in the supernatural was part and parcel of the teaching which, they maintain, could not possibly have risen above the psychological conditions of the times.[1] But its general spirit suggests the view, especially when we recollect that positivistic doctrines were not unknown at the time (p. 104), that Buddha did not recognize anything beyond the sphere of perception and reason. Such a view is also supported by the predominantly rationalistic lines on which, as we shall see, the teaching developed in later times.

(3) It is pragmatic. Buddha taught only what is necessary for overcoming evil whose prevalence is, according to him, the chief characteristic of life. The principle which guided him in his numerous discourses is clearly shown by the following story related in one of the Suttas. Once when sitting under a śiṁśupa tree, Buddha took a few of its leaves in his hand and asked his disciples that had assembled there to tell him whether they were all the śiṁśupa leaves or whether there were more on the tree. When they replied that there were surely many more, he said: 'As surely do I know more than what I have told you.' But he did not dwell upon all that he knew, since he saw no practical utility in doing so. It would on the contrary, he thought, only make his hearers idly curious and delay their setting about the task of exterminating evil. 'And wherefore, my disciples, have I not told you that? Because, my disciples, it brings you no profit, it does not conduce to progress in holiness, because it does not lead to the turning from the earthly, to the subjection of all desire, to the cessation of the transitory, to peace, to knowledge, to illumination, to Nirvana: therefore have I not declared it unto you.'[2] Deliverance from pain and evil was his one concern and he neither found time nor need to unravel metaphysical subtleties. He was thus eminently practical in his teaching. 'Philosophy purifies none,' he said, 'peace alone does.' It is sometimes maintained that Buddha was an agnostic and his silence on matters commonly referred to by other religious teachers is explained as due to a lack of certainty in his knowledge of ultimate

[1] BP. pp. 26 ff.

[2] Oldenberg: *op. cit.*, pp. 204–5.

things.[1] But it is forgotten that to so interpret the teaching of Buddha is to throw doubt upon his spiritual sincerity. 'If he did not know the truth, he would not have considered himself to be a Buddha or the enlightened.'[2]

I

From what we have just stated, it will be seen that we have not to look for any metaphysics as such in the teaching of Buddha. He was averse to all theoretic curiosity. But, though there is no explicit metaphysics in his teaching, there is a good deal of it in an implicit form. There may be no metaphysical *aim* in what he taught; there certainly is a metaphysical *view* underlying it, which in its main outline we shall indicate now. There is a general resemblance, it may be stated at the outset, between this teaching and the assumptions of common sense in that it recognizes a distinction between a soul or self and a material environment in which it is placed. Early Buddhism is thus dualistic and realistic[3]; but at the same time it is necessary to remember that we shall be greatly mistaken if we take it to have been either in the ordinary acceptance of the terms. The Buddhistic view is profoundly different in regard to both for, as we shall presently see, it will be equally correct to say that in another sense it recognizes neither the self nor the physical world. The main features of early Buddhism on the theoretical side are as follows:—

(1) 'At any moment of our experience,' it has been observed, 'we stumble upon some particular perception or other, of heat or cold, light or shade, love or hatred, pain or pleasure.' The common belief is that these sensations and thoughts do not stand by themselves but belong to an unchanging entity known as the self. Buddha admitted the transient sensations and thoughts alone and denied the self in the above sense as an unwarranted assumption. To

[1] BP. p. 63. [2] IP. vol. i. p. 465.

[3] Cf. Prof. Stcherbatsky: *op. cit.*, p. 73, where early Buddhism is described as 'radical pluralism.'

express the same in modern phraseology, he admitted only states of consciousness but not the mind. To him the sensations and the thoughts, together with the physical frame with which they are associated, were themselves the self. It is an aggregate or saṁghāta (literally, 'what is put together') of them; and Buddha declined to believe in anything apart from, or implicated in, it. In the expressive words of Mrs. Rhys Davids, there is in his view no 'King Ego holding a *levée* of presentations.'[1] The aggregate is sometimes described as nāma-rūpa, utilizing an old Upaniṣadic phrase (p. 63), though its meaning is here very much modified.[2] By the first term, nāma, is meant, not 'name' as in the Upaniṣads, but the psychical factors constituting the aggregate; and by the second, rūpa, the physical body so that the compound signifies the psycho-physical organism and may be taken as roughly equivalent to 'mind and body.' That is, Buddha took as the reality—if we overlook for the moment the change in the meaning of nāma—the very things that were explained away as not ultimate in the Upaniṣads and denied the substratum which alone according to them is truly real.[3] There is another description of this aggregate based upon a closer analysis of the psychical factors constituting it. According to it the self is conceived as five-fold, the five factors or skandhas, as they are called, being rūpa, vijñāna, vedanā, saṁjñā and saṁskāra. Of these, the first, viz. rūpa-skandha, stands for the physical, and the rest for the psychical, elements in the self. There is a little uncertainty about the exact connotation of some of the latter, but we may for our purpose here take them respectively to represent 'self-consciousness,' 'feeling,' perception' and 'mental dispositions.' This explanation of the

[1] *Buddhist Psychology*, p. 98.

[2] This expression seems to have retained at one stage in Buddha's teaching its original Upaniṣadic sense of 'name and form,' for nāma-rūpa is reckoned separately from 'consciousness' in what is known as the 'chain of causation.' See later and cf. Oldenberg: *op. cit.*, p. 228 n.

[3] But there was agreement between the two teachings in so far as both conceived the aim of life as escape from nāma-rūpa. Cf. *Id.*, p. 446.

self, by the way, brings out clearly an outstanding feature of early Buddhism, viz. its analytical character and the predominantly psychological basis of its analysis. It is remarkable that of these two divisions, Buddha should have held, contrary to prevalent opinion, the mental to be more shadowy than the physical.[1] He said: Even the non-Buddhist readily grants that the body composed of the four elements—earth, water, fire and air—is not the self, but he sees his own self in that which is called 'mind.' That is, however, nothing more than an obsession. It would be less erroneous to call the body the self, for it may last for a hundred years; the mind, on the other hand, is ever restless, like 'the ape in the forest which seizes one branch, only to let it go and grasp another.'

The explanation given of material things is similar. Common sense believes that when sensations are received from outside, those sensations correspond to certain attributes like colour characterizing an object, say, a jar. To Buddha the attributes or sense-data are themselves the object, and he denied the existence of any self-sustaining substance apart from them. He dismissed it as a superstition, there being no means of knowing it as there are in the case of the attributes themselves, viz. the sense of sight, etc. Material things then, like the self, are also aggregates with no underlying unity whatever.

This doctrine is described in Sanskrit as nairātmya-vāda ('doctrine of no-self'). The term nairātmya, being negative, tells us what objects are not, while saṁghāta, being positive, states what they are. Thus according to Buddhism, when we for instance say 'It thinks' or 'It is white,' we mean by the 'it' nothing more than when we say 'It rains.' There are several parables in Buddhistic literature to bring home to us the full import of this doctrine, one of the best known being that of the chariot. It is mentioned in older books also, but is fully elaborated in the 'Questions of King Milinda,' a work which was composed in the North-west of India about the beginning of the Christian era and purports to give an account of the conversations between the Greek king

[1] Cf. Mrs. Rhys Davids: *Buddhism*, p. 133.

Menander and a Buddhistic sage of the name of Nāgasena.[1] One day when Milinda went to see Nāgasena, the sage discoursed upon the doctrine of no-self; but finding him unconvinced said: 'Great king, hast thou come on foot or on a chariot?' 'I do not travel on foot, sire: I have come on a chariot.' 'If thou hast come on a chariot, great king, then define the chariot. Is the pole the chariot? Are the wheels the chariot?' When similar questions were put about the axle and so forth, the prince was able to see that none of its component parts, when examined singly, is the chariot and that the word is a mere symbol for those parts 'assembled' or placed together in a particular way. Then the sage added: In the same way, the word 'self' also is only a label for the aggregate of certain physical and psychical factors. Not one of the objects of experience stands for an entity apart from the constituent parts. The important thing to bear in mind here is the sameness of the explanation given of both the self and the material world. The doctrine of nairātmya should not accordingly be understood as applicable to the soul alone as it is apt to be done. Both soul and matter exist only as complexes and neither is a single self-contained entity.

(2) So far we have looked at reality in a section as it were, ignoring altogether the element of time. When we take the same in time, this aggregate according to Buddhism does not continue the same for even two moments, but is constantly changing. So the self and the material world are each a flux (saṁtāna). Two symbols are generally used to illustrate this conception—the stream of water and 'the self-producing and the self-consuming' flame, the latter being particularly appropriate in respect of the self in that it suggests also suffering through its tormenting heat. It will be seen thus that every one of our so-called things is only a series (vīthī)—a succession of similar things or happenings, and the notion of fixity which we have of them is wholly fictitious. This theory of the ceaseless movement of all things with no underlying constancy is obviously a compromise between the two opposite views current at the time—one

[1] See Oldenberg: *op. cit.*, pp. 254 ff.

believing in Being and the other in non-Being. 'This world, O Kaccāna, generally proceeds on a duality, of the "it is" and the "it is not." But, O Kaccāna, whoever perceives in truth and wisdom how things originate in the world, in his eyes there is no "it is not" in this world. Whoever, Kaccāna, perceives in truth and wisdom how things pass away in this world, in his eyes there is no "it is" in this world.'[1] Neither Being nor non-Being is the truth, according to Buddha, but only Becoming. From this we should not conclude that he denied reality. He did admit it, but only gave a dynamic explanation of it. There is incessant change, but at the same time there is nothing that changes. 'There is action, but no agent.' Language almost fails to give expression to this view, the like of which is known only twice in the history of philosophy—once in Greece when Heraclitus taught a generation or two later than Buddha and again in our own time in the philosophy of Bergson. Great indeed should have been the genius that enunciated such a doctrine for the first time.

Since there is incessant production, but no new *things* are brought into being, the world becomes the world-process—'a continual coming-to-be and passing away.' Neither the world as a whole, nor any object in it, can be described as subject to the process. The process is the thing. The law governing this process is most vital to Buddhism and needs a few words of explanation here, although its enunciation in a general form applicable to whatever is produced belongs to its later history. We may begin by asking the question: If everything is but a series of similar states, what is the relation between any two consecutive members of it? One explanation given in Buddha's time of the fact of such succession was that it was accidental (p. 103). Another, though recognizing a causal relation as underlying the succession, introduced in explaining it a supernatural element like God in addition to known factors (p. 104). In neither case could man effectively interfere with the course of things. Buddha discarded both these explanations alike and postulated necessity as the sole governing factor. In denying chance, he took his stand on the

[1] Oldenberg: *op. cit.*, p. 249.

uniformity of nature; and in denying supernatural intervention, he dissociated himself from all dogmatic religion. This idea of ordered succession is no doubt really very old. It goes back to the conceptions of ṛta and dharma found in earlier literature. But they both suggest an agency operating in some unknown manner. The peculiarity of order as conceived in Buddhism is that it excludes such an agency altogether. In this, the Buddhistic view resembles the Svabhāva-vāda[1] (p. 104). But it differs from it also in one essential respect. The Svabhāva-vāda regards the necessity to produce the effect as inherent in the cause. We need not, according to it, go outside of a thing to explain its history. Here no such inner teleology is recognized, for production, according to Buddhism, is not the mere self-unfolding on the part of the cause, but the result of certain external factors co-operating with it. It is necessary succession, but yet the constraint implied by it is of a contingent kind. It is contingent in so far as a series does not come into being until certain conditions are fulfilled; and it is necessary in so far as the series once begun will not cease so long as the conditions continue. The flame-series, for example, does not start until the wick, oil, etc., are there; but, when once it starts, it goes on uninterruptedly till one or more of the co-operating factors are withdrawn. Thus, though the law itself is universal and admits no exception, its operation is dependent upon conditions. This is the reason why it is called the law of 'dependent origination' or pratītya-samutpāda—'that being present, this becomes; from the arising of that, this arises.'[2] The Sanskrit expression means literally 'arising in correlation with' and signifies that if certain conditions are present, a certain product arises so that the nature of necessity as conceived here is not the same as in the Svabhāva-vāda. The implication of the 'if' here is that by sundering the causes sustaining the effect, the series can be arrested. This is stated in the remaining part of the causal formula: 'that being absent, this does not become; from the cessation of that, this ceases.' The consequent difference from the practical standpoint between the Svabhāva-vāda and

[1] Cf. BP. pp. 68 ff. [2] Mrs. Rhys Davids: *Buddhism*, p. 89.

Buddhism is immense. In the one, whatever is to happen *must* happen, whether we will it or not; in the other, there is every scope for human effort since a series, though begun, admits of being put an end to. It is only necessary that we should know what are the causes so as to get at them.[1] The causal factors are determinable in their entirety; and the series they give rise to is therefore terminable, according to early Buddhism, at least in respect of the misery of existence whose removal is the chief problem of life. It was the knowledge of these factors, with the law of contingent causation implicit in it, that flashed across Siddhārtha's mind at last and made him the 'Buddha.'[2] Its chief significance for man is that since misery is caused in accordance with a natural and ascertainable law, it can be ended by removing its cause—a discovery which points at the same time to the positivistic and the practical basis of Buddha's teaching. The explanation was then extended to all causal phenomena. In this general form, it states that for everything that is, there is an adequate reason why it is so and not otherwise; and the causes accounting for it are at least in theory completely knowable. We have here the Indian counterpart of what is now known as the Law of Sufficient Reason. Buddhism may accordingly be described as having reached in those early days the modern conception of causation.

This view that everything changes from moment to moment is known as the kṣanika-vāda or 'the doctrine of momentariness'; and it is by that term that Buddhism is commonly alluded to in Hindu philosophical works. Buddha himself seems to have taught only the impermanence or mutability of things, excepting perhaps mind; but soon, through the force of its inherent logic, the doctrine was transformed into the general one of the momentary disintegration of all things. Its full development belongs to later times and we accordingly postpone further observations on it to the chapter on the Buddhistic systems in the next Part. There are, however, two obvious criticisms which may

[1] Cf. *Bodhi-caryāvatāra-pañcikā*, vi. 25–6 and 31–2.
[2] See Oldenberg: *op. cit.*, pp. 224–5.

be urged against such a view of reality to which, as well as to the way in which the Buddhist met them, it is necessary to briefly refer now. If everything is a flux and everything is being continually renewed, we may ask how recognition of objects—the apprehension of a familiar external object as the same we already know—is explained. The Buddhist states in answer that the things in the two moments of our cognition are only *similar* and that we mistake them to be *the same*. In other words, all recognition is erroneous since similarity is mistaken in it for identity. Another criticism is that if the self also be changing every moment, it becomes difficult to account for the fact of memory. Here also the Buddhist has his explanation. He holds that each phase of experience, as it appears and disappears, is wrought up into the next[1] so that every successive phase has within it 'all the potentialities of its predecessors' which manifest themselves when conditions are favourable. Hence, though a man is not the same in any two moments, yet he is not quite different. 'The self is not only a collective, but also a recollective entity.'[2] It is on this basis that Buddhism establishes moral responsibility. What one does, it is true, the same one does not reap; but he that reaps the fruit is not quite alien either and so far merits to come in for the good or evil that belonged to the preceding members of that particular series. In the Devadatta-sutta, which describes a sinner meeting Yama, the latter says: 'These your evil deeds, none other has done. You alone have done them; and you alone will reap the fruit.'[3] The Jātaka stories again which recount the deeds of Buddha in former births all end with the identification of characters, though separated by whole births: 'I was then the wise white elephant: Devadatta was the wicked hunter.' That is to say, Buddhism denies *unity* in the sense of identity of material, but recognizes *continuity* in its place. If we represent two self-series as A_1 A_2 A_3 . . . B_1 B_2 B_3 . . ., though A_1 A_2 A_3 . . . are not identical and B_1 B_2 B_3 . . . also are not so, there is a kinship among the

[1] Mrs. Rhys Davids: *Buddhism*, p. 135.
[2] Prof. Hopkins: *Journal of the Royal Asiatic Society* (1906), p. 581.
[3] Oldenberg: *op. cit.*, p. 244.

members of each series which is not found between those of the two, e.g. A_1 and B_1, A_2 and B_2, etc. We should therefore be careful how we understand the Buddhistic doctrine of the denial of the soul. As a stable entity which, without itself changing, appears amidst changing conditions—bodily and mental—Buddhism does deny the self; but it recognizes instead a 'fluid self' which because of its very fluidity cannot be regarded as a series of altogether distinct or dissimilar states. We may, however, observe in passing that in so stating his view the Buddhist has tacitly admitted a self transcending the experience of the moment. In the very act of analysing the self and dismissing it as but a series of momentary states, he is passing beyond those states and positing an enduring self which is able to view them together, for a series as such can never become aware of itself. Some are of opinion that belief in such a self is not merely the unintended implication of the teaching of Buddha, but an accepted element in it; and that its negation is an innovation introduced by his later followers.[1]

The principles of impermanence and no-self are fundamental to the teaching of Buddha; and by enunciating them he may be said to have reversed at the same time both the truth of the traditional teaching and the belief of the common people. This unique doctrine starts by postulating certain elements as basic which are mutually distinct and which include both the physical and the psychical, and explains the whole world as produced out of them. But the rudimentary elements are as unsubstantial and as evanescent as the things they produce. The only difference is that while the former are simple and represent the ultimate stage in the analysis of the things of experience, the latter are all aggregates and do not, like the chariot of the parable, stand for new things. On the physical side, early Buddhism recognized only four bhūtas or constituent elements of material things, viz. earth, water, fire and air, excluding ākāśa,[2] the fifth commonly admitted by the thinkers of the day. These names,

[1] Cf. IP. vol. i. pp. 386 ff.

[2] Ākāśa also is sometimes included, but then it seems to stand merely for the field of experience emptied of its content. See BP. p. 02.

however, it must be remembered, are only conventional, for they stand for nothing more than the sense-data commonly associated with them, viz. hardness, fluidity, heat and pressure respectively. The material world, our indriyas and our bodies are all aggregates derived from these elements and are therefore termed bhautika to indicate their secondary character. On the psychical side, it similarly recognized a rudimentary form—citta, and explained the other features of mind as caitta or derived from it. Such details, however, strictly belong to stages in the history of the doctrine later than the one we are now concerned with and we need not therefore consider them further here.

II

The practical teaching of Buddhism will become clear in the light of its theory as briefly sketched above. If all things in the world are transient and unsubstantial, our endeavours to secure any of them for ourselves or for others must be labour wholly lost. The very desire for them is a delusion and we should therefore wean ourselves from it as quickly as possible. More powerful than this desire for outside things is the craving for the preservation of the self or the will to be. Buddhism teaches that since there is no self at all, we should first get rid of this craving, if we have to extinguish the pains of existence. Thus self-denial is to be understood in a literal sense in Buddhistic ethics. There is a later Sanskrit saying, derived from a Buddhistic source, which states that belief in the being of oneself simultaneously posits belief in that of others and thereby gives rise to the whole range of narrow love and hatred.[1] With the negation of self, all selfish impulses necessarily disappear. Since the belief in self-identity which is the basis of suffering is false, ignorance (avidyā) becomes the true source of all evil. Here also then, as in Upaniṣadic teaching, evil is traced to ignorance; and in both, the way to escape lies through right knowledge such as is calculated to remove it. But once again, while the word

[1] See *Nyāya-kandalī* (Vizianagaram Sans. Series), p. 279; NM. p. 443.

remains the same, the idea for which it stands is different. Avidyā is not conceived here as a cosmic power explaining how the niṣprapañca Brahman shows itself as the empirical world, but merely as the ground of individual existence as is shown by the first place assigned to it in the 'chain of causation' to which we shall soon refer. Nor is it here, to look at it from another side, as in the Upaniṣads, ignorance of the essential unity of all existence, but the failure to recognize the hollowness of the so-called self. It is generally stated that this ignorance is of the Four Noble Truths (ārya-satya)—those concerning suffering, its origin, its removal and the way to remove it. 'Not seeing the four sacred truths as they are, I have wandered on the long path from one birth to another. Now have I seen them: The current of being is stemmed. The root of suffering is destroyed: there is henceforward no rebirth.'[1] It is evident that in formulating this four-fold truth, Buddha was guided by the medical view of the time in regard to the curing of diseases,[2] such transference of the method of current science to philosophy being not at all uncommon in its history. Buddha, who is sometimes styled the Great Healer, looked upon life with its suffering as a disease and his method was naturally that of a doctor seeking a remedy for it. We might say that the first three of these truths constitute the theoretical aspect of the teaching and the last, its practical. That suffering predominates in life, as we commonly know it, was admitted by practically all the Indian thinkers. The peculiar value of Buddhism lies in the explanation it gives of the origin of suffering, in the manner in which it deduces the possibility of its removal and in the means it recommends for doing so. To take these three in order:—

(1) *The origin of suffering.*—That suffering originates follows from the belief that whatever is, must have had a cause. Buddha found this cause to be ignorance in the last resort, as we have just stated. His foremost aim was to discover how it brings about evil; for if we once know the process, he said, we are on the highway to get rid of the

[1] Oldenberg: *op. cit.*, p. 240.

[2] See BP. pp. 56–7. Cf. BUV. p. 15, st. 28.

result it leads to. The stages of this process were set forth in a somewhat elaborate form which may be described as the special causal formula as distinguished from the general one to which we alluded in the previous section. It consists of a dozen links (nidāna)—Ignorance (avidyā), action (saṁskāra), consciousness (vijñāna), name and form (nāma-rūpa), the six fields, viz. the five senses and mind together with their objects (ṣadāyatana), contact between the senses and the objects (sparśa), sensation (vedanā), desire (tṛṣṇā), clinging to existence (upādāna), being (bhava), re-birth (jāti) and pain or, literally, old age and death (jarā-maraṇa). This 'chain' alludes not to the present life only, but includes a reference to the previous and the coming ones also. It exhibits the life that now is in its relation to the past as well as the future and stands for a sample of saṁsāra or the ever-recurring series of births and deaths. Without entering into a discussion of the details of this formula, about whose interpretation there has been a good deal of controversy, we may say that the first two of the links are retrospective. They refer to the life immediately preceding this one and hit off its general feature by describing it as 'ignorance' and its sequel, 'action.' It means that it is the activity of the past life prompted by ignorance that directly gives rise to the present. The course of the latter is traced in the next eight links, the earlier ones among which allude to the evolution of the organism, suitably equipped for the experiences of life and the later describe the nature of those experiences and their results. The last two links refer prospectively to the birth and suffering that will necessarily follow from the activities of the present life.[1] Confining ourselves to the broadest features of this explanation, we may say that there is, first of all, ignorance which is the root-cause of the individual's existence. From ignorance proceeds desire; desire, leading to activity, brings in its turn rebirth with its fresh desires. This is the vicious circle of saṁsāra—the bhava-cakra or 'wheel of existence' as it is sometimes called.

(2) *Removal of suffering.*—Just as it follows from the Buddhistic view of causation that suffering to exist must

[1] BP. p. 105.

have been caused, it follows from the same that it must admit of being destroyed. According to the principle underlying the view, the removal of the cause removes the effect. So when ignorance is dispelled by right knowledge, the succeeding links of the chain snap one after another automatically. The process which gives rise to suffering, no doubt, involves a necessity; but the necessity, as we have stated already, is not absolute.

(3) *The way to remove suffering.*—The path of self-discipline which leads man to the desired goal is eight-fold: right faith, right resolve, right speech, right action, right living, right effort, right thought, right concentration. It will suffice to refer here to a simpler scheme which also is found in old Buddhistic works[1] and which may be said to consist of the essence of the more elaborate one. According to this scheme, prajñā or right knowledge of the four-fold truth is the basis of the whole discipline. But if it is to result in a sense of freedom, it should be more than mere intellectual conviction, however strong it may be. It should be knowledge that has been transformed into our own experience and prajñā more strictly means this intuitive experience. Buddha insists that his hearers should not borrow their views from him, but should make them their own. He often declares that we must accept only what we ourselves have realized to be right. 'Then, monks, what you have just said is only what *you yourselves* have recognized, what *you yourselves* have comprehended, what *you yourselves* have understood; is it not so?' 'It is even so, Lord.'[2] In other words, every man should win his own salvation. It is salvation through self-reliance, not by the grace of God or under the guidance of any external authority. Even the guru can only show the way. For knowledge to become an internal certainty, śīla and samādhi are necessary. There can be no perception of truth without control of thought and action. Śīla means right conduct which includes virtues like veracity, contentment, and non-injury or ahiṁsā. Samādhi is meditation upon the four verities. It is an aid in

[1] See Oldenberg: *op. cit.*, p. 288; BP. p. 115.
[2] *Majjhima-nikāya*, 38th Discourse.

securing tranquillity of mind and in gaining a clear insight into the truth that has been learnt from others. This part of the training includes, as in the Upaniṣads, diverse forms of yogic exercises, the details of which it is not necessary to consider here. These three together sufficiently indicate the scope of Buddhistic discipline. It is prajñā in the sense of insight or intuition, the outcome of the whole training, that will bring deliverance, while the same, in the sense of knowledge accepted on trust, marks the beginning of the discipline leading to it.

What is meant by right living differs somewhat in the case of a monk and a layman, and either mode of life may be followed, according to the capacity and inclination of the individual; but ultimate release is normally to be attained only after one becomes a monk.[1] Even in the monk's life, there is not that extreme severity of discipline characterizing some of the other Indian creeds, notably Jainism. We have already seen that Buddha's theory strikes a mean between two extreme courses, e.g. believing neither in Being nor in non-Being, but in Becoming; believing neither in chance nor in necessity exclusively, but in conditioned happening. The same spirit is reflected in his ethical teaching also. It is neither self-indulgence, which is the harbinger of pain; nor self-mortification, which is itself pain. Success lies in a middle course. True spiritual life is compared to a lute which emits melodious sounds only when its strings are stretched neither too loose nor too tight. In his very first discourse—the celebrated Sermon at Benares—Buddha said: 'There are two extremes, O monks, from which he who leads a religious life must abstain. What are those two extremes? One is a life of pleasure, devoted to desire and enjoyment: that is base, ignoble, unspiritual, unworthy, unreal. The other is a life of mortification: it is gloomy, unworthy, unreal. The perfect one, O monks, is removed from both these extremes and has discovered the way which lies between them, the middle way which enlightens the eyes, enlightens the mind, which leads to rest, to knowledge, to enlightenment, to Nirvana.'[2]

[1] BP. p. 131; Prof. Poussin: *The Way to Nirvāna*, pp. 114 and 150-1.
[2] Oldenberg: *op. cit.*, p. 127.

The object to be attained by following this discipline is designated nirvāna. The word literally means 'blowing out' (p. 114) or 'becoming cool'; and signifies annihilation—the 'heaven of nothingness' as it has been described. When it is reached, the constant procession of the five-fold aggregate disappears once for all. This of course is the view which accords best with the theoretical position of Buddhism, and salvation then becomes literally 'the unmaking of ourselves.'[1] But the extremely negative character of such an ideal unfits it to serve as an incentive to man for pursuing the course of discipline recommended for its attainment, and thus appears to defeat the very purpose of Buddha's teaching. So other interpretations have been suggested.[2] Some have flatly denied that nirvāṇa can be annihilation, and represented it as everlasting being or eternal felicity—an ideal hardly different from the Upaniṣadic mokṣa. Others again have taken it as a condition of which nothing whatsoever can be predicated—not even whether it is or is not. All that the term means, according to them, is freedom from suffering; and positive descriptions of it—whatever the speculative interest attaching to them—are irrelevant from the practical standpoint. But it does not seem necessary to resort to such explanations to show that nirvāṇa as conceived in Buddhism is worth striving for, because it does not really signify, as seems to be commonly taken for granted, any state following death. It represents rather the condition which results after perfection is reached and while yet the 'individual' continues to live. This would correspond to jīvan-mukti, which, as we know, had been well recognized in India by Buddha's time. It is a state when the passions and the limited interests of common life have been extinguished and the person leads a life of perfect peace and equanimity. It connotes a certain habit of mind; and he that has succeeded in cultivating it is known as an arhant, which means 'worthy' or 'holy.' It is this perfect calm to be reached within the four corners of the present life that the Buddhist *aims at*

[1] IP. vol. i. p. 418.

[2] See e.g. Oldenberg: *op. cit.*, pp. 267–285; Prof. Poussin: *op. cit.*, pp. 115–18.

and means by nirvāṇa, although as stated above an arhant after the dissolution of his body and mind may come to nothing. The idea of nirvāṇa understood in the latter sense (pari-nirvāṇa) need not stultify the teaching, for the goal which it presents as worthy of attainment is not annihilation but the state which precedes it. Annihilation is only a further consequence, not the motive of the training which Buddhism prescribes. That is nirvāna in the sense of 'blowing out' while the state of the arhant, which marks the transition from common life to it, corresponds to the other meaning of the word, viz. 'becoming cool.'

There is one other point to which attention should be drawn before we conclude. The Buddhist believes in transmigration, but the belief seems to be inconsistent with his denial of an enduring self. Some have, therefore, characterized the doctrine as self-contradictory. Deussen, for instance, writes:[1] 'This *karman* must have in every case an individual bearer and that is what the Upaniṣads call the ātman and what the Buddhists inconsistently deny.' But there seems to be no justification for such a criticism. The belief in the karma doctrine really presents no new difficulty to Buddhism; for if there can be action without an agent, there can well be transmigration without a transmigrating agent. Further, we have to remember that according to Buddhism there is transmigration, or, more precisely, rebirth, not only at the end of this life as in other Indian beliefs, but at every instant. It is not merely when one lamp is lit from another that there is a transmission of light and heat. They are transmitted every moment; only in the former case a new series of flames is started. Similarly, the karma belonging to an 'individual' may transmit itself at death as it does during life; and, though the dead person does not revive, another with the same disposition may be born in his stead. If so, it is character, as Rhys Davids has put it, that transmigrates, not any soul or self. When a person dies, his character lives after him, and by its force brings into existence a being who, though possessing a different form, is entirely influenced by it. And this process will go on until the person in question

[1] *Indian Antiquary* (1900), p. 398.

has completely overcome his thirst for being. If we take this explanation along with what has already been stated that the self is here recognized as a continuity, though not as a unity, we see that there need be no inconsistency in Buddhism upholding the karma doctrine. For it admits both the implications of the doctrine, viz. that nothing that we do disappears without leaving its result behind and that the good or evil so resulting recoils upon the doer. Buddha, however, rationalized the doctrine to a considerable extent. For one thing, he dissociated it from all supernatural and materialistic appanages. In the traditional Hindu view, the allotment of pain or pleasure according to one's past actions was in the hands of a divine or some other transcendental power; and in Jainism karma, as we shall see, was taken to be subtle matter adhering to and pulling down the soul from its natural spiritual height. Buddha discarded both these views, and conceived of karma as an impersonal law in the sphere of morality working according to its nature and by itself.

CHAPTER VI

JAINISM

THE word Jainism goes back to jina, which, derived from the Sanskrit root *ji* 'to conquer,' means 'victor,' i.e. one that has successfully subdued his passions and obtained mastery over himself. The creed to which the name is applied is not an off-shoot or a sub-sect of Buddhism as it was once taken to be, but is quite independent of it. It is, as a matter of fact, much older; and Vardhamāna, styled Mahāvīra or 'the great spiritual hero,' was only the last in a series of prophets. Tradition reckons twenty-three prophets as having preceded him, which takes us back to fabulous antiquity. Of these, at least one Pārśvanātha, the next previous to Vardhamāna, who is believed to have lived in the eighth century B.C., can claim historicity (p. 43). There is evidence to show that his followers were contemporaries of Vardhamāna.[1] But corruptions had crept into the older teaching by then,[2] and Vardhamāna gave it fresh impetus by reforming it. It is the only heretical creed that has survived to the present day in India out of the many that were preached in this period in opposition to the Vedic teaching. Though independent of Buddhism, Jainism resembles it in several respects, e.g. in its repudiation of the authority of the Veda, its pessimistic outlook on life and its refusal to believe in a supreme God. But the differences it exhibits are equally noticeable, such as its recognition of permanent entities like the self and matter. In these it resembles Brahminism, justifying the description that it is 'a theological mean between Brahmanism and Buddhism.[3]

Vardhamāna was born about 540 B.C., near Vaiśālī, the capital of Videha. His father Siddhārtha was the chief of a Kshattriya clan; and his mother was Triśalā, sister of the King of Videha. Thus by birth he, like Buddha, was a member of the ruling class. Like him, Vardhamāna also first

[1] Prof. Jacobi: *Jaina Sūtras* (SBE.), Pt. II. p. xxxiii.

[2] *Id.*, p. 122 n.

[3] Prof. Hopkins: *Religions of India*, p. 283.

addressed himself to his kinsmen and through their support succeeded in propagating his teaching. He married Yaśodā; but, unlike Buddha, he lived in the house of his parents till they died and entered upon the spiritual career afterwards when he was twenty-eight years old.[1] For about a dozen years he led an austere life practising penance and at the end of that period attained perfect knowledge or, as it is said, became a kevalin. He did not, like Buddha, look upon this period of severe mortification as time wasted, but felt convinced of its necessity as a preparation for the great work of his life. As a result of this self-discipline he became a Tīrtham-kara (p. 19). He spent the rest of his life in teaching his religious system and organizing his order of ascetics. He died, it is believed, when he was over seventy years of age. The influence of Jainism unlike that of Buddhism is confined to India; and even there it is seen, somewhat strangely, to be wider outside the province of its birth—especially in the West and the South—than within it. The redaction of the Jaina canon or the siddhānta, which like that of Buddhism is written in a Prākṛtic language (Ardha-māgadhī), took place according to tradition under the presidency of Devardhi about the end of the fifth or the beginning of the sixth century A.D. This comparatively late date has led some to doubt the faithfulness of the canonical doctrine to the original teaching. The truth, however, seems to be that Devardhi only *arranged* the texts that were already in existence, and had been handed down from the third century B.C. Even before that date, there were Jaina works called Pūrva, which, as their name signifies, were later superseded by the new canon of the Aṅgas.[2] Thus there is really no cause for doubting the authenticity of the Jaina doctrine, as now known, although this does not mean that additions and alterations, here and there, have not been made in it at all.[3]

[1] There is difference in the tradition relating to Vardhamāna's marriage, etc., between the two important sections of the Jains—the Śvetāmbarás or 'white-clad' and the Digambaras or 'sky-clad.' The statement above is according to the former.

[2] This is again according to Śvetāmbara tradition. The Digambara canon is different and is divided, as it is termed, into four Vedas. See Mrs. Stevenson: *Heart of Jainism*, p. 16.

[3] Prof. Jacobi: *op. cit.*, Part II. p. xl.

I

The Jains bring the whole universe under one or other of two everlasting categories. The two classes of things are respectively described as jīva and ajīva, i.e. the conscious and the unconscious[1] or spirit and non-spirit—the latter including not merely matter but also time and space. The terms show clearly the realistic and relativistic standpoint of Jainism. As surely as there is a subject that knows, Jainism says, so surely is there an object that is known. Of them, the ajīva has its own specific nature; but that nature cannot be properly understood until it is contrasted with the jīva. That is why it is designated as 'not-jīva' or the contradictory of jīva. The latter is the higher and more important category, which accounts for its independent designation, although that also can be well understood only when contrasted with the ajīva or non-spirit :—

(1) *Jīva.*—The notion of jīva in general corresponds to that of ātman or puruṣa of the other schools of Indian thought. But as implied by the etymology of its name—'what lives or is animate'—the concept seems to have been arrived at first by observing the characteristics of life and not through the search after a metaphysical principle underlying individual existence.[2] It would therefore be more correct to take the word in its original significance as standing for the vital principle than for the soul. 'The spirit does but mean the breath.' In its present connotation, however, it is practically the same as the other Indian words for the self. The number of jīvas is infinite, all being alike and eternal. In their empirical form they are classified in various ways, such as those that have one sense, two senses and so forth; but it is not necessary to dwell upon those details here. It will suffice to remark that the classifications imply different levels of development in the souls. The Jains believe not only that the jīva exists, but also that it acts and is acted upon. It is both an experient (bhoktā) and an agent (kartā)[3] Its intrinsic nature is one of perfection and it is characterized

1 SDS. p. 33.
2 Prof. Jacobi: *op. cit.*, Part I. p. 3 n.
3 *Ṣaddarśana-samuccaya*, st. 48.

by infinite intelligence, infinite peace, infinite faith and infinite power[1]; but during the period of its union with matter which constitutes saṁsāra, these features are obscured, though not destroyed. The jīva's 'exterior semblance' accordingly belies its innate glory. Man's personality as it is familiarly known to us is dual, consisting of a spiritual as well as a material element. The object of life is so to subdue the latter as to shake off its malignant influence and thereby enable the jīva to reveal all its inherent excellences in their fulness. One of the curious features of Jainism is the belief in the variable size of the jīva in its empirical condition. It is capable of expansion and contraction according to the dimensions of the physical body with which it is associated for the time being. In this respect it resembles a lamp, it is said, which though remaining the same illumines the whole of the space enclosed in a small or big room in which it happens to be placed.[2] It means that like its other features, the jīva's non-spatial character also is affected by association with matter. The Jaina thus denies the unalterable nature of the jīva which is commonly recognized by Indian thinkers.

The jīva's relation to matter explains also the somewhat peculiar Jaina view of knowledge. Knowledge is not something that characterizes the jīva. It constitutes its very essence. The jīva can therefore know unaided everything directly and exactly as it is; only there should be no impediment in its way. External conditions, such as the organ of sight and the presence of light, are useful only indirectly and jñāna results automatically when the obstacles are removed through their aid. That the knowledge which a jīva actually has is fragmentary is due to the obscuration caused by karma which interferes with its power of perception. As some schools assume a principle of avidyā to explain empirical thought, the Jains invoke the help of karma to do so. This empirical thought is sometimes differentiated from the jīva, but its identity with the latter is at the same time emphasized, so that the jīva and its

[1] Guṇaratna: Com. on *Ṣaddarśana-samuccaya*, p. 74.
[2] SDS. p. 45.

several jñānas in this sense constitute a unity in difference.[1] Perfect enlightenment being of the very nature of the self, its condition of partial or indistinct knowledge marks a lapse from it.[2] Accordingly the senses and the manas, though they are aids to knowing from one standpoint, are from another so many indications of the limitation to which the jīva is subject during its earthly pilgrimage. This leads to the recognition of differences in the extent of enlightenment that a self may possess as a result of the removal of less or more of the obstacles to it. But no self without jñāna is conceivable, or jñāna without a self—a point in the doctrine which well illustrates its distinction from Buddhism (p. 139). The culmination of enlightenment is reached when the obstacles are broken down in their entirety. Then the individual jīva, while continuing as such, becomes omniscient and knows all objects vividly and precisely as they are. That is called kevala-jñāna or absolute apprehension without media or doubt and is what Mahāvīra is believed to have attained at the end of the long period of his penance. It is immediate knowledge and is described as kevala ('pure') since it arises of itself without the help of any external aid like the senses, etc. It is 'soul-knowledge,' if we may so term it—knowledge in its pristine form and is designated mukhya-pratyakṣa or perception *par excellence* to contrast it with common perception (sāṁvyavahārika-pratyakṣa). There are other but lower varieties of this supernormal knowledge recognized in the school, but it is not necessary to describe them here.

(2) *Ajīva.*—The category of ajīva is divided into kāla (time), ākāśa, dharma and adharma (which together may for our purpose be regarded as standing for 'space')[3] and pudgala ('matter'). Their essential distinction from the jīva is that they, as such, lack life and consciousness. Of

[1] SDS. p. 34. [2] SDS. p. 29.

[3] Strictly ākāśa alone is 'space.' Dharma and adharma are respectively the principles of motion and stability. They are found everywhere in the universe or that part of space which is called lokākāśa. Dharma helps movement as water does, it is said, the movement of fish; adharma, on the other hand, makes it possible for things to rest. Dharma and adharma, it should be noted, do not stand here for 'merit' and 'demerit' as they do in Hindu thought. See SDS. p. 35.

these, time is infinite. But there are cycles in it, each cycle having two eras of equal duration described as the avasarpiṇī and the utsarpiṇī—a metaphor drawn from the revolving wheel. The former is the descending era in which virtue gradually decreases; and the latter, the ascending in which the reverse takes place. The present era is stated to be the former. Space which also is infinite is conceived of as being in two parts—one (lokākāśa) where movement is possible and the other (alokākāśa) where it is not. Whatever is, is only in the former and the latter is empty ākāśa, 'an abyss of nothing,' stretching infinitely beyond it. Matter possesses colour, flavour, odour and touch,[1] sound being looked upon not as a quality but as a mode of it (pudgala-pariṇāma).[2] It is eternal and consists of atoms out of which are constituted all the things of experience including animal bodies, the senses and manas. These atoms are all believed to house souls so that the universe should be literally crowded with them. Prof. Jacobi says: 'A characteristic dogma of the Jains which pervades the whole philosophical system and code of morals, is the hylozoistic theory that not only animals and plants, but also the smallest particles of the elements, earth, fire, water and wind, are endowed with souls (jīva).'[3]

Reality is defined as that which is characterized by 'birth' (utpāda), 'death' (vyaya) and 'persistence' (dhrauvya).[4] It means that though eternal in itself, reality shows modifications which come into being and pass out of it. A jīva for instance has several embodied conditions—one for every birth it takes, and each of them has its beginning and end; but, as soul itself, it always subsists. 'To suffer change and yet endure is the privilege of existence.' The changes or modes are known as paryāyas, which, as distinguished from

[1] Sparśa-rasa-gandha-varṇavantaḥ pudgalāḥ-Umāsvāti: *Tattvārthādhigama-sūtra*, v. 23. [2] See Guṇaratna: *op. cit.*, pp. 69–70.

[3] Prof. Jacobi: *op. cit.*, Part I. p. xxxiii. It is necessary to remember that when Jainism states that there are souls in water, for instance, it does not refer to the germs that may be contained therein, but to souls having for their bodies the water particles themselves. See SDS. p. 35.

[4] Utpāda-vyaya-dhrauvya-yuktam sat-Umāsvāti: *op. cit.*, v. 29.

the enduring substance, come into being, persist for at least one instant and then disappear.[1] Thus the minimum duration of empirical objects here is two instants as contrasted with the single moment of all reality as conceived in Buddhism. The notion of reality here is dynamic as in Buddhism; but it is not the same, for the latter altogether repudiates the constant element and the change it recognizes is therefore really the change of nothing. It accepts the many but denies the one. Jainism, on the other hand, admits both, defining reality as a one-in-many. The many as such are distinct, but they are also identical in that they are all of the same substance. To the question how an identical object can exhibit different features—how unity and diversity can co-exist, the Jains reply that our sole warrant for speaking about reality is experience and that when experience vouches for such a character of reality, it must be admitted to be so.[2] It is in connection with this view of reality that they formulate the theory of syādvāda to which we shall allude later. The term dravya or 'substance' is applied to the six entities mentioned above—the jīva and the ajīva with its five-fold division. The dravyas, excepting 'time' alone, are called asti-kāyas, a term which means that they are real in the sense just explained (asti) and possess

[1] In addition to this distinction between substance and mode, the Jains recognize another—that between substance and attribute (guṇa). The two are somewhat discrepant from each other and Prof. Jacobi states, writing on this subject, that 'the ancient Jaina texts usually speak only of substances, dravyas and their development or modifications, paryāyas; and when they mention guṇas, qualities, besides, which, however, is done but rarely in the sūtras and regularly in comparatively modern books only, this seems to be a later innovation due to the influence which the philosophy and terminology of Nyāya-Vaiśeṣika gradually gained over the scientific thoughts of the Hindus. For at the side of paryāya, development or modification, there seems to be no room for an independent category 'quality,' since paryāya is the state in which a thing, dravya, is at any moment of its existence and this must therefore include qualities as seems to be actually the view embodied in the oldest text' (SBE. vol. XLV. pp. xxxiv. and 153 n.).

[2] Cf. Pratīyamāne vastuni virodhāsiddheḥ: *Prameya-kamala-mārtaṇḍa*, p. 93.

constituent parts (kāya). Time is not an asti-kāya because it has no such parts, though an eternal entity.[1]

There are two other aspects of the theoretical teaching of Jainism to which we may briefly refer now:—

(1) *Atomic Theory.*—The term aṇu, the Sanskrit equivalent of 'atom,' is found in the Upaniṣads, but the atomic theory is foreign to the Vedānta. Of the remaining schools of Indian thought, it is, as we shall see, a characteristic feature of more than one, the Jaina form of it being probably the earliest. The atoms, according to it, are all of the same kind, but they can yet give rise to the infinite variety of things so that matter as conceived here is of quite an indefinite nature. Pudgala has, as we know, certain inalienable features; but within the limits imposed by them it can become anything through qualitative differentiation. The transmutation of the elements is quite possible in this view and is not a mere dream of the alchemist. Even the four-fold distinction of earth, water, fire and air is derived and secondary, not primary and eternal as believed by some Hindu thinkers like the followers of the Vaiśeṣika.[2] These so-called elements also, according to Jainism, are divisible and have a structure. By developing the respective characteristics of odour, flavour, etc., the atoms become differentiated, though in themselves they are indistinguishable from one another, and it is from the atoms diversified in this way that the rest of the material world is derived. Matter may thus have two forms—one, simple or atomic and the other compound, called skandha. All perceivable objects are of the latter kind.[3] Jainism also, like the Upaniṣads, does not stop in its analysis of the physical universe at the elements of pṛthivī, etc. It pushes it farther back where qualitative differentiation has not yet taken place. But while in the latter the ultimate stage is represented by the monistic principle of Brahman, here it is taken by an infinity of atoms. It is not qualitatively only that matter is indefinite. Quantitatively also it is regarded as undetermined. It may

[1] SDS. pp. 35–6.

[2] Compare the somewhat similar distinction in the atomic views held by Democritus and Empedocles in ancient Greece.

[3] SDS. p. 36.

increase or decrease in volume without addition or loss—a position which is taken to be possible by assuming that when matter is in the subtle state any number of its particles may occupy the space of one gross atom. It is matter in this subtle form that constitutes karma, which by its influx into the jīva brings on saṁsāra.

(2) *Syādvāda.*[1]—It is the conception of reality as extremely indeterminate in its nature that is the basis of what is known as syādvāda—the most conspicuous doctrine[2] of Jainism. The word syāt is derived from the Sanskrit root *as* 'to be,' being its form in the potential mood. It means 'may be,' so that syādvāda may be rendered in English as 'the doctrine of *maybe.*' It signifies that the universe can be looked at from many points of view, and that each view-point yields a different conclusion (anekānta). The nature of reality is expressed completely by none of them, for in its concrete richness it admits all predicates. Every proposition is therefore in strictness only conditional. Absolute affirmation and absolute negation are both erroneous. The Jains illustrate this position by means of the story of a number of blind people examining an elephant and arriving at varying conclusions regarding its form while in truth each observer has got at only a part of it. The doctrine indicates extreme caution and signifies an anxiety to avoid all dogma in defining the nature of reality. The philosophic fastidiousness to which we alluded in an earlier chapter (p. 41) reaches its acme here.

To understand the exact significance of this doctrine, it will be necessary to know the conditions under which it was formulated. There was then, on the one hand, the Upaniṣadic view that Being alone was true; and on the other the view, also mentioned in the Upaniṣads, but with disapproval, that non-Being was the ultimate truth.[3] Both these views,

[1] See Guṇaratna: *op. cit.*, pp. 85–9; SDS. pp. 41–2. One of the fourteen Pūrvas is said to deal with this topic. See OJ. pp. 139–40.

[2] Regarding the applicability of the doctrine not only to matter but also to other forms of reality, see Guṇaratna: *op. cit.*, pp. 87–8.

[3] See e.g. *Ch. Up.* VI. ii. 2. In several passages in the Upaniṣads, however, asat stands not for non-Being but for undifferentiated Being. Cf. *Id.* III. xix. 1.

according to Jainism, are only partially true and each becomes a dogma as soon as it is understood to represent the *whole* truth about reality. Equally dogmatic in the eyes of the Jains are two other views which also we come across occasionally in the Upaniṣads and which maintained that, because neither Being nor non-Being is the truth, reality must be characterized by both or neither[1]—thus adding, with characteristic love for subtlety, two more alternatives—both 'is' and 'is not,' and neither 'is' nor 'is not'—to the well-known ones of 'is' and 'is not.' The Jains think that reality is so complex in its structure that while every one of these views is true as far as it goes, none is completely so. Its precise nature baffles all attempts to describe it directly and once for all; but it is not impossible to make it known through a series of partially true statements without committing ourselves to any one among them exclusively. Accordingly the Jains enunciate its nature in seven steps, described as the sapta-bhaṅgī or 'the seven-fold formula.' Its several steps are:—

(1) Maybe, is (Syāt asti).
(2) Maybe, is not (Syāt nāsti).
(3) Maybe, is and is not (Syāt asti nāsti).
(4) Maybe, is inexpressible (Syāt avaktavyaḥ).
(5) Maybe, is and is inexpressible (Syāt asti ca avaktavyaḥ).
(6) Maybe, is not and is inexpressible (Syāt nāsti ca avaktavyaḥ).
(7) Maybe, is, is not and is inexpressible (Syāt asti ca nāsti ca avaktavyaḥ).

If we consider for example an object A, we may say that it *is*, but it *is* only in a sense, viz. *as* A and not also as B. Owing to the indefinite nature of reality, what is now or here A, may become B sometime hence or elsewhere. Thus we must remember when we posit A, that we are not stating absolutely what the nature is of the reality underlying it. So far as its material cause is concerned, a thing has always existed and will always continue to exist; but the particular

[1] *Muṇḍaka Up.*, II. i. 1; *Śvetāśvatara Up.*, iv. 18. See BP. p. 137 and also the passage from *Samyuttaka-Nikāya*, quoted in Oldenberg's *Buddha*, p. 249.

form in which it appears now and here has but a limited existence. While the substance remains the same, its modes vary. As a result of this qualification, we get to the third step, which affirms as well as denies the existence of A. It *is* as well as *is not*. That is, it is in one sense, but is not in another. While the opposition between the predicates 'is' and 'is not' can be reconciled when they are thought of as characterizing an object successively, the nature of the object becomes incomprehensible when they are applied to it simultaneously. We cannot identify A and not-A thus wholesale, for that would be to subvert the law of contradiction. So it must be expressible as neither. This gives us the fourth step, which amounts to saying that reality from one standpoint is inscrutable. Hence Jainism insists that in speaking of an object we must state what it is in reference to material, place, time and state. Otherwise our description of it will be misleading. It may seem that the formula might stop here. But there are still other ways in which the alternatives can be combined. To avoid the impression that those predicates are excluded, three more steps are added. The resulting description becomes exhaustive,[1] leaving no room for the charge of dogma in any form. What is intended by all this is that our judgments have only a partial application to reality. There is some enduring factor in all the changes with which experience makes us familiar, but its modes or the forms it assumes, which may be of any conceivable variety, arise and perish indefinitely. There is no self-identity in things as common sense hastily assumes, and nothing is really isolated. Jainism recognizes both permanence and change as equally real; hence arises its difficulty to express in one step the full nature of reality. It has been observed[2] that the Jains are here thinking of empirical being and not of the transcendental, which for instance is what the Upaniṣads have in view when they speak of reality as only Being. But it is clear from the description of kevala-jñāna, the highest form of knowledge,

[1] These seven are the only ways in which 'is' and 'is not' can be taken singly and in combination. Cf. *Prameya-kamala-mārtaṇḍa*, p. 206.

[2] ERE. vol. vii. p. 468.

as comprehending all things and all their modifications,[1] that the Jains made no such distinction. Reality according to them is in itself infinitely complex; only knowledge of it may be partial and erroneous or complete and correct. We shall defer to the end of the chapter the few observations we have to make on this theory.

II

The special feature of Jainism, as signified by its very name, is to be found in its practical teaching; and the chief feature of the discipline it prescribes is its extreme severity. It is not merely the discipline for the ascetic that is characterized by such rigour; that for the householder also, comparatively speaking, is so. Jainism, like so many other doctrines, insists not on enlightenment alone or on conduct alone, but on both. To these it adds faith, describing right faith (samyagdarśana), right knowledge (samyagjñāna) and right conduct (samyak-cāritra) as the 'three gems' (tri-ratna) or the three precious principles of life.[2] Of the three, the first place is given to right faith, for even right activity, if accompanied by false convictions, loses much of its value. It is unshaken belief in the Jaina scriptures and their teaching, and is intended particularly to dispel scepticism or doubt which thwarts spiritual growth. Right knowledge is knowledge of the principles of Jaina religion and philosophy. Right conduct is translating into action what one has learnt and believes to be true. It is the most important part of the discipline, for it is through right activity that one can get rid of karma and reach the goal of life. We need not describe this discipline in detail. It will suffice to refer to what are known as the 'five vows' (vrata) to indicate its general character. They are in the case of the ascetic—(1) not to injure any living being (ahiṁsā), (2) not to utter falsehood (satya), (3) not to steal (asteya), (4) to lead a celibate life (brahma-carya) and (5) to renounce the world (aparigraha).

[1] Umāsvāti: *op. cit.*, i. 30.

[2] Samyagdarśana-jñāna-cāritrāṇi mokṣa-mārgaḥ-Umāsvāti: *op. cit.*, i. 1.

In the case of the layman they are the same except that the last two are replaced by the vows respectively of chastity and contentment or strict limitation of one's wants. Of the various virtues to be cultivated by the Jains, ahiṁsā occupies the foremost place. The doctrine of ahiṁsā is no doubt very old in India,[1] but the way in which it is made to pervade the whole code of conduct is peculiarly Jain. Even Buddha seems to have permitted meat-eating, but it is wholly abjured here. Literally the word ahiṁsā means 'non-injury' where 'injury' should be understood as comprehending injuring in thought, by word or act. It signifies that one should live without harming others even in the least. This is explained as much more than a negative ideal. It means not only abstention from inflicting positive injury, but also the rendering of active service to others; for we shall be really injuring a person when we can help him but do not.[2] It is clear from this that the social or objective side of ethics is not ignored in Jainism; only in so far as its final aim is the development of one's personality, it emphasizes the individualistic aspect. The following Jaina prayer brings out clearly this social and, along with it, the pre-eminently tolerant side of its teaching. 'Let the King be victorious and righteous. Let there be rain in every proper season. Let diseases die and famine and theft be nowhere. Let the Law of the Jaina give all happiness to all the living beings of the world.'

Like Buddhism, Jainism also admits a two-fold training—that of lay life and that of the monk, and places the latter above the former. Naturally the precepts for the ascetic are more rigid and the vows for the layman are therefore called the 'lesser vows' or aṇu-vrata, to contrast them with the former known as the mahāvrata.[3] Thus to take the last of the five vows, while contentment is all that is required of a layman, absolute renunciation is insisted upon in the case of an ascetic so that he can call nothing his own—not even the alms-bowl. But the two institutions of lay and ascetic life are more closely connected here than in Buddhism, which

[1] See Note 4, p. 92.

[2] See OJ. p. xxiv.

[3] SDS. p. 33; OJ. pp. 69 and 133.

emphasizes the latter at the expense of the former. It permits for instance the combination of the two modes of discipline in one or more directions, thus making it possible for the spiritually weak to rise to the level of the monk by easy steps. To give an example, a person while continuing as a layman may follow the higher ideal in regard to food alone.[1] The difference between the training of a layman and that of an ascetic here is thus not one of kind but only one of degree.

The aim of life is to get oneself disentangled from karma. Like the generality of Indian systems, Jainism also believes in the soul's transmigration, but its conception of karma, the governing principle of transmigration, is unlike that of any other. It is conceived here as being material and permeating the jīvas through and through and weighing them down to the mundane level. 'As heat can unite with iron and water with milk, so karma unites with the soul; and the soul so united with karma is called a soul in bondage.' As in so much of Hindu thought, here also the ideal lies beyond good and evil, so that virtue as well as vice is believed to lead to bondage, though the way in which each binds is different. If through proper self-discipline all karma is worked out and there arises 'the full blaze of omniscience' in the jīva, it becomes free. When at last it escapes at death from the bondage of the body, it rises until it reaches the top of the universe described above as lokākāśa; and there it rests in peaceful bliss for ever.[2] It may not care for worldly affairs thereafter, but it is certainly not without its own influence, for it will serve ever afterwards as an example of achieved ideal to those that are still struggling towards it. During the period intervening between enlightenment and actual attainment of godhead—for all liberated souls are gods—the enlightened jīva dwells apart from fresh karmic influence. An enlightened person may lead an active life, but his activity does not taint him as even unselfish activity, according to Jainism, does in the case of others. During this interval the devotee, as in Buddhism, is termed an arhant[3] (p. 152), and he becomes a siddha or 'the perfected'

[1] OJ. p. xxxi. [2] SDS. p. 40.

[3] Jainism is sometimes described as the arhat-creed (ārhata-darśana).

at actual liberation. It will be seen from this that the stage of arhant-ship corresponds to the Hindu ideal of jīvan-mukti and the Buddhistic one of nirvāṇa as explained above.

To describe the Jaina course of practical discipline for reaching this goal, it is enough to explain the scheme of seven principles as it is called. The aim of this classification is to show how the jīva comes to be associated with karma and how it may escape from it. These principles are āsrava, bandha, saṁvara, nirjara and mokṣa together with the jīva and ajīva already mentioned. Karma is the link between the jīva and its empirical outfit, the body. It is, as we know, regarded as consisting of extremely subtle matter which is beyond the reach of senses.[1] We should not think that there was ever a time when the jīva was free from this karmic accompaniment. Yet dissociation from it is admitted to be possible. Karma by its association with the jīva soils its nature and the consequent lapse of the jīva from its pure state is what is termed bondage. In this process of binding, it should be particularly noted, karma acts by itself and not under the guidance of God as in Hinduism. The forging of the fetter of karma takes place in two stages: Certain psychical conditions like ignorance of the ultimate truth and passion lead to the movement of contiguous karmic matter towards the soul. That is āsrava. Then there is the actual influx or infiltration of karma which is known as bandha. The falling away of the karma-fetter is also thought of in two stages. First through right knowledge and self-restraint, the influx of fresh karma is stopped. It is saṁvara. Then the shedding of karma already there takes place. That is nirjara which will result of itself after saṁvara, but may be hastened by deliberate self-training. The condition which results thereafter is mokṣa, when 'the partnership between soul and matter is dissolved'[2] and the ideal character is restored to the jīva. It then transcends saṁsāra and flies up to its permanent abode at the summit of lokākāśa. The final condition is one of inactivity, but it is characterized by

[1] References to a physical or quasi-physical conception of sin are traceable in Vedic literature. See Prof. Keith: *Religion and Philosophy of the Veda*, p. 245.

[2] IP. vol. i. p. 320.

complete knowledge and everlasting peace. These seven principles together with puṇya and pāpa, the outcome respectively of good and bad deeds, constitute what are sometimes stated as the nine categories of Jainism.

There remains yet to consider, before we pass on to our final observations on the doctrine, a question which is sometimes asked, whether Jainism is atheistic. The answer to this question naturally depends upon the meaning we attach to the word 'atheistic.' If we take it in the sense of nāstika, which is its commonly accepted Sanskrit equivalent, the answer is clear. For the word nāstika means one that does not believe in a life beyond (para-loka),[1] i.e. one that does not believe in a surviving self. In this sense there is only one atheistic doctrine, viz. the sensualist Cārvāka. The word nāstika is sometimes used, as the result of a later modification in its meaning, to describe those that repudiate the authority of the Veda. In that sense, Jainism is nāstika for it is antagonistic to the Hindu scriptures and there it sides with Buddhism. If, on the other hand, we take 'atheistic' as 'not believing in God,' which is its sense in English, a doubt may well arise regarding the character of Jainism. For it believes in no God, though it does in godhead. In fact, every liberated soul is divine; and there can be many such, since only addition is possible to their number but no deduction from it. If by 'God,' then, we understand a supreme personality responsible for the creation of the world, Jainism must be declared to be atheistic. It deliberately rejects such a conception of divinity as self-discrepant. If God needs to create the world, it means that he feels a want which is inconsistent with his necessary perfection as the Supreme. So there is no God, and the world was never created. In this view the Jaina is curiously enough in agreement with the Mīmāṁsaka, the upholder of strict orthodoxy. However opposed to the common trend of human belief, this position is not altogether without rational support. Theistic systems are generally anthropomorphic. They bring down God to the level of man. Jainism, on the other hand, looks upon man himself as God when his inherent powers are

[1] See Pāṇini. IV. iv. 60.

fully in blossom. God is here only another word for the soul at its best. It is the ideal man that is the ideal of man; and there is only one way to achieve it—to strive for it in the manner in which others have striven, with their example shining before us. Such an ideal carries with it all necessary hope and encouragement, for what man has done, man can do. In rejecting God who is so by his own right and with it also the belief that salvation may be attained through his mercy, Jainism and other systems of the kind recognize that karma by itself and without the intervention of any divine power is adequate to explain the whole of experience and thus impress on the individual his complete responsibility for what he does. 'Jainism more than any other creed gives absolute religious independence and freedom to man. Nothing can intervene between the actions which we do and the fruits thereof. Once done, they become our masters and must fructify. As my independence is great, so my responsibility is coextensive with it. I can live as I like; but my choice is irrevocable and I cannot escape the consequences of it.'[1]

The Jains recognize matter as well as spirit; and each, according to them, implies the other, for they maintain that nothing is wholly independent and can be fully understood by itself. An old Jaina stanza states that he who knows one thing completely knows all things, and that he alone who knows all things knows anything completely.[2] It means that if we have to understand one thing, we have to relate it to all. Hence the Jaina view may be described as relativistic. It is pluralistic also, for it recognizes an infinite number of jīvas as well as of material elements. These two features of relativism and pluralism point to a first analysis of common experience; and Jainism stops short at it, disregarding its implication. Thus relativism, if pushed to its logical conclusion, leads to absolutism, which the Jains refuse to accept. Let us

[1] OJ. pp. 3–4.

[2] Eko bhāvaḥ sarvathā yena dṛṣṭaḥ sarve bhāvāḥ sarvathā tena dṛṣṭāḥ: Sarve bhāvāḥ sarvathā yena dṛṣṭāḥ eko bhāvaḥ sarvathā tena dṛṣṭāḥ—quoted by Guṇaratna: *op. cit.*, p. 89. Cf. also Prof. Jacobi: *op. cit.*, Pt. I. p. 34.

see how it does so in the case of spirit and matter, overlooking the categories of space and time. So far as matter is concerned Jainism adopts a criterion which enables it to reduce the entire variety of the physical universe to one kind of substance, viz. pudgala. It does the same in the case of spirit also, concluding that all jīvas are of one kind. But when it comes to a question of matter *and* spirit, Jainism abandons that criterion and adopts mere contrast as the guiding principle. If the dualism of spirit and matter were a clear-cut one as it is in the Sāṅkhya, we might somehow understand it; but it is not so here. The distinction between the two ultimate entities of prakṛti and puruṣa which the Sāṅkhya admits is absolute, and neither in reality comes into relation with the other. Here, on the other hand, spirit and matter are admitted to be in actual relation with each other. The very disjunction between jīva and ajīva, as they are termed, shows their interdependence. Yet no attempt is made to look for a common principle behind them, and the two are set side by side, as if they were entirely independent. If now we consider the other aspect of the teaching, viz. pluralism, we are forced to take a similar view. Matter is divided into an infinite number of atoms; but, all being of the same kind, it is impossible to distinguish them from one another. Similarly in the case of the jīvas their empirical distinctions are adequately explained by their physical adjuncts. Even the difference in their moral nature is fully accounted for by them, Jainism electing to explain karma as a form of matter. In these circumstances the intrinsic distinction which is assumed to exist between one jīva and another, or the plurality of spirit, becomes only nominal. The necessary implication of Jaina thought in this respect is, therefore, a single spiritual substance encountering a single material substance. And since these two substances are interdependent. the dualism must in its turn and finally be resolved in a monism and point to an Absolute which, owing to its essentially dynamic character, develops within itself the distinctions of jīva and ajīva as known to us. That is the inevitable consequence of the Jaina view. The half-hearted character of the Jaina inquiry is reflected in the seven-fold mode of predication (sapta-bhaṅgī), which stops at giving us the several partial views together, without attempting to overcome the opposition in them by a proper synthesis. It is all right so far as it cautions us against one-sided conclusions; but it leaves us in the end, as it has been observed,[1] with little more than such one-sided solutions. The reason for it, if it is not prejudice against Absolutism, is the desire to keep close to common beliefs. The doctrine hesitates to deny anything that is familiar. But at the same time its partiality for common views does not mean acquiescence in all popular beliefs, as is clear from its repudiation of the idea of God in the accepted sense. The truth is that the primary aim of Jainism is the perfection of the soul, rather than the interpretation of the universe—a fact which may be supported by the old statement that āsrava and saṁvara constitute the whole of Jaina teaching, the rest being only an amplification of them.[2] As a result we fail to find in it an ultimate solution of the metaphysical problem.

[1] *Proceedings of the First Indian Philosophical Congress* (1925), p. 133.

[2] Āsravo bhava-hetuḥ syāt saṁvaro mokṣa-kāraṇam:
Itīyam ārhatī dṛṣṭiranyadasyāḥ prapañcanam (SDS. p. 39).

PART III

AGE OF THE SYSTEMS

CHAPTER VII

PRELIMINARY

INDIAN thought whose growth we have so far traced may be described as largely consisting of results. These results should of course have been arrived at by processes more or less definite; but we know very little about them now. The philosophy of the present period is different in this respect, and gives us not only conclusions but also the methods of reaching them. In fact, the several systems which develop now do not set about investigating their proper subject-matter until they have given us what may be described as a critique of knowledge and considered how we come by truth. In other words, Indian philosophy becomes self-conscious at this stage; and Logic emerges as an explicit branch of it. It is not easy to discover the exact causes of this change; but it is clear that the growth and consolidation of heterodox doctrines like those of Buddhism and Jainism must have contributed much towards it, especially as some of the latter claimed to base their conclusions exclusively on reason. The increasing opposition in thought forced each party in the controversy to entrench its position properly, and to the efforts put forth in that direction should be ascribed the generally critical character of Indian philosophy in the present period.

This change of standpoint accounts for the systematic attention that now comes to be paid by all the schools without exception to what are known as pramāṇas. The word *pramāṇa* signifies the essential means[1] of arriving at valid knowledge or pramā. The object known is described as prameya; and the knower, pramātā. There is a great variety of views in regard to the nature and scope of pramāṇas; but it will do to refer now to only one or two general points about them. Broadly speaking, the pramāṇas are three—pratyakṣa or perception, anumāna or inference and śabda or verbal testimony. The value of the first two of these as pramāṇas is

[1] Pramā-karaṇam pramāṇam.

recognized by all; but the same cannot be said of the third. Its inclusion under pramāṇas along with perception and inference is indeed peculiar to the Indian view and requires a word of explanation. We should first distinguish here between two aspects of śabda. When we hear a sentence uttered, there is a certain impression produced on our mind through the auditory channel. That is perception and what we apprehend then are sounds occurring in a certain order. Śabda as a pramāṇa does not, of course, mean this, which is rather a prameya. There is another, the expressive or semantic aspect of it, and śabda as we are now thinking of it is of this latter kind. Its utility in life as a means of acquiring knowledge cannot be exaggerated. Of the numerous facts which a person knows, it is only a small portion that he has observed or deduced for himself. For the rest, he has to depend entirely upon the testimony of others which comes to him through spoken or written words. But it may be questioned whether so much is sufficient to constitute it into an independent pramāṇa; and we shall see as we proceed that some Indian thinkers denied to verbal testimony the logical status implied by classing it as a separate pramāṇa. That is, however, to understand śabda in a sense wider than the one which belonged to it at first. In the beginning it stood only for tradition[1] and its scope was extended in course of time so as to comprehend all verbal statements irrespective of their connection with ancient belief. We shall postpone the consideration of the pramāṇa in this extended sense to later chapters and shall confine our remarks now to it regarded as merely a vehicle of tradition.

The reason for including śabda in this sense under pramāṇas will become clear when we remember the vastness of the material of tradition that had accumulated by the time the pramāṇas came to be formally enunciated.[2] The

[1] In the Prābhākara school of Mīmāṁsā, śabda as a pramāṇa continues to this day to represent only the Veda.

[2] The words pramāṇa and prameya are found in the *Maitrī Up.* (vi. 14); and prāmāṇika or 'one who bases his conclusions on pramāṇas' is used for 'philosopher' in the Greek accounts of ancient India (see *Cambridge History of India*, vol. i. p. 421).

main idea underlying the inclusion was that the contributions of history to philosophy should not be ignored. It also indicates the reverence with which the authority of tradition was regarded then (p. 91). But it would be wrong to conclude that the exponents of the systems surrendered their judgments by indiscriminately admitting as valid whatever belief had come down from the past, even though it were taught in the Veda. Such a course was indeed impossible as matters stood at the time. There was, on the one hand, the whole of the complex teaching of the Veda handed down from the past; and there was, on the other, a mass of heterodox thought which as the result of free-thinking in different circles exhibited a good deal of diversity. Philosophy as embodied in tradition was thus largely of a conflicting nature; and the need for testing the mutual compatibility of the elements constituting each creed was felt to be imperative. Both the orthodox and the heterodox accordingly set about examining their traditional beliefs, and tried to interpret them consistently. The interpretation involves a great deal of independent reasoning; and it is the result of this reasoned inquiry that we have to understand by śabda as originally conceived in Indian philosophy. The pramāṇa, therefore, signifies not tradition in general, but systematized tradition. It is such systematic interpretation of the teaching of the Veda that is, for example, the essential aim of the Mīmāṁsā system. Though both sets of thinkers admit tradition as a source of philosophic knowledge, there is an important difference between the ways in which it is conceived by them. For the heterodox, this tradition at no stage goes beyond human (pauruṣeya) experience, including in that expression what can be known not only through perception and reasoning but also through a higher faculty—no matter what name we give it, insight or intuition.[1] In this sense the value of tradition lies in its communicating to

[1] Not all the hererodox schools believe in such a higher faculty. So Indian schools may be classified under three heads: (i.) those that recognize only perception and inference, (ii.) those that recognize intuition in addition, and (iii.) those that substitute revelation for intuition.

us not what is humanly unascertainable, but only what is not knowable through mere reason and perception. In other words, tradition stands for truths that are beyond the reach of common men, but have been directly perceived by those that were possessed of spiritual vision. For the orthodox, on the other hand, it means revelation which, if not exactly divine or coming from God, is, as we shall see, supernatural (apauruṣeya) in some sense or other.[1] The significance of the distinction is that while for the one school the realm of human experience understood in its widest sense exhausts Reality, for the other it does not. Human experience may be sufficient to understand nature; but nature, the latter contend, transcends itself and points to something beyond, and they postulate śruti or revelation as the sole means of acquiring what knowledge is possible of that transcendental sphere of being. According to the former, no such region at all exists; and to place anything beyond the reach of human powers is the same as denying reality to it. The question what śabda or tradition represents in the two schools thus resolves itself eventually into one of general philosophic outlook and connotes a fundamental difference between them in the conception of Reality.

The acceptance of śruti as an authority in this sense, it will be seen, has its danger; for it may lead to belief in anything under the plea that it has been revealed. The ancient Indian realized the danger and has hedged in his view of it by various conditions. They show what exactly revelation as conceived in orthodox circles is, and how it stands related to experience in general and to reason in particular: (i.) The first of these conditions is that the revealed truth should be new or extra-empirical (alaukika), i.e. otherwise unattained and unattainable.[2] The authority

[1] We might understand by tradition āgama in the one case and śruti or, as it is sometimes styled, nigama in the other case. This distinction in the use of the several terms is not, however, strictly followed.

[2] Cf. the expression arthe anupalabdhe—'in respect of an object (otherwise) unknown'—used in *Jaimini-sūtra*, I. i. 5.

of revelation for instance is not to be invoked to show that heat destroys cold, which is a matter of common experience.[1] Now it is clear that revelation should speak to us in terms of our experience, for otherwise it will be unintelligible and will therefore fail of its purpose.[2] Even the scripture cannot teach the unknown through the unknown, so that the theme of revelation cannot be wholly out of relation to human experience. When we take the condition of novelty along with this fact that the terms in which transcendental truth is communicated must necessarily be known to us, we see that what is revealed, so far at least as philosophic truth is concerned, cannot be altogether new, but can only be a new *way* of construing our experience. (ii.) The next condition is that what is revealed should not be contradicted (abādhita) by any of the other pramāṇas.[3] Nor should one part of it be in conflict with another. This means that the content of revelation must be internally coherent and that, though it may be above reason, it cannot be against it. The very fact that conditions are laid down for determining the validity of revelation makes it evident that it cannot be opposed to reason. (iii.) It is not only thus negatively that revelation is related to reason. The relation is also positive in that we find a third condition laid down, viz. that reason should foreshadow what revelation teaches. That is, revealed truth must appear probable. If this condition again is not to clash with the first one of novelty, we must take it as meaning only a rough forecast of the truth under consideration by means of analogies drawn from the empirical sphere.[4] They are not proofs of revealed truth; yet they are not useless, since they serve to remove any 'antecedent improbability' that may be felt to exist about the truth in

[1] The statement—agniḥ himasya bheṣajam—actually occurs in the Veda, but it is explained as an anuvāda or 'echoing' what is known already.

[2] See Śabara on *Jaimini-sūtra*, I. iii. 30.

[3] Cf. the word avyatireka ('not negatived') occurring in *Jaimini-sūtra*, I. i. 5.

[4] Cf. Ānandajñāna's gloss on Śaṁkara's com. on *Bṛ. Up.* p. 8; Saṁbhāvanā-mātreṇa liṅgopanyāsaḥ. Na hi niścāyakatvena tadupanyasyate.

question.[1] The appeal to reason which we come across often in the śruti—particularly in the Upaniṣads—is explained by the orthodox as really of this kind. In their view, reason by itself is incapable of discerning such truths.[2] At best, it may lead to two or more conclusions equally plausible[3]; and, without the aid of revelation, it is impossible to avoid scepticism. The survival of the self after death is a good instance of a truth taught in the Veda which satisfies these conditions. It is not accessible to reason, but at the same time there is nothing in it to contradict reason. Despite these careful reservations, it should be admitted, śruti so defined remains an external authority; and that is the view taken of it in the orthodox schools.[4]

The general name for the results arrived at by means of the several pramāṇas is darśana, which literally means 'sight,' and may be taken to indicate that what the Indians aspired after in philosophy was not a mediate knowledge of the ultimate truth but a direct vision of it. The word in that case would express what is a distinguishing feature of Indian philosophy in general—its insistence that one should not

[1] In this sense they are known as yukti or anukūla-tarka, not anumāna or inference proper.

[2] See VS. II. i. 11. As regards the claim of the rationalists that such truths can be reached through reason, it is pointed out that theirs is a case of reasoning when once the revealed truth is there. They do not know because they reason; rather they reason because they know. See Śaṁkara on VS. I. i. 2. and on *Bṛ. Up.* p. 7.

[3] Cf. Bhartṛhari: *Vākya-padīya* (i. 34).

Yatnenānumitopyarthaḥ kuśalairanumātṛbhiḥ:
Abhiyuktatarairanyairanyathaivopapādyate.

[4] It is obvious, however, that scriptural truth also should at first have been known by some human means—through direct intuition, if not reasoning. If the śruti also thus represents the intuitive experience of ancient sages and is pauruṣeya, it may seem hardly different from the heterodox āgama. But we may deduce a distinction between the two from a fourth condition sometimes laid down (cf. *Kusumāñjali*, ii. 3 and SV. p. 90), that the revealed truth should have proved acceptable to the general mind of the community (mahājana-parigraha), or that it should be in harmony with what may be described as race-intuition. It is this sanction of the community in general that in the end seems to distinguish orthodox śruti from heterodox āgama.

rest content with a mere intellectual conviction but should aim at transforming such conviction into direct experience. It seems, however, more probable that darśana here, like its equivalent dṛṣṭi which is sometimes substituted[1] for it, means 'philosophic opinion'[2] and signifies a specific school of thought as distinguished from others. There are many such schools of philosophic opinion. They are commonly reckoned as six, viz. the Nyāya of Gautama, the Vaiśeṣika of Kanāda, the Sāṅkhya of Kapila, the Yoga of Patañjali, the Pūrva-mīmāṁsā of Jaimini and the Uttara-mīmāṁsā or Vedānta of Bādarāyaṇa. These six systems may be regarded as falling into three pairs—Nyāya-Vaiśeṣika, Sāṅkhya-Yoga and the two Mīmāṁsās—as the members forming each pair agree either in their general metaphysical outlook or in their historical basis or in both. We shall deal here not only with these three groups but also with two more—Indian Materialism, and later Buddhism with its four-fold division of Vaibhāṣika, Sautrāntika, Yogācāra and Mādhyamika. The latter, along with Jainism, are sometimes described as the six heterodox (nāstika) systems to contrast them with the same number of orthodox (āstika) ones just mentioned.[3] The germs of practically all of them are to be found in the literature of the previous periods, but their full development and systematization belong to the present one. The darśanas, when once systematized, determined the main channels in which philosophic thought ran for ever afterwards in India. Though ascribed to individual teachers, they in their present form are really the outcome of the thought of a long succession of thinkers, for the systems have grown with the growth of time. While we may know the names of some of the thinkers, we can hardly say what the nature of their contribution was and to what extent the original doctrine has been remodelled by each of them. For they always thought more of the system of which they were adherents than of claiming credit for their share in developing

1 Cf. NSB. IV. i. 14.

2 See BUV. p. 890. st. 22 (com.) and cf. SBE. vol. XXII. p. xlv.

3 Not all of these, as observed above (p. 107), are orthodox in the strict sense of the term.

it. The several systems are accordingly the result of what may be described as co-operative thinking; and the work of the individual is merged in that of the group. Even profound teachers like Śaṁkara and Rāmānuja were content to work for a system, sinking their individuality entirely, and have thus given proof of the complete disinterestedness with which they sought the truth. As more than one old writer has said, the pursuit of truth served as its own spur —neither glory, nor gain.[1]

These darśanas are described as 'systems' because the thoughts in each are well co-ordinated and constitute a logical whole. They are systems also in another sense; for they are regarded as *closed* (siddhānta) in essentials, though not in matters of detail. Many of them are more than philosophy as we now understand the term, since they include on the one hand religion and, on the other, what would in these days be regarded as science. The value of the science contained in the systems cannot be great now when experimental methods of investigation have advanced so much; and we shall not, therefore, refer to it except when it has a clear philosophic bearing. The case of religion is, however, different; for in India, as already noticed, the line that separates it from philosophy is very faint. But we shall exclude from our purview the purely dogmatic side of the teaching. In particular, we shall leave out as far as possible those aspects which contain an eschatological reference, and shall estimate the value of a system not by the state of existence it promises to an enlightened person hereafter, but by the actual life which it expects him to lead after enlightenment and before physical death, i.e. in that condition which is described in some systems as jīvan-mukti or arhant-ship.

The primary sources of information in regard to the various systems are generally found in what are known as the Sūtras—a unique form of literature which was developed in India some centuries before the Christian era, when writing had not yet come to be used for literary purposes and the whole of the knowledge acquired had to be con-

[1] Cf. NB. IV. ii. 51; Sureśvara: *Naiṣkarmya-siddhi*, i. 6.

served through mere memorizing. The sūtras or aphorisms of which they consist are extremely laconic in form, and are hardly intelligible without explanation. They were originally handed down by word of mouth from teacher to pupil together with their authoritative explanations and were reduced to writing much later. The explanations, which in the course of time had become more or less divergent, were also reduced to shape then and committed to writing under the name generally of bhāṣyas or commentaries written in the common or vernacular tongue (i.e. Sanskrit, not Vedic). This species of aphoristic literature continued to be produced long after the need for it had ceased; and some, if not all, of the philosophical Sūtras, as distinguished from the earlier ones like the Kalpa-sūtras (p. 88), are to be ascribed to this later stage. They are generally assigned to the period between 200 and 500 A.D.[1] But it is essential to remember that it does not imply that the schools of thought, whose doctrines they expound, are themselves so late. They are undoubtedly considerably older and their high antiquity is indicated by the term ṛṣi or 'ancient seer' applied to their first exponents like Gautama and Kapila. The dates given above should, therefore, be taken as only indicating the period of their reduction to a definite form. Thus, though representing in one sense the starting-point of the darśanas, the Sūtras in reality presuppose a long course of development the details of which are lost to us, perhaps for ever. While they do not, therefore, correctly represent the real antiquity of the systems, they at the same time have received emendations at the hands of teachers and commentators since their first formulation. But there is no means now of determining exactly what parts are really original and what later modifications. The new is so inextricably blended with the old. The aim of the Sūtras may be described as two-fold—to establish the particular doctrine which they inculcate and to refute all others which are at variance with it. They are thus critical as well as constructive. The literature of a school consists, in addition to the Sūtra, of one or more commentaries upon it with works explaining

[1] *Dates of Philosophical Sūtras*, by Prof. Jacobi.—JAOS. xxxi. (1911).

those commentaries themselves and treatises (prakaraṇa)—written in prose or verse or both—dealing with select phases of the doctrine. This literature in each case ranges over a very long period, beginning soon after the time to which the Sūtras are assigned and ending only a century or two ago.

CHAPTER VIII

MATERIALISM

THE first school of thought we propose taking into consideration is Materialism or the Cārvāka-darśana, as it is termed in Sanskrit. The significance of the term 'Cārvaka' applied to it is not quite clear. Some say that it was originally the name of the disciple to whom the doctrine was first communicated by its founder.[1] More probably the word is to be understood as the equivalent of 'sweet-tongued' (cāru-vāka),[2] which aptly describes the advocates of a doctrine characterized by so much of superficial attractiveness. We have already referred to the Yadṛcchā-vāda as its possible source (p. 104) and pointed out its distinguishing feature, viz. the abolition of the idea of causality altogether. Neither the world, nor any event that takes place in it, has anything beyond accident to account for it. As indicated by the other name of Lokāyata-darśana sometimes given to it, there seems to have merged in it the Svabhāva-doctrine, which also had only an empirical basis. The Cārvāka school has been the butt of ridicule for long.[3] The very designations of its followers—cārvāka and lokāyata—have acquired a disparaging sense, much as the term 'sophist' did in ancient Greece, and have become bye-names for the infidel and the epicure.[4] It is in this degenerate form that we find the doctrine summarized even by so early an author as Śaṁkara.[5] One does not expect to find any treatise expounding such a doctrine. Yet a Sūtra on it, ascribed to Bṛhaspati, whom the *Maitrī Upaniṣad* describes as a heretical teacher,[6] is mentioned in old works; and since a few extracts from it are

[1] SS. p. 99. [2] Whitney: *Sanskrit Grammar*, p. 80.

[3] See e.g. *Naiṣadhīya-carita* (xvii. 39–83), whose author Śrīharṣa was also a great philosophic thinker.

[4] Cf. SV. p. 4 st. 10. Compare also the description of the Cārvāka as nāstika-śiromaṇi or 'arch-heretic' in SDS. p. 2.

[5] See his account of it in the bhāṣyas on VS. III. iii. 53–4. and on *Bṛ. Up.* pp. 552 ff. [6] vii. 9.

quoted[1] and a bhāṣya or formal commentary upon it also seems to be alluded to,[2] we need not doubt that it existed. But the book is not extant, and it is therefore difficult to say to what extent the teaching deserved the name of darśana or merited the wholesale condemnation to which it has been subjected. The only account of the doctrine we now have is in the *résumé* given in the works of the other schools of thought for purposes of refutation. It is unfortunate that in forming an estimate of its value we have to depend entirely upon the statements of its several opponents. For one thing, they are too meagre to enable us to speak of many details relating to the system. The *Sarva-darśana-saṁgraha,* no doubt, contains a chapter on it, but it is very brief and adds nothing to what may be gathered from other sources. Again these statements in all probability exaggerate the weak points of the doctrine and may even misrepresent its tenets. Thus it is commonly assumed by the critics that the Cārvākas denounced reasoning totally as a pramāṇa; but to judge from the reference to it in one Nyāya treatise,[3] they seem to have rejected only such reasoning as was ordinarily thought sufficient by others for establishing the existence of God, of a future life, etc. Such a discrimination in using reason alters the whole complexion of the Cārvāka view. But this is only a stray hint we get about the truth. What we generally have is a caricature. The special ridicule to which the Cārvāka is held up by the orthodox may be due to the denouncement by him of Vedic authority and of the priestly profession[4]; but this by itself cannot explain it fully, for the Buddhists and the Jains also were hostile to the Veda. We have, therefore, to seek for its cause at least in part in the deficiencies of the doctrine itself, especially on the ethical side, which tended to undermine the foundations of social order and of moral responsibility. The chief importance of the system for us lies in the evidence it affords

[1] See Bhāskara on VS. III. iii. 53; NM. p. 64.

[2] See SAS. p. 85.

[3] NM. p. 124.

[4] Cf. stanzas quoted at the end of SDS. ch. i. The Veda is here characterized as unintelligible, self-contradictory, untrue and so forth.

of the many-sidedness of philosophic activity in India in ancient times and of the prevalence of a great deal of liberty of thought as well as of freedom of expression.

I

The most important of its doctrines is that perception (pratyakṣa) is the only means of valid knowledge. Every other pramāṇa including inference (anumāna) is rejected so that philosophy, which according to the common Indian view ought to be a discipline of life, ceases here to be even a discipline of the mind. The reason assigned for rejecting inference is that there is not sufficient warrant for believing in the truth of the inductive relation or vyāpti which forms its basis. The ascertainment of this relation, even supposing that it actually exists,[1] depends upon observed facts; and since observation is necessarily restricted in its scope, it does not entitle us, it is urged, to universalize the conclusion reached with its help. It may be granted for the sake of argument that observation can comprehend *all* present instances coming under a general rule; but even then it should be admitted that there are others which are removed in time and which, therefore, lie beyond the possibility of investigation. While a general proposition may be all right so far as investigated cases are concerned, there is no guarantee that it holds good of uninvestigated cases also. Even the suspicion that it may not is enough to render the general proposition useless for purposes of exact investigation. If to avoid this difficulty we assume that it is not the examination of isolated particulars that is really the basis of induction but only the proper linking up of essential features or universals[2] which are permanently associated with them, the Cārvāka objects that such a course would leave unrelated the particulars which alone are of practical concern. Nor can the universals themselves be taken as its subject, for in that case there would be no inference at all, the so-called

[1] NM. pp. 119–20.

[2] This does not mean that the Cārvāka admitted universals as objectively real. They are assumed here only for the sake of argument.

inferred truth connecting one universal with another being identical with the observed fact itself as stated in the major premise. It is in the quagmire of such a dilemma, as a well-known stanza[1] has it, that a logician finds himself floundering when he tries to maintain the validity of inference. Our familiar belief in the validity of inference, the Cārvaka explains as due to associations established during observation so that it is purely a psychological process with no implication whatsoever of logical certitude. Otherwise how can we account for the notorious differences even in essential matters among rationalistic philosophers themselves?[2] Where the belief is verified in practical life, it is due to accidental coincidence as in the case of omens, etc., which also sometimes come true. In other words, inference is nothing more than guess-work. If the Cārvāka specifically formulates his view in such a manner, it would certainly be a stultifying position for him to assume, because this negative conclusion that inference is not valid is itself the result of induction and points to a conviction that in one case at least the relation of vyāpti holds true. It would then refute itself, for what is rejected would be admitted in the very act of rejecting it. Moreover, his very attempt to convince others of the correctness of his view would imply a knowledge of their thoughts which, not being directly knowable, could only have been inferred by him. But the probability is that the Cārvāka did neither state his view so formally, nor try to convince others of its rightness, but was content with merely refuting the position of the opponents.[3] Usually, however, it is assumed that he did so formulate his view; and it is criticized as above by the representatives of the other systems. They vindicate inference directly also, stating why and in what circumstances a universal proposition may be taken to be valid, though it may be based on a limited examination of the

[1] Cited for example in SD. p. 63.

Viśeṣenugamābhāvat sāmānye siddha-sādhanāt:
Anumā-bhaṅga-paṅkesmin nimagnā vādi-dantinaḥ.

[2] Cf. Note 3 on p. 182.

[3] Cf. NM. p. 270: Vaitaṇḍika-kathaivāsau na punaḥ kascidāgamaḥ.

cases falling under it. But the answers vary according to the systems and it would, therefore, be preferable to deal with them under those systems themselves. We shall accordingly postpone their consideration for the present.

As a consequence of the view taken by him of knowledge, the Cārvāka cannot speak of any order or system in the world. He no doubt admits perception as a means of valid knowledge, but that gives rise only to a piecemeal knowledge of things without connecting them by means of any *necessary* relation. Yet he is stated to have postulated four elements (bhūtas)—each with its own character. So far he is a realist and a pluralist. The elements are to be understood as gross in form; for the Cārvāka, discarding inference as he does, cannot believe in any subtle state which can be deduced only by reason. Commonly Hindu thought recognizes five elements—earth, water, fire, air and ākāśa. While the first four of these are matters of ordinary sense-experience, the last is the result of inference. The Cārvāka, because he admits only the immediate evidence of the senses, denies the last. For the same reason he denies also the soul or ātman as a surviving entity. It comes into being, according to him, with that peculiar concatenation of the elements which we call the living body. The Cārvāka accordingly does not deny a conscious or spiritual principle; only he refuses to regard it as ultimate or independent. It is a property of the physical aggregate of the body and disappears when the latter disintegrates. It is compared to the intoxicating quality that arises by the mingling of certain ingredients such as yeast which separately do not possess it.[1] The entire dependence of consciousness on the physical organism, it is added, is also indicated by the fact that it is *always* seen associated with it and is never found apart from it. The theory may thus be taken as a rough Indian counterpart of the view that mind is a function of matter. His view, as it is sometimes set forth, borders upon

[1] The illustration probably suggests the idea of an 'emergent characteristic,' because the Cārvāka does not admit consciousness as characterizing the factors constituting the body, taken severally. See *Bhāmatī*, III. iii. 53.

modern behaviourism. According to Śālikanātha's summary, for instance, the Cārvāka regards feeling as directly characterizing the physical body and describes it in terms of bodily expression.[1] 'Pleasure, pain, etc., should be regarded as only attributes of the body, for they bring about change in its condition. What is a characteristic of one entity cannot affect another, for then the cause would be operating where it was not. And it is a matter of common experience that the body is affected when pleasure, etc., arise as shown by expanding eyes, a graciousness of look, horripilation and so forth.'

Naturally the denial of the ātman, which occupies an important place in the other Indian systems, provoked the keenest controversy; but theoretically the position of the Cārvāka, it must be admitted, is irrefutable. It cannot be *demonstrated* that the soul or ātman in the accepted sense *is*. That indeed is recognized by some orthodox thinkers themselves, who accordingly lay stress in their refutation of the Cārvāka doctrine upon the indemonstrability of the opposite position that the body and the soul are *not* distinct.[2] We may also note here some of the more important among the 'arguments' advanced directly against the Cārvāka position: First, if consciousness be a property of the body, it should be either essential to it or accidental. If the former, it should be inseparable from the body and last as long as it does; but it does not, for in a swoon or in dreamless sleep the body is seen without it. If the latter, it implies another agency (upādhi)[3] at work in producing consciousness and cannot, therefore, be wholly ascribed to the body. Moreover, a person waking from a dream owns the dream experience while disowning the dream body, say that of a tiger, as Vācaspati[4] puts it. If the one were a property of the other, both would be avowed or disavowed together. Again it may be true as the Cārvāka holds, that consciousness is always found in association with the physical organism; but it is far from certain that it ceases to be, when the organism

[1] PP. p. 147.
[2] See e.g. SD. p. 122.
[3] See SP. III. 20. and Mr. J. C. Chatterji's *Hindu Realism*, p. 70.
[4] *Bhāmatī*, II. i. 14.

breaks up. For aught we know, it may continue to exist in another manner; and though that such is the case is not proved, even a doubt of the kind is sufficient to reject the position of the Cārvāka that it is a property of the body. Nor can such association of the two in itself, even if constant, prove that one is a property of the other. The eye cannot see, for example, except with the aid of some kind of light; yet it cannot be said that visual perception is a property of light. Similarly in the present case also, the body may only serve as an auxiliary (upakaraṇa) or condition for consciousness to manifest itself. Lastly, if consciousness were really a property of the body, it would, if knowable by one, be knowable in exactly the same way by others as well. The form or complexion of our body, for instance, is perceived not only by ourselves, but also by others. A person's thoughts, feelings, dreams and memories, on the other hand, while they are immediate facts to him, are not known to any other in the same way. The knowledge which a philosopher has of his toothache is different from that of the dentist who treats it. This important difference suggests that consciousness is not a property of the physical body, but of something else or is itself an independent principle which only finds its medium of expression in the body.[1]

II

The doctrine dismisses necessarily all belief in a supernatural or transcendental being, and with it also belief in everything that constitutes the specific subject-matter of religion and philosophy. It recognizes neither a God who controls the universe nor conscience which guides man; and it does not care for belief in a life after death which, so far as right conduct is concerned, matters more according to the Indian than even belief in the existence of God. It thus draws away

[1] Cf. Śaṁkara on VS. III. iii. 54. The view set forth above represents but one type of Indian Materialism. There were other types also which, though admitting the self to be other than the body, endeavoured to identify it with the senses, vital power (prāṇa) or some other non-spiritual principle. Cf. NM. pp. 440–1.

man's mind altogether from the thought of a higher life and fixes it upon the world of sense. It smothers all consciousness of a deeper reality. Accordingly the ideal, if such an expression is admissible at all in this case, is one of hedonism, pure and simple. Pleasure in this life—and that of the individual—is the sole aim of man. Collective happiness, if it is ever thought of, is regarded as expressible in terms of individual happiness; and there is no conception of a general good to which the interests of the individual are to be subordinated. Of the four puruṣārthas or 'human values' (p. 109) the Cārvāka rejects two, viz. dharma and mokṣa, thus restricting the scope of human effort to the attainment of sensual pleasure (kāma) or securing the means therefor (artha). Whatever virtues are cultivated are either based upon convention or are the result of worldly prudence. The useful is the only good which the doctrine knows of. Pain is recognized as an inevitable feature of existence; but that affords no reason, it is argued, for denying ourselves pleasure which appeals to us as desirable and towards which we are instinctively drawn. 'Nobody casts away the grain because of the husk.'[1] The Cārvāka is so impatient of obtaining pleasure that he does not even try to secure freedom from pain. He makes a compromise with evil, instead of overcoming it. Every man, according to him, must make the best of a bad bargain and 'enjoy himself as long as he lives.'[2] The repudiation of the traditional teaching and all the moral and spiritual discipline for which it stands is a necessary corollary to this crude utilitarianism, whose motto is 'Sufficient unto the day is the good thereof.' One may think of a school of thought without the ideal of mokṣa, but not without that of dharma also. It may be that death is final and nothing remains afterwards; but to believe in an ideal of life devoid of dharma is to reduce man to the level of the brute. It is difficult to believe that there could ever have existed such a school of thought. Even if we explain its extreme views as due to a reaction against the free specula-

[1] SDS. p. 3.

[2] Yāvajjīvet sukham jīvet, which seems to be a parody of the Vedic injunction—Yāvajjīvam agnihotram juhoti.

tions and the austere asceticism that were widely current in ancient India, the system, we must admit, should once have inculcated less objectionable principles. The form in which it is now presented has an air of unreality about it. If any proof were required, it is found in its lesson of self-indulgence, which needs not to be taught. It is also somewhat suspicious that the Cārvāka doctrine should consist so much in denying what is accepted by the other schools and so little in contributing any new ideas of its own to the sum of Indian thought.[1]

[1] See SS. p. 100.

CHAPTER IX

LATER BUDDHISTIC SCHOOLS

WE know that there was some vagueness in Buddhism as it was originally taught. It was this vagueness, combined with the wide and rapid spread of its teaching not only in the country of its birth but also outside, that in course of time gave rise to a great divergence of views among its followers. There are several schools mentioned by Buddhist tradition, the number of those that arose in India itself being as many as eighteen[1]; but we shall take into consideration here only the most important among them—especially those that are commonly mentioned in Hindu and Jaina philosophical works and may therefore be regarded as of particular significance in Indian thought, whose development we are tracing here. The various views falling under later Buddhism are broadly classifiable under two heads, which go by the name of Hīnayāna and Mahāyāna. These terms are variously explained, the most common explanation being that they signify respectively the 'small way' and the 'great way' of salvation. It is clear from the inferiority indicated by the word hīna ('low') that the names were devised by the followers of Mahāyāna. Of these, the Hīnayāna had an earlier origin; but the distinction between the two is not merely one of chronology. In their philosophic and ethical outlook also they differ widely. For instance the adherents of Hīnayāna believe in the reality of outward objects—however they may conceive of reality itself—and are for that reason often described in Hindu works as sarvāstitva-vādins,[2] while the adherents of Mahāyāna adopt the opposite view. Another important difference is that while the Hīnayāna is content to stop at pointing out the means for the individual releasing himself from the bondage of saṁsāra, the Mahāyāna teaches that the

[1] BP. pp. 149–50.

[2] Cf. Śaṁkara on VS. II. ii. 18. In Buddhistic tradition the term is sarvāsti-vādin.

awakened individual should work, without resting, for the spiritual welfare of the world. Such radical differences between the two forms of the doctrine in essential matters have led some to suggest that the Mahāyāna has been influenced by alien thought[1]; and the suggestion may look plausible as there were foreign incursions into India in the formative stages of this phase of Buddhism. Without entering into the merits of this historical question, we may state that it is not at all difficult to account for the development of the characteristic tenets of Mahāyānism from the ideas latent in early Buddhism. The exponents of Mahāyāna were themselves of this opinion, and held that their doctrine represented the *whole* truth of Buddha's teaching, ascribing the variations found in the Hīnayāna schools either to an attempt on the part of the Master at adjusting the teaching to less qualified disciples or to inability on the part of the latter to grasp its complete significance.[2] Whatever the truth may be, both forms of the doctrine alike exhibit several important changes and neither can be taken as representing exactly the teaching as it was originally imparted. In our present treatment, we shall refer only to the new developments and shall not dwell upon points already mentioned in the chapter on early Buddhism.

Several Buddhistic works of this period are written in Sanskrit. Some of them are probably renderings from Pāli originals, which shows that Buddhism gradually assumed a more and more scholastic character, although this should not be taken to mean that it ceased to exist as a popular creed. Buddha, as we have seen, preferred to dwell upon the practical bearing of his teaching passing over the theory underlying it. There springs up now a remarkable development of theoretic interest which for its keenness is almost unrivalled in the whole history of thought. This result is in no small measure due to the sharp conflict that gradually developed between the Buddhists and their Hindu opponents—a conflict in which each party gained and through which Indian speculation as a whole became much richer and

[1] See V. A. Smith: *Early History of India*, p. 266 (3rd Edn.).
[2] Cf. Śaṁkara on VS. II. ii. 18; BP. pp. 216–221.

more varied than it would otherwise have been. All the different shades of philosophic theory—realistic and idealistic—are found within Buddhism itself; and we have, so to speak, philosophy repeated twice over in India—once in the several Hindu systems and again in the different schools of Buddhism. The prominence which the Buddhistic schools acquired gradually declined chiefly under the stress of strengthening Hindu thought. To judge from extant Sanskrit literature, the first great onslaught, so far as the scholastic side of the teaching was concerned, came from Kumārila Bhaṭṭa (A.D. 700) and it was continued by Śaṁkara and others with the result that the doctrine once for all lost its hold on the Indian mind. In regard to minor points of a purely technical character, controversies were carried on for some time longer; but from the twelfth century onwards the discussions of Buddhistic thought in the various Hindu schools became for the most part academic and unreal. For the history of this great teaching after that time, we should look outside India—in Tibet, China and Japan.

The literature bearing upon the later phase of Buddhism, which began to appear as early as the first or second century A.D., is vast; and we can refer here only to a small portion of it, remarking by the way that several of the works in Sanskrit have been lost.[1] To take only the four schools (p. 183) to which we confine our attention here: The chief exponents of the Vaibhāṣika views were Diṅnāga[2] and Dharmakīrti. The former is usually assigned to about 500 A.D. His works, such as the *Pramāṇa-samuccaya*, in their Sanskrit form are not extant. The latter is known as an interpreter of Diṅnāga and is anterior to Śaṁkara. His *Nyāya-bindu*, which is a treatise on logic, is available, as also a very valuable commentary upon it by Dharmottara. Numerous quotations from the works of these two thinkers are found cited by Hindu writers. Kumāralabdha (A.D. 200)[3]

[1] Some of the works lost have in recent times been fortunately recovered in translations in Chinese and Tibetan.

[2] See *Nayana-prasādinī* on Citsukha's *Tattva-pradīpikā*, p. 244 (Nirṇayasāgara Press):—Vaibhāṣikāṇām sūtra-kṛto Diṅnāgasya.

[3] BP. p. 156 n.

is reputed to have been the founder of the Sautrāntika school, between which and the Vaibhāṣika it is not always easy to discover the dividing line. The chief teachers of the Yogācāra[1] school were Asaṅga and Vasubandhu, who were brothers and flourished probably in the third century A.D. Vasubandhu seems to have started as a Sautrāntika and to have been afterwards converted into an idealist under the influence of his brother. His *Abhidharma-kośa* with his own commentary—only partly preserved in Sanskrit—is a source of great authority not only on this school but on the Buddhistic doctrine as a whole. 'It covers the whole field of ontology, psychology, cosmology, the doctrine of salvation and of the saints, and a vast proportion of its matter is common to all Buddhistic belief.'[2] Another of the chief works of this school is *Laṅkāvatāra*, so called because the teaching there is fictitiously represented as having been imparted by Buddha to Rāvaṇa, the demon king of Laṅkā. The chief exponent of the last school—the Mādhyamika—is the renowned Nāgārjuna, who was probably a pupil of Aśvaghoṣa (A.D. 100),[3] the saintly preceptor of King Kaniṣka and also a celebrated Sanskrit poet and dramatist rivalling in fame the great Kālidāsa himself. Nāgārjuna's *Mūla-madhyama-kārikā* with the commentary of Candrakīrti, which is only one of several upon it, has been published and is a most valuable work in the whole range of Sanskrit philosophical literature. The *Śata-śāstra* or *Catuḥ-śataka* of Āryadeva, a pupil of Nāgārjuna, is another important work belonging to the same school.

I

The Cārvāka rejects inference (p. 189) on the ground that there is no warrant for assuming the validity of the inductive truth from which it proceeds. The Buddhist adduces cogent reasons against such a position. He does not indeed believe in all the types of vyāpti or inductive relation recognized by the Hindu logicians; but he does not discard the notion itself as the Cārvāka does. A general statement relating two things

[1] BP. pp. 155 and 230. [2] Ibid., p. 156. [3] Ibid., p. 229.

or events must be admitted to be true, according to the Buddhist, when it is based upon a principle which is universally accepted and is made the ground of everyday activity. To question a statement thus supported would be to question the very foundation of practical life, which is clearly a stultifying position for any disputant to assume. The Buddhist refers in this connection to a maxim[1]—vyāghātāvadhirāśaṅkā—which means that we cannot go on doubting for ever, but must desist from doing so when it results in a self-contradiction in thought or leads to a practical absurdity. Such legitimate vyāptis are of two kinds. (i) *Sphere of Causation:* We can for instance connect smoke always with fire. If anyone should question the correctness of the two being thus linked, we may point to its basis, viz. the law of causation. Smoke is caused by fire; and no one can maintain that an effect may come into being without its cause, for to do so would be to divest almost the whole of life's activity of its meaning. (ii) *Sphere of Identity:*[2] When we know for instance that a thing is a śiṁśupa, we know that it is a tree. A tree may or may not be a śiṁśupa; a śiṁśupa on the other hand must necessarily be a tree, for otherwise we shall be questioning the law of identity—a position as stultifying as the one referred to above. This constant relation between genus and species may be made the basis of a valid inference, provided we take care to see that what is inferred is not narrower than that from which it is inferred; for while it is right to conclude that a śiṁśupa is a tree, the conclusion when reversed is certainly wrong. Here, it will be seen, the predicate is obtained by analysing the subject and the conclusion, though trivial and so perhaps not always of much practical value, is necessarily true. According to the Buddhist then, amongst relations of succession, it is only that of cause and effect (tadutpatti) that warrants inductive generalization; and among relations of co-existence, it is only the identity of essence (tādātmya)

[1] See *Kusumāñjali*, iii. st. 7.

[2] This should be regarded as stated only from the common standpoint and not as committing the Buddhist to the view that two or more things can have any common features.

that does so. He would not believe for instance in the proposition 'All animals with cloven hoofs have horns,' although the concomitance of the two, so far as our knowledge goes, is invariable; for its truth cannot, as in the cases mentioned, be referred back to any general principle whose validity is unquestioned. There is no clinching argument to meet the question 'Why should the cloven hoof be associated with horns?' and any doubt that may be entertained about the matter will, therefore, remain unremoved. In other words, the Buddhist admits the principle of the uniformity of nature only in the two spheres of causal sequence and necessary co-existence. By thus restricting the scope of vyāpti, he insists not only on the condition of invariable concomitance, but also on that of an inner necessity connecting the two terms of the relation. We shall see later that some Indian logicians were content with the first only of these two conditions.

It may be assumed that there is practical agreement in regard to this point among the several Buddhistic schools, but no express statement to that effect can be quoted. That inference is a pramāṇa, however, is admitted by all the Buddhists, though, as we shall see, it can have only a provisional value according to them. But they differ sharply from one another in respect of the view they hold of perception. In fact, according to Hindu writers, the division of Buddhistic thought into the four schools which alone they seem to recognize and with which we are concerned here is based chiefly upon the difference in this respect. To explain that difference, we may divide the four schools first into two classes—realistic and idealistic. The former which are Hīnayāna believe in the existence of objects outside and independently of knowledge, though the objects according to the general postulate of Buddhism are conceived as momentary. The latter, on the other hand, which are Mahāyāna deny such objects altogether. Of the former, the Vaibhāṣikas[1] hold that objects are directly

[1] Vibhāṣā is the commentary on the Abhidharma books; and the Vaibhāṣikas were so called because they accepted this commentary as finally authoritative. The Sautrāntikas on the other hand were of

perceived; and the Sautrāntikaṣ that they are known indirectly since according to the doctrine of momentariness objects cannot be present at the time they are perceived. If they are, they would endure for at least two instants—that when they served as the cause or stimulus of perception and that when they were actually perceived. If things are really momentary, it is only a past thing that can be perceived. So what is present externally when perception takes place is only the successor in the object-series in question of the member that served as its cause. The previous member, however, before it disappears, leaves its impression on the percipient mind; and it is from this impression or idea (ākāra) that we infer the prior existence of the corresponding object. Accordingly, though what is apprehended in perception actually exists, it is not apprehended at the moment when it exists. The explanation is similar to the one which modern science gives, for example, in the case of our seeing a star. Owing to the vastness of its distance from us, the rays proceeding from a star take a considerable time to reach us; and what we perceive, therefore, is not the star as it is at the moment of perception, but as it was at the moment when the rays left it. Thus the so-called perception really refers to the past and is in the nature of an inference. The star, for aught we know, may have disappeared in the interval. Analogous is all perception according to the Sautrāntika. It is not the object which we directly know, but rather its representation through which we indirectly come to know of it. In modern phraseology, the Sautrāntika view of perception involves the doctrine of representative ideas.

The Vaibhāṣika, who holds that objects are known directly, is able to dismiss the intervening psychic medium. His view agrees with the description of perception found in early Buddhistic writings, viz. that it is like fire produced by the rubbing of two sticks,[1] which implies direct causation.

opinion that, being a human composition, it was liable to contain error. They maintained that Buddha taught Abhidharma doctrines in certain Sūtras or Sūtrāntas and recognized their authority alone. Hence their name. See ERE: vol. xi. 'Sautrāntika' and BP. p. 155.

[1] BP. p. 53.

The chief objection which he urges against the Sautrāntika view is that it totally contradicts experience, which is to the effect that the object we perceive is present at the time. He adds also that if perception be abolished, there would be no inference. All inference is supported by a vyāpti or inductive truth which depends upon observation, and we cannot therefore make observation itself a form of inference. The latter argument seems to be somewhat wide of the mark, for the existence of the external object does not seem to be really a matter of inference according to the Sautrāntika, though it is described as anumeya.[1] The statement that it is indirectly known only means that the object is postulated as a *hypothesis* to account for the fact of perception consistently with the doctrine of momentariness. So far from being a weak point in the doctrine, this way of solving the problem indicates great cautiousness in the Sautrāntika. Moreover, the Vaibhāṣika seems to take for granted that the object as perceived should be absolutely contemporaneous with the act of perception. But as a matter of fact the two must always be, at least slightly, separated in time; for light, to instance only visual perception, takes time to travel as also the transmission of a current along the optic nerve.

The criticism of the Sautrāntika view by the Vaibhāṣika does not signify that he believes in the truth of everything that is perceived and takes things at their face value. He, like the Sautrāntika, refuses to admit the distinction between substance and attribute; and there is no object, according to him also, of which anything may be predicated. Perceptual judgments, in all of which this distinction is found, are therefore necessarily wrong. When we see something and say or feel 'This is blue,' we are predicating blueness of 'this' (idam). It is perception as it is familiarly known, and is described as 'determinate' (savikalpaka). The position of both the Vaibhāṣika and the Sautrāntika is that it is erroneous. But it is not wholly so, for it contains a core of truth known as the sva-lakṣaṇa, which in the present case is the colour blue. It is the bare unrelated particular and is supposed to be given in an earlier stage of perception,

[1] Cf. SV. pp. 283–4, st. 51 (com.).

described as 'indeterminate' (nirvikalpaka),[1] which we may perhaps regard as mere sensation. Here the mind is passive; but in the next stage of determinate perception it becomes active leading to a subjective elaboration of the sva-lakṣaṇa and the consequent blurring of it, to speak from the metaphysical standpoint. Thus common perceptual experience is true only so far as the sva-lakṣaṇa is concerned. Whatever is associated with it then—all the conceptual elements or sāmānya-lakṣaṇas as they are termed—whether a universal like cow-ness or an attribute like whiteness—is superposed by the mind (kalpanā) upon it and is not to be taken as an ontological fact.[2] The particular alone is real, not the general. The latter is in fact as unrelated to the former as the name or verbal sign by which we refer to it. The general feature is nothing more than a working fiction, a convenient device in thinking. So the realism of the Vaibhāṣika, as that of the Sautrāntika, does not indicate the being of anything except the sva-lakṣaṇas; but while the one admits that a sva-lakṣaṇa is directly cognized, the other views it as known indirectly. Both alike endow the perceiving mind with a constructive side on account of which reality becomes vastly transformed when it is experienced. The resemblance between such a view and Kant's will be obvious to the student of Western philosophy. The Buddhistic realist also, like Kant, assumes a thing-in-itself (sva-lakṣaṇa) and explains the actual content of perception as the result of the mind imposing its own forms[3] upon it. But the two views are not identical, since the Buddhist assumes that the sva-lakṣaṇa is known, whether directly or indirectly; and it is not, therefore, unknowable like Kant's 'thing-in-itself.' Reality is not only given but is also known. There is also the fact that the forms imposed by the mind upon it are not, as we shall see in the next section, exactly the same as they are in Kant's view.

Buddhistic idealism also is of two types: The first of them

[1] These are respectively termed adhyavasāya and grahaṇa (See SDS. p. 22), which names imply that the former is a judgment while the latter is bare sensation.

[2] Cf. NM. pp. 93 and 303.

[3] Kalpanā hi buddhi-viśeṣaḥ: SV. p. 306 (com.).

is pure subjectivism; and the complicated explanation of perception which the Sautrāntika gave may be supposed to have directly led to it. The followers of this view are known as Yogācāra—a term whose significance is not very clear.[1] While, according to the two previous schools, knowledge is true so far as the sva-lakṣaṇa is concerned and is false only in respect of the conceptual elements involved in it, according to the Yogācāra it is the sole truth and its whole content is false. In fact in the triple factor commonly assumed wherever experience arises—'knower,' 'known' and 'knowledge'—the last alone is here taken to be true. There is neither subject nor object but only a succession of ideas. The specific form which cognition at any particular instant assumes is determined in this view, not by an outside object presented to it, but by past experience. That is, the stimulus always comes from within, never from without. It is in no way dependent upon objects existing outside, but is to be traced to an impression (vāsanā) left behind by past experience, which in its turn goes back to another impression, that to another experience and so on indefinitely in a beginningless series. At no particular stage in the series, it must be noted, is the experience due to an external factor. In other words, the ideas signify nothing but themselves. Since the Yogācāra believes in the reality of nothing but these ideas (vijñāna), he is also designated as vijñāna-vādin.

We may mention some of the main arguments by which this extreme view is maintained.[2] First comes the obvious analogy of dreams where experience arises without corresponding objects, and internal thoughts appear as external. The second argument is based upon the view which the Yogācāra holds in common with the rest of the Buddhists that cognition becomes aware of itself. In self-cognizing cognition, we have a case in which what is known is identical with what knows; and the Yogācāra argues that the same may be the case in all experience, there being no reason why an explanation which is not absurd in one case must be so in another. In the awareness of a jar also, knowledge and the

[1] The Chinese rendering of the term suggests 'Yogācārya' as the Sanskrit form. See BP. p. 243 n.

[2] Cf. Śaṁkara on VS. II. ii. 28.

known may be identical. All knowledge is thus only self-knowledge and the distinction felt between jñāna and content is a delusion, comparable to the single moon illusorily appearing double. A third support which the Yogācāra cites in favour of his view is the invariable association (sahopalambha-niyama) existing between cognition and its content. Thoughts and things always appear together; and neither without the other. There is consequently no need to assume that they are distinct, and they may well be viewed as different phases of one and the same factor. Lastly, it is argued that the so-called objects are seen to impress different persons differently and even the same person at different times—a circumstance which would be inexplicable if the objects were real, each having its own defined character.[1] The arguments are much the same as those commonly advanced whenever subjectivism is sought to be maintained, except for the additional circumstance that everything is conceived here as momentary. But they are by no means convincing. To take the last of them as an example: It is stated that objects of experience cannot have any intrinsic nature, for no two persons agree in their perceptions of them. The argument assumes not only that there is no agreement whatever between one perceiver and another in this respect, but also that when anything is presented, it must be apprehended precisely as it is. But it is forgotten that the content apprehended may have a subjective side and may, at the same time, point to a real object outside. Individual variations in the matter of perception do not, therefore, necessarily mean the non-existence of external objects. Yet the Yogācāra reasoning has a negative force which cannot be easily thrust aside. They point to the indemonstrability of the opposite view maintained in realism.

The second school of Buddhistic idealism which we have to consider is known as the Mādhyamika.[2] In one sense it is

[1] Cf. SV. p. 286, st. 59. This argument is common to the two idealistic schools of Buddhism.

[2] Strictly it is the followers of the school that are 'Mādhyamikas,' the doctrine itself being known as Mādhyamaka. See ERE. vol. viii. 'Mādhyamaka.' The term signifies an adherent of the 'middle path,' which is a distinctive feature of Buddhism. See p. 132 *ante*.

the most important outcome of Buddha's teaching and, at the same time, the most difficult to evaluate properly. The standpoint of the Mādhyamika in regard to knowledge is altogether novel. So far we have seen that some aspect of common experience is assumed to be true, all the three schools having taken for granted the subject-series at least as real. The Mādhyamika is quite revolutionary in his view and questions the validity of knowledge as a whole. He holds that if criticism of knowledge is necessary, it must be so in the case of all knowledge and that the validity of no part of it should be taken as self-evident. We commonly believe that we get into touch with reality through knowledge. When, however, we begin to inquire into the nature of this so-called reality, we discover that it is riddled with all sorts of self-discrepancies. Reflection at once shows its hollowness. 'No sooner are objects thought about than they are dissipated.'[1] What for instance is the nature of a jar which appears to be given in knowledge? If we ask ourselves whether it is an aggregate of parts or a whole, we are not able to maintain either position satisfactorily. For if it be an aggregate of parts, it should eventually be an aggregate of atoms; and an aggregate of invisible atoms must necessarily be invisible. If to avoid this difficulty we assume it to be an integral whole over and above its constituents, we shall be at a loss to explain satisfactorily the relation between the two. Similarly we cannot describe what passes for a real thing as either existent or non-existent. If a jar always exists, it is difficult to see why it needs to be made; and the efficiency of its maker becomes superfluous. If on the other hand we assume that it is at one time non-existent and then comes into existence, we shall be predicating both existence and non-existence of the same object whose nature for that reason becomes unintelligible. The only escape from such difficulties is to regard objects as having no intrinsic character (nissvabhāva)—a position which is diametrically opposed to that of the Svabhāva-vāda (p. 104). The same argument is extended to vijñāna, and it is also dismissed as devoid of self-essence or as a thing which is *not* in itself. This line of

[1] Yathā yathārthāścintyante viśīryante tathā tathā. SDS. p. 15.

reasoning leads the Mādhyamika to conclude that, though knowledge serves the purposes of empirical life and so far may be valid or not as the case may be, it is impossible to attach any metaphysical significance to it. All knowledge, whether perceptual or inferred, is relative; and there is none that is absolutely true. He accordingly believes neither in outer reality nor in the inner; and his doctrine is therefore described as that of the void (śūnya-vāda). The unique method of establishing this position, though utilized by other thinkers also, seems to have originated with him. It may be described as the method of dichotomy and bears a resemblance to that adopted by Bradley in modern times. By the use of this method, he tries to show how the common concepts of philosophy are self-discrepant and are nothing more than dogmatic assumptions. In more than one chapter of his *Kārikā*, Nāgārjuna passes in review conceptions like 'motion,' showing how they are utterly unintelligible.

If perception and inference are both of provisional value for the Mādhyamika, the latter is so for all the four schools alike; because, according to the Buddhistic doctrine, relations are all false and inference which is based upon a supposed relation between two terms cannot, therefore, be valid. Moreover, this pramāṇa, even according to the realistic schools, has reference only to the ideal constructions or sāmānya-lakṣaṇas,[1] the sva-lakṣaṇas being the objects exclusively of pratyakṣa; and it can, therefore, lay claim to no final validity. Diṅnāga says that the whole process of inference refers to what is imposed by thought and has no relation to external reality.[2] As regards perception, the Yogācāra doctrine may be placed on the same footing as the Mādhyamika, because it also refuses to recognize external objects. It no doubt admits vijñāna or 'momentary idea' to be real and as directly known; but it becomes aware of itself and is not, therefore, perception in the ordinary sense of the word. In the Sautrāntika view also the validity of perception cannot be absolute, for, as already explained, it postulates the external world as a mere hypothesis which,

[1] *Nyāya-bindu*. ch. i. NM. p. 30.

[2] See SV. p. 258, st. 168 (com.).

therefore, carries no certitude with it. It is only in the Vaibhāṣika school which admits that external objects are real and are directly known that perception can claim any ultimate logical value.

The Buddhist recognizes only these two pramāṇas and brings others like verbal testimony (śabda) under inference. From this we should not understand that he discards tradition (p. 179). He only denies to it the logical status implied by designating it a pramāṇa. In this respect his view is at one with that of the Vaiśeṣika, to which we shall refer in the succeeding chapter.

It is clear from what has been said so far that the place which Buddhism assigns to jñāna is very precarious. Knowledge may have value for life, but its metaphysical significance is next to nothing. This position accounts for the Buddhistic criterion of truth, viz. that it consists in fitness to secure for us the object in question (prāpakatva).[1] That knowledge is true which confirms the expectation it raises. There is nothing strange about such a view in itself, and it has found supporters both in the East and the West. The peculiarity of the Buddhistic view lies in that the practical verification of knowledge which is possible is held to be only approximate. This is rendered necessary by the unusual way in which it conceives of reality. Even in the nirvikalpaka, where according to the Vaibhāṣika a sva-lakṣaṇa is actually given, that very sva-lakṣaṇa cannot be reached for it ceases to be in a moment. So the utmost that knowledge can do is to direct us to the series of which the sva-lakṣaṇa cognized *was* a member. That is what is presented is a particular; but what is attained is not that particular but the corresponding series. This is what is meant by approximate verification. Such verification is held to be quite adequate to meet the demands of practical life, and the discrepancy that exists between knowledge and realization consequently passes unnoticed. Knowledge merely lights up, as it were, the path of action; and, so long as it successfully does so, it is regarded as true. And the analogy is given here of a person who sees only the lustre of a shining jewel, but mistaking it for the

[1] *Nyāya-bindu-ṭīkā*, p. 3; NM. p. 23.

jewel itself stretches forth his hand and happens to secure it.[1] In inference, the objects are invariably sāmānya-lakṣaṇas, which are by hypothesis unreal. Yet it can be serviceable in life by leading us to an object-series with which its content is associated. Thus not only is the ultimate significance of knowledge little; its practical value also is of an indirect kind.

So much about truth. But knowledge may not be valid even in this restricted sense. A person through a defect of sight may see a patch of black where there is one of blue. It is error or illusion (viparyaya). Inference also may go wrong, for it may not comprehend the right sort of general features. Thus the validity of pramāṇas, even in the qualified sense in which it is understood, is not necessary and can be accepted only after verification. It is not, therefore, surprising that all knowledge should in the doctrine be described as presumably wrong and standing in need of validation by an external circumstance.[2] Postponing for the present the consideration of the question whether knowledge needs to be tested or not, we may indicate the distinction between the content of error and ideal constructions (kalpanā), both of which are alike unreal. The kalpanās are in their very nature false and are always found where perception takes place. They are in fact the necessary condition of perception as ordinarily known—the frame into which the mind fits reality as it apprehends it. But errors are occasional and affect only individual percipients. Moreover, the former are classifiable, unlike the content of illusions, into definite groups. They may be described in Kantian terminology as forms of the mind. What these groups or categories are, we shall see later.

II

In dealing with their theories of knowledge, we have to a large extent anticipated the ontological views of the four Buddhistic schools. It is still desirable to bring together the

[1] SDS. p. 23.

[2] Aprāmāṇyam svataḥ: prāmāṇyam parataḥ. SDS. p. 129.

statements already made, filling them out where necessary with details so that we may have a connected idea of the world-view of each school. The distinguishing features of primitive Buddhism were (1) its belief that everything is a flux (saṁtāna), and (2) its belief that everything is an aggregate altogether lacking self (saṁghāta). These features continue to characterize the teaching in the present stage also; but naturally they receive greater emphasis and are more formally enunciated. We shall add a few words on the former of these, viz. the doctrine of momentariness.

Change is ordinarily understood to imply something that endures through it. If we represent a changing object by XA, it becomes, according to the common view, XB under certain conditions, where X stands for the element common to the two phases. This view that a changing object persists amidst varying features does not commend itself to the Buddhist; and he maintains that all change is necessarily *total*. That is, change means revolution, not evolution. His arguments are as follows: In the example given above, if the conditions bringing about the change alter A to B without at all affecting X, then X is merely a conventional adjunct of A; and it may well be dispensed with as superfluous. The result is that A becomes B, and we have total change. If on the other hand we assume that the conditions in question do affect X, altering it thereby, it is again total change, for we now have YB as the result in place of XA, and not XB as supposed. To express the same more generally, the ordinary view of change is based upon the supposition that Being may be related to Becoming while the Buddhist altogether denies the possibility of such a relation. In his view there is no Being at all, and the only reality is Becoming. Change is not only total; it is also *perpetual*. This follows directly from the conception of reality entertained in the system, viz. that it consists in causal efficiency or the capacity to effect something. A seed for example causes the shoot and, according to the principle of total change, it then becomes wholly different without any the least part of what was the seed surviving in it (niranvaya-nāśa). Its capacity as a seed to produce the shoot must manifest itself *at once*, for otherwise we shall have prolonged or suspended efficiency which Buddhism describes as a contradiction in terms. That a thing should be capable of producing something and yet should not produce it or do so only bit by bit, is inconceivable. Potentiality is only another expression for lack of efficiency; and the distinction between 'can' and 'does' is fictitious. It should, therefore, be admitted that whatever capacity a thing has, is at once and fully manifested; and since a thing is, only *when* it acts, it must be momentary. Yat sat tat kṣaṇikam.[1] If now in the light of this view that practical efficiency or 'the pulse of the moment' is the sole test of reality, we consider the same seed in the instants previous to its becoming a shoot, we should agree to associate it in those instants also with some sort of activity; for, if it then be idle and do nothing, it will be unreal and cannot give rise to a positive something—the shoot. The only way to think of it as active in each of those instants is to take it as producing its like in the next instant. The seed is thus never inactive. The difference when it becomes a shoot instead of continuing as a seed, is that the nature of the series is altered; but the one series is as much a flux as the other. The theory gives us, instead of a static seed which at some stage is transformed into a shoot, a seed-series which is replaced by a shoot-series when certain new conditions make their appearance. This causal efficiency is described in Sanskrit as artha-kriyā-kāritva, which may be taken as equivalent to 'making become.' The same conclusion is reached by showing that no extraneous causes are necessary for destroying a thing.[2] The germs of destruction are inherent in every object, which cannot, therefore, last beyond one instant. What are ordinarily regarded as the causes of destruction such as a stick in the case of breaking a jar, it is explained, give rise to a different series—that of the potsherd; for there is no meaning in speaking of non-existence (abhāva) being brought bout. If a thing does not annihilate itself, nothing else can do it; and if it does not end itself in the instant following its appearance, there is no reason on earth why it should disappear at all at any time. Hence if things are not momentary,

[1] SDS. pp. 9–12; NM. pp. 444 ff.

[2] NM. pp. 447–8.

every one of them will have to be eternal—a conclusion which is accepted by none.

This conception of reality is criticized in several ways by the exponents of the other Indian systems. If everything be a flux and is being continually renovated, no recognition would be possible. The Buddhist meets this objection, as briefly remarked before (p. 145), by explaining away recognition. It is according to him not a single piece of knowledge at all, but a compound of memory and perception; and what we apprehend in it is not one object as we commonly assume, but two distinct ones though both are members of the same series. How can the same object, he asks, appear in two different temporal settings?[1] In other words, the things in the two moments are only similar, and similarity is mistaken for identity in recognition. He admits that our feeling, then, is that we perceive the same thing which we did once before, as is implied in the conative response resulting from recognition; but he explains the feeling as a mere delusion. He cites in illustration the example of the lamp-flame where, if recognition were valid, the identity of the flame-material in two different moments, which though ordinarily assumed is known to be false, would be established. All recognition involves a reference to past time which perception is not competent to apprehend as well as to present time which memory cannot refer to. To regard it as a single unit of knowledge, overlooking its hybrid character, is clearly erroneous. The main argument of the critics of this view is based upon the postulate that the invalidity of knowledge is established by its being contradicted by other knowledge which is better supported. In the case of the lamp-flame that has been mentioned as an illustration, the gradual consumption of the oil, for example, is a sign that the flame-material is not the same in any two stages. But no such indication exists in regard to everything. Rather inquiry in other cases generally confirms the identity of the thing. What the lamp-flame illustrates is only that recognition is not always true. That, indeed, is so in the case of all knowledge. The definition of the real as the 'causally efficient' is also criticized. Though

[1] NM. pp. 459–61.

commonly, according to Buddhism, a series never ends, but may only be transformed into another as in the case of the seed becoming the shoot, certain exceptions are admitted of which one is the cessation of the ego-series (pratisaṁkhyā-nirodha) when an arhant dies and attains nirvāṇa. Here the question arises as to whether the final member of the ego-series in question is real or not. Since by hypothesis it gives rise to no successor, it is not causally efficient and cannot, therefore, be real. And if that is unreal, it must follow that the next previous one is unreal and so on backwards until the whole series disappears as a figment,[1] with the result that either the ideal of nirvāṇa should be given up as never achievable or the ego-series representing the aspirant for nirvāṇa should be admitted as absolutely non-existent.

These are specimens of the arguments advanced in Hindu philosophical works against the Buddhistic doctrine of momentariness. They are ingenious, though they are not all convincing; and it is not necessary to mention more of them here. The chief argument to refute the Buddhistic position in this respect, it seems, should be based upon quite a distinct consideration. According to modern science, the present is to be regarded as a duration.[2] The duration may be of any breadth, but the point to be noted is that it is never a mere instant. This truth, it may be added, was not unknown to old Indian thinkers[3] and we sometimes find allusions to it in Sanskrit philosophical works. The Buddhist supposes that what is given in perception is the instantaneous present.[4] In fact, one of the arguments for the doctrine of momentariness is based upon the assumption that perception is necessarily confined to the present instant.[5] The Buddhist does not admit time as a reality; and it may, therefore, appear as not legitimate to speak of any 'instant' in criticizing

[1] Cf. Śaṁkara on VS. II. ii. 22.

[2] Cf. Prof. Whitehead: *The Concept of Nature*, pp. 68 and 72.

[3] See NS. II. i. 39–43, and *The Quarterly Journal of the Mythic Society*, Bangalore (1924), pp. 233–7.

[4] Cf. SDS. p. 25: pūrvāpara-bhāga-vikala-kāla-kalāvasthiti-lakṣaṇa-kṣaṇikatā.

[5] NM. p. 450.

his position. But he accepts a momentary thing or state as representing the ultimate stage when the things of experience are analysed, which is equivalent to the admission of an instantaneous present. He only substitutes for a minimal time a minimal real, which is open to exactly the same criticism. So our reference to it in terms of time, while it facilitates exposition, does not affect the theory. The duration of the present may be reduced to any extent, but it will always remain a duration, however small, with its own boundary moments so to say. The absolute instant is only a limiting concept—an ideal of thought and not an actual existent. To base an ontological theory upon such an abstraction is not right; and it is for this reason that the Buddhist view of change, however subtle in itself, fails to convince us. This criticism may be said to receive support from the history of the Buddhistic doctrine itself. For Buddha did not think that things were momentary. He was content with the conclusion that they were impermanent (p. 144). It was his followers that in later times devised this novel theory which has all the merits and all the defects of a purely speculative solution.

Of the four schools of Buddhism, the Vaibhāṣika may be described as pluralistic realism. It believes in the existence of an indefinite number of fleeting sva-lakṣaṇas and regards them as the only basis of the external world. They are all diverse with no principle of unity underlying them. That is the reason why they are called sva-lakṣaṇas, a term which signifies that every one of them is unique and can be described only as itself.[1] Each sva-lakṣaṇa is produced by the preceding one in its series and gives rise in its turn to the succeeding one in the same series; but it is otherwise absolutely independent and relationless.[2] Since these sva-lakṣaṇas are supposed to be apprehended directly by the senses, they may be represented as the material of bare sensation. When they are perceived, they are invariably accompanied by certain subjective determinations (kalpanā), which are divided into five classes—generality (jāti), quality (guṇa),

[1] Svam asādhāraṇam lakṣaṇam tattvam sva-lakṣaṇam: *Nyāya-bindu-ṭīkā*, p. 15.

[2] Cf. NM. p. 30.

action (karma), name (nāma) and substance (dravya) or, to state the same differently, relation to other substances.[1] We may call them 'categories,' but we should remember that they are only categories of thought. Everything that appears to us appears through their medium—not as mere sva-lakṣaṇa, but as a thing belonging to a class or bearing a name, as a substance characterized by an attribute or related to another substance. Thus perception includes much more than what is actually presented to the senses. The additions are not material attributes, but only mental forms which are superimposed ready-made on the sva-lakṣaṇa. Though thus imaginary they are of the utmost importance to practical life, for it is through the discrimination and agreement between one thing and another, which by their aid we are able to make, that we carry on our everyday activities. Time and space also are equally mental devices and no sva-lakṣaṇa in itself has either extension or duration,[2] but they are not reckoned separately because their conception is relational and are, therefore, already included under the last category.

So far we have considered the external world as it is presented to us. It is largely subjective though based on reality; and the realism of the doctrine is therefore far from naïve. The sva-lakṣaṇas of which we have spoken, however, are not ultimate, but are constituted of certain primary elements and are, therefore, all secondary. The ultimate elements of reality or the bhūtas, already alluded to (p. 146), are described as atoms so that the world-conception of the Vaibhāṣika may be taken as atomistic. But by 'atom,' in this case, we should not understand an enduring thing[3] as

[1] NM. p. 93–4. See Prof. H. N. Randle: *Fragments from Diṅnāga*, p. 71.

[2] NM. pp. 450–1; Prof. Stcherbatsky: *The Conception of Buddhistic Nirvāṇa*, p. 142 n.

[3] This is said from the standpoint of Hindu works. Compare, for example, Śaṁkara on VS. II. ii. 22, where a passage is cited to show that all positive things are momentary. According to some modern works dealing with Buddhism, these fundamental factors are permanent and unchanging, though everything derived from them is unstable and changing. Such a doctrine, though perhaps placing

in the Jaina or Vaiśeṣika doctrine. As regards the inner world of mind, a parallel classification is adopted with citta and caitta corresponding to bhūta and bhautika. Of the five skandhas, which together stand for personality (p. 139), the vijñāna-skandha is what is known as citta; and the other four are explained as caitta or 'derived from citta.' The idea is that self-consciousness as a succession of momentary ideas is fundamental and that the other psychical features are modifications which show themselves therein.[1] They depend not merely on outside factors presented at the time, but also on the predispositions of the individual so that in mental life the past has always a very important part to play in determining the present.[2] While the description as caitta is quite intelligible in the case of feeling (vedanā), perception (saṁjñā) and mental dispositions (saṁskāra), it presents a difficulty in regard to rūpa-skandha because it stands for the material frame and cannot, therefore, be represented as psychical. The difficulty is noticed by Hindu writers and their explanation is that matter, in so far as it constitutes the senses which are the apparatus of thought, may justifiably be included in the knowing subject. Or perhaps, we should say, its inclusion implies a view of personality which comprehends within it not only the mind and its organs, but also that aspect of the physical universe which the individual perceives and which, being relative to his ends, may be regarded as *his* world.[3]

An obvious criticism of the Vaibhāṣika world-view is that a sva-lakṣaṇa of the kind in which it believes is as good as nothing and may as well be dispensed with. It is, as the exponents of the other Indian systems point out, an unwarranted addition of which really nothing can be said or known. The Vaibhāṣika no doubt claims for it knowability; but its knowledge, as Uddyotakara puts it, resembles 'a dumb man's dream.'[4] The doctrine however, so far as it

the Vaibhāṣika view on a more secure basis, would remove it very far from the spirit of early Buddhism, which insists upon change being fundamental. Cf. *Aristotelian Society Proceedings* (1919–20), p. 161.

[1] NM. p. 74; PP. p. 48.

[2] Cf. *Bhāmatī*, II. ii. 18.

[3] Cf. Prof. Stcherbatsky: *Central Conception of Buddhism*, p. 7.

[4] Mūka-svapna-sadṛśam: NV. p. 43.

retains belief in an external world, is more loyal to the old teaching than the subjectivism of the Yogācāra, though it also marks a departure in the investigation for its own sake of objective reality. The inquiry here is not merely practical and psychological as in primitive Buddhism, but also logical and metaphysical or, to express it in a different way, the study of matter now comes to be added to the study of man. The Vaibhāṣika, like the rest of the Buddhists, has attempted to work out the implications of Gotama's teaching, but seems to have stopped short at the penultimate stage lest he should do violence to it, while the other schools have carried on the investigation farther. One unsatisfactory character of the doctrine, viewed by itself and not in relation to its traditional basis, is due to the attempt it makes to think of reality after abolishing time and space from the objective sphere. Its dimensionless sva-lakṣaṇas can have no verity about them. Herein lies its chief weakness which should have suggested to the Yogācāra the doctrine of pure subjectivism. As regards the Buddhistic view of the conceptual elements or sāmānya-lakṣaṇas also, criticisms are met with in Hindu philosophical works; but the criticisms are often based upon postulates which differ in different systems and not on such as are equally acceptable to them all. In the case of 'generality' (jāti), for example, the Hindu schools themselves disagree—some taking it as objectively real and others regarding it as only a concept conveniently holding together the features common to several objects. It would accordingly be more convenient to postpone whatever criticisms we have to offer on this aspect of the Vaibhāṣika doctrine to the later chapters dealing with those systems.

There is not much to be said about the next two schools. The Sautrāntika position is identical with that of the Vaibhāṣika, except that instead of dogmatically asserting the existence of sva-lakṣaṇas, it only admits them as a hypothesis to account for experience. It probably marks a conscious advance on the Vaibhāṣika, as the latter is known to have preceded the Sautrāntika in the systematization of its doctrine.[1] The Yogācāra view is essentially different; but

[1] See ERE. vol. xi. p. 213.

it is more consistent inasmuch as it explains the whole of the external world as a creation of the mind and thus abolishes the logical distinction between the sva-lakṣaṇa and the sāmānya-lakṣaṇa. If, as stated by the Sautrāntika, the image or idea is a necessary link between the mind and its object, there is no need to assume the object, provided we otherwise account for the appearance of its image or idea in the mind; and that is just the view which the Yogācāra takes. He abolishes what according to the Sautrāntika is the hypothetical outer circle by assuming that the mind itself can generate the respective ideas. Objects according to the Yogācāra are not accordingly encountered by the mind, but are created by it. In this doctrine, we have not only to explain generality, quality, etc., as subjective, but also the concept of externality itself, the only reality admitted being vijñāna which is 'internal,' if the word can be used at all when nothing outside is recognized. In the case of each vijñāna, we must assume the fictitious diversification of 'knower,' 'knowledge' and 'known,' so that the subject and the object are only aspects of vijñāna or knowledge itself. So far as the evidence of Hindu philosophical works goes, the presumption is that the number of vijñāna-series is unlimited; and the doctrine, though idealistic, is pluralistic. But the position that 'externality' is merely a mental construct, if strictly adhered to, renders the recognition of more than one self impossible and we shall be led into solipsism.[1] But even then the plurality of selves would be granted on the empirical plane to explain life and its common activities on the analogy of dreams. There is no evidence in Sanskrit works to show that such a position was actually reached in the Yogācāra school. But there are indications, on the other hand, that by some among its adherents a cosmic or absolute vijñāna-series[2] was postulated of which everything was regarded as but an appearance. Thus we find the doctrine described as Vijñānādvaita[3] and classed with

[1] See Guṇaratna on *Ṣaḍdarśana-samuccaya*, st. 56. Tarhi bahirarthavat sva-jñāna-saṁtānāt anyāni saṁtānāntarāṇyapi viśīryeran.

[2] See e.g. Vidyāraṇya: *Vivaraṇa-prameya-saṁgraha*, p. 80.

[3] Cf. NM. pp. 526 and 537.

monistic doctrines like the Ātmādvaita of Śaṁkara. The absolutistic development which the doctrine underwent outside India was thus already known to Buddhism in its Indian form and was not, therefore, peculiar to its extra-Indian history. Its very character suggests Upaniṣadic influence; but this ultimate vijñāna also, it should not be forgotten, is only Becoming.

The last school we have to consider is the Mādhyamika, which believes in no reality whatsoever, and is therefore described as sūnya-vāda. Its general position is one of complete distrust in knowledge, so far as metaphysics is concerned, and is reached by scrutinizing the things of common experience and showing that the scrutiny leads nowhere. This will be best indicated by explaining how the old conception of pratītya-samutpāda (p. 143) is interpreted here. The other Buddhistic schools believe in things originating, though their view of causation is quite singular. The Mādhyamika denies the possibility of origination itself. The very first verse of Nāgārjuna's *Kārikā* tries to unsettle the notion by subjecting it to the test of a negative logic. 'Nothing exists anywhere, whether we conceive of it as born of itself or of others, or of both or of no cause whatsoever.' It means that the notion of causation is an illusion; and, since the doctrine of Buddha admits nothing that is uncaused, the whole universe must be illusory. The teaching is thus entirely negative. All experience is a delusion[1]; and the world, a tissue of false things falsely related. It is illustrated by citing the case of the mock-elephant by which Udayana, the adventurous hero of Indian folk-lore, was undone.[2] This view, it is maintained, is not inconsistent with the relative or provisional reality (saṁvṛti-satya) of the common things of experience. They are all real so far as empirical purposes go, but they vanish like mist when they are subjected to philosophic investigation. They may be intelligible from a practical standpoint, but they altogether fail to satisfy a philosophic criterion, being wholly of a self-discrepant nature.

It may be pointed out how small, in spite of this extreme

[1] Anubhava eṣa mṛṣā: Nāgārjuna's *Kārikā* (St. Petersburg Edn.), com. p. 58.

[2] *Id.* xiii. 1, com.

position of the Mādhyamika, is its difference from the remaining three schools. According to all of them alike, common knowledge contains elements which are superimposed by the mind. Thus general features like cow-ness have no objective reality according to any of them and are entirely due to the nature of thought. In the Yogācāra school, this illusory character is ascribed to the whole of the physical world. That is, scholastic Buddhism as a whole regards the greater part of common knowledge as only conventionally true. The Mādhyamika merely extends this principle to all experience. But it may be asked whether the system is altogether devoid of the notion of a positive ultimate. Our object here being chiefly to present later Buddhism as it was understood by Hindu thinkers and is found set forth in their works, it is easy to answer this question; for they all alike agree in holding that the void is the only truth according to the Mādhyamika. They describe the school as nihilistic and have no difficulty in refuting that apparently absurd position. Some even go so far as to say that such a view needs no serious refutation, because it stands self-condemned.[1] It may appear to us that the negation of everything is inconceivable without implying a positive ground (avadhi) thereby, and that the ultimate truth cannot therefore be the void. Nothing can be proved false, if nothing is taken as true. That is the very criticism of Hindu philosophers passed on the Mādhyamika.[2] So we cannot doubt that in their view the Mādhyamika was a nihilist in the literal sense of the term.[3] It would seem that

[1] Cf. Śaṁkara on VS. II. ii. 31 and on *Bṛ. Up*. p. 577.

[2] See e.g. *Bhāmatī*. II. ii. 31. The Mādhyamika shows great impatience at this criticism and characterizes the critic as obsessed to an incurable extent in favour of the positive. Candrakīrti ridicules him by comparing him to a person who, when told that he would get nothing, expected that 'nothing' would actually be given to him. See com. on Nāgārjuna's *Kārikā*, xiii. 8.

[3] The only other conclusion that can be drawn from the references to the doctrine in Hindu philosophical works is that the Mādhyamika was concerned *solely* with showing that the several explanations given of the world by the others were untenable, but that he had no solution of his own to offer about it. This is the significance of the term Vaitaṇḍika applied to him sometimes.

this view is not different from the one held by the Mādhyamika himself, at least in one stage in the history of the doctrine, if we may judge from certain statements appearing in Buddhistic works. To mention only one such statement: When the charge of nihilism is brought against his view, Candrakīrti, the seventh-century commentator on Nāgārjuna's *Kārikā*, instead of trying to repel that charge merely points out that the doctrine is different from common or vulgar nihilism.[1] From this it is clear that the Mādhyamika view also is negative, though it may not be identical with nihilism as ordinarily understood. It differs from the other, it is stated, in that its negation is the result of a logical scrutiny of experience and is not merely a dogmatic or whimsical denial. The difference is illustrated by comparing the Mādhyamika to a witness who speaks in a court of law against a thief, fully knowing that he has committed the theft; and the common nihilist, to one who also speaks against the thief and who, though not uttering a falsehood, is speaking not from knowledge, but through some bias or other. The belief among some modern scholars is that the Mādhyamika could not really have been a nihilist and that he also believed in a positive something as the Ultimate, the word śūnya applied to it only meaning that it is *as nothing* from the empirical standpoint.[2] But we cannot with the evidence available in Hindu philosophical literature reach such a conclusion. Not the Hindus alone, but the Jains also,[3] we may add, hold the Mādhyamika to be a nihilist.

III

It has been observed that while school after school of epistemological and ontological inquiry arose, the Buddhistic practical teaching remained almost unchanged. That may be true of Hīnayānism, but not of Mahāyānism. The belief that all is suffering and that pleasure itself is 'attenuated

[1] Nāgārjuna's *Kārikā*, xviii. 7, com. [2] See e.g. IP. vol. i. pp. 662–6.
[3] Cf. *Pramāṇa-naya-tattvālokālaṁkāra*, i. 15, com. Sarva-śūnyataiva param tattvam. (Benares Edn.) See also *Prameya-kamala-mārtaṇḍa*, p. 25. (Nirṇaya Sāg. Pr.)

pain' continues to characterize the latter doctrine as also the belief that right knowledge is the means of overcoming it. The course of discipline laid down for the attainment of nirvāṇa is also the same as before—partly moral and partly intellectual. But the conception of the ideal of life becomes vastly transformed. There had all along been the two ideals (p. 114) of action (pravṛtti) and of contemplation (nivṛtti). Like so many other heretical doctrines Hīnayānism adopted the latter, while Mahāyānism, largely under the influence of Hindu thought, modelled its practical teaching on the former. Although saving oneself still continues to be the aim of life, it ceases to be commended for its own sake and comes to be regarded as but a qualification to strive for the salvation of others. This is the ideal of the Bodhisattva as distinguished from that of the arhant of the Hīnayāna schools. The Bodhisattva, having perfected himself, renounces his own salvation to work for the spiritual good of others. He is not content with his own enlightenment or Buddha-hood, but yearns to help his suffering fellow-creatures, and is ready for any sacrifice on their account. In fact, self-sacrificing love or disinterested activity may be described as the chief spring of Mahāyānism. Thus Nāgārjuna before his birth, it is believed, was a deva living in a happy world and came down to the earth to spread the great teaching of Buddha. The same spirit is abundantly illustrated in the Jātaka stories, which profess to recount the doings of Buddha in his former lives. The altruistic aim was so prominent a feature of Māhāyanism that we find poets and dramatists laying special stress on it when characters that have come under the influence of that doctrine are introduced. Thus in the *Nāgānanda*,[1] a Sanskrit play of the seventh century A.D., which dramatizes a Buddhistic legendi the hero censures the saint who flees from the world seeking his own peace: 'A hermit is no doubt happy in the forest—with the meadow for his bed, the white rock for his couch, the shady tree for his dwelling, the cool water of the cascade for his drink, roots for his food and the deer for his companions. Yet there is one drawback in such a life. Being all lonely, it

[1] Act iv. 2. Cf. also Bhavabhūti's *Mālatī-mādhava*, x. 21.

gives no scope for helping fellow-men and is therefore led to no purpose.' In this connection also comes about a great change in the Buddhistic view of karma; and the rigour of the law that one can under no circumstances escape from reaping the fruit of what one has done is mitigated by the belief that a Bodhisattva can transfer his good deeds to others or 'turn them over' (parivarta) to them, thus helping them in their struggle for freedom from suffering. All his merit (puṇya) he can thus dedicate to the saving of his fellow-beings. Whatever may be said of such transfer from the strictly ethical standpoint, this new feature is not without its special religious appeal; and it prompts the devout, in its turn, to an act of absolute self-surrender (bhakti) to the lofty-minded and compassionate Bodhisattva. There are other changes also, like the deification of Buddha, whose influence on practical life is great; but such developments of later Buddhism, however interesting, are outside our purview and need not detain us now.

CHAPTER X

NYĀYA-VAIŚEṢIKA

WE now begin the study of what are commonly styled the orthodox systems.[1] The Nyāya and the Vaiśeṣika, which form the subject of this chapter, were independent in their origin. Our justification for dealing with them as one here is that they are closely allied in their realistic and pessimistic outlook and that, in the course of history, they have actually been amalgamated by their exponents themselves. Thus the popular manuals of the *Tarkasaṁgraha* of Annaṁbhaṭṭa and the *Bhāṣā-pariccheda* or *Kārikāvalī* of Viśvanātha, which belong to about the same period (A.D. 1650), treat of the two systems together. The syncretic spirit exhibited in these works is much older and may be traced as early as Vātsyāyana,[2] whose bhāṣya is the earliest extant commentary on the *Sūtra* of Gautama. But a formal synthesis of the two systems does not appear till about the tenth century, when works like the *Sapta-padārthī* of Śivāditya began to appear. Besides these two stages in the history of the systems, we may also perhaps note a third when the Nyāya-Vaiśeṣika as representing an independent world-view was practically ignored and it became reduced as mere logic to a position ancillary to the study of philosophy in general and of the Vedānta in particular. There are certain marked differences in the doctrine as taught in the two schools and in the several periods of its history. We shall, as we proceed, draw attention to the more important among them. The word 'Vaiśeṣika' is derived from viśeṣa,[3] which means 'difference,' and the doctrine is so designated because, according to it, diversity and not unity is at the root of the universe. The word 'Nyāya' is commonly understood as meaning 'argumentation' (literally 'going back'). It indicates the method followed in the system which is predominantly intellectualistic and analytical; and the fact is borne out by the other designa-

[1] See Note 3 on p. 183. [2] Cf. I. i. 9.
[3] Pāṇini. V. iv. 34. See ERE. vol. xii. p. 570.

tions like hetu-vidyā or 'the science of causes' which are sometimes applied to it. It is this characteristic that accounts for the special attention paid in the system to questions of formal logic, with which it is in fact ordinarily confounded. Thus the compound designation 'Nyāya-Vaiśeṣika' refers to the method followed in the system as also to the result finally reached, viz. pluralistic realism. Of the chronological relation of the two doctrines it is difficult to say anything definite. Speaking of the systems, as distinguished from the *Sūtras* in which their teaching is embodied, we may perhaps state that the Vaiśeṣika is the older of the two.

The literature of the Nyāya-Vaiśeṣika is next in extent only to that of the Vedānta. We can mention here only a few of the outstanding works. The *Vaiśeṣika-sūtra* of Kaṇāda is in ten chapters, each of which is divided into two sections. Though aiming chiefly at the explanation of the various categories recognized in the system, the treatise incidentally refers to several problems of general philosophic interest. The earliest extant commentary upon it is that of Praśastapāda, known as the bhāṣya, which probably belongs to the fifth century A.D. But it does not in its exposition follow the order of the sūtras. It is a 'restatement rather than a commentary'; and in restating the position of the school, it considerably develops it. For instance the clear formulation of the doctrine of creation with God as creator is found for the first time in it in the history of the Vaiśeṣika school. On account of such developments, the work is to be looked upon more as an independent authority on the doctrine than as a commentary. It has been expounded by several writers of whom Udayana and Śrīdhara, both contemporaries, are the most important. Of them Udayana (A.D. 984) is the more celebrated, particularly on account of his *Kusumāñjali*, which has become a classic of Indian theism. His commentary is known as the *Kiraṇāvalī* while Śrīdhara's bears the title of *Kandalī*. Both give a most lucid exposition of the Vaiśeṣika doctrine. The *Upaskāra* of Saṁkara Miśra (A.D. 1650) is a commentary on the *Sūtra* in the common acceptation of that term, but owing to the lateness of its author it cannot always be regarded as faithful to the original. The *Nyāya-sūtra* of Gautama is in five chapters each of which again is divided into two sections. Its bhāṣya is by Vātsyāyana (A.D. 400), who mentions still earlier Naiyāyikas, from whose views he dissents.[1] It seems to have been unfavourably criticized by the eminent Buddhist thinker Diṅnāga and was defended against him by one described as Uddyotakara ('the illuminator') in his *Vārtika*. Uddyotakara probably belongs to the reign of Harṣavardhana (A.D. 608–648) and may have been patronized by that sovereign. This work has been explained in the *Tātparya-tīkā* by Vācaspati (A.D. 841), who, though a follower of the Advaita, has written works of authority on all the systems. This work in its turn has been commented upon by Udayana, already mentioned, in his *Tātparya-ṭīkā-pariśuddhi*. One more writer whom we may name is Jayanta Bhaṭṭa, of doubtful date, whose *Nyāya-mañjarī*, though professing only to be a commentary on a select few of Gautama's sūtras, is a rich store-house of information on Indian philosophic thought as it was known in his time. This concludes the 'old' or prācīna phase of the history of the Nyāya. Its 'new' or the navya phase[2] commences about the twelfth century with the epoch-making *Tattva-cintāmaṇi* of Gaṅgeśa of Eastern Bengal (A.D. 1200). This great work gradually threw into the shade the earlier ones, including the two *Sūtras*, and it is only in recent years that they have been restored to their legitimate place in the study of the system, through the awakening of interest in India's past. In Gangeśa, it has been said, the logic of the Nyāya attains its final shape. The study of the system as representing an independent philosophic doctrine thereafter declines. But what was lost in one direction was gained in another, for the new Nyāya influenced all the other schools of philosophy. It helped especially the cultivation of precision in thought as well as in expression. But discussions came to be confined more and more to matters of detail, and formal perfection

[1] Cf. I. i. 32.

[2] Neither of the words prācīna and navya, as applied to the doctrine, always refers to the same stage in its history. What is spoken of as 'new' at one stage may be 'old' at another.

became the chief object of attainment. However acute these discussions and whatever their value as means of mental discipline, they must be pronounced as for the most part philosophically barren. They are subtle rather than profound. Several commentaries and sub-commentaries on the *Tattva-cintāmaṇi* have been written. It will suffice to mention here those of Vāsudeva Sārvabhauma (A.D. 1500), the first of what is called the 'Nuddea school' of logicians and of Raghunātha Śiromaṇi—his pupil along with Caitanya, the renowned Bengali religious teacher. Raghunātha's commentary on Gangeśa's work, which is the best of its class, is known as the *Dīdhiti*. Gadādhara, who belonged to the same school, commented upon it; and it is his commentary in its various sections or Vādas that has since become the staple of advanced study in schools that teach Nyāya not only in Bengal, but all over the country. Gadādhara has been described as the prince of Indian schoolmen. Roughly speaking he lived in the same time as Lord Bacon whose denunciations of scholasticism, as a modern writer observes, may be 'most appositely illustrated by extracts from Gadādhara's writings.' Amongst the numerous manuals treating of the system, we have already mentioned the two most important—the *Tarka-saṁgraha* and the *Kārikāvalī*, which have been explained by the authors themselves in the *Dīpikā* and the *Siddhānta-muktāvalī* respectively.

I

The system starts with the postulate that all knowledge by its very nature points to an object beyond it and independent of it.[1] These objects, it is added, are independent not only of knowledge, but also of one another, whence the doctrine may be described as pluralistic realism. But by this description we should not assume that the data of knowledge are all disconnected. The multifarious things of experience are divisible into certain classes of which one called dravya, or 'substance,' as it is commonly translated in English, is

[1] Na cāviṣayā kācidupalabdhiḥ: NSB. IV. i. 32.

the most important. The dravyas are nine in number—(1) 'earth' (pṛthivī), (2) 'water' (ap), (3) 'fire' (tejas), (4) 'air' (vāyu), (5) ākāśa, (6) 'time' (kāla), (7) 'space' (dik), (8) the 'self' (ātman) and (9) manas; and they, together with their various properties and relations, explain the whole universe. They are all ultimate, and as such are either infinite or infinitesimal, the system viewing things made up of parts as necessarily transient. The dravyas are not all material so that the Nyāya-Vaiśeṣika is not, like the Cārvāka, materialistic. At the same time the doctrine treats all dravyas alike; and even the self, it regards, is one object among others possessing properties, exhibiting relations, and knowable like them. It will be best to begin our account by describing the nine dravyas:

(1) to (4) *'Earth,' 'Water,' 'Fire'* and *'Air.'*—By these four, we should not here understand the discrete things of common experience bearing those names, but their ultimate material causes which are supra-sensible—the atoms (paramāṇus) which are partless and eternal. Objects like a jar are constituted out of or derived from such atoms. They come into being and pass out of it. The exact manner in which they are produced, we shall explain presently.

(5) *Ākāśa.*—This and the four dravyas just mentioned are together known as 'elements' (bhūtas); but, while the latter are found in two forms—primary and secondary—ākāśa appears only in one form. It is partless and infinite and does not, therefore, produce anything as the infinitesimal atoms of the other elements do.

(6) and (7): *Time* and *Space.*—These are conceived as objective realities; and they are infinite and partless like ākāśa. Time cannot be measured except indirectly by means that possess parts, e.g. the movements of the sun. Similarly space cannot be defined except by reference to determinate objects, say, the pole star. In other words, time and space are not of atomic structure; and points and instants are conventional divisions of them. The primary dravyas are not in time and space while all secondary or derivative objects like the jar necessarily are in them. Space, it should be added, is not the same as ākāśa. The latter stands

here for what fills space—some ethereal substance of which sound is supposed to be the distinctive quality.[1] Ākāśa is, in fact, postulated solely to account for it, which as a quality requires a substance to abide in. Its affinity with the first four dravyas is shown by its being grouped along with them under elements.

(8) *Self.*—It is many, each being regarded as omnipresent and eternal. Though theoretically present everywhere the feelings, thoughts and volitions of a self are confined to the physical organism with which it is, for the time being, associated. So, for all practical purposes, the self is where it acts. A peculiar feature of the system is that it makes jñāna or knowledge an attribute of the self, and that too, not an essential, but only an adventitious one. Its adventitious character is taken to be shown by dreamless sleep where the self is supposed to endure without being characterized by knowledge. The self thus differs from matter only in that it *may* become conscious and not in that it is itself mental in nature. Two other attributes of it, viz. desire (icchā) and volition (yatna), are conceived more or less similarly. They, like knowledge, refer to an object (saviṣayaka) and are meaningless without such reference. The really mental or spiritual element in the doctrine accordingly is not the self, but these three attributes which are all transient. Our own self we know directly; but the selves of others can be known only indirectly through their behaviour, etc.[2] Whether it be our own self or that of another, we never know it by itself, but always as the subject of which something is predicated, e.g. 'I am pleased,' 'He is hungry.'

(9) *Manas.*—This is atomic and eternal but, unlike the first four dravyas, does not give rise to any product. Each self has its own manas, which is merely an instrument of knowing and is therefore as inert as any other sense. It is consequently incorrect to translate it as 'mind.' The really mental element in the system, as we have just said, is different. But the co-operation of the manas is a necessary condition of all knowledge whether it refers to external objects or internal states. The fact that occasionally,

[1] Cf. NV. III. i. 72.

[2] SM. p. 209.

though our eyes and ears are open, we do not see or hear has been made the basis for concluding that there should be a different and common aid to all knowledge which the system terms manas.[1] Sometimes we purposely look at a watch, for example; but we do not yet see the time, for our manas has meanwhile come to be otherwise occupied. It may thus be described as exercising a double function: It helps the self in acquiring knowledge, but at the same time acts as a check upon it by narrowing its field to a single object or a single group of objects. It is through the manas that the relation of the self to the senses and the body is established; and through them the self comes to be related to the external world. Association with it is, indeed, the basic cause of bondage[2]; for though the body and the senses also accompany the transmigrating self, they are, unlike the manas, completely renewed at every birth.

The dravyas do not by themselves explain the whole universe. They serve merely as its framework; and we should now refer to their various properties and the relations into which they may enter. In other words, we have now to consider the categories other than dravya. By the term 'category' (padārtha) here we have to understand, with one exception alone to which we shall soon draw attention, the several groups or classes into which objects can be divided and not mere modes of predication. They are guṇa, karma, sāmānya, viśeṣa, samavāya and abhāva; and, together with dravya, they constitute the seven categories of the Vaiśeṣika, which are also accepted in the Nyāya.[3] Originally only six of them appear to have been recognized,[4] the last, viz. abhāva, being unknown. We have already spoken about dravya; and we shall now say a few words about each of the remaining six:—

Guṇa ('Quality').—These are attributes which pertain to one or more dravyas and do not, as in Buddhism, by themselves stand for a thing. Though thus dependent upon dravya, they are conceived as altogether distinct from it; for they can by themselves be known and as such must, according to

[1] NS. I. i. 16.
[2] Bandha-nimittam manaḥ: NM. p. 499.
[3] NSB. I. i. 9.
[4] *Vaiśeṣika-sūtra*, I. i. 4.

the doctrine,[1] be independent realities. They are what they are in complete independence of everything, including the dravyas to which they belong; but they are not necessarily eternal.[2] Yet being simple and not further analysable, they are placed among the fundamental components of the universe. Another important feature is that none of these is explained as subjective, the system viewing as self-contradictory the explanation of some entities as subjective and others as objective. The guṇas have been enumerated as twenty-four, which include not only material qualities, but also the mental that are referred to a distinct centre, the self. The arbitrary number at which they have been fixed clearly shows the rather conventional nature of the category. It is not necessary to mention them all, as their significance is more scientific than philosophical. We may merely notice in passing that, while several of these qualities such as magnitude (parimāṇa) are common to two or more dravyas, a few characterize or serve as the special mark of only a single dravya. The latter are known as 'specific qualities' (veśeṣa-guṇa). They are odour, of earth; flavour, of water; colour, of fire; touch, of air; and sound, of ākāśa.[3] These, it will be seen, are the so-called secondary qualities; and the doctrine not only takes them as quite real, but also considers consistently with its pluralistic standpoint that the true nature of dravyas is revealed by the qualities in which they differ rather than by those in which they agree. Of the remaining dravyas, only one, viz. the self, has specific qualities to which we shall refer later.

Karma ('Action').—This represents various kinds of movement whose relation to the dravya in which alone they are found is exactly the same as that of the guṇas, and whose independent reality also should be understood as in their case. The significance of recognizing it as a distinct category is that the doctrine admits stability as a possible charac-

[1] Pratīti-bhedāt bhedosti: NM. p. 312.

[2] They are eternal when they belong to dravyas that are so. Nitya-gatam nityam; anitya-gatam'anityam: TS. p. 16.

[3] See SM. st. 90–2. Pṛthivī possesses also flavour, touch and colour; ap, touch and colour; and tejas, touch.

teristic of reality. In this it differs from some other doctrines, e.g. the Sāṅkhya, which has no conception of static objects at all in the physical world. Infinite dravyas are always stable, for the doctrine recognizes only change of place (parispanda), but not change of form (pariṇāma); atomic and finite dravyas may or may not be moving.

Sāmānya ('Universal').—The manifold entities, so far alluded to, are reducible to types. There is order in them which is due to objective features and is not imported into them by the perceiving mind. It is by virtue of this order that objects are divisible not only into the three classes of dravya, guṇa and karma, but also into sub-classes like cows, redness or flying. It is necessary to caution the student against taking sāmānya as the equivalent of 'genus.' It stands for merely a feature or property common to two or more things and not like genus for a class of things exhibiting such a feature. The category dravya includes jars, cloths, etc., but the sāmānya of dravyatva which characterizes every dravya does not include the lower sāmānyas of 'jar-ness' (ghaṭatva), 'cloth-ness' (paṭatva), etc. The term sāmānya may be better rendered by the word 'universal,' without, however, suggesting a complete resemblance to the Platonic 'idea.'[1] It is in all and in each; and yet it is not different in different particulars. Thus cow-ness is one and unanalysable. It always subsists, but it can be apprehended not by itself but only through a particular cow. Though appearing together, cow and cow-ness are conceived as two distinct entities.[2] Of these universals, sattā or Being is the highest, for it is found to characterize the largest number of entities; and the others follow it in a descending order, like dravyatva, pṛthivītva and ghaṭatva; guṇatva and śuklatva; and so forth, each characterizing less and less numerous things.

We find the keenest controversy raging round this conception. Some, like the Jains, admit a basis for it in the

[1] For instance, the particulars are not here viewed as copies of the universal.

[2] We are here taking into consideration only the more important variety of sāmānya known as jāti. There is also recognized another variety called upādhi, e.g. 'blue-potness' (nīla-ghaṭatva) or 'cap-wearing.' The description given above does not apply to it.

outer world, but they do not elevate it to the rank of a universal. Cow-ness for instance stands for something objective, but it is for them only a special disposition of pudgala which disappears with the cow in which it is found.[1] The Buddhists on the other hand deny it altogether, explaining it away as merely ideal (p. 204). What is there for instance, they ask, that is common to a mountain and a mustard seed which are both classified as 'earth'? They point out that its admission in the Nyāya-Vaiśeṣika sense leads to all sorts of absurdities. First of all, it involves the difficulty of accounting satisfactorily for the presence of the one in the many. Again we cannot say whether the so-called universal abides everywhere (sarva-sarva-gata) or is confined only to the respective particulars (vyakti-sarva-gata). In the former case only chaos would be the result, because a cow would then be characterized not only by cow-ness, but also by horse-ness, etc., which are everywhere by supposition; in the latter, it would be difficult to account for its sudden appearance in a new particular which springs into existence at a spot where the universal in question was not found previously and whereto it could not have moved from the place in which it was, being by hypothesis incapable of movement. The Buddhist admits that we do regard certain things as similar rather than others; but that, in his opinion, is due to a subjective interference and has to be explained negatively as signifying their difference from the rest without implying any actual agreement, contrast being sufficient for knowing things. When we describe an animal as a cow, we do not mean to assert cow-ness of it as a positive predicate; we rather deny of it horse-ness and such other features.[2] The main part of the Nyāya-Vaiśeṣika answer to such objections is that they are based upon a spatial view of universals—that they are *located* in the particular. But the particular is not the seat of the universal; it is only the means of revealing it (vyañjaka), so that we may view it as being everywhere or only where the corresponding particulars are.[3]

[1] See *Parīkṣā-mukha-sūtra*, iv. 4.

[2] Cf. SDS. pp. 13–14.

[3] NM. pp. 312–13.

Viśeṣa ('Individuality').—This is the differentia of ultimate things which are otherwise alike. Thus two atoms of earth or two selves in their intrinsic form resemble each other in every respect and if they should still be two, there must be a distinctive feature in each. That feature is its viśeṣa. The need for it arises only in the case of such objects as cannot be distinguished otherwise; and they are ultimate entities like those we have just mentioned. Two jars may be exactly alike in size, colour, etc., but they can be distinguished from each other by means of the separateness of the material out of which they are made. So it is not necessary to assume viśeṣas in their case. Nor is it incumbent to seek their aid in distinguishing even ultimate entities like an earth-atom and a water-atom, for the difference in the qualities that characterize them is sufficient for the purpose. The question will of course now arise as to how the viśeṣas differ from one another. To this there is no more satisfactory answer forthcoming than that they differentiate not only the ultimate entities to which they belong, but also themselves (svato-vyāvartaka). This category has been given up by the later followers of the doctrine.[1]

Samavāya ('Necessary Relation').—We have mentioned that relations in this system are conceived as real. They are generally included in guṇas,[2] but there is one relation which is elevated to the rank of an independent category. It is samavāya which may be described as an intimate relation, for the separation of the relata connected by it necessarily implies the destruction of one at least of them. Such relata are described as ayuta-siddha, which means that of them one is invariably found associated with the other. There are five types of ayuta-siddha objects, which alone admit of samavāya relation. They are (1) dravya and guṇa, (2) dravya

[1] See Prof. Keith: *Indian Logic and Atomism*, p. 196 n. We have not taken into account the view of the *Sūtra* in regard to sāmānya and viśeṣa about which there is some ambiguity.

[2] For example, 'priority' (aparatva). Strictly, however, there is only one relation included in the guṇas, viz. saṁyoga, which is parallel to samavāya. These are the only two cases in which one of the relata can be described as being in the other.

and karma, (3) particular and universal, (4) ultimate things and viśeṣa and (5) whole and parts or, as the same may otherwise be put, material cause and product. It will be observed that in one case, viz. the last, both the relata are dravyas and in another, viz. the third, neither may be a dravya, for guṇas and karmas also, as conceived here, are particulars and reveal universals. The necessity for this category arises from the pluralistic postulate of the system, which takes 'distinguishable' as equivalent to 'different.' If a dravya be altogether distinct from its attributes, the particular from the universal, the material cause from the effect and they are yet found together, they must be related; and the relation itself must be unique since one at least of these in each pair does not exist apart from the other. In order to get a clear view of this relation it is necessary to contrast it with the parallel conception of saṁyoga ('conjunction') which is classed under the category of guṇa and is an occasional or separable connection. Saṁyoga obtains only between dravyas while samavāya, as we have seen, may or may not. While again samavāya is only between relata that are never found separate, samyoga is between normally separate (yuta-siddha) things. Two objects now in conjunction must once have been separate and may again be separated, the nature of the objects in either case remaining unaffected by the process. For this reason, viz. that it makes no difference to the relata, saṁyoga should be taken as an external relation. Even samavāya, it is necessary to add, has to be explained as an external relation, although it is usual to represent it as internal in modern works on the Nyāva-Vaiśeṣika. To take it so would be to go against the very spirit of the doctrine which views the relata involved in the one case quite as distinct as those in the other. One of the relata here, no doubt, is never found apart from the other. That, however, is no disproof of its distinctness. The reason why while one of them can exist without the other, the other cannot do so is that it becomes related to its correlate *as it comes to be*. We should not think that redness, for example, comes to characterize the rose *after* that colour has sprung into existence. Its origination is simultaneous with its relation.[1] In other words, unlike saṁyoga which is adventitious or contingent, samavāya is necessary, though the necessity is only one-sided. The red colour presupposes the rose (say), but the reverse does not hold good, because the rose may, according to the theory, exist out of this relation even though it be, as it is stated, but for one instant.[2] Hence when we describe samavāya as an external relation, it is not in the sense that both its terms are equally independent as in saṁyoga, but only one.[3]

Abhāva ('Negation').—This is a later addition, and the addition is the result of working out in full the realistic hypothesis of the system. If all knowledge points to something outside it, so also should the knowledge of negation do and imply its existence apart from such knowledge. As in the positive sphere, here also knowledge must be different from the known.[4] In other words, absence of an object is not the same as the knowledge of its absence. By abhāva, however, we should understand only the negation of something somewhere and not absolute nothing (śūnya) which the Nyāya-Vaiśeṣika dismisses as unthinkable or as a pseudo-idea. We may speak of the negation of a jar or of cloth in a room or on a table, but never of negation itself. Accordingly this category, unlike others, is relative in its conception. It represents in reality what corresponds to the predicate in a negative judgment—'the lotus is *not* blue'—and so far is an exception to the sense in which the term 'category' is to be understood in the system. Four varieties of negation are enumerated: In the case of a jar there is first the 'antecedent non-existence' or 'prior negation' (prāgabhāva) before the object is made and there is only the clay or, as it is usually put, the two halves (kapāla) of it. This variety of negation is

[1] Jātaḥ saṁbaddhaśca ityekaḥ kālaḥ: NV. II. i. 33.

[2] Cf. TSD. pp. 4 and 7: Utpannam dravyam kṣaṇam aguṇam akriyākam ca tiṣṭhati.

[3] For a further discussion of this topic see *Proceedings of the Indian Philosophical Congress*, vol. iii. pp. 159–66.

[4] Compare: ' "Socrates is not living" must have an objective fact as its basis. This is a *negative fact*. If the correspondence theory of Truth is to work, "negative facts" must be admitted'—Bertrand Russell.

obviously beginningless, but comes to an end when the object in question is produced. When again the jar is destroyed leaving only the potsherd behind, there is 'subsequent non-existence' or 'posterior negation' (dhvaṁsābhāva). It has a beginning, but is endless, since the identical jar will never again come into being. It should be added that these two negations characterize the clay and the potsherd respectively, but are not identical with them. The third variety, known as 'absolute or total negation' (atyantābhāva), we have when there is the bare ground with no jar on it. Though really temporal it is for certain technical reasons, into which it is not necessary to enter here, regarded as eternal. The last variety is mutual negation (anyonyābhāva) which is only another word for distinction (bheda) between two objects each having its own identity and which finds expression in judgments like 'The jar is not cloth,' 'A is not B.' It is, of course, eternal owing to the law of identity.

We have seen that the first four dravyas have a two-fold form as atoms and as discrete objects originating from them. How are the latter derived? The answer to this is found in the Nyāya-Vaiśeṣika atomic theory. The first point of importance about it is that, unlike the Jaina theory (p. 162), it admits a qualitative distinction among the ultimate particles of matter, so that the atoms of any particular element can give rise only to products of that element. Commonly, no doubt, it is thought that more than one element may enter into the making of objects. But, according to the Nyāya-Vaiśeṣika, it is wrong to think so. The human body, for instance, is the product, in the strict sense of the term, of pṛthivī atoms only and not of the other elements also, like water, though they are found in it. It is the belief that there is difference in the manner in which dravyas may come together which is at the bottom of the conception of samavāya. When dravyas of the same kind are brought together so as to give rise to a new product, there is saṁyoga as well as samavāya; when, on the other hand, there is no such product but merely an aggregate, there is only saṁyoga—whether the dravyas coming together are the same or are different in kind. In deciding what is new, the system is guided solely by the common-sense view (pratīti). Aggregation and production do not, as one might think, correspond to mechanical combination and organic growth, for the Nyāya-Vaiśeṣika explains a piece of cloth also which is only mechanically produced as involving samavāya, exactly like a tree that grows from a seed. When a piece of cloth is woven, we have in it the threads in conjunction; and, *over and above* the conjoined threads, the cloth which has come into being afresh. It is this new product that is in samavāya relation with the threads. But in a bundle of threads there is only saṁyoga, for no fresh product, as commonly understood, results therefrom. All the material things of common experience are supposed to have been produced in this manner and are to be taken as new. This view of causation, which signifies that new things can be added to those already in existence, is known as ārambha-vāda ('doctrine of new creation'). It is also termed asat-kārya-vāda ('doctrine of non-existent effect') because it maintains that the effect, once non-existent, comes into being afterwards. This does not mean that it can exist apart from the cause. The effect inheres in the material cause as a quality may be said to do in a substance. The second point to be noticed in the theory is that all such products are impermanent.[1] That is, the asat-kārya-vāda signifies not only that the non-existent comes to be, but that an existent product sooner or later also ceases to be. In contrast to Buddhism, it is maintained here that nothing can last for less than two instants[2]—those of origination and persistence, so that a product can disappear at the earliest only in the third instant after it is made. Lastly, all such products necessarily abide in two or more dravyas. The insistence that produced things are not only in time and space but also abide in dravyas is noteworthy. When we remember that guṇas and karmas also—whether produced or not—are so by their very nature,

[1] Utpannam nirudhyate: NSB. i. 29.

[2] This limitation applies also to what falls under the other categories and is produced. Jñāna, for instance, lasts only for two instants (SM. p. 425).

we see that the world as a product is in its entirety dependent upon the permanent dravyas. The doctrine does not admit of our using the term 'phenomena'; but if we might use it, we could describe the permanent dravyas as the ground of all phenomena. The universe thus consists of (1) a primary one that subsists always which was never made and will never be destroyed—the various kinds of atoms, the other dravyas like the selves, the universals and so forth; and (2) a derivative one which is dependent on it and which is the world we ordinarily know. This theory, by the way, makes an attempt at solving the well-known problem of change. The solution is that there is really no change in the sense of successive modifications within the unity of a thing. There are certain things that never change, and it is the transient things which they give rise to that explain our notion of change. The solution is thus different from the two we are so far familiar with—the Buddhistic one that change is total and perpetual (p. 211) and the Jaina one (p. 161) that it takes place in an enduring substance.[1]

The existence of the atoms is deduced from the known divisibility of perceivable material objects—a divisibility which, it is said, must terminate at some stage; for, if all objects be alike divisible indefinitely, it would be difficult to account for the observed variations of magnitude in them. The terminal stage in this process of division gives the atoms which are the uncaused cause of all that is transient in the material universe. They are simple and partless and their size is infinitesimal so that their presence in ākāśa does not interfere with its all-pervading nature. They have neither an exterior nor an interior; and their number in each of the four classes is infinite. The process of origination of objects is as follows: Two atoms of earth (say) come together and the resulting binary compound (dvyaṇuka), like the primary atoms constituting it, is infinitely small (aṇu) in size and therefore supersensuous. Three such binaries,[2] suitably adjusted, produce a triad (tryaṇuka) which is identified with the dust mote we see dancing in the sun-beam and is

[1] Kṣaṇa-bhaṅga-pariṇāmayoḥ nirāsāt: *Upaskāra*, VII. ii. 9.

[2] There are also other views in this respect.

taken as the minimum visible entity. Its magnitude is finite and all other finite objects are made out of such triads. To the question how the finiteness of the triad arises from the infinitesimal size of the atoms, the answer given is that it is due to the *number* of the constituent atoms and not to their magnitude as in the case of common things. This is, however, a point which is not very clear, and has accordingly been severely criticized by the adherents of the other doctrines.[1] When material things from binary compounds onward are produced, their qualities also are produced, their nature being determined by the qualities of the respective causal substances. Thus the whiteness of a cloth is effectuated by the whiteness of the threads woven into that cloth. Not only is the whiteness of the cloth different from the cloth, it is also equally different from the whiteness of the threads, so that there are several whitenesses. They are, as already pointed out, the particular instances of white colour which all exhibit the universal 'white-ness' (śuklatva). The only other aspect of the world of things that can be produced is karma. In this case also many particulars are recognized of each variety, so that the flying of one bird (say) is not the same as that of another though both belong to the same class. The process of destruction, which is the reverse of that of creation, is somewhat differently explained by the old and the new exponents of the doctrine.[2] According to the former, a jar for example is destroyed one instant after the destruction of the halves (kapāla) out of which it is made. The only exception to this order is in the case of the very first product, viz. the binary compound. The material cause of it being indestructible, the destruction of the effect is explained as brought about by the mere disjunction of the atoms constituting it. There is in this view the difficulty of satisfactorily explaining the continuance, for however short a time it may be, of the effect after its material cause is gone. To avoid this difficulty as well as to secure uniformity of explanation, the later exponents hold the disjunction of the several parts of the material cause as throughout the cause, so that the disappearance of the material cause, where it

[1] See e.g. Śaṁkara on VS. II. ii. 11.

[2] TSD. p. 10.

takes place at all, is subsequent to the destruction of the effect.

In connection with this theory we have to draw attention to the idea of God in the system. There are no references to it in the *Sūtra* of Kaṇāda, though commentators profess to find them there. Gautama makes only a casual mention of God, and some have doubted whether the Nyāya was originally theistic. But both Praśastapāda and Vātsyāyana recognize God[1] and the belief later becomes a well-established part of the doctrine. Śrīdhara for instance tries to prove God's existence; and Udayana, as already noted, gives what has come to be regarded as a classical exposition of the problem and its solution. While this is the historical position, logically the teaching undoubtedly stands in need of an all-powerful Being that can initiate the process of world-production.[2] It is possible that this necessary implication of the doctrine as first conceived was developed and made explicit by Vātsyāyana and others. The God that is recognized is classed under ātman and described as paramātman to distinguish him from the jīvātman or the individual self. He, like the other ātmans, is omnipresent and eternal; but while consciousness and related attributes may or may not characterize the jīvātman always, they do so characterize God. His knowledge is not only eternal but also universal and perfect. He can desire and will, but unlike the jīva has no pain or pleasure[3] and is devoid of evil desire or hate. He is regarded as responsible for the creation of the universe, by which expression we must understand here only suitable dispositions of the primary objects—atoms, etc., though according to the view of causation held in the school the dispositions themselves give rise to new things. God not only creates but also protects and in due course destroys the world, but only to create it again. The guiding factor in the whole process is the past karma of the beings that are to play their part on the stage of the world in the particular kalpa. It is difficult to say whether we have here the conception of a

[1] NSB. IV. i. 21; PB. pp. 48–9. [2] See Śaṁkara: VS. II. ii. 12.

[3] NSB. pp. 200–1. Some of the later exponents, with their Vedāntic bias, ascribe eternal bliss to God. See *Dinakarīya* on SM. p. 467.

personal God; but the voluntary agency ascribed to him would indicate that the notion of personality is not altogether excluded. No doubt, God here cannot be described as conceived in man's image, yet he is styled ātman which does suggest some kinship of nature with man. One special point about God as understood here is that his existence is established through inference and not through revelation as in the Vedānta. The doctrine thus gives prominence to reason here as elsewhere in accordance with its generally rationalistic spirit. If we exclude those[1] that are based upon the special postulates of the system, the arguments are of a commonplace character and their consideration need not detain us long. We shall merely note the chief of them as set forth by Udayana. They are: (1) the world is an effect and like all other effects points, among other causes, to an efficient cause or agent who is by knowledge as well as power equal to the task of creating it; (2) there is observed in the created world physical order which indicates a controller or law-giver; and (3) the moral government of the world implies a governor who dispenses justice in accordance with desert. We may also refer to one other argument which is somewhat out of the way. In trying to establish the existence of God, Udayana takes full advantage of the lack of any proof to the contrary. He devotes one whole chapter out of the five in the *Kusumāñjali* to the examination of this point and shows how none of the pramāṇas can be adduced to make out that God does not exist. This is no doubt a point of only dialectical value; but it cannot be denied that it has some force, especially against those that make much of the opposite fact that the existence of God can never be proved.

It is necessary to say a few words now about the notion of 'cause' in the system. The cause should be antecedent to the effect, i.e. should exist in the just previous instant. It should also be an invariable antecedent (niyata-pūrva-vṛtti). This description, however, is too wide, for it includes in any particular case several factors which cannot be regarded as causes. Thus when a jar is being made, there is

[1] See for instances, Prof. Keith: *op. cit.*, p. 268.

the sound produced by the play of the staff on the clay; but, though an invariable antecedent, it can by no stretch of imagination be taken as the cause of the jar. Hence exclusions are made, which are technically termed anyathā-siddhas, to render the definition of cause accurate. Whatever answers to the description of 'invariable antecedent' after such exclusions are made is a cause of the effect in question. The exclusions are stated to be of five kinds, but the distinction between them is vague and indefinite and they can all be brought under one head and described as 'conditional factors' as J. S. Mill does. One or two instances will suffice to indicate the general nature of the five-fold scheme of anyathā-siddhas: (1) the attributes of a cause are not causes, e.g. the colour of the staff in respect of the jar is not a cause, while the staff itself is; (2) the cause of a cause also is not to be regarded as a cause. To give the standing example, the father of the potter is not a cause, though the potter is. It is clear that these are 'conditional,' since their invariable antecedence is dependent upon that of others, viz. the staff and the potter respectively. All positive effects are regarded in the other systems as having two sets of causes—one the material cause (upādāna-kāraṇa) and the other the efficient cause (nimitta-kāraṇa). But here, while the efficient cause is retained in the same form, the place of the material cause is taken by two, known as the samavāyi and the asamavāyi kāraṇas, in consonance with the view that a substance is different from its attributes. The samavāyi-kāraṇa is invariably a dravya; and the asamavāyi-kāraṇa, a guṇa or karma. Accordingly the Nyāya-Vaiśeṣika speaks of three causes instead of only two for a positive effect. In the case of cloth, say, the threads—a dravya—are the samavāyi-kāraṇa, and the saṁyoga or conjunction between them—a guṇa—the asamavāyi-kāraṇa. In the case of the whiteness of the cloth, the cloth itself is the first kind of cause and the whiteness of the threads the second, it being believed that the whiteness is produced in it one instant after the cloth has come into being. For a negative effect neither of these is required, but only the efficient cause, as for example a stick in breaking a jar.

We may now call attention to an important difference in the general standpoint of the two systems considered separately. The Vaiśeṣika views the world from the ontological standpoint while the Nyāya does so from the epistemological. This will be clear from the nature of the categories acknowledged in the two systems. We have described the seven padārthas of the Vaiśeṣika. The Nyāya recognizes sixteen padārthas; and all the seven of the Vaiśeṣika are included in but one of them—prameya or 'the knowable,' the second of the sixteen. The first category is pramāṇa. These two terms—pramāṇa and prameya—are sufficient to make clear the specific view-point of the Nyāya. It does not concern itself with things as such, but rather with how they are known or demonstrated. This should not be taken to mean that the Nyāya felt any doubt as regards the independent existence of objects. It admitted their independent reality as readily as the sister system, but it felt that knowledge might easily mislead us, and therefore set about investigating the laws of correct thought. This standpoint becomes clearer still from the nature of the remaining fourteen categories,[1] which are all serviceable either in the discovery of truth or in safeguarding it against irrational attacks. The aim of the Nyāya thus is first to win the field of truth and then to secure it with the fence[2] of dialectics against the encroachment of error and sophistry. The Nyāya is not accordingly mere logic, but also a theory underlying the art of controversy. The logical part seems at first to have been even overladen with dialectical devices, but having been relieved of much of this encumbrance it became fully prominent in course of time. Works like the *Nyāya-sāra* of Bhāsarvajña, exhibit this change by adopting a new classification of their subject-matter and treating of it under the four heads of perception, inference, verbal testimony

[1] These are saṁśaya (doubt), prayojana (aim), dṛṣṭānta (example), siddhānta (conclusion), avayava (members of the syllogism), tarka (hypothesis), nirṇaya (settlement), vāda (discussion), jalpa (wrangling), vitaṇḍā (cavilling), hetvābhāsa (fallacy), chala (fraud), jāti (wrong objection), and nigraha-sthāna (occasion for reproof).

[2] NS. IV. ii. 50. It is interesting to note that the same figure was used by the Stoics also.

and upamāna—all coming under pramāṇa, the first of Gautama's categories. The transformation is complete in Gaṅgeśa's *Tattva-cintāmaṇi* where the Nyāya becomes pre-eminently a pramāṇa-śāstra, casting off for the most part its features as a vāda-vidyā. The epistemological standpoint adopted from the beginning in the Nyāya thus comes to be emphasized and the dialectical character of Gautama's scheme, so far as it remains, is subordinated to it.

II

We have seen that in India psychology never succeeded in getting itself separated from philosophy. Accordingly each system has its own psychology which is coloured by its metaphysics. The Nyāya-Vaiśeṣika believes in a permanent self and makes consciousness, which it describes as the basis of all life's activity,[1] one of its possible attributes. In addition to this, five other specific attributes which the self may have, have a bearing upon psychology. They are, 'love' (rāga), 'aversion' (dveṣa), 'pleasure' (sukha), 'pain' (duḥkha) and 'volition' (yatna). Of these six attributes, jñāna and yatna correspond to cognition and conation; and the remaining four may be viewed as roughly representing what would now be described as the affective side of the mind. Love and hatred are the result of pleasure and pain respectively. We like things that have given us pleasure and dislike those we associate with pain. But while in modern psychology these three phases are not regarded as in reality separate and the mind is looked upon as a unity, in the Nyāya-Vaiśeṣika the distinction between them is taken to be fundamental. The three attributes of cognition, feeling and volition are in any specific case supposed to manifest themselves in the self in a particular order: first, knowledge; then, desire; and last, volition.[2] We have to know a thing before we can feel the want of it; and it is to satisfy that want that we will to act. Feeling thus mediates between cognition and conation. There is not much that is psychologically important which we find stated in the system about feeling and volition. It

[1] TS. p. 21.

[2] Jānāti icchati yatate.

contents itself with viewing them from the ethical standpoint, and we shall refer later to its view of them in that respect. The psychology of cognition, on the other hand, is very fully treated. Before describing it, it is necessary to call attention to the distinction between presentative cognition (anubhava) and representative cognition (smṛti). The former generally leaves behind a trace or impression called bhāvanā or saṁskāra which abides in the self and, when revived, leads to recollection of what was previously cognized. That is smṛti or memory. Such bhāvanā is a seventh specific quality of the self.

Presentative cognition may be broadly divided into two, viz. mediate and immediate, the manas being a necessary aid to both. The latter is termed pratyakṣa which may roughly be taken as equivalent to sensation and perception; and the former, such as inferential knowledge, is known as parokṣa which is based upon pratyakṣa and needs no further reference in this section. On the primary character of pratyakṣa is based its definition as knowledge which does not presuppose other knowledge. When we infer that there is fire on the hill, we should previously have observed smoke there, not to mention our acquaintance with the inductive relation between smoke and fire. But to cognize blueness, say, no such preliminary knowledge is necessary. That is, our first ideas are furnished by the senses. There is another definition which is more useful in understanding the psychology of perception. It states that it is knowledge which arises by contact of a sense-organ (indriya) with an object. Such contact is not the sole condition of perception, but it is its distinctive feature. The actual process is usually described as follows: The self comes into contact with the manas; the manas with the senses; and the senses with the object, when, if certain external conditions like the presence of sufficient light are satisfied, perception takes place.[1] It is obvious that the description applies only to cases involving voluntary attention; and the process is reversed when, for instance, a man waking from sleep perceives the things about him casually.[2] The word indriya here denotes not only the five organs of

[1] NSB. I. i. 4. [2] NS. II. i. 26.

sense as elsewhere in Indian philosophy, but also the manas. The last is the means of experiencing pain, pleasure, hunger, etc. Thus the manas is not only an aid in the acquisition of knowledge through the other senses; it is also a direct means of securing for the self the knowledge of certain internal states. The senses, excepting the manas which is both simple and ultimate, are explained here as derived from single elements (bhautika)—the sense of sight, from fire-atoms; the sense of taste, from water-atoms; the sense of touch, from air-atoms; and the sense of smell, from earth-atoms. The sense of hearing is ākāśa itself, but as delimited by the corresponding physical organ, the ear (karṇa-śaṣkuli). The principle underlying the explanation is that like only can affect like—since without kinship between a sense and its object its distinctive capacity cannot be satisfactorily accounted for. The organ of sight alone for example apprehends colour, for it alone is made of tejas-atoms whose characteristic quality is colour. This, by the way, is how the doctrine maintains the objective character of the secondary qualities—a point to which we have already alluded.

What are the kinds of objects that can be known through pratyakṣa? That some qualities and actions out of the seven categories are apprehended directly needs no special mention. But does pratyakṣa apprehend any of the objects falling under the remaining categories? Here the system holds certain peculiar views which we must now consider: (1) Realists commonly believe that the existence of substances is inferred or indirectly known after their attributes are perceived. The Nyāya-Vaiśeṣika considers that substances also are directly cognized. But not all the senses are capable of doing this. In regard to external substances, it is only the organs of sight and touch that can do so; and in regard to the internal, viz. the self, it is the manas. In other words, while all the indriyas can sense, some can perceive also. This position is not merely assumed; attempts are made to substantiate it by a reference to experiences like the following: 'I am now touching what I saw.' Here what the two senses are able to apprehend are clearly different, but yet an identity is experienced which is explained as referring to the underlying substance perceived alike in the two moments.[1] (2) We have seen in the previous section that the Nyāya-Vaiśeṣika views universals as distinct ontological entities. The means of apprehending them is identical with the means of apprehending the corresponding particulars so that when the latter are perceivable the former also are so. That is, some universals are directly apprehended. We perceive that a rose is red through the eye; and the same organ of sense is also able to show the universal red-ness (raktatva) characterizing the red colour. Again let us suppose that with the aid of touch we cognize that a certain animal is a cow; the same sense of touch gives us the idea of the universal cow-ness (gotva) also. (3) We are able to know directly not only dravyas and sāmānyas in addition to some guṇas and karmas, but also abhāva or negation provided it is of perceivable objects, the aid to it being the same sense-organ as is necessary for apprehending those objects. A jar is visible to the eye and its absence also is perceivable by the same sense-organ.[2] But atoms for example being supersensuous, their absence cannot be perceived but has to be inferred or known otherwise. The reason adduced in support of this view is that the apprehension of the absence of such objects is invariably preceded by the functioning of the respective organs of sense. Nobody for instance can say that there is no chair in a room without using his eye or some other appropriate sense-organ. We shall recur to this point when dealing with the Mīmāṁsā system which postulates a distinct pramāṇa for the knowledge of negation.

All these kinds of pratyakṣa are described as laukika or ordinary. The system recognizes a different variety of it also which it designates alaukika-pratyakṣa or transcendental perception. This is of three kinds: (1) We have stated that when a cow, say, is seen cow-ness also is seen in exactly the same manner. The range of pratyakṣa extends farther still, and with the aid of this knowledge of the universal cow-ness we are able to apprehend directly, it is

[1] NSB. I. i. 30.

[2] Yenendriyeṇa yā vyaktiḥ gṛhyate tenaivendriyeṇa tajjātiḥ tadabhāvopi gṛhyate.

said, but in a transcendental manner all the particular cows that exist now or ever existed or are going to exist, though only as belonging to that class. This knowledge of all the particulars falling under a universal when that universal itself becomes the object of perception is regarded as a case of alaukika-pratyakṣa. (2) Again when we see a rose at a distance we apprehend its redness, form, etc., directly; and we may also become conscious then of its fragrance by virtue of the impression left on our mind by a past experience of that quality in the rose. But the flower being by supposition too far from us we cannot ascribe it to ordinary perception. This is regarded as another case of alaukika-pratyakṣa. The psychological truth involved here is the familiar one that all percepts are partly presentative and partly representative. (3) The last variety is termed yogic perception. It brings man face to face with supersensuous objects like atoms, dharma, etc.; and its acquisition means the development of mystical power through a long course of discipline which is as much moral as mental. It is described as perception, though the senses do not co-operate in it, on account of the complete vividness of view which it is supposed to yield.

We have yet to draw attention to the distinction between savikalpaka and nirvikalpaka pratyakṣa. All perceptual knowledge, according to the doctrine, is expressible in the form of a judgment. Even what appears as an isolated percept really stands for a judgment—something predicated of something else. 'A horse' for example is equivalent to 'an object possessing the characteristic of horse-ness.' In other words, perception as familiarly known to us is complex in its character, and it is therefore described as determinate (savikalpaka). Now, according to the atomistic standpoint of the system, all complex things are explained as the result of a putting together of the simples constituting them. The complex of savikalpaka also is brought under this rule, and it is assumed that it presupposes necessarily simple or nirvikalpaka pratyakṣa, which presents the isolated object altogether uncharacterized.[1] Thus if at any time we cognize

[1] SM. p. 255.

that a cow is white, we must, it is assumed, necessarily have perceived previously a cow by itself, the whiteness by itself, and the relation of samavāya between them also by itself.[1] So the savikalpaka becomes a process of compounding units separately given and not one of 'discrimination within a mass.'[2] The fact of this preliminary cognition, however, it is admitted, is not a matter of which we become directly aware; it is only the result of logical deduction from a fundamental postulate of the system. The savikalpaka, on the other hand, is a matter of observation and is given in introspection. We become aware of it not as it arises, but later in a second knowledge termed anuvyavasāya ('after knowledge'). We first know the object; and then, if we choose, we may become conscious of this fact, i.e. of the self as characterized by the jñāna in question. That is inner perception or self-consciousness.

III

One of the distinguishing features of the doctrine is the belief that whatever is, is knowable. It not only asserts a reality outside knowledge, but also admits that it can be known. In fact, to say that anything is unknowable is equivalent in the system to denying it. According to this view, even knowledge can be known so that jñāna is not only about objects but also about itself. But it is *primarily* directed to the object which is therefore known before either the subject or knowledge is. The two latter are revealed together and later in self-consciousness or reflection upon experience (anuvyavasāya). Though thus the reality of the external world stands on its own footing, knowledge is necessarily the means of reaching to it: and that is how the problems of logic come to be considered in the system.

[1] The nirvikalpaka is not here restricted to the sva-lakṣaṇa as it is according to Buddhism. See p. 204 *ante*.

[2] In current expositions of the doctrine the preliminary knowledge, it is stated, need only refer to the viśeṣaṇa or attributive element: Viśiṣṭa-jñānam viśeṣaṇa-jñāna-janyam (TSD. p. 30. Cf. SM. p. 253). But a knowledge of the other constituents also seems once to have been thought necessary. See NM. pp. 93 and 95.

The Nyāya differs from the Vaiśeṣika in admitting two pramāṇas—verbal testimony (śabda) and comparison (upamāna)—in addition to perception and inference which alone the Vaiśeṣika, like Buddhism, allows. We shall now consider these pramāṇas in order:—

(1) *Perception* (pratyakṣa).—The psychological aspect of this variety of knowledge has been treated of already and we have here only to look at it from the logical side. The main point to realize about it is that the scope of the postulate that knowledge invariably points to a real object beyond itself is restricted to the nirvikalpaka. Its data can never be false, for we are then in direct contact with reality and get an immediate knowledge of it. An erroneous nirvikalpaka is a contradiction in terms. Error may, however, creep in when we relate two or more objects thus given in it, for though all the things we are thinking of may be severally there, the content of our knowledge as a complex may be false. In other words, it is the judgment with its synthetic character or the savikalpaka that is the subject of logic. If the complex content of our knowledge has a complex corresponding to it in the objective world, we have truth; otherwise error. Thus when one sees the conch to be yellow (pīta-śaṅkha) owing to one's jaundiced eye, the conch, the yellow colour, and the relation of samavāya are all facts of the objective world and are given at the nirvikalpaka level; but while the yellowness is not related to the conch by samavāya there, it appears so in knowledge. It is therefore an error. In the case of a red rose when it is cognized as such, the two schemes—the mental and the actual—agree; and we have therefore truth. While the three elements involved in judgment do not constitute in error a single complex whole in the objective world, they are thus perceived by us. In truth, on the other hand, they are not only thus perceived but are actually so. This explanation of error will have to be altered in a matter of detail when we take other examples. In the case of the yellow conch or the white crystal appearing red when placed in the vicinity of a red flower, the several elements constituting them are presented to the mind in the ordinary or laukika sense; but there are cases of error

in which it is not so, as in the stock example of shell-silver (śukti-rajata). Here also the doctrine maintains that not only the subject but also the predicative element is 'presented,' but the presentation is of the alaukika kind—the second variety of it, where the impression of a former experience serves as the means of re-presenting a thing to our mind. The silver is not here, but elsewhere. It is āpaṇastha ('in the shop'), as it is stated. Thus in such cases also, error is due to a wrong synthesis of presented objects only. The argument may appear specious, but all that is meant is that even the content of error has a complete objective basis, and what does not exist at all (asat) can never be known. What serves as the subject of an erroneous judgment ('this') is actually given; the predicate also *is*, though elsewhere and not here. This theory, which is directly opposed to the Mādhyamika view that the non-existent is perceived (asat-khyāti), is known as anyathā-khyāti, a term which indicates that the discrepancy found in error is in regard to the predicative element.[1]

It may be asked how the correspondence with reality, which is said to constitute truth, can be known. There can obviously be no direct testing of correspondence, for we cannot get outside of our knowledge. Hence the Nyāya-Vaiśeṣika proposes an objective or indirect test—through putting the knowledge in question to practice. If we doubt whether a thing we cognize as water is really water or not, we have to see whether it will quench our thirst. The proof of the pudding is in the eating of it. This is what is known as saṁvādi-pravṛtti or 'fruitful activity.' The verification is pragmatic; but the definition of truth, it should be remembered, is not so. Truth is not what 'works'; it is what conforms to reality. Knowledge is for its own sake, and it need not necessarily have a practical end in view.[2] Unlike the Buddhists (p. 209), the followers of the Nyāya-Vaiśeṣika lay stress on the cognitive significance of knowledge. The practical activity to which it leads is only a further result. It

[1] Anyathā implies prakāra. Cf. Sarvam jñānam dharmiṇyabhrāntam, prakāre tu viparyayaḥ: *Sapta-padārthī* (Vizianagaram Sans. Series), p. 25.

[2] NM. p. 171.

implies a motive operating subsequent to cognition, viz. to attain what is liked or to avoid what is disliked. In its absence, knowledge may remain without a practical consequence, but its logical validity cannot on that account be questioned.

(2) *Inference* (Anumāna).—The conception of vyāpti here is much widened when compared with that in Buddhism. Thus we can reason not only from smoke to fire, but also from the cloven hoof to the horns—features which, so far as we know, are not necessarily related[1] (p. 201). An attempt seems to have been made by the Buddhists[2] to bring cases of the latter kind also under causation. It is quite possible that the association between the 'cloven hoof' and 'horns' is a necessary one, though how it is so is not known to us. Yet the Nyāya-Vaiśeṣika on principle postulates invariable concomitance as the criterion of vyāpti, adducing as the reason therefor that even supposing that the features in question are causally related, a person that connects them inductively is not conscious of that relation when he does so. To the Cārvāka contention that neither the universals nor the particulars can be thus related (p. 189), the Nyāya-Vaiśeṣika reply is that the relation is between the particulars but as belonging to a class. The justification for this view is found in the recognition of universals as a separate objective category and in the belief that through the apprehension of a universal all the corresponding particulars are in some sense apprehended (alaukika-pratyakṣa).

Gautama refers to a triple classification of inference. The terms denoting the three classes—pūrvavat, śeṣavat and sāmānyatodṛṣṭa—are ambiguous and they have been so from the time of Vātsyāyana. The classification in itself is not very important; but we shall refer to one of the explanations given by Vātsyāyana, for it brings out very well a characteristic feature of inference as understood in the system. According to it, pūrvavat stands for reasoning based

[1] Hence the more comprehensive terms of liṅga ('sign') and liṅgin ('the signified') are generally used here for the middle and major terms in preference to hetu and sādhya, which are applicable strictly to cases based on causation.

[2] PP. p. 67.

upon resemblance to what has been observed in the past (pūrva) as in the case of seeing smoke on a hill and concluding to fire therefrom on the strength of former experience. This is the common form of reasoning. Śeṣavat is reasoning, by the method of elimination. It is indirect proof such as is sometimes met with in Euclid's *Elements*. The third variety of sāmānyatodṛṣṭa is that in which, with the support of what is found in the sphere of sensuous objects, we reason about parallel cases in the sphere of the supersensuous. For example we know that an instrument like an axe needs a sentient agent to wield it before it can function. Assuming that manas is such an instrument (karaṇa), we may conclude that there should be behind it an agent—the self, to explain its activity though neither the self nor the manas is perceivable. This, it will be seen, is merely analogical reasoning, and the Nyāya-Vaiśeṣika arguments for the existence of God are of this type. It was such an extension of the scope of inference that was questioned, as we mentioned before (p. 188), by the Cārvāka. The Nyāya-Vaiśeṣika here undoubtedly claims too much for inference, for it mistakes analogy for evidence. It in fact gives this variety of inference, as we shall presently see, a place in its scheme of pramāṇas resembling that of revelation in the Mīmāṁsā.

Inference is two-fold—that which resolves a doubt in one's own mind (svārtha) and that which does so in another's (parārtha).[1] The latter is necessarily couched in language, but the verbal form in itself constitutes no part of the inference. It only helps to direct the mind of the listener to think in the required manner, and thereby gives rise to the same process of thought in his mind as the one in that of the speaker. So if the syllogistic *form* is described as anumāna, it is only by courtesy. That is, the verbal view of logic which is common in the West is rejected here. It was never forgotten in India that the subject-matter of logic is thought and not, in any sense, the linguistic forms in which it may find expression. This anti-verbalist character of Indian Logic is referred to as follows by the Italian philosopher Croce: 'Indian Logic studies the naturalistic

[1] TS. p. 37.

syllogism in *itself* as internal thought, distinguishing it from the syllogism *for others*, that is to say, from the more or less usual, but always extrinsic and accidental forms of communication and dispute. It has not even a suspicion of the extravagant idea (which still vitiates our treatises) of a truth which is merely syllogistic and formalist, and which may be false in fact. It takes no account of the judgment, or rather it considers what is called judgment, and what is really the proposition, as a verbal clothing of knowledge; it does not make the verbal distinctions of subject, copula and predicate; it does not admit classes of categorical and hypothetical, of affirmative and of negative judgments. All these are extraneous to Logic, whose object is the constant: knowledge considered in itself.'[1]

The following is a typical Indian syllogism:—

1. Yonder mountain has fire.
2. For it has smoke.
3. Whatever has smoke has fire, e.g. an oven.
4. Yonder mountain has smoke such as is invariably accompanied by fire.
5. Therefore yonder mountain has fire.

The syllogism stands for what was described above as 'reasoning for another,' i.e. reasoning for convincing another. This explains for instance the statement of the conclusion at the outset known as the pratijñā or proposition. It is intended to draw attention to the point under consideration and keep the discussion within limits. In a purely logical syllogism—unmixed with rhetorical appurtenances—it is admitted that the first two or the last two of the five members (avayava) may be dropped. Dropping the first two and taking the last three, we shall contrast the Indian syllogism with the well-known Aristotelian one:—

(i) The first is the major premise. It does not stand by itself but is supported by an example. This step in inference seems to have consisted originally of only the example. It is even now designated udāharaṇa or 'illustration.' The general statement was introduced later. That is, according to early

[1] See *Logic*, pp. 584–5.

Indian logicians, reasoning even when restricted to the sphere of the sensuous was taken to be from particulars to particulars. In its present form the statement implies that it was realized in course of time that reasoning proceeds from particulars to particulars through the universal. This innovation is now commonly ascribed to the Buddhist logician Diṅnāga.[1]

(ii) The Indian logician is not content to leave the universal proposition by itself. He illustrates it by an example. This is, no doubt, due to an historical circumstance, viz. a change in the view taken of the character of the inferential process. But by retaining the example in the major premise even in its changed form, he desires to point out that it is a generalization derived from observation of particular instances. In other words the reasoning process, as represented by the above syllogism, is not purely deductive but inductive-deductive.

(iii) In the next step we have a synthesis of the major and minor premises. In the Aristotelian syllogism, the two stand apart although there is the middle term to link them together. The Nyāya-Vaiśeṣika syllogism makes this connection quite explicit by bringing all the three terms together in the same proposition. The formulation of the conclusion then becomes very simple indeed. The doctrine lays special stress on this synthesis, but other doctrines like the Vedānta do not agree with it,[2] and refuse to accept the synthesis as necessary.

(3) *Verbal Testimony* (Śabda).—We have already drawn attention (p. 178) to the distinction between śabda as a pramāṇa and as a prameya and pointed out the value of the former as a means of communicating information to others or of enriching our own experience. We have also stated that some Indian logicians like the Buddhists (p. 209) hold that it cannot be a separate pramāṇa. They bring it under inference because the ascertainment of the meaning of a verbal statement, they say, in no way differs from the inferential process. When we hear uttered significant words

[1] Cf. Prof. Keith: *op. cit.*, p. 109.

[2] VP. p. 191.

bearing certain syntactical relations to one another, we infer on the basis of our past experience that they must stand for a connected meaning. Or to express the same in another way, we take the words uttered as the characteristic mark (liṅga) of an idea in the mind of the speaker; and since we can always go back from the sign to that of which it is the sign, we conclude that there must be a corresponding idea in the mind of the speaker, the exact nature of that idea being determined by the sense of the words in question. This argument is commonly met by an appeal to our introspection which shows, it is contended, that the two processes of inference and interpretation are not identical.[1]

The Nyāya, unlike the Vaiśeṣika, admits śabda as an independent pramāṇa and defines it as the testimony of a trustworthy person (āpta)—one that knows the truth and communicates it correctly.[2] We find out that a person is trustworthy by the truth of his statements and by his unselfishness.[3] That is, the doctrine makes the value of śabda as testimony depend upon the virtue of its source—the honesty and competence of the speaker. On this principle, it regards what is taught in the Veda as valid because its author, God, is all-knowing.[4] It does not in this involve itself in a circle since it bases its belief in the existence of God not on revelation as the Vedānta does, but on reason. According to the Mīmāṁsā, on the other hand, the Veda, as we shall see, is self-existent and authority is inherent in it. But it must be added that in proving the existence of God, the Nyāya utilizes a form of inference—sāmānyatodṛṣṭa—whose validity can easily be questioned. If we do not reckon it as inference from which it materially differs, we have in the system an additional pramāṇa whose bearing is extra-empirical quite as much as that of revelation in the Mīmāṁsā. Thus there seems eventually to be little difference

[1] TSD. p. 54; SM. st. 140–1.

[2] TS. p. 50.

[3] That the process so far is inferential is admitted even in the Nyāya. See NM. p. 155. What is contested is the view that the psychological process involved in passing from the sounds heard to an idea as existing in the mind of the speaker is also inferential.

[4] NS. II. i. 68.

from the logical standpoint between the two systems in regard to their attitude towards the Veda.[1]

(4) *Comparison* (Upamāna).—This is commonly rendered as 'analogy' in English, but the student should be careful not to confound it with reasoning by analogy. We shall best explain what the Nyāya means by it by taking an example. Suppose we are familiar with an object X and there is another object Y resembling it. Suppose also that while we do not know Y, we have been informed of its resemblance to X by one who knows both. Now if the object Y is casually presented to us, we notice the resemblance in question, and recollecting what we have been told we at once come to know that that is the object which bears the name Y. It is this connection between a name and the thing it signifies that forms the *sole* sphere of upamāna here; and it is so called because it arises through the previous knowledge of *resemblance* between two things. The immediate cause (karaṇa) of the knowledge that Y is the object bearing a certain name is the perception of Y after one has learnt that it resembles X. The scope of the pramāṇa is quite narrow. Yet in practice it is very useful, as for instance in teaching where explanations accompanied by apt illustrations help us in extending our acquaintance with language.

In treating of perception, we referred to the nature of truth as understood in the system. It is such knowledge as represents reality faithfully.[2] There are two other points of an allied character, usually considered in Indian philosophy, to which we have hitherto alluded only incidentally (p. 210). As it is judgments that are true, we may view truth to be a property of the savikalpaka form of knowledge; but it does not appear to be essential to it. Hence a question arises as to how knowledge *comes to be true*. We know the manner in which knowledge arises according to the Nyāya-Vaiseṣika, though it is hard to understand how when the aids to its

[1] It is instructive to note in this connection that in all probability the belief neither in God nor in the Veda was originally a part of the Nyāya-Vaiśeṣika teaching.

[2] Tadvati tat-prakārakam jñānam pramā: TS. p. 23; *Kārikāvalī*. st. 135.

genesis—the self, manas, senses and object—are wholly inert (jaḍa), it can be knowledge at all.[1] The point to determine now is what conditions determine the added feature of truth when it is found in it (utpattau prāmāṇya). This is the first of the points to be considered now. Some maintain that knowledge does not become true as we have assumed, but is by its very nature so; and that where it is otherwise, its erroneous character is the result of some extraneous interference. Knowledge as such is valid, but it may deflect from its nature owing to some disturbing factor. That is, it is not truth that needs explanation, but only error—a view which stands opposed to the Buddhistic one according to which all knowledge is suspect until it is proved to be true. To this theory of the self-validity or svataḥ-prāmāṇya, as it is termed, of knowledge we shall recur later in speaking about the Mīmāṁsā and shall confine our attention at present to the Nyāya-Vaiśeṣika view. According to it, neither truth nor falsity is a normal feature of knowledge. Whether any particular knowledge is the one or the other depends entirely upon circumstances other than those that account for the rise of knowledge itself. To state the view in general terms: If *a*, *b* and *c* are the causes of knowledge, its truth or falsity is caused by another circumstance, say *m* or *n*. This additional circumstance, however, does not stand for anything altogether distinct from the causes of knowledge, but means only their excellence or deficiency respectively.[2] And since the doctrine holds that the causes must necessarily have either of these features, all knowledge as it arises will be either true or false and there can never be what may be called neutral knowledge.[3] A similar discussion is carried on in reference to the criterion of truth—that by which we *discover* what knowledge is true (jñaptau prāmāṇya). This is the second of the two points mentioned above. The question here is not how knowledge comes to be true or false, but how we become aware of its truth or falsity. Here also

[1] The position is scarcely distinguishable from that of the Cārvāka.
[2] TSD. pp. 55–6; *Kārikāvalī*, st. 131.
[3] Cf. NM. p. 171: Nirdoṣam nirguṇam vāpi na samastyeva kāraṇam. See also *Id.*, p. 161.

two answers are given by Indian logicians, but we shall refer only to the Nyāya-Vaiśeṣika one at present. According to it, the validity or invalidity of knowledge is not revealed in anuvyavasāya, which apprehends it. That gives us only knowledge. To know whether the knowledge so given is true or not, we require an additional means, viz. fruitful activity (saṁvādi-pravṛtti), as pointed out already. That is, when we know knowledge, we do not know its logical worth. It is known only subsequently—as the result of an appeal to facts, which is what fruitful activity means. And there may be knowledge known of which the truth or falsity is not yet seen. That is 'doubt.' The view that the validity of knowledge depends, in respect of its origin (utpattau) or of its ascertainment (jñaptau), upon the fulfilment of an extra condition is known as parataḥ-prāmāṇya-vāda or 'the theory of validity from outside.'

IV

Before describing the practical teaching of the doctrine, it is necessary to refer to the notions of dharma and adharma which in one form or another all systems alike associate with the self, indicating thereby that man's life has not only a mental but also a moral or spiritual side to it. The Nyāya-Vaiśeṣika speaks of dharma and adharma as two specific qualities (viśeṣa-guṇa) that belong to the self in addition to the seven already mentioned. They thus directly characterize it. But then the words do not stand for right and wrong deeds; they signify rather the merit (puṇya) and demerit (pāpa) resulting respectively from the performance of the one and indulgence in the other.[1] The Mīmāṁsā and the Vedānta systems accept an external standard for distinguishing a right deed from a wrong one, viz. the revealed authority of the Veda; here in the Nyāya-Vaiśeṣika, the law that constrains us in the field of conduct, is in the last resort internal. It believes that dharma as well as adharma is directly perceived. It is not, however, every one that can discern the difference between them, but only he that has purified

[1] TS. pp. 58–9.

his nature by continuous self-discipline and has succeeded in developing yogic power. Hence their perception is stated to be of the alaukika kind—the third of the varieties mentioned above. When we say that morality as conceived here is obedience to an inner law, we mean the intuitive judgments of such 'seers' who alone can speak with the voice of the true self. To the average man, who is still under the sway of particular desires and passions, the standard remains external inasmuch as his knowledge of dharma, to confine ourselves to only one of the two notions we are considering, is acquired through another and is second-hand. Strangely enough the doctrine in its present form accepts the authority of the Veda also in this respect as shown by its adoption of the whole of the karma discipline as taught in it,[1] and the need for two pramāṇas is justified on the supposition that dharma can be intuited only after it is known from the Veda.[2] But if we remember that when once dharma is known, the most important thing to do is to strive not for acquiring an immediate or direct knowledge of it, but for realizing it in action, it becomes clear that one of the two pramāṇas is superfluous. And it is the Veda that is so, if we may judge from the general tenor of the doctrine and the repudiation of verbal testimony as an independent pramāṇa in the Vaiśeṣika part of it.

So far as the preliminary discipline is concerned, we can trace the influence of the Gītā teaching as early as Praśastapāda,[3] but the training really appropriate to the Nyāya-Vaiśeṣika and originally recommended in it is akin to what we have noted in connection with the heretical schools in an earlier chapter (p. 113). Its object, however, is the same as that of karma-yoga, viz. sattva-śuddhi or 'cleansing of the heart,' as is clear from Gautama's reference to it as ātma-saṁskāra or 'self-purification,' and is to be achieved by eliminating narrow love (rāga) and hate (dveṣa). Only the course of conduct laid down here is not disinterested activity in the Gītā sense but the practice of yama and niyama.[4] There is some uncertainty regarding the original connotation

[1] PB. pp. 7 and 272–3.
[2] NM. p. 108.
[3] See p. 281. Cf. TSD. p. 67.
[4] NS. IV. ii. 46.

of these terms as understood in the Nyāya-Vaiśeṣika. But in the later works treating of the doctrine, they come to be identified with the same as defined in the Sāṅkhya-Yoga.[1] We shall, therefore, defer the explanation of these terms to the next chapter, merely remarking now that they respectively represent the negative and positive sides of ethical training. Love and hate are found to a greater or less extent in all men; and together with their causes—pleasure and pain—they are reckoned as specific qualities of the self in its empirical condition. All voluntary activity is traced to these sources so that the view which the Nyāya-Vaiśeṣika takes of conduct may be described as hedonistic. Only we must not forget that it regards the desire to avoid pain to be as strong a motive in prompting the will as the desire to obtain pleasure.[2] The selfish activity (pravṛtti) to which narrow love and hate give rise leads in its turn to pain and pleasure, and they again to likes and dislikes. Thus life, as it is commonly led, moves in a vicious circle in which no point can be regarded as the beginning. By restraining man from indulging in certain activities and by encouraging him to cultivate certain positive virtues, the training implied in yama and niyama helps him to break away from this circle and pursue undistracted the path by which he may reach the ultimate goal of life.

The nature of the goal is determined by the pessimistic attitude of the doctrine towards life as a whole. The doctrine does not deny the reality of pleasure as a positive experience[3]; but pain is equally real, and the two, in its view, are so inextricably connected with each other that avoiding pain necessitates avoiding pleasure as well. Further, it believes that pleasure in life is so uncertain and pain so much predominates over it that it is not worth one's while to strive to secure it. All pleasure again being transient—lasting only for two instants, like jñāna—continuous pleasure means perpetual effort. Hence the ideal of life is represented as apavarga or 'escape.' It is negative and consists not in the

1 See NSB. IV. ii. 46; Vācaspati: *Tātparya-ṭīkā*, IV. ii. 46; *Nyāya-kandalī*, p. 278.

2 *Kārikāvalī*, st. 146 ff.

3 NS. I. i. 9; IV. i. 56.

attainment of happiness, but in the removal of pain. The removal, being a dhvaṁsa or 'posterior negation,' will endure ever afterwards and no lapse from that condition will take place. Such an ideal is quite operative, for, according to the Nyāya-Vaiśeṣika, conative activity is prompted as much by a desire to shun pain as by a desire to obtain happiness, and the prospect of rising above all pain once for all is strong enough to impel a person convinced of the misery of empirical existence to do his utmost for reaching that end. But the aim of life should not only be desirable; it should also be possible of attainment and the doctrine holds, as we know, that evil though real can be avoided.[1] For pain like pleasure is only an adventitious feature of the self and its removal means no loss to its intrinsic character. For instance in deep sleep, the self remains without either, which may be taken to indicate the possibility of mokṣa being a similar but permanent condition.[2] It is not only pain and pleasure that are adventitious, but also knowledge, desire, volition, etc., so that the state of mokṣa is one in which the self is able to cast off all its nine specific qualities. Accordingly, the self then not merely transcends empirical life, but also ceases to be the subject of experience in all its forms.

It is interesting to compare this ideal with that of Buddhism. Buddha taught that avoiding pleasure and pain or eliminating selfishness is not possible until we cease to believe in the self as a persisting entity. The Nyāya-Vaiśeṣika differs in admitting an enduring self; but it insists that the ideal of life is not reached until we feel convinced that the self in reality is beyond all experience. Thus the source of evil in this system lies not in our belief that there is a permanent self, but in the belief that it must needs have pain or pleasure while in its intrinsic nature it is devoid of both. Such a wrong view of the self gives rise to love and hate; and the rest of life's selfish activities follow from them. This theory which is implicit in the Vaiśeṣika analysis of the springs of action into desire for pleasure (rāga) and aversion from pain (dveṣa), the Nyāya makes explicit by resolving them into something more ultimate, viz.

[1] NS. I. i. 20–1; NM. p. 501. [2] NS. IV. i. 63.

delusion[1] (moha). Our aim should be to free ourselves from the tyranny of this wrong conviction by realizing the true nature of the self. This initial folly of moha or mithyā-jñāna is not a mere lack of right knowledge but positive error or wrong knowledge.[2] It may be represented as two-fold: (i) mistaking things that are not really of the self as belonging to it, viz. manas, body and so forth; and (ii) mistaking the non-essential or accidental features of the self such as knowledge, pain and pleasure arising through association with its empirical vesture, for its essential features. Neither separation from the former nor the elimination of the latter can affect the integrity of the self; but man commonly loses sight of this fact and feels that with their deficiency is bound up that of himself. In one word, there is nothing which the self can or has to obtain for itself; and it is the knowledge of this truth that is the immediate means of release.[3] But if it is successfully to dispel the delusion, it should be ripened into direct intuition through constant meditation. Mere reasoned conviction is of no avail. Thus the acquisition of right knowledge and the practice of yoga constitute the chief features of the discipline directly leading to release. The way of securing the saving knowledge is as follows: (1) Formal study of philosophy which is to be carried on under a competent teacher who can properly instruct us; and (2) reflection upon what has been thus learnt with a view to get conviction for oneself about it. These two stages secure mediate knowledge or 'knowledge by description' as we might say. Then follows (3) meditation upon the true nature of the self.[4] It leads to direct experience of the truth which will banish ignorance at once. A person who has such experience, it is supposed, will reach the final goal of life (apavarga) as soon as he is dissociated from the physical body at death.

In thus conceiving of the goal of life, the Nyāya-Vaiśeṣika

1 NṢ. IV. i. 3–8; NM. pp. 500–1.

2 Na tattva-jñānasya anutpatti-mātram: NSB. IV. ii. 1.

3 NS. I. i. 1.

4 NSB. IV. ii. 38 and 47–9. These correspond to śravaṇa, manana and nididhyāsana of the Upaniṣads and are so termed in the *Nyāya-kandalī*, p. 282.

is tacitly denying that there is any difference between soul and matter. The self that has reached it is divested of all experience and it is not even conscious of itself then. Such an ideal is surely repugnant to the common mind, whatever justification it may or may not have in theory. It may successfully avoid evil, but it is a success which is worse than defeat. The straightforward attempt of the Buddhist to secure annihilation is far better than this formal admission of a self in unconscious mokṣa. But it is mokṣa only in the eschatological sense. The complete elimination from the self of all its specific qualities in the case of an enlightened person is supposed to take place only after death. So far as the present life is concerned, such elimination is not only not aimed at but is impossible. If we then, according to our plan (p. 184), try to determine the Nyāya-Vaiśeṣika ideal of life from the positivistic side, much of what is undesirable disappears from it. Jīvan-mukti, no doubt, is not formally recognized here as in some other systems; but a stage corresponding to it, when a person has succeeded in obtaining enlightenment though he has not yet become 'free' in the technical sense, is admitted (p. 19) both by Vātsyāyana and Uddyotakara. Such a person will not be divorced from his physical or mental adjuncts; but narrow love and hate will have disappeared from him together with the selfish activity that proceeds from them. Nor will his life be one of passivity, if we may judge from Gautama's statement[1] that activity taints only when it is prompted by selfishness. The best support for putting this forward as the Nyāya-Vaiśeṣika ideal of life is to be found in its conception of God, 'the highest soul' (paramātmā) as he is termed, who is not bereft of knowledge or desire or will, but only has no pain or pleasure, no likes or dislikes and therefore, though ever active, never engages himself in any selfish activity. From this view-point, then, man's effort here should be directed towards acquiring enlightenment, refining desire and will by purging them of all selfishness, learning to endure pain and wholly abolish hate—an ideal which, whatever it may lead to ultimately, is not without an excellence of its own.

[1] NS. IV. i. 64.

CHAPTER XI

SĀṄKHYA-YOGA

THIS should once have been a widely influential school to judge from references to it in the Mahābhārata and kindred literature[1]; but its vogue, especially on the Sāṅkhya side, is not very great now.[2] The surviving part of its literature also is relatively poor. Modern scholars, as we have already had occasion to notice (pp. 106, 132), are divided in their opinion as regards its origin. All agree that references to what appear as the Sāṅkhya-Yoga doctrine are found in the Upaniṣads, especially in the later ones among them. But while some are of opinion that the system is independent in origin and almost as old as the Upaniṣads, others maintain that it is an offshoot of the teaching of those ancient treatises. There is indeed a reference in one of the Upaniṣads[3] to Kapila ṛṣi, the supposed founder of the Sāṅkhya according to tradition; but both old Indian thinkers[4] and present-day scholars[5] agree that it is only apparent. The expression there means the 'red wizard,' not 'Kapila, the seer,' as it may at first appear and denotes not a real person at all but Hiraṇyagarbha or some other mythical being. As the discussion of this question requires an acquaintance with the details of the doctrine, we cannot enter upon it now. We shall merely state in passing that whatever its true origin, there was one stage in the history of the system when its adherents traced it to the Upaniṣads. Bādarāyaṇa, as is well known, has systematized the teaching of the Upaniṣads in his *Vedānta-sūtra*, and one of the topics to which he recurs time and again is whether the Sāṅkhya is the teaching of the Upaniṣads.[6] His conclusion is that it is not, and his repeated

[1] See SS. p. 227.
[2] ERE. xi. p. 189.
[3] *Śvet. Up*. v. 2.
[4] Cf. Śaṁkara on VS. II. i. 1.
[5] See PU. p. 200; Prof. Keith: *The Śaṁkhya System*, pp. 8, 40–1.
[6] Cf. Śaṁkara on VS. I. i. 5–11; II. i. 1–3. This refutation is different from the one in VS. II. ii. 1–10, where the Śāṅkhya is criticized on rationalistic grounds.

reference to it cannot be satisfactorily accounted for without assuming that there were Sāṅkhya thinkers in his time who contended that that was the teaching of the Upaniṣads. Even so late as the sixteenth century A.D. Vijñāna Bhikṣu, the author of the *Sāṅkhya-pravacana-bhāṣya*, which is a commentary on the *Sāṅkhya-sūtra*, maintained a similar view. This may of course be the result of later Sāṅkhya teachers trying to find support for their doctrine in the Upaniṣads, whose authority had come to prevail, but it may also indicate a desire on their part to trace it to its real source even when the modifications in it had changed its character so very much.

The relation between the Sāṅkhya and the Yoga again is difficult of settlement. It is not even clear that one of them is later than the other, for they may well have been due to differentiations in what was originally a single doctrine. In the form in which the two have come down to us, there is no doubt that the Yoga is later. If the view adopted here, viz. that the doctrine is derived from the Upaniṣads, be right, it appears probable that its starting-point should be sought in a primitive Sāṅkhya-Yoga with belief in a supreme God to whom the individual selves and prakṛti, the source of the physical universe, though distinct are yet subordinate; for such a doctrine is nearer to the teaching of the Upaniṣads than the atheistic Sāṅkhya or the theistic but dualistic Yoga of classical times.[1] We have to assume that under naturalistic influence such as that of the Svabhāva-vāda, the capacity to unfold the universe was transferred completely to prakṛti, rendering the idea of God superfluous; and on that was later grafted a belief in his existence by the exponents of the Yoga[2] probably as a matter of theological expediency—'to satisfy the theists and to facilitate the propagation of the theory of the universe expounded in Sāṅkhya.'[3] This point will become clear when we trace the origin of the doctrine and point out its relation to the Vedānta.

[1] Cf. Dr. Belvalkar: *Bhandarkar Commemoration Volume*, pp. 183–4

[2] Vācaspati in his *Bhāmatī* (II. i. 3) seems to give support to two such stages in the history of the doctrine on its Yoga side.

[3] ERE. vol. xii. p. 831.

The earliest book of authority on classical Sāṅkhya we now have is the *Sāṅkhya-kārikā*, which is a work of about the fifth century A.D. Roughly speaking, we may take its author Īśvarakṛṣṇa to have been a contemporary of Kālidāsa. It consists of seventy stanzas and is on that account sometimes designated as the *Sāṅkhya-saptati*. It contains a brief but exceedingly lucid exposition of the theoretical teaching of the system and has been described as 'the pearl of the whole scholastic literature of India.' It has been commented upon by several, including Vācaspati—the well-known advaitic scholar of the ninth century A.D. This book, with a commentary whose identity is not quite certain, was translated into Chinese under the name of 'the Golden Seventy Discourse' by one Paramārtha, a Brahmin of Ujjain who went to China in A.D. 546 on the invitation of its then Emperor and spent the rest of his life there. Another work of note on the system is the *Tattva-samāsa*, which, as its name indicates, is very brief—hardly more than a table of contents, as it has been characterized. It was regarded by Max Müller as the oldest work on the subject,[1] but that view is not generally accepted now.[2] A third work of importance on the system is the *Sāṅkhya-sūtra*, ascribed to Kapila himself; but the work, though much of its material may be really old, is clearly a very late production and cannot be assigned to a date earlier than the fourteenth century A.D. It is in six chapters of which four are concerned with the elucidation of the doctrine, one criticizes the rival systems and one gives the parables (ākhyāyikā) illustrating the chief points of the doctrine—rather a novel feature in a Sūtra work. It has been commented upon, among others, by Vijñāna Bhikṣu, to whom reference has already been made. In this commentary the Sāṅkhya appears considerably modified, the general effect of the modification being to bring it nearer to the Vedānta. We may regard it as *later* Sāṅkhya. We shall refer to its divergences from the earlier where they are of importance. As regards the Yoga system, Patañjali's *Yoga-sūtra* is the

[1] SS. p. 242.

[2] Prof. Keith: *op. cit.*, p. 89. But see *Journal of Oriental Research* (Madras) for April 1928, pp. 145–7.

recognized text-book. It has been assigned to about the end of the fifth century A.D.[1]; and if this date be correct, the traditional identification of its author with Patañjali, the grammarian who is known to have lived in the second century B.C., must fall to the ground. It consists of four chapters which deal respectively with the nature of mental concentration (samādhi), the pathway to it (sādhana), the supernatural powers that may be acquired through it (vibhūti), and the nature of the goal of life which consists in the isolation of the self (kaivalya). It has been commented upon by Vyāsa[2] (A.D. 500) and King Bhoja (A.D. 1000) among others. The former's commentary has a splendid gloss by Vācaspati and another by Vijñāna Bhikṣu.

I

The Sāṅkhya-Yoga like the Nyāya-Vaiśeṣika admits a plurality of selves, called puruṣas, and is likewise realistic since it regards objects as existing independently of the mind that cognizes them. But while the latter traces the physical universe to a multiplicity of sources, the former derives it from a single one, viz. prakṛti. In other words, the Sāṅkhya-Yoga, unlike the Nyāya-Vaiśeṣika, is—if we overlook for the moment the plurality of selves—dualistic, prakṛti and puruṣa or nature and spirit being the only two ultimate entities recognized. We shall now consider in some detail how each of these is conceived:—

(1) *Prakṛti*.—This is the first cause of the universe—of everything excepting only spirit which is uncaused, and accounts for whatever is physical, both matter and force. Out of it, the whole variety of the universe evolves. Hence the doctrine is known as *pariṇāma-vāda* or a 'theory of change.' Even space and time are represented as aspects of prakṛti and do not, therefore, exist apart from it[3] as independent entities. This is a point which is worthy of note, for it shows that the system does not, like the generality of philosophic

[1] Prof. Jacobi: *Dates of Philosophical Sūtras*, JAOS. (1911).

[2] It is difficult to say who this Vyāsa was. Tradition identifies him with the well-known author of that name.

[3] STK. st. 33; SPB. ii. 12.

doctrines including much of Western thought till quite recent times, start by positing matter *in* space and time, but looks upon the primordial physical entity as including and explaining them both. The nature of prakṛti is deduced from the nature of the common things of experience by the aid of reason alone. As the material cause of these things, it should consist of what is common to all of them; for the effect, according to a fundamental postulate of the system, must be essentially the same as the material cause. By a process of analysis, the essential characteristics of the physical universe are reduced to three—named sattva, rajas and tamas; and prakṛti is conceived as constituted of them. It is thus complex in its nature, though single. These three factors are termed guṇas, whose conception is of the utmost importance in the system. The chief point about them is that they are not what their name might suggest, viz. qualities of prakṛti. That would be admitting the distinction between substance and attribute as the Nyāya-Vaiśeṣika does, but the Sāṅkhya-Yoga regards it as a pure abstraction. The guṇas are to be understood here as the components of prakṛti. They might be described as substances, if that again did not suggest the same artificial distinction. They are still termed guṇas because, it is said,[1] they by intertwining make a rope (guṇa) or forge a chain for binding the self. This explanation is somewhat inconsistent with the spirit of the Sāṅkhya-Yoga teaching, for prakṛti not only binds but also liberates the self from bondage. Indeed puruṣa's liberation, as we shall see, is the ultimate purpose for which it evolves. There is another explanation, which again seems to run counter to the dominant thought of the doctrine. It is stated that the guṇas are so called because they form a category *subordinate* to the puruṣa, which implies that spirit here is more important and that prakṛti is only something that ministers to it. The explanation, though supported by certain statements of old authorities,[2] would destroy the avowed dualistic character of the teaching by making one ultimate entity depend upon another. As regards the nature of the guṇas: sattva represents whatever is fine or light; tamas whatever is coarse or

[1] SPB. i. 61. [2] YS. ii. 23; YSB. i. 4.

heavy; and rajas whatever is active. It is clear from this description that the conception is arrived at as a hypothesis in accounting for the diversity of the world in its material as well as its mechanical aspects. Their triple character merely signifies that *three* is the minimum number of elements necessary for such an explanation.[1] If only one guṇa is postulated, it would not explain variety at all; if two, they would either cancel each other's effect, thus leading to no transformation whatever, or one would dominate over the other always, thus leading to a monotonous movement in a single direction. In later Sāṅkhya is found the important development that each of the three guṇas is manifold and that the infinity of prakṛti is due to their indefinite number. In this case the triple division would be the result of grouping together like guṇas. Such a view undoubtedly explains better the discord and diversity of the world of experience; but at the same time it makes the doctrine more like the Vaiśeṣika[2] with its belief in an infinity of atomic reals with qualitative distinctions.

The guṇas form the substratum of change which as in Buddhism is taken to be perpetual (p. 211). But change is not total here and the guṇas persist while only their modes appear and disappear. This solution of the problem of change leads to the postulating of a two-fold condition for all things—one, latent or potential and the other, potent or actual. When all the modes of prakṛti are latent, we have the state of dissolution (pralaya); at other times, evolution (sarga). Even in the state of dissolution, prakṛti is supposed to maintain its dynamic character; only then, instead of producing unlike forms, it reproduces itself (sajātīya-pariṇāma) so that perpetual motion is a fundamental postulate of the system so far as the physical world is concerned (p. 233).[3] The ground for the conclusion that there is per-

[1] The idea of guṇas here, if not derived from the medical theory of the three dhātus, has at least a parallel in it. Cf. STK. st. 13.

[2] SPB. i. 127–8. As regards the antiquity of the guṇa-doctrine, see OST. vol. v. p. 377. The conception occurs as early as AV., and the Mbh. is full of references to it.

[3] Pratikṣaṇa-pariṇāmino hi sarva eva bhāvā ṛte citi-śakteḥ: STK. st. 5.

petual movement in prakṛti is to be found in the conviction that if it ceased to be dynamic at any stage, it would be impossible to account for the reappearance of motion in it again. Here we see a realization of the truth of Newton's First Law of Motion that a body in motion or at rest continues to be so unless it is disturbed from outside. There is no such external agency recognized in the doctrine to interfere with its movement. No doubt the change from the state of dissolution to that of evolution is accounted for by introducing an outside influence, viz. the presence of spirit (puruṣa-saṁnidhi)[1]; but the explanation is given only in a half-hearted manner and is, as we shall see, one of the unsatisfactory features of the system, so far at least as the Sāṅkhya part of it is concerned.

There are certain special features of evolution as conceived here which deserve notice. First, it is based on a belief in the indestructibility of matter and the persistence of force. Something cannot come out of nothing; and whatever is, has always been. Production is only the manifestation (abhivyakti) of what is already in a latent form, and is not a new creation (ārambha). The so-called beginning of an object is only an event in its history; the object itself is not, and cannot be, made. Similarly, destruction means only change of form, for there can be nothing like absolute annihilation. Secondly, evolution is conceived as cyclic or periodical. That is, there are periods of evolution and dissolution alternating so that it is not a process of continuous progress in one direction only. It would seem also that dissolution is the normal state, for there is a persistent tendency in prakṛti when in evolution, to revert to that state. Next, evolution is here regarded as teleological; but, as prakṛti is by hypothesis not sentient, we cannot take it wholly so. We may characterize it as quasi-teleological, however hard it may be to understand that term. What is meant is that the whole process serves a purpose, though it cannot be described as consciously pursued. Lastly evolution, so far as it is teleological at all, has reference to the individual and not to the species. Its object is not the elevation or improvement of

[1] SP. i. 96.

the latter, even at the expense of the former, but securing worldly experience (bhoga) for the individual or bringing about his liberation (apavarga) from the ties of saṁsāra. We shall later explain the probable meaning of this double aim involved in the evolution of prakṛti.

The order of evolution of the twenty-four principles (tattvas) known to the system, if we exclude the puruṣas which stand outside the realm of change, will be seen from the following scheme:—

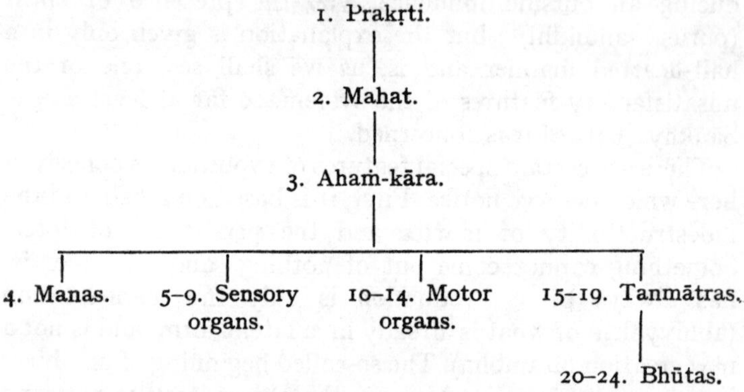

The complete significance of this scheme and of the various terms used in it will become clear as we proceed. For the present it will suffice to refer to only a few points in it:—

(i) The evolutionary series includes in addition to what are clearly physical, viz. the five subtle (tanmātras) and the five gross elements (bhūtas), certain others like the manas which appear to be psychical in character; and it may seem a contradiction to make prakṛti, which by hypothesis is non-sentient, their source. Really, however, there is no contradiction, for the latter are not themselves psychical, but owe that character to the influence of the self, the sole principle of consciousness acknowledged in the doctrine. An illustration may make the Sāṅkhya-Yoga position clear in this respect. A mirror can reflect our features, but the surface of the wall, upon which it hangs, cannot; and yet both are alike material. Similar is the case of the two sets of entities above referred to which, though originating from the same prakṛti, behave differently towards the self—one responding to its influence readily and the other not doing so. The difference between them is therefore one of degree, not of essence. The 'psychical' factors have in fact been compared to the nervous system on its physical side.[1]

(ii) In the state of dissolution, the three guṇas of prakṛti, though perpetually active, are in perfect equilibrium. At the beginning of a period of evolution, this state ceases and is followed by one in which sattva predominates. It marks the starting-point of heterogeneous evolution and is called mahat ('the great'), or buddhi. The initial stimulus for this alteration, according to the Yoga, comes from God or Īśvara.[2] According to the Sāṅkhya on the other hand which acknowledges no such supreme Being, the change is ascribed to the 'mere presence' (sāmnidhya-mātra),[3] as it is termed, of the puruṣa; and the possibility of its influencing prakṛti, though continuing to be passive, is illustrated by a magnet attracting iron. This is a point which is far from satisfactory. In the first place, the puruṣa is eternal and omnipresent like prakṛti so that the condition determining the evolution of the latter is ever fulfilled while its course is supposed to be interrupted at intervals by dissolution. To explain the break in the course of evolution by the past karma of beings will not do, for the puruṣa, being really untouched by good or evil, karma and its effects should be taken to characterize the buddhi and therefore as internal to prakṛti.[4] There is again the difficulty due to the admission of many selves in understanding what exactly is meant by the presence of purusa—whether it is of one or of all. To assume, as Vijñāna Bhikṣu does,[5] that it refers to the influence of a chief Puruṣa in each kalpa or cycle of creation would virtually be to abandon the atheistic position and side with the Yoga.

(iii) Now as regards the last group in the evolution, viz. the elements: When we remember that the ultimate reals out of which the produced part of the universe is constituted according to the Nyāya-Vaiśeṣika are these elements, it will

[1] ERE. xi. p. 190. [2] See *Bhoja-vṛtti* on YS. i. 24.
[3] SPB. i. 96. [4] SP. i. 16. [5] SPB. i. 96.

be seen that the Sāṅkhya-Yoga carries its investigation farther back than that system until it arrives at a single principle. How are these elements derived and what are their characteristics? Their immediate causes are the five tanmātras; and they are named after the distinguishing features of the five elements as śabda-tanmātra ('essence of sound'), sparśa-tanmātra ('essence of touch'), etc. The gross elements which spring from them show greater and greater differentiation. Their mode of origin is as follows: From śabda-tanmātra emerges ākāśa with sound as its manifest quality. From śabdatanmātra and sparśa-tanmātra combined emerges air, which therefore has the two qualities of sound and touch; from these two and rūpa-tanmātra springs fire, which has the three qualities of sound, touch and colour; from these three and rasa-tanmātra emerges water with four qualities, viz. sound, touch, colour and taste; and last, earth comes into being from all the five tanmātras and is therefore characterized by all the five qualities of sound, touch, colour, flavour and odour. The elements beginning with ākāśa are consequently more and more concrete. Each element is conceived as manifold, and consists of finite and disparate particles termed paramāṇus,[1] though the expression does not signify here precisely what it does in the Nyāya-Vaiśeṣika. It is out of these atoms that the whole of the physical universe as known to us is produced.

(iv) The scheme indicates only what we may describe as primary evolution. Evolution does not stop at it. It goes further on as is shown, for example, when pṛthivī is transformed into a tree[2] or a caterpillar becomes a butterfly. This secondary evolution is in fact what we are familiar with and what takes place within any single period of evolution. When an object that has evolved in this sense breaks up, it is reduced to the form of the gross elements and the process of dissolution does not extend beyond except when the evolutionary period in question itself comes to an end. Primary evolution is described as the differentiation into

[1] Cf. YSB. i. 40, 45; iii. 44, 52.

[2] As in the Nyāya-Vaiśeṣika, no distinction is made here between mechanical and organic products. See p. 239 *ante*.

distinct principles (tattvāntara-pariṇāma)[1]; but what constitutes distinctness is not well defined. It is clear, however, that this amounts to a recognition of grades or degrees in change.

An attempt is made in the system to deduce the being of prakṛti, not merely its nature, with the aid of reason. The deduction depends upon two principles which the system takes as its postulates. The first of them to which we have already alluded is described as the sat-kārya-vāda. According to it, nothing new can come into being which is in clear opposition to the Nyāya-Vaiśeṣika doctrine of asat-kārya-vāda. The totality of what exists now is given from the very beginning. But what is, may be implicit or explicit—the two forms being respectively termed 'cause' and 'effect.' The jar is ever there and is so really eternal; but it is not perceivable when in a subtle or latent form. In other words, a thing always is *in itself* though it may not be *for us*.[2] It subsists always although it may exist only for a while, and existence necessarily signifies subsistence. The bearing of this postulate on the present question is that the physical world which is now explicit must once have been implicit; and it is just that implicit state which is prakṛti. That is indeed the literal meaning of the term pradhāna ('what is put before or presupposed'),[3] which is sometimes used for prakṛti. The second postulate is that the finite always implies the infinite, which reminds one of the dictum of Hegel that the finite transcends itself. The notion of finitude here requires a word of explanation. Things as understood in the Sāṅkhya-Yoga cannot be said to be limited by time or space, for neither of them is recognized as a separate entity. So the word 'finite' is taken to mean 'not self-sustaining' or, as it is otherwise expressed, 'not pervasive' (avyāpi).[4] For example, ākāśa is finite in this sense because while it sustains all that is derived from it in the process of evolution, it itself is sustained by its cause, viz. śabda-tanmātra. This tanmātra again reveals another element more fundamental by which it is sustained; and so forth backwards until we reach an entity

[1] STK. st. 3.
[2] Cf. YS. iii. 13.
[3] SPB. i. 125.
[4] STK. st. 15–16.

which is all-pervasive and self-sustaining. That is prakṛti. In prakṛti itself or, what amounts to the same, in the three guṇas, we may think that there is mutual exclusion, none being caused by the others, and that they are all therefore finite. But the theory is that, though not causally related, they are absolutely dependent upon one another (anyonyāśraya-vṛtti),[1] and that none of them is self-sustaining. In other words, prakṛti is not a mere unity of aggregation, but a systematic unity of parts each of which has its special place and function in the whole. This, by the way, shows the existence of a limit to the investigation of the cause for the physical world; for, if we proceed farther back, we do not get anything *different* from prakṛti. It is therefore regarded as paramavyakta, 'the final unmanifest'[2] or the first cause whose being is unconditioned and necessary. It will be seen that the reasoning is based upon the observation of common things emerging from their respective material causes and disappearing into them again. A jar is made out of clay; and, when destroyed, it turns into clay again. Emergence and absorption thus have a terminus, viz. clay here. This process of reasoning is only extended beyond the visible material world to arrive at prakṛti; or, to state the same differently, primary evolution is postulated on the analogy of the secondary. Even supposing that a principle which has a basis in experience may be extended to what transcends experience, it may well be asked what warrant there is for assuming the very principles —mahat, ahaṁ-kāra and tanmātras—and only so many, to account for the bhūtas which alone are given in experience; and it is significant that the basis for this part of the doctrine is stated to be not inference but verbal testimony (āptāgama) or the *ipse dixit* of the Sāṅkhya-Yoga teachers.[3] That the physical world has evolved out of a certain number of elemental principles given in our experience, or perhaps from one, is a doctrine of the Svabhāva-vāda (p. 105); but the further reference to mahat, etc., as intermediate stages in the

[1] STK. st. 12; YB. ii. 15. Such a view, of course, is open to criticism with reference to spirit which neither pervades nor is pervaded by the guṇas, leading to the conclusion that both prakṛti and puruṣa are finite. See *Bhāmatī* II. ii. 1. [2] STK. st. 15–16. [3] STK. st. 6.

evolution, which distinguishes the Sāṅkhya-Yoga, suggests that it is to be traced to a different source. We shall see in the sequel what reasons there are for concluding that source to be the Upaniṣads.

(2) *Puruṣa.*—Puruṣa is mere sentience. It is changeless, eternal and omnipresent. It is also entirely passive, all activity being restricted to prakṛti. It may accordingly be said to represent the affective or receptive side of the mind and is consequently described as an enjoyer or experient (bhoktā) without being a doer or agent (kartā). Like prakṛti, the self also is here sought to be established with the help of reason alone. Various arguments are adduced to prove why such a psychic entity should be supposed to exist.[1] First of all it is stated that the physical universe, being insentient, requires a sentient principle to experience it or that objects suggest a subject, although such an argument by recognizing a necessary relation between the two militates against the fundamental dualism of the system. Equally inconsistent with the same aspect of the doctrine is the second argument that prakṛti, which is complex, implies by contrast the existence of something which is simple, viz. the self. Again the design[2] that is found in nature, particularly in the living body, it is argued, leads to the same conclusion. A noteworthy point here is the manner in which the 'design argument' is utilized. It is explained as pointing not to the designer but to one that profits by the design. The Sāṅkhya concludes from the presence in nature of means adapted to the accomplishment of particular ends, not to God as their author, but to the self for whom it supposes them to exist. This conclusion may be taken as being on a par with the other, for any contriver must necessarily have in view one whose need his contrivance meets. No watches for example would be made if there was none to use them. But it may be asked why it should not equally well imply God as the contriving mind whom the Sāṅkhya, as an atheistic doctrine, declines to accept. Here is a point of much importance in the

[1] SK. st. 17.

[2] This argument is foreshadowed already in the Upaniṣads. See p. 66 *ante*.

doctrine, especially in contrast to the Nyāya-Vaiśeṣika. In the latter, the material out of which the visible universe is made possesses no spontaneity of its own. Its various parts have accordingly to be brought together and also kept together by some external factor—God or karma or both. But here there is a great advance in the conception of prakṛti in that it is of an organic entity.[1] It is able to develop of itself. Such an entity has no need for an external manipulator. This is at the bottom of the atheism of the Sāṅkhya and shows the futility of attempts like that of Vijñāna Bhikṣu to read theism into the doctrine.[2] But prakṛti, though its conception is different from that of the Nyāya-Vaiśeṣika atoms, does not evolve for itself and therefore points to sentient puruṣa. It is this teleology implicit in prakṛti that the design argument here makes use of. It serves as the point of departure from the Svabhāva-vāda with which the doctrine has much in common, and tells us by the way that spirit is the only true ultimate in the Sāṅkhya-Yoga. Unlike prakṛti, it is not a unity of parts; nor is it non-sentient like it. So it does not in its turn refer to anything beyond itself. A fourth argument is drawn from man's longing for escape from saṁsāra or the spiritual instinct to be free. What strives to escape must be other than what it is to escape from, viz. prakṛti. The puruṣas are conceived as many; and various arguments are put forward in support of that view,[3] such as the divergent histories of men and the differences in their endowment—physical, moral and intellectual. But such reasoning only shows the plurality of the empirical selves. In themselves, it is hard to see how the puruṣas can differ from one another. There is not even a semblance of explanation here as in the Nyāya-Vaiśeṣika, where each self is stated to be inherently characterized by its own viśeṣa (p. 235).

The view of causation in the system is the very reverse of that in the Nyāya-Vaiśeṣika. It is described as sat-kārya-vāda, for the product, according to it, is supposed to be there in the material cause always in a latent form. But sat-kārya-vāda like asat-kārya-vāda, it must be remembered, refers

[1] SK. st. 57. [2] SPB. i. 92–8. [3] SK. st. 18.

only to the material cause. The system recognizes two other kinds of cause—the efficient and the final. The latter points to something outside the sphere of prakṛti, it being always either worldly experience (bhoga) or release (apavarga), both of which have reference to the self. This statement, however, does not seem to signify that the final aim of evolution is two-fold. Apavarga or escape means, as in the Nyāya-Vaiśeṣika, the restoration of the self once for all to its natural condition. Prakṛti evolves for bringing about its release in this sense, and it ceases to do so for a self when that particular self becomes free. When we take this along with the point already noticed, viz. that the state of pralaya or world-absorption and not that of evolution is normal to prakṛti, apavarga will be seen to be the only true aim. We may look upon the other aim of bhoga as its necessary antecedent. If the two aims be considered as independent or external to each other, it will not be possible to explain how blind prakṛti, albeit that it is omnipotent, can exercise a choice between them and decide which is to be secured for which puruṣa and when. The introduction of karma, as already indicated, will not help the argument, for the traces which past karma leaves behind abide not in the self but in the buddhi and are therefore of prakṛti. Such an interpretation saves the doctrine to some extent from the charge of self-contradiction in the conception of prakṛti, viz. that while it is stated to be non-sentient, it is supposed to be endowed with activity which implies conscious choice. The final cause is the most important of the causes and in one sense it may be said to be the only cause,[1] for in its absence there would be no progressive movement at all in prakṛti. Its recognition signifies what we have already pointed out, that the conception of prakṛti is that of a systematized unity of parts or a teleological whole. The efficient cause is conceived as negative in its nature. It is useful only in removing obstacles and not in making any positive contribution towards the product, for by hypothesis whatever manifests itself is already there in the material cause. Prakṛti is characterized by universal potency, and holds in itself the possibility of all forms. It can

[1] Cf. SK. st. 31: Puruṣārtha eva hetuḥ.

become anything and the efficient cause is required only to determine the direction in which it is to exhibit movement by removing the obstacle in that direction. As analogous to this, we may think of water stored up in a reservoir which at every point of its sides is trying to find an outlet and flows out only where the resistance to its effort is removed.[1] Finally, we must point out that this view of causation holds solely within the sphere of prakṛti and its transformations. The self, in reality, remains untouched by it. It is neither a cause nor an effect of anything.

The most important distinction between the Sāṅkhya and the Yoga is the belief of the latter in God. Some scholars, old as well as new,[2] have tried to maintain that there was no intention on the part of Kapila to deny God and that all that he meant to assert was the impossibility of *rationally* establishing his existence. But this seems to be contrary to the spirit of classical Sāṅkhya as already observed; and it may here be added that the attempt to give a theistic colour to the doctrine appears quite late in its history. Vijñāna Bhikṣu is anxious to find a place for God in the Sāṅkhya scheme, but the support for it even in the late *Sūtra* is slender. We have already indicated how the notion of God or Īśvara as he is termed here came to be included in the Yoga; and it is therefore only loosely related to the doctrine. The very sūtras in which it is postulated in Patañjali's work stand disconnected with the rest of the work.[3] As conceived here, he is a puruṣa like others, though a perfect one. He is omniscient and omnipresent; but, unlike the Vedāntic Īśvara, he is external to matter (prakṛti) as well as to the individual selves (puruṣas). In other words, he is not the Absolute and in this he resembles the Nyāya-Vaiśeṣika God (p. 242), the chief difference being in the part they play in shaping the world owing to the difference in the conception in the two doctrines of the material out of which it is shaped. The only argument adduced by Patañjali in support of his theistic position is the existence in our experience of a graded scale of knowledge, wisdom, etc., which, he supposes, points to

1 YS. iv. 3. 2 See SPB. i. 92–8; v. 2–12; SS. pp. 302–4.
3 YS. i. 23–9. Cf. ERE. vol. xii. p. 831.

infinite knowledge, wisdom, etc., as their limit. He to whom these latter belong is God. But it may be asked how these super-excellences can belong to God if he also, being a puruṣa, is bare spirit and stands aloof from prakṛti. To ward off such an objection the doctrine views God as endowed with a sort of personality implying actual contact with a physical adjunct which consists mainly of sattva and does not bind him. Besides affording the initial impetus for the evolution of prakṛti, he in his mercy helps his devotees in finding release from empirical existence. But God's help is not the only means of securing it, the successful practice of yoga, as we shall see, being another.

Before concluding this section, we may bring together the several postulates of the Sāṅkhya-Yoga to which we had occasion to refer. They are:—

(i) Whatever is, always is; and whatever is not, never is.
(ii) Change implies something that changes.
(iii) The effect is essentially the same as its material cause.
(iv) All variety can eventually be traced to three sources, which are not, however, independent but inter-dependent.
(v) Matter is characterized by perpetual motion.
(vi) Neither mind is derived from matter, nor matter from mind.

II

Here as elsewhere in Indian philosophy generally the term 'psychology' is to be understood in its etymological sense as the science of the soul. But what is the soul that can be thought of as the subject of experience in this system? We have the puruṣa, no doubt, but it really remains external to everything and cannot therefore stand for the subject of experience. There is another element that serves as an important aid in the process of knowing, viz. mahat or buddhi; but that is equally unsuited to be the subject though for quite a different reason. It is non-sentient (jaḍa) being derived from prakṛti, and experience cannot therefore be ascribed to it. Though neither by itself can serve as the subject, it is stated, they do so together, the buddhi contributing all the activity involved in it and the puruṣa the element of awareness (caitanya). The puruṣa illumines or is reflected in the buddhi, which though physical is fine enough to receive the reflection; and, thus illumined, it serves as the conscious subject. The buddhi may therefore be viewed as the physical medium for the manifestation of spirit. We may call their unity in this sense the empirical self to distinguish it from the puruṣa or the transcendental self. Owing to such association, each of the two elements in the empirical self appears completely transmuted—non-sentient buddhi becoming sentient, as it were, and passive puruṣa, active.[1] The illustration commonly given in this connection is the 'red-hot iron ball' where the formless glow of fire appears spherical and cold iron, hot. Every jñāna is a state of this blend. When we consider its two parts separately, the modification of the buddhi which such a state involves is called a vṛtti and the reflection of the puruṣa in it jñāna. Owing to the felt identity of the two elements, the vṛtti also is sometimes designated jñāna.[2]

It will be noticed that in the evolutionary scheme are included the eleven indriyas or sense organs (including manas), ahaṁ-kāra and buddhi; but there they represent successive stages in the evolution of the universe from prakṛti. These thirteen factors have also another aspect with which we are at present more particularly concerned. In this aspect they assist the individual in acquiring experience, and together constitute the psychic apparatus with which every puruṣa is endowed in the empirical state. The exact relation between these two aspects, viz. the cosmic and the individual, is a matter which shall immediately engage our attention. For the present it will suffice to recall the explanation already given of 'psychic' as applied to these factors. They are psychic in the sense that they lend themselves to be lighted up by the puruṣa unlike the other products of prakṛti, viz. the elements whether subtle or gross. It is this that distinguishes the two series, the subjective and the objective as we may call them. They are the result on the part of prakṛti to adapt itself to the requirements of the

[1] SK. st. 20.

[2] YSB. ii. 20; iv. 22.

puruṣa.[1] In other words, the functions that we describe as mental are really mechanical processes of physical organs, which assume a psychical character only when illumined by spirit. The senses are here derived from the aham-kāra, and not from the elements (bhūtas) as in the Nyāya-Vaiśeṣika (p. 248). Though traceable to one and the same source, each sense functions differently—the eye apprehending colour; the ear, sound; and so forth—owing to the difference in the collocation of the guṇas in them.

The Sāṅkhya-Yoga, like the Sautrāntika but unlike the Nyāya-Vaiśeṣika, believes that perception is effected by means of a psychic sign, viz. an image or idea (ākāra) of the object in question. The image is not transferred to the buddhi and found *in* it as may be supposed, but the buddhi itself assumes the form of the object, when a suitable stimulus is received from outside. The modification of the evolvent buddhi, viz. vṛtti, is a characteristic not only of perception but also of all forms of consciousness, and when it is inspired by spirit, experience results. The psychic apparatus as a whole mediates between the puruṣa and the outside world thereby securing for the former the experiences of life (bhoga) or, if the time for it is ripe, final freedom (apavarga) through right knowledge (viveka). The details of the process of knowing are as follows: The object first impresses one or other of the senses, and the jñāna that arises then is quite vague and general. It is 'bare awareness' (ālocana-mātra) and marks the nirvikalpaka stage. The first stage in perception does not accordingly refer, as in the Nyāya-Vaiśeṣika (p. 251), to the isolated and discriminate particular. It becomes properly explicated later when interpreted by the manas, and is therefore termed 'determinate' or savikalpaka. Pratyakṣa does not accordingly start here from detached elements and synthesize them, but from an indistinguishable whole into which it introduces order afterwards.[2] This completes the process from the objective

[1] Instead of saying, as we ordinarily do, that we adjust ourselves to our environment, we should here say that prakṛti adjusts itself to our needs.

[2] SK. st. 27, 28 and 30. Vijñāna Bhikṣu somewhat modifies this view which is based upon STK. See SPB. ii. 32.

standpoint; but there follow two other stages before perception is psychologically fully explained. The first is the appropriation of the experience by the aham-kāra or the reference of it to the self in question. If now the perception is to lead to any action the buddhi intervenes and decides upon what action has to follow and issues instructions, so to say, to the proper motor organ (karmendriya), the result being either some action or desistence from it. The buddhi thus corresponds to the will-aspect of conscious life. If we use a single term—antaḥ-karaṇa—for the last three elements of the psychic apparatus, we see how the internal organ in one or other of its phases is engaged, when once the senses have been stimulated, in reacting to the stimulus. The order in which the psychic organs function, it will be seen, is the reverse of that in which they appear in the evolutionary scheme given above. In internal perception such as that of pain or pleasure, as also in mediate knowledge, the process is exactly the same; only the co-operation of the external senses (jñānendriya) is not required and they do not therefore function then. This analysis of the psychic process, which takes perception as an increasing differentiation in a presented whole, is very much sounder than that of the Nyāya Vaiśeṣika; but owing to the denial in the doctrine of direct interaction between the buddhi and spirit, there is even here a difficulty in understanding how experience emerges all at once out of a purely physical or physiological process. The illustration of a glowing iron ball is not apt, for the iron ball and fire are actually in relation there unlike the buddhi and the puruṣa here.

Now as regards the double sense in which the principles from mahat onwards, excluding the elements in their twofold form, are to be understood in the system. It is not difficult to understand their significance from the standpoint of individual experience. The process of perception, as just set forth, makes it quite clear. But the same cannot be said of their cosmic aspect, and it is impossible from the premises of the system to discover why these psychical terms should be applied to the ontological entities in question. The only way of explaining this obscure point is to assume a cosmic

Puruṣa and regard the whole process of evolution as an *ideal* presentation to him. That will give us at once a rendering in psychical terms of these ontological principles. If we identify the mahat—as cosmic buddhi illumined by spirit—with this Puruṣa, the next stage in evolution, viz. the ahaṁ-kāra will stand for the sense of self-hood which arises in him, positing on the one hand what we have described as the objective series or not-self; and on the other the subjective series, or more strictly, the apparatus of thought adapted to cognize it.[1] Since in the case of such a cosmic subject the order of psychological presentation coincides with that of actual evolution,[2] the above assumption also accounts for the order in which the several principles occur in the evolutionary scheme which, as observed already, is the reverse of that in which they function in individual mental life. When we remember that this is exactly the position of the Upaniṣads and that they mention more or less the same stages[3] in describing the creation of the world by the personal Brahman (mahān ātmā), it will be clear that the inclusion by the Sāṅkhya of these principles in its scheme is to be traced to the teaching of those treatises. But in its reaction against Absolutism, the doctrine has discarded the idea of a universal soul and by sundering it into two—prakṛti and puruṣa—has reduced each to a mere abstraction. For the activity of prakṛti is meaningless with puruṣa; and puruṣa, were it not for its association with prakṛti, would be hardly distinguishable from nothing. The result is that while the system professes to be dualistic, its implication is quite the reverse.[4]

[1] According to YSB. ii. 19, it would seem, the tanmātras are derived from mahat and not from ahaṁ-kāra. Such a view would give us the notion of the not-self at the same level at which the notion of the self is given. But see YSB. i. 45.

[2] See IP. vol. ii, p. 277; Prof. Keith: *Religion and Philosophy of the Veda*, pp. 535 ff.

[3] Cf. *Kaṭha Up.* I. iii. 10–13, II. iii. 7–11; *Praśna Up.* iv. 8; *Bṛ. Up.* I. iv. 1.

[4] In connection with the early history of Sāṅkhya, reference may be made to Prof. Dasgupta's *History of Indian Philosophy*, vol. i. pp. 213–22.

III

The view that knowledge arises through a psychic medium (buddhi-vṛtti) may easily lead to subjective idealism as it does in the Yogācāra school; but the Sāṅkhya-Yoga lays down a postulate at the very outset that all knowledge necessarily points to some object outside it. Belief in the plurality of selves which is an essential part of the doctrine furnishes a support for the postulate, since the agreement between what different people experience may be taken to vouch for the existence of a common or trans-subjective basis for it all.[1] The psychic medium accordingly is here but a connecting link between the knower and the known and does not displace the latter (p. 206). A natural corollary to this view is the correspondence theory of truth. That knowledge is true in which the form assumed by the buddhi rightly represents the object perceived. This is the Nyāya-Vaiśeṣika view as well; only the theory of representative ideas (vṛttis) is not accepted there. A more important difference between the two is that whereas in the Nyāya-Vaiśeṣika which makes the manas merely the pathway of knowledge, knowledge is supposed ordinarily to show objects *as they are*, there is here no guarantee that it does so. The buddhi, which so far as our present purpose is concerned may be taken as the equivalent of the manas of the Nyāya-Vaiśeṣika,[2] is conceived here not as passive but as endowed with self-activity and as the abode of numberless impressions acquired through experience during a beginningless past. Owing to this circumstance, every buddhi has its own special bent and different persons may not therefore be impressed in the same manner by the same object. Though one, the object becomes 'severalized,' as it were, in the act of being apprehended on account of the bias of individual percipients. These two factors, viz. the objects and the particular bent of the percipient, co-operate in all knowledge and the result-

[1] This is the significance of the words viṣaya and sāmānya used in SK. st. 11. Cf. also YS. iv. 15.

[2] Strictly it is the antaḥ-karaṇa, of which the buddhi is only one element, that corresponds to the manas of the Nyāya-Vaiśeṣika.

ing image may not, and generally is not, an exact copy of the former. It is in this power of meddling with the object which the buddhi possesses that we have to seek for the source of error. But the power only emphasizes one aspect rather than another of what is given and does not add any new feature to it. In other words, the activity which the buddhi exercises is selective, the theory being that only so much of the nature of an object is known as is in kinship with the perceiver's mood at the time. Like only appeals to like.[1] This alters very much the complexion of the resulting error. It is one of omission and not of commission as in the Nyāya-Vaiśeṣika. It is right so far as it goes; only it does not go sufficiently far. To get at the true nature of the object, we have accordingly to supplement our personal view by taking into consideration all other possible views of it. The doctrine admits, like Jainism (p. 159), that such comprehensive knowledge[2] is possible, but it can be attained only when the buddhi is purified by continuous self-discipline, so that generally speaking what we perceive is only partially true. Incompleteness is a common deficiency of our knowledge, and much of the evil in life is to be traced to viewing it as complete. Two people may disagree about an object though both may be right in part, because each is obsessed by the idea that he is in possession of the whole truth about it. There is also another deficiency characterizing all knowledge excepting only that of a 'freed man' or jīvan-mukta. As neither the buddhi by itself, nor the self by itself can, according to the system, be the conscious subject, we have to seek for it, as has already been pointed out, in the two together; and no experience is possible until we mistake them for one, or to be more correct, we fail to notice that there are two factors constituting it. This failure, termed aviveka or non-discrimination,[3] which again is an error only in a negative sense, is a pre-condition of all experience. It leads to a fatal confusion

[1] Compare the illustration of one and the same damsel appearing differently to different persons, given in STK. st. 13.

[2] See STK. st. 4, where such knowledge is described as ārṣam jñānam. Cf. YS. i. 48.

[3] For the use of this term or its equivalents see STK. st. 2, 21, 66, etc

between the puruṣa and the buddhi in which the characteristics of each are ascribed to the other and we talk of the buddhi as knowing and of the puruṣa as acting. It is the removal of this error, we may add by the way, through discrimination (viveka) between the two factors constituting the empirical self that the doctrine holds to be the chief aim of life.

Error may thus be of two kinds: (i) where only one object is involved, it is mistaking a part for the whole; and (ii) where two objects are involved, it is overlooking the distinction between them and so virtually identifying them with each other. The two kinds can be reduced to the same form, for the second may be looked upon as a particular case of the first. Not knowing the puruṣa or the buddhi completely we confound the one with the other; and when complete knowledge of them is attained the mistake will of itself disappear so that it also, like the first, may be said to result from incomplete knowledge. The two instances of incorrect knowledge given above may together be described as 'metaphysical error.' They are what vitiate all experience, and there is no escape from it until jīvan-mukti is achieved. But apart from this basic error of which man is not commonly aware, there is another with which he is quite familiar. Thus a white crystal appears red when it is placed by the side of a red flower; and we sometimes think we see silver when closer scrutiny discovers it to be only shell. Their explanation is similar: In the case of the first, the red flower as well as the white crystal is given, and it is because we lose sight of the fact that they are two that we mistake the colour of the crystal. It is non-discrimination (aviveka) as in the case of the puruṣa and the buddhi, the confusion between which is the cause of empirical life. The moment we realize that there is the flower *in addition to* the crystal, the error vanishes. In the case of the second, only one object, viz. shell, is presented and our error is owing to our stopping short at grasping its features which it has in common with silver for which it is mistaken. That is, it is incomplete knowledge that gives rise to error here, as in the case of the other variety of what we have termed 'metaphysical error.' Though thus the two forms of common illusion correspond to the two forms of the other, there is an important difference between them from the practical standpoint. To dispel the latter, *complete* knowledge is necessary; but in the case of the former it will suffice if we acquire such knowledge as does not leave out the feature which is *relevant* in the given context to distinguish the objects confounded with each other. To take the second of the two illusions we are considering, such a feature is the lightness of the shell as compared with the heaviness of silver. Because we overlook the fact that the object before us is too light to be silver, we fall into the error; and the moment we discover it, the error disappears.

Though the explanations of the several kinds of error may differ in matters of detail, their underlying principle is the same. Error is lack of sufficient knowledge (akhyāti),[1] not wrong knowledge (anyathā-khyāti) as in the Nyāya-Vaiśeṣika (p. 253); and the way to avoid it is to acquire more, if not complete, knowledge. The most important point in this explanation is that when the error is discovered, nothing of what was cognized before is sublated (bādhita). What is given in knowledge is always and necessarily a fact; only it may not be the whole of the fact. In other words, there is no subjective element in error. Truth does not supplant, but only supplements what is given in the so-called error. This view is what is generally found expressed in early Sāṅkhya-Yoga works.[2] But the *Sāṅkhya-sūtra* modifies it in a fundamental manner by admitting an ideal element in explaining error.[3] Thus it describes the illusion of the red-crystal as involving a positive relation between the two objects—the crystal and redness, which is not given, but is fancied so that, though the relata as such are real, the relation between them is not so. That is, error shows what is given as well as what is not (sadasat-khyāti)[4]—an explanation which seems

[1] This may also be described as sat-khyāti as nothing but the given is apprehended.

[2] See references given in footnote 3 on p. 289 as well as YS. ii. 26; *Bhoja-vṛtti* on YS. iv. 33.

[3] SP. v. 56.

[4] SPB. v. 26 and 56.

to be inconsistent with the fundamental postulates of the doctrine.[1] This later Sāṅkhya view of error, we shall see, is very much like the explanation given by Kumārila (viparīta-khyāti), while the earlier one resembles that given by Prabhākara (akhyāti).

The pramāṇas accepted here are only three: perception, inference and verbal testimony. The system, being derivative, has not developed these details separately and seems to have borrowed them from the Nyāya-Vaiśeṣika, so far as they are not inconsistent with its metaphysical view-point.[2] In perception alone is there any difference which is worth mentioning; and that difference is mainly due to the view taken of the process of knowing as already explained. In the case of inference and verbal testimony, the agreement with the Nyāya-Vaiśeṣika is almost complete. As regards validity (prāmāṇya), the Sāṅkhya-Yoga represents a position which is the exact opposite of the Nyāya-Vaiśeṣika. Validity and invalidity are both stated to be normal aspects of jñāna,[3] since according to the sat-kārya-vāda the potential alone can become the actual, and whatever manifests itself at any time should be regarded as already there. Both are therefore regarded as inherent in jñāna; and which of them shows itself at any time is determined by the circumstances that explain the genesis or apprehension of the jñāna in question. This is a statement which seems self-contradictory; but it is not out of keeping with the Sāṅkhya-Yoga principle that the phase of reality which reveals itself to us is always relative to our standpoint.

IV

The Sāṅkhya-Yoga, like the other systems, believes in karma and transmigration. What transmigrates, however, is not the self, which because it is all-pervading does not admit of change of place, but the subtle body (liṅga-śarīra) consisting of the eleven organs of sense together with buddhi,

[1] See for a further discussion of this point *Indian Philosophical Quarterly* (1929), pp. 99–105.

[2] SK. st. 4; YS. i. 7. See also STK. st. 5. [3] SD. p. 20; SDS. p. 129.

aham-kāra and the five rudimentary elements (tanmātras). This is a permanent annexe, so to speak, to each self which leaves it only at release. Death and birth mean only the change of the gross body and not of the subtle. In the latter are stored up all traces of past thought and action; and the acquisition of right knowledge depends upon the cleansing of this empirical outfit or more strictly of the buddhi which forms its pre-eminent element. Dharma and adharma are here conceived not as qualities of the self as in the Nyāya-Vaiśeṣika (p. 261), but only as modes of the buddhi which, owing to the congenital confusion between it and the puruṣa, are mistaken to belong to the latter.[1] It means that, like experience, morality also has significance only on the empirical plane. Intrinsically, neither the puruṣa nor the buddhi can be described as moral. In the Nyāya-Vaiśeṣika likewise is the ethical life confined to the empirical sphere; but while it constitutes there an actual, though only a temporary, phase in the history of the self, here good and evil do not so much as touch the puruṣa. To remain always absolutely untainted is, in fact, the essence of spirit as conceived here. The *Kārikā*[2] says: 'No puruṣa is bound or liberated; nor does any migrate. It is prakṛti in its manifold form that is bound, is liberated and migrates.'

The ideal is kaivalya or aloofness from prakṛti and all its transformations, which is quite in consonance with the pessimistic attitude of the doctrine. It is also termed apavarga, for the self in that state *escapes* from the realm of suffering. But no positive bliss is associated with it. The self not only has no pain or pleasure in that condition; it is also without knowledge, for it has not the means, viz. the buddhi and its accessories, wherewith to know. This reminds us of the Nyāya-Vaiśeṣika ideal; but sentience being conceived here as the very substance of the self, the charge of insentience cannot be brought against it as in the other system. The immediate cause of such aloofness is viveka or discriminating knowledge, which removes the cause of bondage. But the knowledge should be more than a mere belief that nature is different from spirit. It should be an immediate experience and the

[1] See SP. v. 20–5.

[2] St. 62.

truth should become known by the practical, we might say, as distinct from the theoretical reason. Thus in this doctrine also ignorance or ajñāna is the cause of suffering. It is not wrong knowledge as in the Nyāya-Vaiśeṣika (p. 265); but, according to the view of error set forth in the previous section, incomplete knowledge.

The Sāṅkhya, as it has been handed down to us, is almost silent regarding the method of acquiring the intuitive experience that results in release; the Yoga, on the other hand, is mainly concerned with its elaboration. The only reference to the disciplinary means found in the basic work of the Sāṅkhya, viz. the *Kārikā*, is meditation upon the truth that prakṛti and puruṣa are distinct[1]; and the rest of it has to be gathered from the sister system. As in so many other doctrines, the path to salvation here also lies through detachment (vairāgya) and meditation (yoga).[2] Detachment in the beginning can only be provisional (apara-vairāgya), for in its mature form (para-vairāgya) it presupposes complete knowledge. The provisional detachment which results from an awakening to the ills of life as it is commonly led, will gradually lead to the higher form of it, if meanwhile the disciple engages himself in learning and meditating upon the ultimate truth—a view which shows that the means of achieving the ideal is as much intellectual as it is moral. The discipline laid down by Patañjali is what is familiarly known as yoga. We cannot enter into the details of this training, which are somewhat technical, but can mention only its broad features:

(1) The preliminary moral training is included under the first two heads, which we had occasion to mention already (p. 263), of yama and niyama of the eight-fold means (aṣṭāṅga) of yoga.[3] Yama is mostly negative—consisting of non-injury (ahiṁsā), truth-speaking (satya), abstention from stealing or misappropriation of others' property (asteya), celibacy (brahma-carya) and disowning of possessions (aparigraha).[4] Niyama, which signifies the cultivation of

[1] St. 64. [2] YS. i. 12–16. [3] YS. ii. 29 ff.

[4] The resemblance of this part of the training to the 'five vows' of Jainism may be noted. See p. 166 *ante*.

positive virtues, comprises purity (śauca), contentment (saṁtoṣa), fortitude (tapas), study (svādhyāya) and devotion to God (Īśvara-praṇidhāna).[1] These are so to speak the ten commandments of the Yoga, and their general tendency is ascetic. Of the first group, non-injury is the most important and is stated to be the end and beginning of yama.[2] The remaining four virtues must not only be rooted in it, but also help to perfect it so that it may finally come to be practised irrespective of time, place and circumstance.

(2) After this ascetic preparation begins the yogic training proper. This is a form of discipline which is very old in India and was known both to the orthodox and heterodox circles. It finds a prominent place in the Upaniṣads as well as in doctrines like Buddhism. The references to it in the Mahābhārata also indicate its great vogue. But there were important differences in the way in which it was understood in the various schools. It was for instance practised by some with a view to acquire occult or supernatural powers and by others for the attainment of mokṣa. Among the latter, some took it as the means of becoming one with the Absolute; others, like the followers of the present doctrine, as that of merely shaking off the yoke of matter. Yoga as treated of by Patañjali, is very much rationalized; and, though he refers to the acquisition of certain supernatural powers, he dismisses them as really hindrances[3] to self-realization. This yogic training may be divided into two stages—the first comprising the next three of the eight-fold help—āsana ('posture'), prāṇāyāma ('control of breath') and pratyāhāra ('withdrawal of senses from their objects')—which aim at restraining the mind from the physical side; and the second comprising the remaining three of dhāraṇā, dhyāna and samādhi, which are different forms of concentration and aim directly at control-

[1] This is explained as cultivating a spirit of absolute self-surrender to God in whatever one does, suggesting the influence of the Gītā ideal of disinterested action. Here it appears as part of the preliminary discipline; but in YS. i. 23 such devotion to God is represented as a means, alternative to yogic practice, of attaining samādhi and, through it, kaivalya. For a possible explanation of this contradiction, see Prof. Dasgupta: *The Study of Patañjali* (Calcutta Uni. Pr.), pp. 166–7.

[2] Cf. YSB. ii. 30–1.

[3] iii. 27.

ling the same. The principle underlying the whole discipline is that man's faculties are by long habit adjusted to the preservation of the empirical self and that they must be readjusted[1] so as to secure the totally opposite aim of restoring the puruṣa-element in it to its true condition. Of these several stages in reaching yogic perfection, it is necessary to add a few words of explanation only on the last, viz. samādhi, which directly leads to kaivalya. It is divided into a lower and a higher form known respectively as saṁprajñāta and asaṁprajñāta samādhi. The latter is the goal,[2] the former serving but as a stepping-stone to it. In both alike there is need for the highest power of concentration. The first is a state in which the buddhi continues to function though it is wholly absorbed in the contemplation of a particular object, everything else being excluded—even the fact that one is having a vision of it. It is accordingly described as 'conscious samādhi.' All sources of distraction are eradicated here and the buddhi shines forth with its sattva element in the ascendant. In asaṁprajñāta-samādhi, the consciousness of the object also disappears, and it is therefore described as 'superconscious.' The buddhi ceases to function then or its vṛttis, as it is expressed, become latent or get lost in their source.[3] In that condition not only are the inferior vṛttis arising from the dominance of rajas and tamas overcome, but also those arising from sattva. When in the final form of asaṁprajñāta-samādhi the buddhi is thus concentrated on the self, it vanishes once for all, leaving the puruṣa apart and alone. If we compare our common mental state to the ruffled surface of water in a lake which reflects an object like a tree on the bank as a distorted image, the saṁprajñāta condition may be likened to the calm surface containing a steady and faithful image of it and the asaṁprajñāta to the condition where the tree is by itself and there is no image at all for the lake has dried up. There are thus altogether three levels of life that may be distinguished: the first in which rajas or tamas is the chief governing factor, the second in which sattva predominates and the third which transcends sattva also. The lower

[1] YSB. ii. 33. [2] YS. i. 3 and 4. [3] YS i. 2.

samādhi is quite intelligible psychologically; but the higher, because it presupposes the suppression of the mind, takes us beyond normal psychical life. We pass in it to the realm of mysticism.

A person that has reached this stage, when his lease of life runs out, attains kaivalya once for all and there is no return thence. But that is the goal of life in the eschatological sense (videha-mukti). There is another that can be reached in this life, viz. jīvan-mukti, which the doctrine explicitly admits.[1] In this condition the puruṣa continues to be related to the buddhi, but it is the buddhi which has been purged of its defects and is fully enlightened. The attitude of the jīvan-mukta towards the world is very much like that of the perfected man according to the Nyāya-Vaiśeṣika ideal (p. 266). He participates in its life, but is detached from it Though in the world, he is not of it.

[1] SK. st. 67–8.

CHAPTER XII

PŪRVA-MĪMĀṀSĀ

THE distinguishing feature of this system, as compared with the others so far considered, is its adherence to the Veda as in itself an infallible authority. We have seen systems like Jainism refusing altogether to recognize its authority and others like the Nyāya attempting to subordinate it to some other. The Mīmāṁsā differs from them all in that it places the Veda or śruti on a footing peculiarly its own. As to the exact place it assigns to reason, we have to refer the reader to what was stated in an earlier chapter (pp. 180–2). It will suffice now to observe that though thus authoritative in its own right, revealed truth comes to us through the medium of words whose interpretation is by no means easy. Hence the need for mīmāṁsā or the investigation of the principles according to which the texts enshrining that truth are to be interpreted.[1] It is only when thus assisted by reason that the Veda will disclose its true import. The primary aim of the Mīmāṁsā as a branch of learning may, therefore, be described as getting back from the expression to the idea behind it, the solving of the important problem of the relation of speech and thought. Since the view taken of language here is that it is independent of the individual using it,[2] the system involves a great deal of discussion relating to social or folk psychology. This psychological inquiry contains much that is valuable for the modern science of Semantics or the branch of knowledge dealing with meaning in relation to linguistic forms. The Mīmāṁsā in this respect serves as a necessary complement to Vyākaraṇa or Grammar, whose treatment of words is mainly formal. The indirect advantage thus resulting to psychology and philology, forms one of the most important

[1] See e.g. PP. p. 104. Mīmāṁsā is viewed as a form of tarka, since it assists a pramāṇa. Cf. Note 1 on p. 182.

[2] Compare SD. Śabda-sādhutve hi prayoga-paravaśā vayam na svayam īśmahe (p. 122). Yathā-lokam ca śabdārthāvadhāraṇam na yatheccham (p. 127).

features of the study of Mīmāṁsā. The laws of interpretation formulated by Jaimini and his successors are quite general, and they are applicable as much to works outside the Veda as to that ancient text. They have, in fact, become widely current and are utilized for arriving at a right interpretation of all old texts, particularly legal treatises (dharma-śāstra).

Speaking generally, we may say that the Mīmāṁsā attaches greater importance to the Brāhmaṇas than to the Mantras, which means that it looks upon the Veda as essentially a book of ritual. It not only subordinates the earlier Mantras, but also the later Upaniṣads. Its designation as Pūrva-mīmāṁsā has reference to this latter phase, viz. its being concerned with the teaching of those portions of the Veda that come *before* the Upaniṣads, the darśana dealing with the latter being termed Uttara-mīmāṁsā. The sacrificial inquiry which forms the main subject-matter of the Mīmāṁsā is, no doubt, very old. It is the chief purpose of the Śrouta-sūtras and is found even in the Brāhmaṇas. Doubts and discussions regarding ritual are but natural, especially when once the stage of its inception is passed. The Mīmāṁsā only extends the scope of the inquiry and makes it more systematic. We must not understand from this that it deals with sacrifices precisely as taught in the Brāhmaṇas. Separated as it must have been in its origin from the Brāhmaṇas by several generations, the Mīmāṁsā marks both growth and decay in its conception of ritual. It does, as a matter of fact, reinterpret and in reinterpreting considerably modify the old system of rites. The doctrine as known to us also exhibits a far more important change, viz. the subordination of the idea of sacrifice itself to that of the attainment of mokṣa. The aim of life as originally conceived was, to state it in general terms, the attainment of heaven (svarga). The replacement of this aim by the ideal of mokṣa points to a radical transformation of the doctrine. By it, the Mīmāṁsā ceases to be a mere commentary on Vedic ritual and becomes a darśana. It is therefore in its present form vastly different from what its other name, Karma-mīmāṁsā, may suggest. The emphasis that it lays on the performance of rites, so far as that emphasis is still preserved, has now in effect become quite secondary. This important change should have been brought about by a desire on the part of the later exponents of the Mīmāṁsā to bring it into line with the other systems of thought and not allow it to remain a mere liturgical discussion bearing upon rites which probably had by that time become more or less defunct. The change has not taken place in the Kalpa-sūtras, if we leave out the few references to self-realization (ātma-lābha) in them[1]; but it is clearly seen in Upavarṣa and Śabarasvāmin, early commentators on the *Sūtra* of Jaimini, and is very common in their successors. The darśana aspect of it is, therefore, comparatively late. The speculative spirit underlying it is not new to the Veda as a whole, for it is found in the Upaniṣads and in the allegorical interpretations of rites sometimes given in the Brāhmaṇas themselves. But the special type of philosophic theory which it now represents follows quite other lines. It is not derived from the philosophy of the Mantras; neither does it continue Upaniṣadic speculation. It is traceable to sources other than the Veda and is therefore neither a religion of nature nor a philosophy of the Absolute. Some of its minor tenets may be allied to what is found in the philosophic portions of the Veda; but, strange as it may seem, the larger part of them and the more important among them have, as we shall see, been borrowed from the Nyāya-Vaiśeṣika. The spirit of the Brāhmaṇas was to supersede the simple nature-worship of the Mantras; the spirit of the fully developed Mīmāṁsā is to supersede ritualism as taught in the Brāhmanas and later systematized in the Śrouta-sūtras. But the supersession in neither stage is complete, so that the Mīmāṁsā as now known is an admixture of the rational and the dogmatic, the natural and the supernatural and the orthodox and the heterodox. It is with the darśana aspect of the system that we shall deal here and not with its ritualistic theories or its exegetical principles.

The main source of authority in regard to this system is Jaimini's *Mīmāṁsā-sūtra.* Its date, as in the case of the other philosophical Sutras, is quite indefinite; but it is commonly believed now to have been the earliest of them all and assigned

[1] See Note 1 on p. 93.

to about 200 A.D. The system of thought itself, however, is much older, references to it being found in such early works as the Dharma-sūtras[1] and possibly also in the *Mahābhāṣya* of Patañjali (150 B.C.).[2] The sūtras are considerably over 2,500 in number and are divided into twelve chapters with sixty sub-sections in all. There are nearly a thousand topics discussed so that the work is by far the biggest of the philosophical Sūtras. Like the others of its class the work when read by itself is for the most part unintelligible, and the aid of a commentary which preserves the traditional interpretation is indispensable for understanding it. Such an aid we have in the bhāṣya of Śabarasvāmin, who wrote it probably about 400 A.D. Tradition fondly associates Śabara with King Vikramāditya, who is supposed to have lived in the first century B.C., but there seems to be no truth in it. There was at least one earlier commentary on the work by Upavarṣa (A.D. 350), but nothing of it is known to us, except a possible extract from it in Śabara's bhāṣya.[3] The bhāṣya has been explained in two ways by Prabhākara (A.D. 650) and Kumārila Bhaṭṭa (A.D. 700), who differ from each other in certain essential respects. Prabhākara's 'great commentary' known as the *Bṛhatī* is yet in manuscript, except for a small fragment which has been published; and the same is the case with the *Ṛju-vimalā*, commentary upon it by Śālikanātha, believed to have been a pupil of Prabhākara. The views of the school have therefore to be gathered from the *Prakaraṇa-pañcikā* of the latter, which also has unfortunately not been recovered completely. Bhavanātha was another influential writer of the school with his yet unpublished *Naya-viveka*. As regards the second school, which for a long time has practically superseded the first, we have adequate material for reference. Kumārila's own huge and important work is fully printed and consists of a general or philosophical part called the *Śloka-vārtika* and two others—*Tantra-vārtika* and *Ṭup-ṭīkā*. The first of these has been commented upon in a most lucid manner by Pārthasārathi Miśra in his *Nyāya-ratnākara*. Maṇḍana Miśra, probably a pupil of Kumārila,

[1] See Prof. Keith: *Karma-mīmāṁsā*, p. 2.

[2] Cf. IV. i. 14.

[3] I. i. 5.

was a famous thinker who has to his credit many works on the Mīmāṁsā like the *Vidhi-viveka* and the *Bhāvanā-viveka.* Several other works of this school are also known, amongst which we may note Pārthasārathi's *Śāstra-dīpikā*, Mādhava's *Nyāya-mālā-vistara* (A.D. 1350) and Khaṇḍadeva's *Bhāṭṭa-dīpikā* (A.D. 1650). These follow in their explanation the order of the sūtras of Jaimini. Several independent treatises also are known which serve as useful manuals on the ritualistic or the interpretative side of the system. Such is the *Mīmāṁsā-nyāya-prakāśa* of Āpadeva (A.D. 1650) and a digest—or, according to some, the chief basis[1] of it—by Laugākṣi Bhāskara, the *Artha-saṁgraha*. Another work which deals with the philosophic teaching of the school of Kumārila or the Bhāṭṭa school, as it is termed, is the *Māna-meyodaya.* It has come to light only latterly and is the composition of two writers who lived about the sixteenth century A.D. Our treatment of the system will be general; but wherever there are important divergences between the two schools from the philosophical view-point, we shall notice them. The chronological relation of these schools is yet a matter of dispute; but, speaking on the whole, the Prābhākara school seems to be the older and to preserve better the distinctive lineaments of the original Mīmāṁsā or at least to be nearer in spirit to it than the other.[2]

I

The conception of ātman is somewhat different in the two schools, but both agree regarding its plurality. To consider first the school of Kumārila: The view is very much like the Nyāya-Vaiśeṣika one and ātman is conceived as both an agent (kartā) and an enjoyer (bhoktā). But while the Nyāya-Vaiśeṣika admits no action in the self—neither change of place (spanda), nor change of form (pariṇāma)—here though the former is denied, the latter is admitted.[3] That is, the system recognizes the possibility of modal change in the self. Though undergoing modifications it is regarded as

[1] Prof. Edgerton: *Mīmāṁsā-nyāya-prakāśa* (Yale Uni. Pr.), pp. 22–3. [2] Prof. Keith, *op. cit.*, pp. 9–10. [3] SV. p. 707, st. 74.

eternal, for Kumārila rejects the view that even internal change militates against permanence. Experience acquaints us daily with many things that change almost constantly, but yet maintain their identity. Jñāna or knowledge is a mode of the self. It is described as an act (kriyā) or process (vyāpāra)[1] and is naturally spoken of as supersensible, since it is found in so ethereal a 'substance' as the self. This change or disturbance which takes place in the ātman brings about a certain relation with the object known. The self, being by hypothesis omnipresent, is necessarily in relation with all existent objects; but that relation is not the same as the one we are now considering. If it were, jñāna would arise in respect of all objects as long as they existed. The relation resulting from jñāna is unique and is described as 'comprehension' (vyāptṛ-vyāpyatva). The act or process of jñāna is viewed as transitive so that its result (phala) has to be sought in something other than where it manifests itself. The act of cooking, for example, is seen in the agent, but its result—'softness' (vikleda)—is found in the material cooked, viz. the rice-grain. The former is the subject; and the latter, the object. When jñāna arises in the self relating it to an object, the latter is affected in a particular way so that experience is not wholly a subjective modification, but has also an objective modification corresponding to it. The object becomes 'illumined' (prakāśa-viśiṣta) thereby; and its being thus illumined or made known (prākaṭya or jñātatā) serves as the means for our concluding that jñāna must have arisen in the self previously. The arising of jñāna is thus only to be inferred. While it can reveal other objects, it has no power to manifest itself. Though knowable, jñāna is conceived here as known indirectly through inference and not directly through introspection as in the Nyāya-Vaiśeṣika (p. 251). The new feature of being illumined which characterizes the object, as a consequence of jñāna arising in respect of it, may mean that it is known mediately or immediately. According to this double nature of the result, jñāna is either mediate (parokṣa) or immediate (pratyakṣa).

The proximate cause of perception which leads to direct

[1] SD. pp. 56–7.

knowledge (viśadāvabhāsa) is the contact of the senses with their respective objects. The knowledge that we so get is in the first instance quite vague and indefinite and is named ālocana as in the Sāṅkhya-Yoga (p. 285). It gains clarity and definiteness only afterwards. The earlier stage in this process is described as 'indeterminate' (nirvikalpaka); and the later, 'determinate' (savikalpaka).[1] The conception of the two stages here is therefore different from that in the Nyāya-Vaiśeṣika. Another important divergence from the Nyāya-Vaiśeṣika is that the nirvikalpaka here is not merely a theoretical supposition which, beyond explaining the savikalpaka, serves no practical purpose (p. 251). It is quite useful and the Mīmāṁsaka admits that activity may be, and actually is, based upon it. Children and animals whose mental growth is incomplete or imperfect act only under the promptings of this primitive stage of perception and even elderly people do the same when in a flurry.[2] That is, the nirvikalpaka is not here a mere hypothesis formulated to account for some known phase of experience, but is a part of normal experience itself. Like the Nyāya-Vaiśeṣika, the Mīmāṁsā also recognizes manas as a sense (indriya) in addition to the five admitted by all and its co-operation is laid down as indispensable for all jñāna. Regarding the structural character of the senses also, there is a general agreement—the first four senses of sight, flavour, odour and touch being taken as derived from the elements whose distinctive qualities are their respective objects. In the case of the manas, the view is that it may or may not be derived from the elements (bhūtas). As regards the remaining sense, viz. that of sound, the school, relying on the Vedic statement that 'the organ of hearing proceeds from dik,'[3] makes it delimited space (dik)[4] and does not connect it with ākāśa. The senses including the manas, with or without contact with objects according as the knowledge is immediate or mediate, furnish the external conditions which induce

[1] SD. pp. 36 and 40.

[2] SD. p. 40 (com.). The reference to the behaviour of animals and children is noteworthy.

[3] *Muṇḍaka Up.* II. i. 4.

[4] See SD. p. 36.

change in the self constituting knowledge; and it is the dissociation once for all from them in MOKṢA that will set the self free as in the Nyāya-Vaiśeṣika.

So far we have taken into consideration the waking state. More or less the same description applies to dream also; only the co-operation of the five external organs of sense is there withdrawn. In regard to sleep (suṣupti), Kumārila holds a somewhat peculiar view. He admits of course that the self endures in it as other Indian thinkers generally do; but in consonance with his view of knowledge, he regards the self as characterized then by the potency to know (jñāna-śakti). In this, he differs from the Nyāya-Vaiśeṣika, which denies jñāna in every form to the self in sleep. He also dissents from the Upaniṣads because he recognizes no happiness then. The later reminiscence of happiness to which the Vedāntin pointedly draws our attention (p. 72), Kumārila explains negatively—as due to the absence at the time of all consciousness of pain. If the self were really in the enjoyment of the highest bliss then, it would be impossible, he says, to explain the feeling of regret which a person feels afterwards if he comes to know that by going to sleep he has missed some common pleasure.[1]

There is one other point to which we must allude before we leave this part of the subject and it is the way in which, according to Kumārila, we become aware of our own self. It is known directly through the ahaṁ-pratyaya or the 'I-notion' as we may render it.[2] This forms an important point in the teaching and requires explanation. Kumārila understands 'self-consciousness' literally and holds that the self can at once be both subject and object—the knower as well as the known (jada-bodhātmaka) and adduces as evidence therefor the common saying: 'I know myself.'[3] Ascribing such an apparently contradictory character to the self is quite in harmony with the ruling principle of his thought, which, as we shall see, is that the nature of things cannot

1 SD. p. 124. 2 Ibid., p. 122.

3 This saying is to be viewed as only partially representing experience as it actually occurs, for it necessarily includes a reference to an object (say, a 'jar') other than the self which is left out here.

be rigidly determined as such and such (bhedābheda-vāda).[1] In a sample of knowledge like 'I know the jar.' there are two elements—one comprehending the self (ahaṁ-vṛtti) and the other comprehending the object in question (e.g. ghaṭa-vṛtti). That is, self-awareness is constant and accompanies all states of consciousness, being absent only in deep sleep where no object is known. When we say that the self is thus known in all experience, we must not take it to mean that it is known as the *subject* in the act of knowing. The fact of knowing is itself not known at the time and has, as already pointed out, to be inferred later. We cannot, therefore, know the self then as characterized by or as owning such knowledge, which is what is meant by the term 'subject.' But yet the self cannot be unknown, for that would go against the felt personal identity in all one's experience. It is therefore explained as being known then as the *object* of the 'I-notion.' If we take this along with the view that the self to be known at all must at the time become aware of some object or other, we see that self-consciousness, according to Kumārila, implies not only an internal difference—a self which is opposed to itself as its object, but also an external difference —a self which is distinguished from the not-self.

Prabhākara disagrees with Kumārila in two important respects in his view of the self, and in both he sides with the Nyāya-Vaiśeṣika.[2] Not believing in pariṇāma, he does not admit that the self suffers change. Again he objects to the description of the self as 'knowable,' and avers that agent and object can never be the same in any act. It is only objects that are knowable. The self, on the other hand, is a subject and is revealed *as such* in all jñāna. If it were not so revealed simultaneously with the object, one's jñāna would be indistinguishable from another's. From this, it should not be thought that the ātman is self-luminous. It is wholly non-sentient (jaḍa), and therefore requires for its revelation the presence of some knowledge to which the character of self-luminousness is assigned.[3] Though thus dependent upon an aid the self, to be realized, does not require a separate

[1] SD. p. 101.
[2] See PP. chap. viii, especially pp. 152 ff.
[3] PP. p. 51.

mental act, it being manifest equally whenever any object is known. The word which the Prābhākaras use for knowledge or experience is saṁvit which, being self-luminous (svaprakāśa), needs nothing else to make it manifest. Though ultimate in this sense, it is not eternal. It appears and disappears; and, as it does so, reveals both the object and the self simultaneously with itself. This triple revelation is what is described as tripuṭī-jñāna. So far as other psychological details are concerned, it will suffice to remark that there is a still closer approximation here to the Nyāya-Vaiśeṣika than in the previous school.

II

The main object of the Mīmāṁsaka is to establish the authority of the Veda; but he does not like to do so solely on dogmatic considerations and therefore tries to seek rational grounds for it. He contends that his system does not consist merely in delivering settled judgments (upadeśa-śāstra), but is a reasoned inquiry (parīkṣā-śāstra).[1] The very classification by him of revelation along with perception and inference under pramāṇa shows it. The testimony of the Veda is but a particular means of knowing truth; and whatever value there is in it, the Mīmāṁsaka holds, is due to its being a pramāṇa like perception or inference. It is thus that he enters the arena of logic; and, though he may not be a rationalist in the full sense of the term, he cannot at the same time be described as a mere dogmatizer.

The system starts by postulating what is called the svataḥ-prāmāṇya or the self-validity of knowledge (p. 260) both in respect of its origin (utpattau) and ascertainment (jñaptau).[2] If *a*, *b*, and *c* (say) account for the genesis of knowledge, those causes themselves explain its validity also. Similarly the validity of knowledge is known when the knowledge itself is known; and no additional means is required therefor. All knowledge is presumably valid and an explanation is called

[1] See SD. p. 18 and cf. *Jaimini-sūtra*. I. i. 3.
[2] SD. pp. 19–23 and 48–50; PP. ch. iv.

for only where any particular knowledge fails to be so. We proceed to act always on the supposition that the knowledge we get is true; but if any part of it is discovered to be not so, we seek for the cause of its invalidity in extraneous circumstances that must have interfered with the free functioning of this means. The cause of invalidity is some defect in the means or source of knowledge (karaṇa-doṣa). Thus a person may think that he sees a particular thing, silver, while it is only shell because his eyesight is defective. This is how wrong knowledge arises. It is found out by its incompatibility with subsequent experience (bādhaka-pratyaya). When the person, who fancies that he sees a serpent, at a distance, approaches it and discovers it to be a rope, he concludes that his previous knowledge was erroneous. While thus the Mīmāṁsā agrees with the Nyāya-Vaiśeṣika in its view of the invalidity of knowledge (aprāmāṇya), it disagrees with it in respect of the view it takes of its validity (prāmāṇya). The chief reason for the disagreement is the disaccord between the nature of truth as defined in the Nyāya-Vaiśeṣika and the manner in which it proposes to verify it. Truth is stated to be correspondence with reality, but the test does not, indeed cannot, ascertain that correspondence. So the doctrine proposes an indirect test—fruitful activity (saṁvādi-pravṛtti). What serves as the test is thus really another experience—that of thirst being quenched, to cite the example already given. Now this second experience cannot validate the first without itself being similarly validated; and setting about verifying it would only mean going on *ad infinitum*. Even supposing that this second experience needs no verification, it cannot vouch for the presence of a corresponding reality outside knowledge. A person may dream of water and also of quenching his thirst by drinking it. There is fruitful activity here, but no objective counterpart. What the test actually finds out is only whether two experiences cohere, and to accept such a test as adequate is virtually to give up the realistic position because the supposed correspondence with reality is left wholly unverified. Thus we see that though the Nyāya-Vaiśeṣika starts as realism, it fails to maintain its position in the solution of what is one of the crucial problems of philosophy—that of truth and error. The fact is that a realistic doctrine cannot adhere to the view that validity is determined *ab extra* (parataḥ-prāmāṇya). That is why the Mīmāṁsā, which likewise upholds realism, advocates the opposite view of svataḥ-prāmāṇya and, by presuming all knowledge to be valid, normally dispenses with the need for testing it.

We may now point out the bearing of such a view of pramāṇa upon the authority of the Veda which is of paramount importance to the Mīmāṁsaka. Neither the circumstance that renders knowledge invalid nor that which leads to its discovery exists in the case of the Veda. There can be no flaw at the source (karaṇa-doṣa); for the source in the case of verbal testimony is the speaker or writer, and the Veda, according to the Mīmāṁsaka, is self-existent and has had no author at all (apauruṣeya). Nor is there the possibility of its coming into conflict with perceptual or other form of common experience, for what it teaches refers, by hypothesis, only to matters beyond this life and is therefore empirically unverifiable (p. 180). We may think that though not contradicting common experience, the Veda may be discrepant with itself by teaching one thing here and another there. But no such discrepancy will be found, it is maintained, if we properly understand the Veda. It is in determining what a proper understanding of it is that the rules of interpretation, to which we referred above, are laid down. This view, which is peculiar to the Mīmāṁsā, requires further elucidation.

The Veda here stands for a form of uttered words and it is in this sense that the Mīmāṁsaka holds it to be self-existent. He bases his view mainly upon the following considerations:

(1) The relation between a word and its meaning is natural and therefore necessary and eternal. We ought not to think that things were there already before they were named. The word and the thing it names go together and it is impossible to think of either as having had a beginning in time.[1] But we must carefully note what in this view is meant by the terms 'word' and 'thing.' In order to know the character of the

[1] SD. pp. 90–7 and 116–17. See also p. 44, com.

former, it is necessary to distinguish first between varṇa and dhvani. A varṇa is an articulate sound. It is conceived as integral (niravayava) and omnipresent (sarva-gata) and therefore also eternal (nitya). That a varṇa can be uttered several times or in several ways does not mean that there are as many particular cases of it with a universal running through them. What thus diversify it are its accidental features; and, however much they may change, a varṇa remains the same. One of the important arguments adduced in support of its permanence is the ready recognition we have when the same varṇa is uttered more than once, which implies that all those utterances refer but to an identical thing. We say for example that the *a*-sound is uttered ten times and not that ten *a*-sounds are uttered. If they did not refer to the same the recognition would have to be explained —without adequate reason for doing so—as an illusion, no identity being possible between the fleeting utterances themselves. The latter, viz. dhvani, is viewed as the means of manifesting the varṇa which has all along been there; and it may be compared to the written symbol, the chief difference being that, when there are several varṇas, we have a temporal series of utterances in the one case, but a spatial series of written signs in the other. The variety of ways in which a varṇa may be uttered, as e.g. with different stresses, is explained as due to differences in this means of utterance. The nature of dhvani is explained in alternative ways, but we need not enter here into a discussion of such details. It is enough for our purpose to regard it as 'tone' which, as the means of revealing varṇas, must be different from them. It is also transient and limited to the place where it is heard. A 'word' (śabda) is two or more of these varṇas, and is regarded as merely an aggregate (samudāya) and not as a whole (avayavin) distinguishable from each of its constituent parts and from all of them. But yet the necessity is recognized in the case of every word for the varṇas in it occurring in a specific order; for otherwise words like dīna ('pitiful') and nadī ('river'), which consist of the same varṇas but placed in a different order, would not differ in their connotation. This order, however, can refer only to their manifestation and not to the varṇas themselves which are, by hypothesis, present everywhere and at all times. Their gradual or progressive utterance does not interfere with the unity of the word as the perceptual process, for instance, which also is gradual, does not affect the unity of an object like a tree when it is seen. As regards the 'things' signified by words, we are not to understand the particular facts of experience which come into being and disappear, but the corresponding universals which are eternal and of which the passing individuals are nothing more than signs. That is, the significance of the word is general[1] though, when associated with other words to form a sentence, it may come to denote a particular. The word and the meaning being both eternal, the relation between them also is necessarily so. It does not follow from this that the Mīmāṁsaka rejects the conventional element in language. He only assigns a subordinate place (sahakāri) to it though a necessary one, the purpose it serves being illustrated by that of light in seeing.[2] If the conventional element were not admitted, tuition or instruction regarding the meanings of words by one who is already familiar with them, which is known to be necessary for learning a language, would become superfluous. The problem discussed here is a philological one and the solution reached is that language is not a creation of the human or even of the divine mind—the former being the view held in modern and the latter, in ancient Nyāya[3]—but a natural phenomenon.[4] In holding such a view, the Mīmāṁsā resembles the older school of modern philolologists, which maintained that philology was a natural science.

(2) The permanence of the relation between a word and its meaning, even though it be granted, does not establish the

[1] The meaning of proper names is regarded as due to mere convention (See PP. pp. 135–6 and SV. p. 674, st. 120). But even here the connotation is general, e.g. Devadatta' means not the person so named in any particular stage of life but the individual who, in spite of minor changes, endures throughout life. Cf. Mammaṭa's *Kāvyaprakāśa*, ii. 8.

[2] SD. p. 91.

[3] SM. p. 361.

[4] It is social also in so far as it involves a conventional element. The diversity of existing languages is explained as the result of corruption in an original ideal speech. That is to put the cart before the horse.

eternity of the Veda. It merely serves as a negative aid to it by precluding the conclusion which one may draw at once that whatever is verbal in form must necessarily have had an origin in time. The Veda consists of words, and so far it is like any other literary work. If the permanence of the word and meaning constituted the criterion of eternity, all literary works, in fact all uttered statements, would alike be eternal. If the Veda alone is so and not other works also, it should be traced to some unique feature it possesses; and such a feature, it is said, is the *particular order* (ānupūrvī) in which the several words occur in it. When the Mīmāṁsaka states that the Veda is eternal, it is this permanence of the text that he means. He views the Veda as produced by no author—human or divine; and he maintains that it has been preserved intact during a beginningless period by being handed down from teacher to pupil with scrupulous care.[1] This belief is based on the circumstance that tradition, though going back to a far-distant antiquity, has throughout been silent in regard to the authorship of the Veda, while in the case of even very ancient works—like those of Buddha or the Mahābhārata—mention is made of some author or other. While the order of the words in those works was determined by their authors, it is self-determined in the Veda. This argument again, granting that tradition is really silent on the authorship of the Veda, is negative and can lead to nothing that is decisive.

Thus the Mīmāṁsaka doctrine of the fixity of the Vedic text rests upon a certain view of language it takes and upon the supposed absence of all reference in long-standing tradition to its having been composed by one or more authors. In neither case, it is clear, is the premise adequate to support the important conclusion that is drawn from it. The belief in its present form is therefore nothing more than a dogma. This 'idolatry of scripture' appears comparatively late and seems to have been arrived at by extending to the form of the Veda what was once taken to hold good of its content. The truth concealed under this purely scholastic view, therefore, is that the Veda embodies eternal verities. In the case of

[1] *Jaimini-sūtra*. I. i. 27–32.

smṛtis, as distinguished from the śruti, it is even now held that this content constitutes the truth revealed, though an attempt is made, under the influence of views similar to the one we are now considering, to trace it (p. 91) eventually to some śruti which is no longer extant. In this connection it is instructive to cite the opinion of the grammarian Patañjali of the second century B.C., that while the sense of the Veda is eternal the order of the words in it is not so. 'Is it not said that the Vedas were not composed—but are eternal? Quite so; but it is their sense that is so, not the order of the syllables in them.'[1]

Coming now to the Mīmāṁsaka theory of knowledge, we have to note that it is realistic, both according to Kumārila and Prabhākara; and there is no knowledge which does not point to a corresponding object outside it.[2] But all knowledge is here presumed to be true, according to the theory of self-validity and verification becomes necessary only when any doubt is cast upon its validity. The one kind of knowledge that does not come under this description is memory. According to the Bhāṭṭas, recollection is not valid for novelty is a necessary condition of validity.[3] Truth should not only be not contradicted by subsequent knowledge (abādhita); it should also point to something not hitherto known (anadhigata). Prabhākara does not accept this condition, for all experience (anubhūti)—whether the object be already known or not—is valid for him. Even the so-called error, as we shall immediately see, satisfies this requirement. But he also differentiates recollection from anubhūti, for it is not experience in the primary sense of the term, being dependent upon a former one (sāpekṣa).[4] If all experience by its very nature is valid, it may be asked how error arises at all. Kumārila and Prabhākara differ considerably in their answers to this question and their explanations are known respectively as viparīta-khyāti and akhyāti. It would be better to begin with a description of the latter and then contrast the former with it.

(1) *Akhyāti.*—The word khyāti means 'knowledge' and

[1] IV. iii. 101.
[2] See e.g. SV. p. 217, st. 3; PP. iv. 66.
[3] SD. p. 45; SV. p. 431, st. 104–6.
[4] PP. pp. 42–3, 127.

the term akhyāti, which is literally equivalent to 'no knowledge,' is applied to Prabhākara's theory to indicate that error, according to it, is not a unit of knowledge, but a composite of two jñānas.[1] When shell is mistaken for silver and we say to ourselves, 'This is silver,' the 'this' is actually perceived as also certain features of the shell which it possesses in common with silver. The knowledge of those features revives in our mind the impression of a former experience and we recollect silver. The so-called error here really consists of these two jñānas—perception immediately followed by memory. Of these the first is true so far as it goes, though it may not go sufficiently far. Its object 'this' is not sublated afterwards since, even when the error is discovered, we feel '*This* is shell.' The same, no doubt, cannot be said of the second jñāna because its object, silver, is not found in the given context. But in this it only exhibits its normal character; for it is memory—although we at the time lose sight of that fact (smṛti-pramoṣa)[2]—and does not as such signify that the object is present then. That is, the former knowledge claims to be valid and the claim is justified; the latter does not put forward any such claim at all. Indeed, Prabhākara does not admit that knowledge can ever play false to its logical nature; and there is consequently no error, according to him, in the common acceptance of the term. In what passes for error, we overlook the fact that there are two jñānas;[3] and, as a natural consequence, we also fail to notice the separateness of their respective objects. This failure to know, however, cannot by itself account for the 'error'; because, if it did, errors would occur in dreamless sleep,[4] which also is characterized by absence of knowledge. The negative factor of failure is therefore viewed as operating

[1] Strictly this should be 'saṁvit.' But to secure uniformity of terminology in considering this topic of truth and error in the two schools, we use 'jñāna.'

[2] Dreams, according to Prabhākara, are memory without the consciousness at the time that they are so. See NM. p. 179.

[3] Recognition likewise partakes of the character of both perception and memory, but one is aware at the time of the recollective element there. It is therefore different from the instance we are considering. See SD. p. 45.

[4] PP. iv. st. 5.

in giving rise to error with a positive one to which we have already referred, viz. the perception of the 'this' as characterized by the features that are common to shell and silver. We may therefore describe what is commonly supposed to be error as partial or incomplete knowledge; only in so doing we must be careful to remember that there is no single unit of knowledge to which that term is applicable. To take another instance: A white crystal placed by the side of a red flower may be wrongly regarded as a red crystal. There also we have two jñānas, viz. the perception of the crystal *minus* its true colour and the sensation of the redness alone of the flower. Each of these jñānas is quite valid so far as it goes; only here both the jñānas are derived through the senses. As before they convey a partial knowledge of the objects, viz. the crystal and the flower; but the basis of error here lies in the contiguity of the objects, not in their similarity as in the previous example. Further, there are two objects bodily given here instead of one and the features comprehended are what characterize them singly and not their common ones. But the distinction between the two jñānas as well as that between their objects is not as before grasped and we are therefore said to fall into error. Here also the akhyāti view lays down two conditions—one positive and the other negative for error becoming possible at all—a partial knowledge of the things presented and a failure to note the distinction between them.[1]

(2) *Viparīta-khyāti*.[2]—Kumārila also maintains that knowledge always points to an object beyond itself. In shell-silver, for instance, there is something directly given, viz. the 'this'; but the silver is not so given. Yet it should not on that account be taken as ideal or non-existent, for its notion, being due to the suggestion of a former experience, goes back eventually to an objective counterpart. This view, like the previous one, splits up the object of erroneous knowledge into two parts—the 'this' (viṣaya) and the 'what' (parakāra)—and explains them separately. The first of them as before is not sublated when the mistake is rectified; and the

[1] Compare the earlier Sāṇkhya view of error, set forth in the previous chapter.

[2] SV. pp. 242–6; SD. 58–9.

explanation of the second element also is practically the same as before. Though not given here and now, the silver must have been experienced before; for otherwise it could not at all have been fancied in the shell. The difference between the two views is that while, according to akhyāti, error is due to a losing sight of the fact that the presentative and the representative factors stand apart unrelated (asaṁsargāgraha), here in viparīta-khyāti it is ascribed to a wrong synthesis of them (saṁsarga-graha). In the former case error, so far as that term is applicable at all, is due to omission because it only fails to grasp some relevant part of what is given. Hence its discovery, when it takes place, does not mean the discarding of any feature previously cognized. In the latter, the error becomes one of commission, for it includes as its content more than there is warrant for in the reality that is presented. In other words, illusion is here explained as *unitary* knowledge instead of as two jñānas. The subject and predicate elements consequently seem related in it, while they are not so in reality. Similarly in the case of the red crystal, the two relata, viz. the crystal and the redness, are actually given; but while they are not unified in fact, they appear so in error. As a consequence the redness of the flower, instead of standing apart, shows itself in the crystal and makes it appear differently (viparīta) from what it is.[1] This view is no doubt more in accord than the previous one with experience which points to the object of illusion as a synthetic whole, but epistemologically it presents a difficulty, viz. the inclusion of an ideal element within the content of knowledge. However unconvincing the akhyāti view may be, it is true to its realistic postulate in admitting no subjective element whatsoever. Knowledge may not be adequate to the given reality, but it never goes

[1] This, by the way, accounts for the name viparīta-khyāti, which literally means 'appears as other.' See SV. p. 245, st. 117 and p. 312, st. 160 (com.). The Bhātta view is commonly identified with the Nyāya-Vaiśeṣika one. There is no doubt much that is common between the two, but there are differences in matters of detail. The Bhāṭṭas do not, for example, recognize what is known as alaukika-pratyakṣa which is essential to the Nyāya-Vaiśeṣika explanation of errors like 'shell-silver.'

beyond it. Here, on the other hand, it overshoots the mark.[1] That is, error is partial misrepresentation; and to admit that knowledge can misrepresent its object, even though it be only in part, is to abandon to that extent the realistic principle on which the doctrine claims itself to be based.

These views of error imply a fundamental contrast between the two schools of Mīmāṁsā in their conception of knowledge. Kumārila recognizes error as such, and it can therefore be easily distinguished from truth. According to Prabhākara, on the other hand, there being truly no error at all the distinction disappears. The distinction, however, being universally recognized must have some basis; and if Prabhākara would explain it, he cannot like Kumārila do so from the purely logical point of view, but has to seek another. The new standpoint he finds in the view he takes of knowledge—that it is essentially a means to an end and that its sole function is to guide action or subserve vyavahāra, as it is said. All knowledge, according to him, prompts activity[2]; and, judged by this fresh criterion of practical utility, truth becomes quite distinguishable from error. Knowledge, no doubt, can never deceive on its logical side; but it may be such as does or does not 'work.' In the one case, we have truth; in the other, error. The latter has cognitive value as much as the former, but it lacks practical worth; and when we describe it as error, we only mean this—that it is deceptive in respect of the claim it puts forward to be serviceable.[3] Accordingly when after rectification error yields place to truth, what happens is not any modification of its logical meaning but only the abandonment of the activity that has been prompted by it.[4] In other words, the effect of the discovery of error is seen on the reactive side of consciousness—not on its receptive side. In viparīta-khyāti also its discovery arrests activity; but that is looked upon as only a further result, the immediate one being a readjustment of

[1] Compare the later Sāṇkhya view of error as stated on p. 291 *ante*.

[2] Compare the view of śabda-pramāṇa as stated in PP. pp. 91–94.

[3] PP. iv. st. 37 ff.

[4] In cases where error has led to suspension of activity, its discovery will prompt it.

our cognitive attitude towards the object. Any effect this readjustment may have on our volition is only subsequent to it. Kumārila's attitude towards knowledge is thus primarily detached and scientific; that of Prabhākara, pragmatic.

The Mīmāṁsakas of the Bhāṭṭa school recognize six pramāṇas, while those of the other accept only five of them:—

(1) *Perception* (pratyakṣa), which has already been considered.

(2) *Inference* (anumāna).—There is a general resemblance here with the Nyāya-Vaiśeṣika, as, for example, in the view taken of inductive generalization (vyāpti). But there are differences also. It will take us too far away from our purpose here to dwell upon them or upon the features distinguishing the views of the two Mīmāṁsā schools in their conception of this pramāṇa.

(3) *Verbal Testimony* (śabda).[1]—The place of this pramāṇa in Mīmāṁsā logic has been indicated already and it now remains to point out one or two of the more important differences between the two schools: The Prābhākaras, unlike the Bhāṭṭas, adhere to what appears to have been the earliest view of śabda as a pramāṇa (p. 178) and equate it with the Veda, explaining other forms of verbal testimony as mere inference (p. 257).[2] Again a verbal statement, according to Kumārila, may point to an existent something (siddha) or to something that is yet to be accomplished (sādhya). For example, the sentence 'There are fruits in the next room' refers to a fact, while 'Fetch a cow' refers to a task. Though thus admitting the two-fold character of the import of propositions, he restricts it to the sādhya or what is yet to be done, when he comes to speak of the Veda.[3] Prabhākara declines to admit that verbal statements, whether Vedic or not, can ever point merely to existent things and limits their scope to the sādhya, in keeping with the pragmatic view he takes of all knowledge. All utterance should be relevant to some context in practical life and therefore point to an action as its ultimate meaning. What-

[1] SD pp. 72–3; PP. pp. 87 ff.

[2] See PP. p. 94.

[3] *Jaimini-sūtra*, I. ii. 1–18.

ever be the difference between the two thinkers in this respect, we see that they agree in holding that action is the final import of the Veda. Assertive propositions found in it, they explain, as fully significant only when construed with an appropriate injunction or prohibition found in the particular context. On this view depends the well-known division of the Veda broadly into two parts, viz. vidhi or 'injunction' and artha-vāda or 'explanatory passage.' The latter, consisting of statements describing things as they are or were, have accordingly no independent logical status and are to be understood as complementary to what is taught in the other portion, viz. vidhi. As complements of injunctions they commend what is prescribed; as complements of prohibitions, they condemn what is forbidden.[1] The bearing of this view of scripture on Upaniṣadic statements like Tat tvam asi, which are not injunctive, is that they also are to be construed with reference to some action taught in the Veda—a point to which we shall recur when treating of the Vedānta.

(4) *Comparison* (upamāna).[2]—The Mīmāṁsaka like the Naiyāyika disagrees with the view that this is not an independent pramāṇa and can be brought wholly or partly under one or other of the other pramāṇas. But he conceives it altogether differently from the latter. According to the Nyāya, it may be remembered, this pramāṇa has for its sole object the relation between a word and its meaning learnt under certain conditions (p. 259). Here it is reciprocal similarity that is known through it. When a person who is familiar with the cow (say) casually comes across a gavaya, an animal of the same species, and notices the resemblance of the latter to the former, he discovers that the cow is also similar to the gavaya. It is this second resemblance or, to be

[1] To give the stock illustration: There is in the Yajurveda (II. i. 1. 1) an injunction 'One should sacrifice a white (animal) to Vāyu,' and in the same context is seen the assertive proposition 'Vāyu verily is the swiftest deity.' The latter is a glorification of Vāyu and is, according to the principle stated above, to be construed with the former. When so construed, it signifies that it is good to offer this sacrifice; for the reward will be *speedy*.

[2] SD. pp. 74–6; PP. 110–12.

more exact, the recollected cow characterized by it that is known through upamāna. This view, no doubt, renders the pramāṇa liable to be classed under inference. But the Mīmāṁsaka defends his position by pointing out that the basis for inference, viz. a knowledge of inductive relation (vyāpti) is not needed here. The relevant major premise here would signify that if one thing, say B, is similar to another, say A, that other is similar to the first. As giving expression to a general truth, it implies the simultaneous observation of both A and B. But the conditions of upamāṇa do not require it, as even a person who has never seen two similar things together but meets with a cow and thereafter a gavaya in the manner described above is able to arrive at the conclusion in question. A matter of metaphysical importance here is that 'similarity' (sādṛśya) is conceived as dual, the similarity of A to B being distinct from that of B to A.

(5) *Presumption* (arthāpatti).[1]—This is postulating something to account for what apparently clashes with experience and is therefore in the nature of a hypothesis. We may otherwise state it as rendering explicit what is already implicit in two truths both of which have been properly tested, but which appear mutually incompatible. Thus if we know that Devadatta is alive and do not find him in his house, we conclude that he should be somewhere else. Another example commonly given in this connection is that of a person who, though not eating by day, continues to be healthy and strong, which leads to the conclusion that he should be eating by night. That this is a valid form of discovering the unknown from the known is clear, but it may appear to be only inference. Some like the Naiyāyika therefore class it under anumāna, and do not regard it as a distinct pramāṇa. The argument in support of the opposite view is as follows: The result here cannot be represented as reached through inference inasmuch as there is no middle term at all to serve as its means. To take the first of the above examples, 'being alive' *by itself* cannot serve that purpose, for that does not necessarily lead to the conclusion in question viz. that Devadatta is outside his house. He may then as

[1] SD. 76–83; PP. pp. 113–18.

well remain in his house as elsewhere. Nor can 'not being in his house' *by itself* take that place, since that reason may equally properly lead to the conclusion that Devadatta is no longer alive. So we are forced to view the middle term as formed by combining both these—'being alive' and 'not being at home.' But in this combined form it involves a reference to what is to be established through the inference viz. that Devadatta is somewhere outside his house.[1] That is, the conclusion is already included in the middle term which is never the case in inference. We might add another reason: while in inference the ground ('the fact of smoke') is explained by the conclusion ('fire'), here the ground ('being alive and not being found in the house') explains the conclusion ('being elsewhere').[2] The truth is that arthāpatti is disjunctive reasoning and is not syllogistic in the ordinary sense of the expression. If we reduce it to the syllogistic form, the major premise will be a negative universal referring to things beyond the universe of discourse; and it therefore ceases to be significant. In this connection it may be stated that, unlike the Naiyāyikas, the Mīmāṁsakas of both the schools reject the negative universal as the major premise in a syllogism. They consider that it can generally be expressed in a positive form. The scope for arthāpatti is just where it cannot be so expressed.

(6) *Non-apprehension* (anupalabdhi).[3]—This is the specific pramāṇa by which negation, not nothing, is known, e.g. the absence of a jar or of atoms somewhere. Like the Nyāya (p. 237), the Bhāṭṭa school of Mīmāṁsā admits negative facts (abhāva); but, unlike it (p. 249), it formulates a separate pramāṇa for knowing them. The word anupalabdhi means the 'absence of apprehension,' i.e. the absence of knowledge derived through any of the five foregoing pramāṇas. This means that, as knowledge got through any of the pramāṇas points to the existence (bhāva) of objects, the absence of such knowledge indicates, other conditions remaining the same, their non-existence (abhāva). Only it should be remembered that the absence, to serve as the index of non-existence, must be aided by the mental presentation of the

[1] SV. p. 455, st. 19 ff. [2] NM. p. 44. [3] SD. pp. 83–7.

relevant object. There may be several objects not found in a particular place; but we think of the absence of that alone among them all, which some other circumstance has made us think of. The Naiyāyika divides 'negations' into two classes according as their correlate (pratiyogin) is perceivable or not. The means of knowing the former kind, he holds, is perception; that of the latter, inference. Here in the Mīmāṁsā, this sixth pramāṇa is postulated as the common means of knowing both varieties of negation. The knowledge of no negation, it is contended, is perceptual. For, in the first place, no sense-contact which is necessary for such knowledge is conceivable in the case of negation.[1] Secondly, there are instances where a knowledge of the negation of perceivable objects arises even when no organ of sense is functioning. Thus a person who did not think of an elephant at all in the morning on a particular day, may later come to realize, owing to some circumstance or other, that he did not see it *then*. The knowledge, because it refers to the past, cannot be connected with the functioning of the senses at the time of realizing the negation. Nor can it be ascribed to their functioning in the morning, since the correlate (pratiyogin), viz. the elephant, was by hypothesis not thought of then for its negation to be apprehended. Again the pramāṇa by which negation is known cannot be brought under inference; for, if it is, the major premise of the syllogism will be 'Wherever there is absence of knowledge of a thing, there is—other circumstances being the same—absence of the corresponding object.' This premise relates two negations and, as an inductive generalization should eventually be based upon perception, it assumes that their knowledge is perceptual which is against the present contention that it is inference. The Prābhākaras do not admit this pramāṇa, for they do not recognize negation which is its sole object. They explain abhāva in terms of the positive factors involved in it, as we shall see in the next section.[2]

[1] SV. p. 479, st. 18.

[2] PP. pp. 118–25.

III

The Mīmāṁsaka is a realist, and his realism has some features of its own. Unlike the Sautrāntika and the Vaibhāṣika, for example, he believes in the existence of permanent dravyas which are the substrata of qualities and are not merely aggregates of fleeting sense-data. So far, the doctrine agrees with the Nyāya-Vaiśeṣika. But it differs from that doctrine also—to confine our attention first to the Bhāṭṭa school—in not admitting that a dravya can be produced anew, and recognizing the principle of change instead. Every dravya is eternal, and endures however much its forms or attributes may change. The clay that we see before us may at one time be made into a jar, at another time into a saucer; it may be brown now, and red hereafter. But in all these transformations the same material persists. The dravya endures; its modes alone appear and disappear.[1] In other words, Kumārila dismisses the notion that things are self-identical units which ever remain the same, excluding all difference.[2] This view of reality exhibits kinship with the Sāṅkhya-Yoga in general. It is pariṇāma-vāda, and the relation between the material cause and the effect is, as in the other system, one of identity in difference (bhedābheda). One important difference between the two doctrines is that here the changing dravyas are ultimately many and not only one. Another difference, by the way, is in that the Mīmāṁsā extends the notion of modal transformation to the ātman also which is absolutely static and passive according to the other doctrine. The change that characterizes the physical reality is ever in progress. It never began and is never going to end, the Mīmāṁsaka recognizing no creation (sṛṣṭi) or dissolution (pralaya) of the universe as a whole.[3] 'There was never a time,' he says, 'when the world was otherwise than now': Na kadācit anīdṛśam jagat. Individual things, no doubt, come and go; but that is accounted for by the self-evolvent character of reality. Whatever stimulus is required

[1] SV. pp. 443, st. 32–3.
[2] Cf. SV. p. 476, st. 12.
[3] SV. p. 673, st. 113.

for such change to take place comes from the past karma of the selves that are on life's pilgrimage at the time. This means the abolition of the idea of God[1] from the system, which is indeed a strange tenet to be held by a school claiming to be orthodox *par excellence*. To characterize the whole view in one word, it is pure empiricism[2] excepting only in one point, viz. the recognition of a supernatural sphere of being and of a revealed authority through which a knowledge of it can be attained. As regards the other sphere—that of common experience—it beats every naturalistic school of thought known to history. In fact, a standing charge against the Mīmāṁsā, at least in one stage of its growth, was that it was thoroughly materialistic in its outlook.[3]

The Mīmāṁsaka is also a pluralist and believes that variety is at the root of the physical universe.[4] The school of Kumārila accepts all the nine dravyas known to the Nyāya-Vaiśeṣika and its conception of them is more or less the same. It adds two more to them, viz. tamas or 'darkness' and śabda or 'sound.'[5] Time is perceivable,[6] the view being that all perceptual experience, no matter through what sense it is acquired, includes a reference to this element. It cannot, however, be apprehended by itself, but only along with some other object. Other dravyas also are regarded as perceivable excepting only the manas which is known mediately.[7] It is curious that darkness should be regarded as a positive dravya in preference to the Nyāya-Vaiśeṣika view, which is also Prabhākara's,[8] of equating it with the absence of light. The reason assigned, viz. that it is characterized by colour and movement which can only be found in dravyas, is too naïve to appeal to anyone. Śālikanātha describes it as 'crude.' The statement that it cannot be negation (abhāva), since its supposed correlate (pratiyogin),

[1] The gods of Indian mythology also are repudiated, and sacrificial offerings, it is explained, are made *as if* there were gods. See p. 36 *ante*.

[2] Cf. Yatha saṁdṛśyate tathā: SV. p. 552, st. 29.

[3] SV. p. 4, st. 10.

[4] Cf. Vilakṣaṇa-svabhāvatvāt bhāvānām. SD. p. 102.

[5] *Māna-meyodaya*, p. 66.

[6] SD. pp. 45–6.

[7] *Māna-meyodaya*, pp. 78–80.

[8] PP. pp. 144 ff.; *Māna-meyodaya*, p. 68.

'light,' is not thought of wherever darkness is seen is equally unconvincing. Of these dravyas, the first four as well as darkness are stated to be of atomic structure and the remaining ones, including soul, are described as infinite and ultimate. By 'atom' in this system should not be understood the infinitesimal paramāṇu of the Vaiśeṣika, but the smallest particle which experience acquaints us with, viz. the mote in the sunbeam which corresponds to the tryaṇuka of the other doctrine. The Vaiśeṣika conception of atom is described as purely speculative, but it does not seem to be altogether rejected.[1] From all the atomic substances, objects of different magnitudes may, as in the Nyāya-Vaiśeṣika, be derived; only the relation between the material cause and the effect is here viewed as bhedābheda or tādātmya ('identity in difference'), instead of samavāya (p. 239), in accordance with the Bhāṭṭa belief in sat-kārya-vāda. These dravyas form only the support, as it were, of the universe. There are also other features of it which are divisible into three classes—guṇa, karma and sāmānya or jāti, which together with dravya form the four positive categories of Kumārila's system. But it must be remembered that they are not conceived as entirely distinct from the dravyas to which they belong. The relation between them is one of identity in difference,[2] so that the significance of 'category' here is not the same as in the Nyāya-Vaiśeṣika. Kumārila's list also includes negation (abhāva), and we therefore have five categories in all.[3] The first of them has already been described and it is sufficient for our purpose to state that the notion of the others is for the most part like that in the Nyāya-Vaiśeṣika.

The Prābhākaras accept four more positive categories of which we need refer here only to one, viz. samavāya. Its recognition means the entire rejection of the relation of identity in difference (bhedābheda) admitted by the Bhāṭṭas.[4] As a consequence substance and attribute, universal and particular, material cause and effect come to be conceived as altogether distinct, and the doctrine does not subscribe to

[1] SV. p. 404, st. 183–4.
[2] *Māna-meycdaya*, p. 6.
[3] *Id.* p. 65.
[4] PP. p. 27.

the sat-kārya-vāda. This signifies a vast difference between the two schools in their conception of reality. While siding with the Nyāya-Vaiśeṣika in this respect, the Prābhākaras differ from it in discarding abhāva as an independent category, their view being that it can always be represented as a positive something. Thus the absence of a jar in a room is the mere empty room; its prior negation, the clay; and so forth.[1] Amongst the eight positive categories recognized, the dravyas are nine as in the Nyāya-Vaiśeṣika, and their conception also is generally the same.

IV

The admixture of the rational with the dogmatic which we noticed in connection with the theoretical teaching of the Mīmāṁsā is equally striking on its practical side. So far as ordinary morality goes, the doctrine adopts a point of view which is severely secular and explains virtue as a conscious or semi-conscious adjustment of conduct to interest. Śabara says that charitable acts like providing water-huts (prapā), though for the benefit of others and therefore good, are not yet dharma.[2] That is, the Mīmāṁsā judges conduct by a utilitarian standard; but it is not egoistic and, as is indicated by the very example given by Śabara, is based upon the realization of the social nature of man. A scheme of morality founded upon such a principle is not without parallels in the history of ethics. But what is peculiar about the Mīmāṁsā is that it refuses such morality the highest place in life's ideal. As in metaphysics, here also it conceives of another sphere of activity whose significance is extra-empirical and confines the title of dharma to it alone. Common morality, according to the Mīmāṁsaka, is purely an empirical affair which none but the short-sighted fail to understand. True spirituality consists in fixing one's attention on dharma or such acts of duty as lead to success in the life beyond. It may appear that such a shifting of the attention from the present life to the coming one will throw morality into the shade and thus tend

[1] Cf. SD. pp. 83 ff.

[2] I. iii. 2.

to reduce its value in the eyes of man. It does nothing of the kind. For, as conceived in the Mīmāṁsā, ceremonial life does not exclude common morality; it is, on the other hand, founded in it. 'The Vedas cleanse not the unrighteous.'[1] Though not viewed as the highest, ethical purity is regarded as a pre-condition as well as a necessary accompaniment of religious or spiritual life. The few occasions on which the dictates of common morality seem to be neglected, as for example in the immolation of an animal in a rite, are explained as only the exceptions that prove the rule. However unconvincing the explanation given in justification of these acts, it should be admitted that generally the Veda supports conclusions that are ethically quite unexceptionable. In the present case, for instance, it explicitly forbids injury to living beings: Na hiṁsyāt sarvā bhūtāni.

When dharma is understood in this unique sense, it naturally requires an equally unique pramāṇa to make it known (p. 109). That pramāṇa is the Veda.[2] While the standard of judgment for common morality is human, that for dharma is superhuman. 'We should distinguish,' Kumārila says, 'between what relates to dharma and mokṣa which is known from the Veda and what relates to artha and kāma which is learnt by worldly intercourse.'[3] It is not merely common human experience that is of no avail in knowing dharma and adharma, but also the higher faculty of yogic perception recognized for the purpose in doctrines like the Nyāya-Vaiśeṣika (p. 262). The single name of apūrva[4] (literally meaning 'never before') which Prabhākara gives to dharma and adharma emphasizes their inaccessibility to the other pramāṇas (mānāntarāpūrva). It is conceived by him as the result of sacrificial and such other acts—not those acts themselves as in the Nyāya-Vaiśeṣika—and corresponds to the puṇya and pāpa of the other doctrine. But it abides like the latter in the self (ātma-samavāyi), so that apūrva is a subjective feature to be distinguished from the objective act leading to it. According to Kumarila these forms of activity

[1] Ācāra-hīnam na punanti Vedāḥ: Quoted by Śaṁkara in his com. on VS. iii. i. 10.
[2] *Jaimini-sūtra*, I. i. 2.
[3] *Tantra-vārtika*, I. iii. 2.
[4] See PP. pp. 187, 195.

are themselves dharma and adharma[1]—the former standing for permitted or obligatory deeds like a sacrifice, the latter for prohibited deeds like drinking or killing an animal; and it is to know what is prescribed or prohibited that we have to seek the aid of the Veda. That is, though there is nothing transcendental about the acts themselves described as dharma and adharma, the fact of their being the means of a supernatural good is not humanly ascertainable. It is from this standpoint that they are represented here as known through revelation and revelation alone.

The Veda reveals dharma, according to both the schools, as the subject of a mandate (vidhi or niyoga)—as something to be accomplished, in accordance with the Mīmāṁsā conclusion that action is the final import of the Veda. But they differ considerably in their view of the motive for obeying that mandate. In fact, this question of the motive has split the Mīmāṁsakas into several camps.[2] It is not necessary to refer to them all.[3] We shall only note the commonly recognized distinction between the two schools. According to the Bhāṭṭas, the Veda not only acquaints us with dharma and adharma, but also specifies the desirable results to be obtained by following the one and abstaining from the other, viz. the attainment of some pleasure or the avoidance of some pain. In the usual example of the jyotiṣṭoma sacrifice, it is heaven (svarga) that is held out as the end; in the case of destroying life, it is hell (naraka) against which one is warned. Thus the Bhāṭṭa school, like the Nyāya-Vaiśeṣika (p. 263), believes that pleasure and pain are the only ultimate motives. 'Not even the stupid act,' Kumārila

[1] Yāgādireva dharmaḥ: SD. pp. 25–6. The term yāga strictly stands for a certain resolve which is the prelude to the performance of a sacrifice and is explained as tyāga, or, the spirit of renunciation involved in giving away what belongs to oneself. (Cf. the formula 'no more mine'—na mama—uttered at the time of the offer.) Devatām uddiśya dravya-tyāgo yāgaḥ (*Nyāya-mālā-vistara,* IV. ii. 27–8). In this sense, dharma would of course be a characteristic of the subject.

[2] See *Tantra-rahasya,* ch. iv.

[3] For a fuller discussion of this and allied topics, reference may be made to *Ethics of the Hindus,* by Dr. S. K. Maitra (Calcutta Uni. Pr.).

remarks in a parallel context, 'without some good in view.'[1] But we should not conclude from this that the end is included in the behest and that it commands us either to seek pleasure or to shun pain.[2] The desire for good is already there in man, and the Veda merely admits it as a psychological fact without pronouncing any judgment on the value of pleasure or on the lack of it in pain. In other words, we have here what is described as psychological hedonism and not ethical hedonism. But it should be acknowledged that the injunction, in this view, utilizes subjective desire by appealing to it as the incentive to make itself operative. The Prābhākaras demur to the admission of a hedonistic aim as necessary for the Vedic imperative to operate. The Veda, they say,[3] is not so helpless as to need an extraneous aid in enforcing its mandatory power. It neither coaxes nor threatens anyone; and the only motive it presupposes is reverence for the mandate itself. But Vedic injunctions like 'one should sacrifice' (yajeta) do no apply to all. They are addressed only to some, and expressions like 'he that desires heaven' (svarga-kāma) found in them do not point to any benefit to be derived by obeying them, as the Bhāṭṭas assume, but only limit the sphere of its applicability by specifying the persons (niyojya) whose duty those injunctions set forth.[4] In the case of any particular injunction, only those will respond who answer to the description contained in it. What prompts them to act is this consciousness that it is their duty to do so (kāryatā-jñāna), and never the prospect of satisfying any desire that they may have (iṣṭa-sādhanatā-jñāna).[5] The good or evil that may result therefrom is accordingly looked upon as a consequence rather than as an end directly aimed at. There is no doubt that the idea of the fruit resulting from ritualistic activity is pushed farther into the background here than in the other school; but for all practical purposes the two views are the same, because both alike admit that an end is attained—no matter what name they give it.[6] The

1 Prayojanam anuddiśya na mandopi pravartate: SV. p. 653, st. 55.
2 SV. p. 125, st. 266.
3 NM. p. 350.
4 PP. p. 191.
5 Ibid., pp. 177 and 180.
6 It is termed here not phala but niyojya-viśeṣaṇa: PP. p. 191.

specially important point to note here is the concern which both the schools exhibit to maintain that it is not of the *essence* of a command to contain either a promise or a threat and the consequent exclusion from Vedic teaching proper of the idea of recompense, which doubtless constituted originally the sole motive of sacrifices.

We have thus far considered what are termed kāmya and pratiṣiddha karmas or optional and forbidden deeds (p. 108), which constitute the sphere of the hypothetical imperative, and seen that there is practically no difference between the Bhāṭṭas and the Prābhākaras in their attitude towards them. There is, however, an important distinction between the two views and it comes out clearly in the case of the third variety of 'unconditional duties' (nitya-karma) like the regular offering of twilight prayers (sandhyā), which after all constitute, as we shall see, the essential part of the discipline of the Mīmāṁsā regarded as a darśana. In accordance with the hedonistic basis of conduct accepted in the Bhāṭṭa school, these duties also are conceived as serving an end, viz. overcoming past sin (durita-kṣaya). Further, by adherence to them, one keeps off the sin (pratyavaya) that is sure to result from their neglect.[1] In neither case does their performance bring any positive gain, but they are not without an aim. According to the other school, such deeds have no consequence whatsoever and are to be performed for their own sake. They are not a means to an end, but are themselves the end.[2] While according to the Bhāṭṭas dharma even in its form of nitya-karmas is only of instrumental value, this school pursues it as the supreme good, regarding it as definitely above artha and kāma or empirical motives taken in their totality. Here we have a conception of duty for duty's sake, and that in a sense far more rigorous than in the Gītā, since even motives so pure as 'cleansing the heart' and 'subserving the purposes of God' (p. 125) are excluded and the doing of duty is placed on a basis of absolute disinterestedness. The law governing dharma here may there-

[1] SD. p. 130.

[2] Apūrva, in general, is described as svayaṁ-prayojana-bhūta. See *Tantra-rahasya*, p. 70.

fore be said to correspond to the 'categorical imperative' of Kant. But what, it may be asked, is the penalty, according to the Prābhākaras, if one should disobey such mandates? The reply to this question, we shall state in the words of the *Tantra-rahasya*,[1] one of the few published works of the school:—

> 'The personal ending such as that of the potential mood (liṅ), you say, teaches apūrva as a duty to be accomplished. In that case one may not set about it, although it is known as a duty, because it serves no end.'
>
> 'Even in respect of optional deeds, which are known to have an end, one may not act. What is to be done? The function of a pramāṇa ceases with the mere revealing of its object.'
>
> 'Well, in the case of the optional deeds, the failure to perform them means missing their fruit and that is the penalty. What is the penalty in the case of unconditional duties?'
>
> 'The Vedic mandate will not then have been carried out.'
>
> 'What of that?'
>
> 'That itself is the punishment, for obeying the Vedic mandate itself is of ultimate value (puruṣārtha). It is on the analogy of these karmas that we say that carrying out the mandate is the true end even in the case of optional deeds and that the attainment of the so-called phala is incidental.'
>
> 'How can their non-accomplishment be itself the punishment?'
>
> 'The good, who praise those that obey the Vedic behest and blame those that do not, will answer that question. Or one's own conscience, which feels guilty of having proved faithless to it, will do so.'

The appeal here, it will be seen, is first to the judgment of the better mind of the community and then to the verdict of our own conscience.[2] But it is conscience not in the sense

[1] P. 66.

[2] The former of these two explanations seems to be more in keeping with the Prābhākara ideal; the latter is hardly different from the Gītā teaching of sattva-śuddhi.

that it is an independent guide in discriminating right from wrong, but in the sense that it constrains us to follow dharma when it is once known. The communication of what is right or wrong is still left to an external code. The appeal in its double form, we may add, implies that man is conceived here not merely as a spiritual being himself, but also as a member of a society of spiritual beings.

In one important respect the aim of the Mīmāṁsā, it is clear, should differ from that of the other systems. It should pursue not the ideal of mokṣa but dharma, whether as a means to an end or as an end in itself. Such seems to have been its aim till a certain stage was reached in the history of the system. In that early period in the growth of the Mīmāṁsā, only dharma, artha and kāma (tri-varga) were accepted (p. 109) as human values and not the fourth one of mokṣa also.[1] To speak generally, dharma is still the highest ideal in the Kalpa-sūtras; but the doctrine in its present form has practically thrown it overboard, and replaced it by the ideal of mokṣa. The transformation means the virtual abandonment of many of the rites taught in the Veda.[2] But the change is of a far more subversive kind in the case of the Prābhākara school than in that of Kumārila. The latter conceive of dharma as a means to an end and the introduction of the mokṣa ideal means only the substitution of one end for another. If the old aim was svarga, the attainment of some positive good, the new one is apavarga, the negative one of escape from saṁsāra. But in the case of the former, which pursued dharma as its own end, the acceptance of the new ideal means deserting its cherished principle of doing duty for its own sake, and going over completely to the side of the Bhāṭṭas; for its idea of mokṣa, to judge from Śālikanātha's

[1] Compare NM. pp. 514 ff; VS. III. iv. 18.

[2] In this connection we may draw attention to the view of some later exponents of the doctrine who, following the teaching of the Gītā, replace the divergent phalas of the several karmas by the single one of 'pleasing God' by their performance (*Mīmāṁsā-nyāya-prakāśa*, p. 273). This change is quite against the atheistic spirit of the Mīmāṁsā and shows how completely the Gītā ideal influenced orthodox thought.

description, is also the seeking of an end, viz. escape from the trials and travails of saṁsāra.[1]

We shall now briefly touch upon the nature of this new ideal and the discipline laid down for its attainment. Our knowledge of the Nyāya-Vaiśeṣika conception of bondage and release will be of much use here, for the two doctrines resemble each other in this respect so very much. We may add that almost the same criticism applies to the one ideal as to the other. The self is conceived in the Mīmāṁsā as eternal and omnipresent; but, as a matter of fact, it is conditioned by various adjuncts which are not at all indispensable to it. Its empirical encumbrance is three-fold[2]: To begin with, there is the physical body as limited by which alone it enjoys pain or pleasure; secondly, there are the organs of sense which are the sole means relating it to the outside world; and lastly, there is that world itself so far as it forms the object of the individual's experience. It is this connection with things other than itself that constitutes bondage, and release means separation from them once for all. The Mīmāṁsaka refutes the Vedāntic view that the physical world is sublated or transcended in mokṣa. Nor does he admit that the relation between the world and the individual self is unreal as the Sāṅkhya-Yoga does. According to him, the world is real and endures in exactly the same form even when a self becomes free; and mokṣa means only the realization that the relation of the self to it though real is not necessary. This state is described negatively as excluding all pain and along with it all pleasure also.[3] There seem, however, to have been one or more interpreters of Kumārila who maintained that it is a state of bliss or ānanda.[4] It is controverted by Pārthasārathi[5] and a consideration of Kumārila's remarks[6]

[1] PP. pp. 156–7. This glaring discrepancy can be explained only by supposing that the stress laid upon dharma as the ultimate puruṣārtha, or the disinclination to bring duty and pleasure into relation with each other, was a characteristic of an earlier phase of the Prābhākara doctrine and that it remains as but a relic in Śālikanātha's exposition of it. For evidence in support of the existence of such a phase, see *Journal of Oriental Research* (Madras) 1930, pp. 99–108.

[2] SD. pp. 125.

[3] SD. pp. 126–7.

[4] *Māna-meyodaya*, pp. 87–9.

[5] SD. pp. 127–8.

[6] SV. p. 670, st. 107.

in that connection seems to support him. No such difference of opinion seems to have existed in the case of the other school. In this condition, all the specific characteristics of the self such as jñāna, pain and pleasure disappear. The self is not conscious then even of itself, for the manas has ceased to operate. But unlike the Nyāya-Vaiśeṣika, the Mīmāṁsā of the Bhāṭṭa school maintains that the capacity for manifesting such features persists. The only advantage gained by this deviation from the Nyāya-Vaiśeṣika is the maintenance of consistency in regard to the pariṇāma-vāda which the school advocates; for the latent capacity to know, to feel or to will which is supposed to persist in the self then is never manifested again. Distinctions like these, moreover, affect only the state attained after death. So far as mokṣa may be taken to represent the condition of the enlightened in this life, there is entire agreement with the Nyāya-Vaiśeṣika.

As in the other doctrines, detachment from worldly concerns and faith in the teaching are needed here also as preliminary requirements. Without them, no serious effort is possible towards securing final freedom. The direct means of release is deduced from the general Indian belief which the Mīmāṁsaka shares that karma is the cause of bondage. When the cause is removed, the effect must necessarily cease to be; and abstention from karma, the Mīmāṁsaka thinks, should automatically result in restoring the self to its original state. The karmas to be abstained from, however, are not all but only those of the optional (kāmya) and the prohibited (pratiṣiddha) types. The performance of the one gives rise to some merit; that of the other, to some demerit. They are thus a means of renewing bondage and have to be eschewed by a person that is seeking freedom. The third or the nitya variety of karma, even the seeker after mokṣa should perform; for otherwise he will be disobeying the Vedic law enjoying them.[1] That would be equivalent to indulging in prohibited deeds, the only difference being that while the first counts as a sin of omission, the second does as one of commission. It is to avoid becoming entangled again in the

[1] The influence of the Gītā is again clear in this restriction of activity to nitya-karmas.

miseries of saṁsāra as a consequence of such sin, that one should carry on the nitya-karmas. Thus the course of discipline laid down here is two-fold: (1) abstention from the optional and forbidden deeds, and (2) adherence to the obligatory ones. In neither case, it should be added, is there anything positive effected, the conception of mokṣa being negative in the system, viz. the restoration of the self to its normal condition. As regards the exact part which a knowledge of the self, according to Kumārila, plays in securing freedom, there is some doubt owing to a discrepancy between the *Śloka-vārtika* and the *Tantra-vārtika* in that respect.[1] Without entering into the polemics of this question we may state, following Pārthasārathi's interpretation, that a knowledge of the self or more strictly the insight born of meditation upon its true nature, is a contributory aid to freedom, so that the doctrine is what is technically described as jñāna-karma-samuccaya-vāda. The followers of Prabhākara agree in this respect; only they do not admit any purpose in the performance of nitya-karmas beyond obeying the call of duty. Their acceptance of the need for jñāna as a means of release, along with the performance of unconditional duties, is quite explicitly stated.[2]

[1] Cf. SV. pp. 669 ff. and *Tantra-vārtika*, I. iii. 25.

[2] PP. p. 157.

CHAPTER XIII

VEDĀNTA

INTRODUCTORY

ALL schools of Vedānta claim to be based upon the Upaniṣads. Whether this claim can be fully established in every case or not, there is no doubt that they derive a considerable part of their material from that source.[1] In dealing with the Vedānta, we shall accordingly have to refer to the Upaniṣads frequently; but, as we have already given an account of their teaching, it will not be necessary to go into details. It will suffice merely to refer to the relevant points or even to assume the reader's familiarity with what has already been stated. The teaching of the Upaniṣads, we know, is predominantly monistic, though it is not easy to determine what particular form of monism is taught in them. But this did not prevent dualistic interpretations being put on them, and the chief form of dualism that was traced to the Upaniṣads in olden times was the Sāṅkhya. There is a clear indication of this, as already noticed (p. 267), in the *Vedānta-sūtra*, which has for long been the universally recognized manual of Vedānta. One of the chief objects of Bādarāyaṇa in his treatise is to refute this view that the Upaniṣads teach the dualistic Sāṅkhya. There is also another object equally important which he has in view, viz. the refutation of ritualistic Mīmāṁsā, according to which the essential teaching of the Veda is contained in the Brāhmaṇas; and the Upaniṣads, though as a part of revelation are not unauthoritative, are only of secondary significance and should be finally construed with reference to some ceremonial act or other (p. 319). They may for instance be looked upon as speaking of the self which is the agent in the performance of rites or as glorifying the deities whose propitiation is their aim. In any case it is

[1] The *Upaniṣads*, the *Bhagavadgītā* and the *Vedānta-sūtra* are known as the prasthāna-traya or, as we might say, the triple foundation of the Vedānta.

certain, the Mīmāṁsaka contended, that karma is the sole theme of the Veda and that the Upaniṣads, which form a part of it, cannot be taken to point to Brahman or any other principle as the highest entity whose realization constitutes the end and aim of man.[1] The inherent ambiguity of the Upaniṣads, the glaring contradiction between the pūrva- and the uttara-kāṇḍas of the Veda and, we may add, the growing power of heterodox beliefs, thus account for the attempts made in the Vedānta to systematize the teaching of the Upaniṣads.

There is evidence to show that this systematization was effected in more than one way. In the *Sūtra* of Bādarāyaṇa there is reference to as many as seven Vedāntic teachers—whether they were his predecessors or contemporaries is not known; and he alludes to differences of view among them in respect of essential points like the nature of mokṣa[2] and the need of saṁnyāsa[3] for the spiritual aspirant. Even in regard to such an important question as the relation of the jīva to Brahman, Bādarāyaṇa mentions two views other than his own,[4] both implying vital distinctions in general philosophic outlook. Differences like these on fundamental issues show that the teaching of the Upaniṣads was from very early times understood in several ways by Vedāntic teachers. Bādarāyaṇa's exposition is only one; and, in all likelihood, the most influential of them. All current schools of Vedānta, though differing from one another in important matters, alike claim to represent precisely what Bādarāyaṇa himself taught. The extremely laconic form of his sūtras has rendered such variety in interpretation possible. In fact, they are more cryptic than the Upaniṣads, and it is consequently much more difficult to get at their meaning than at that of those old treatises. The result is that even as regards the most essential points there is ambiguity. We do not for instance know for certain whether, according to Bādarāyaṇa, the world actually emerges from Brahman (pariṇāma) or is only

[1] Cf. VS. I. i. 4 and Śaṁkara's com. on it. The Mīmāṁsakas are styled 'deniers of Brahman' (Brahma-nāstika) in Rāmānanda's gloss on the latter.

[2] VS. IV. iv. 5–7.

[3] VS. III. iv. 18–20.

[4] VS. I. iv. 19–21.

a phenomenal appearance of it (vivarta). There seem to have been once commentaries[1] on the *Vedānta-sūtra* upholding both these views with all their implied differences under theory as well as practical discipline; but they were all superseded by Śaṁkara's great commentary upholding the latter view and are now lost. Attempts were made later to revive some of the superseded views wholly or in part by commentators like Bhāskara and Yādavaprakāśa, but without much success. Though these interpretations do not abolish the conception of God, they prefer to look upon Brahman as the Absolute and may therefore be described as predominantly philosophic. There have also been purely theistic interpretations of the *Sūtra*, especially subsequent to Śaṁkara; and among them again we find distinctions due to the identification of the supreme God with Viṣṇu or Śiva. Thus Rāmānuja and Madhva uphold the supremacy of Viṣṇu, while Śrīkaṇṭha exalts Śiva above him. Of these various schools of Vedānta, we shall consider here only two—one, that of Śaṁkara to represent the philosophic interpretation and the other, that of Rāmānuja to represent the theistic. Before proceeding to this consideration, we may add a word about the relation between the *Mīmāṁsā-* and the *Vedānta-sūtras*. The two are regarded by all Vedāntins now as complementary to each other and as together exhibiting the totality of Vedic teaching, though they differ in regard to the place that should be assigned in the scheme of Vedāntic discipline to karma as taught in the former. Historically the two treatises were probably independent with different authors—Jaimini and Bādarāyaṇa respectively; and they were later put together with suitable emendations by someone who is described as Vyāsa—'the arranger.'[2] Upavarṣa, the Vṛttikāra to whom we alluded in the previous chapter (p. 301), seems to have commented upon them in this combined form. The date of the original work by Bādarāyaṇa is now believed to be about 400 A.D.

[1] See Dr. S. K. Belvalkar: *Vedānta Philosophy* (Poona) Lecture v.
[2] See Deussen: *System of the Vedānta*, pp. 24–5 and 28.

A. Advaita

The particular type of monism taught by Śaṁkara is very old, though in its final form it owes a great deal to his contribution. Its most distinguishing feature on the theoretical side is its conception of nirguṇa Brahman as the ultimate reality with the implied belief in the Māyā doctrine, the identity of the jīva and Brahman and the conception of mokṣa as the merging of the former in the latter; on the practical side, it is the advocacy of karma-saṁnyāsa or complete renunciation with its implication that jñāna and jñāna alone is the means of release. The earliest extant formulation of this doctrine is found in Gauḍapāda's *Karikā*, which purports to summarize the teaching of the *Māṇḍūkya Upaniṣad*, but really accomplishes much more by giving an admirable summary of advaitic teaching. The main points of Śaṁkara's philosophy—its basic principles such as the inapplicability of the notion of causality to the ultimate reality—are already there. The most important of Śaṁkara's works is the bhāṣya on the *Vedānta-sūtra*, which is as remarkable for the charm of its style as for the logical consistency of its arguments. We have already mentioned that he therein maintains the vivarta-vāda or the doctrine that the world is a phenomenal appearance of Brahman. According to him, the belief to be refuted before the Advaita is established is not so much the Sāṅkhya or Prakṛti-pariṇāma-vāda as Brahma-pariṇāma-vāda. On account of the fact that the treatise on which he comments alludes so frequently to the Sāṅkhya, Śaṁkara also considers it at length and shows how far removed it is from the Upaniṣadic doctrine; but his real objective is to establish the vivarta-vāda or Maya-vāda as against the pariṇāma-vāda of certain commentators on the *Vedānta-sūtra*, especially Bhartṛ-prapañca that preceded him. Śaṁkara has also another aim in his bhāṣya: Owing to the resemblance, though only seeming, of his doctrine of nirguṇa Brahman to that of the śūnya or 'void' of the Mādhyamika form of Buddhistic idealism,[1] one might

[1] Cf. Yat śūnya-vādinaḥ śūnyam tadeva Brahma māyinaḥ. Madhva: *Aṇubhāṣya* on VS. II. ii. 29.

identify the two and regard the Advaita as alien to the Upaniṣads. So he emphasizes now and again the fact that his teaching is not negative or nihilistic. How far this contention can be maintained, we shall see later. He does not expressly mention this phase of Buddhism except in one place[1] and there he dismisses it summarily; but there is no doubt that he throughout tries to steer clear of these two doctrines opposed to his own, but yet so similar to it, viz. the Brahma-pariṇāma-vāda of some Vedāntins and the śūnya-vāda of the Mādhyamikas.

Besides the bhāṣya on the *Vedānta-sūtra*, Śaṁkara wrote commentaries on the principal Upaniṣads and the *Bhagavad-gītā*. Those especially on the *Bṛhadāraṇyaka* and *Chāndogya Upaniṣads* treat of several points that are not dealt with in detail in the *Sūtra-bhāṣya* and are of immense value in the comprehension and appreciation of the doctrine of Advaita. In addition to them, we have his *Upadeśa-sāhasrī*, which, though somewhat terse, gives a splendid account of his views. Śaṁkara's doctrine was defended and amplified in matters of detail by various thinkers after him, and this has given rise to some diversity of opinion among his followers. Two of the schools resulting from such divergences of view are in particular well known—the Vivaraṇa school which goes back to the *Pañca-pādikā*, the fragment of a commentary on Śaṁkara's *Sūtra-bhāṣya* by his own pupil Padmapāda, and the slightly later Bhāmatī school represented by Vācaspati (A.D. 841). The *Pañca-pādikā* was commented upon by Prakāśātman (A.D. 1000) in his *Vivaraṇa*, from which the first school takes its name. The Vivaraṇa has a gloss known as *Tattva-dīpana* by Akhaṇḍānanda, and its teaching has also been most lucidly summarized by Vidyāraṇya (A.D. 1350) in his *Vivaraṇa-prameya-saṁgraha*. The *Bhāmatī* has been explained by Amalānanda (A.D. 1250) in his *Kalpa-taru*, which in its turn has been annotated by Appaya Dīkṣita (A.D. 1600) in the *Parimala*. There are also various other commentaries of greater or less value on the *Sūtra-bhāṣya*, such as the *Brahma-vidyābharaṇa* of Advaitānanda (A.D. 1450). Of the numerous hand-books written to

[1] VS. II. ii. 31.

explain the Advaita system, we may mention here the *Naiṣkarmya-siddhi* of Sureśvara, who was at first probably a Mīmāṁsaka, and the *Saṁkṣepa-śārīraka* by his pupil, Sarvajñātman. Another work of particular value, especially in regard to the Māyā doctrine, is the *Iṣṭa-siddhi* of Vimuktātman (A.D. 1050). Later still are the *Nyāya-makaranda* of Ānandabodha (A.D. 1050) and the *Pañca-daśī* of Vidyāraṇya, a popular treatise. The *Siddhānta-leśa-saṁgraha* of Appaya Dīkṣita describes the divergences of view, already mentioned, which arose within the doctrine as a result of its wide expansion in the centuries following Śaṁkara. The *Vedānta-paribhāṣā* of Dharmarāja Adhvarīndra gives a technical and systematic exposition of the doctrine, especially on its logical and epistemological side; and the *Vedānta-sāra* of Sadānanda (A.D. 1550) is an easy introduction to Advaita philosophy. Among the exclusively polemical works written on the system should be mentioned the *Khaṇḍana-khaṇḍa-khādya* of Śrīharṣa (A.D. 1100), the poet of the *Naiṣadhīya-carita* and the *Advaita-siddhi* of Madhusūdana Sarasvatī (A.D. 1650) with its commentary, the *Laghu-candrikā* by Brahmānanda, whose study is now regarded among the pundits as quite essential to true advaitic scholarship.

I

The Advaita resembles the Sāṅkhya-Yoga in regard to its conception of the psychic apparatus; and it also believes like the other in the theory of representative knowledge. The only difference that may be noticed is that while, according to the Sāṅkhya-Yoga, the ten senses are traced to ahaṁ-kāra, here they are supposed to be derived from the elements much as in the Nyāya-Vaiśeṣika.[1] The internal organ (antaḥ-karaṇa) also is here conceived as bhautika and as constituted of all the five elements. Though it consists of all the five elements, tejas predominates, which accounts for its

[1] It may be noted that the Nyāya-Vaiśeṣika does not recognize karmendriyas, and explains their functions as those of prāṇa or vital air.

being sometimes described as taijasa ('made out of tejas'). It accordingly partakes more of the character of that element than of any other and is unstable—always liable to alter its form either where it is or where it reaches by 'streaming out,' as it is said, through a sense. That is, the antaḥ-karaṇa is always active, except only in states like suṣupti, where it becomes latent. Each of the forms it assumes by exercising this activity is known as a vṛtti as in the Sāṅkhya-Yoga. The explanation that all these organs are bhautika is important on account of the recognition it implies of the indispensableness of physical aids for the manifestation of consciousness. Though indispensable, their distinction from the psychical element is not in the least ignored. It is in fact the constant association of these two incompatibles as implied in common experience that forms, as we shall see, the crux of the philosophic problem according to Śaṁkara.

As regards the nature of the conscious element also, the explanation is almost the same as in the Sāṅkhya-Yoga. It is conceived as extraneous to the apparatus, which yet in some way helps its manifestation. It is not, however, ultimately different from the apparatus here as in the other system; for according to the Advaita the apparatus goes back eventually to the same source, viz. Brahman or spirit, the sole reality acknowledged. For this reason, the interaction between the two—the physical apparatus and the psychical principle—is more satisfactorily explained here than in the other doctrine. But, whatever the metaphysical difference, it does not affect the explanation with which we are concerned in this section. Accordingly we may assume for our present purpose that the two are distinct as in the Sāṅkhya-Yoga. The psychical element is viewed as wholly inactive. The activity it manifests only seemingly belongs to it and is in reality to be traced to its physical accompaniment, viz. the internal organ. The element of consciousness is known as the sākṣin[1] and corresponds to the puruṣa of the Sāṅkhya-

[1] The word means 'witness' or a disinterested looker-on. The conception is thus relative; and the sāksin *as such* is not therefore Brahman.

Yoga—the passive observer of the states of the internal organ as they unfold themselves. It appears never by itself, but always in association with the internal organ in its latent or manifest form. The reverse also is true and no internal organ is conceivable without involving a reference to some sākṣin or other. Thus it is only the unity of the passive sākṣin and the active antaḥ-karaṇa that is real for all practical purposes. That is what knows, feels and wills. In this complex form it is known as the jīva or the empirical self. Such a conception satisfactorily accounts for what would otherwise be wholly unintelligible, viz. the double character of subject and object which one and the same jīva exhibits in so-called self-consciousness. But for the presence within it of the objective complement of the antaḥ-karaṇa one could not, it is said, speak of knowing oneself, since what knows can never be the same as what is known—a view which is entirely opposed to that of Kumārila who regards the ego to be simple and yet ascribes this double character to it (p. 305). This complex entity is believed to endure in one form or other till the time of release. When at last it breaks up, the internal organ is absorbed by or loses its identity in its source, Māyā, which for the moment we may take to be the same as the prakṛti of the Sāṅkhya-Yoga, and the sākṣin losing its sākṣi-hood, as will become clear later, becomes Brahman indeed. The sākṣin and the jīva are thus not identical, though at the same time they are not quite different either. While the jīva may become the object of self-consciousness on account of the objective element it includes, it is wrong to speak of the sākṣin as knowable, for it is the pure element of awareness in all knowing; and to assume that it is knowable would be to imply another knowing element—a process which leads to the fallacy of infinite regress. But the sākṣin does not therefore remain unrealized, for being self-luminous, by its very nature, it does not require to be made known at all. Its presence is necessarily equivalent to its revelation and it is therefore never missed. 'That is self-luminousness,' says the *Pañcadaśī*, 'which is revelation without any aid.'[1] In other words,

[1] xi. 32.

the jīva is spirit as immanent in the antaḥ-karaṇa, while the sākṣin is spirit as transcendent.[1]

By jñāna or knowledge in general we must understand in the system neither a vṛtti of the internal organ nor the sākṣin by itself, but a blend of both—the vṛtti as inspired by the sākṣin. In jñāna thus understood, the vṛtti element is contingent; the other, viz. the element of consciousness, is eternal, being intrinsically Brahman itself which, owing to its association with the vṛttis that appear and disappear, only seems to be characterized by change, but is really untouched by it. It is sometimes termed sākṣi-jñāna to distinguish it from vṛtti-jñāna or empirical knowledge which is a result of the interaction of subject and object. It is present always and it is impossible to think it away. It is 'the light of all our seeing' and does not cease to be even in deep sleep. The antaḥ-karaṇa may have modal transformations (pariṇāma) other than vṛtti-jñāna, such as pain and pleasure. In fact, all internal states are viewed as its modes. But the system does not in theory regard those other states as states of consciousness so that they have to be known through a vṛtti-jñāna. This distinction does not mean that pain and pleasure, for instance, may exist and yet be not experienced; for as states or modes of the internal organ they are necessarily illumined by the sākṣin and are therefore known as they arise just as jñāna itself is.[2] It only shows that the doctrine differentiates the cognitive from the other phases of the mind. If we take this explanation with what we have already stated, viz. that except in states like sleep the internal organ will be ceaselessly operating we see that the jīva is never without some jñāna or other.

Knowledge may be mediate or immediate, the distinction between the two being that while in the former only the 'that' of an object is known, in the latter, the 'what' also is revealed.[3] Both kinds of knowledge are alike vṛttis of the

[1] This is expressed as follows in Sanskrit:—Antaḥ-karaṇa-viśiṣṭo jīvaḥ; antaḥ-karṇopahitaḥ sāksī: VP. p. 102.

[2] VP. pp. 79–82.

[3] Mediate knowledge removes only the ignorance concerning the

internal organ in which the sākṣin is immanent. Knowledge which gives the object directly is not here equated with sensory perception, and there may be immediate knowledge not involving sense-perception. The empirical self for instance is immediately known, but it cannot be said to be *presented* to any sense. Hence the word pratyakṣa, which literally means 'presented to a sense,' is here usually replaced by the wider term aparokṣa or 'not mediate.' If the following conditions are satisfied, knowledge will be immediate, no matter whether it comes through a sense or not. First, the object must be such as can be directly known (yogya). For example, a table can be so known but not virtue. This is not so much a condition of immediacy as an indication that not all things are perceivable. Secondly, the object must be existent at the time; otherwise even a perceivable object will not be immediately known. Our recollection of a table that no longer exists cannot for this reason be immediate. Lastly, there should be established a certain intimate relation between the subject and the object in question. The means of such relation is the vṛtti which flows out[1] in the case of external objects, but remains within where it originates in the case of internal ones like pain or pleasure. It will be convenient to take the former variety of immediate knowledge for finding out the meaning of this condition. The subject and object are here by hypothesis removed from each other and occupy different positions in space; and the vṛtti which relates them brings about for the time being what may be described as an identity of ground for the two. The exact manner in which this takes place is stated as follows: When an organ of sense is brought into contact with an object, the antaḥ-karaṇa, like a searchlight as it were, goes out towards it and gets itself determined by it or assumes the 'form' of that object. The existence of the object previous to the appearance of knowledge is thus necessary so that

existence of an object (asattvāpādakājñāna); immediate knowledge, that regarding its exact nature also (abhānāpādakājñāna). See SLS. pp. 94 and 147; *Pañca-daśī*, vi. 16.

[1] The metaphor is drawn from water in a tank flowing through the sluice to a field to be irrigated and assuming its shape. VP. p. 57.

psychologically the theory is realistic. When the vṛtti coincides with the object, perceptual knowledge arises. The coincidence of these two, since the vṛtti is a mode of the internal organ, is really the coincidence of the jīva and the object. They thus come to have the same ground; or the being of the object, as it is stated, ceases then to be different from the being of the subject.[1] It is their identification in this manner that constitutes the third and the last of the conditions for an object being known immediately. Perception as conceived here is accordingly the result of a communion between the knower and the known; and it would therefore be more appropriate to describe the object as 'felt' then rather than known.[2] In the case of internal perception, when the first two conditions are satisfied, i.e. when the object is perceivable and is actually present at the time, the last condition is invariably fulfilled, for internal states like pain or pleasure are not, as already explained, different in fact from the vṛtti through which they are supposed to be experienced. So if those states admit of being directly perceived at all (yogya),[3] they do become immediately known whenever they exist. If knowledge occurs when one or more of these conditions are lacking, it will be mediate. The table beyond the wall can be known only mediately, for the vṛtti cannot flow out to it to bring about the needed relation, contact with one or other sensory organ being a necessary condition for the starting out of the antaḥ-karaṇa towards the object. But even here, we should remember, a vṛtti is recognized, though it remains internal.

The above view of knowledge implies a classification of objects into those that can be directly known and those that cannot be so known. They may belong to the external world or may be states or modes of the internal organ. External

[1] VP. p. 77.

[2] 'The theory of perception adopted by the Advaita Vedānta is rather crude on the scientific side, though its metaphysical insight is valuable.' IP. vol. ii. pp. 492–3.

[3] For example, religious merit (puṇya) and demerit (pāpa), which also are regarded as modes of the antaḥ-karaṇa, are not perceivable because they lack this condition of yogyatva or fitness. They are only inferable or knowable through verbal testimony.

objects may be perceivable and may also be present at the time; yet they may or may not be directly known. Internal states, on the other hand, when they satisfy those two conditions are necessarily known immediately. To these two kinds of objects must be added a third which is not only necessarily known immediately but is always so known. That is the empirical ego—the jīva or ahaṁ-padārtha as the same is sometimes designated. It is no doubt the object side that is commonly attended to in knowledge; but it does not mean that the subject remains unrevealed in it, although it may not always show itself quite explicitly. As in the Prābhākara school, all knowledge alike involves a reference to it; and since the jiva, according to the Advaita is never without some jñāna or other, the consciousness of self becomes a constant feature of all experience. It is this sense of self that explains how one person is able to distinguish his experience from that of others. It is absent only in states like suṣupti or fainting.

So far we have treated of knowledge during the waking state. But there is dream experience as well and even sleep is not quite bereft of experience. We have now to consider these states specifically. As already stated in the chapter on the Upaniṣads, the essential distinction between dreams and waking is that the senses co-operate in the latter, but not in the former. Further, unlike waking, dreaming is not marked by an association with the gross body. Yet there is in it the feeling that the senses are co-operating and that a gross body—not necessarily similar to that of the waking state—is also present. We may dream of an elephant and we may feel that we are riding on it. The consequence is that we experience objects as existent at the time. This peculiarity precludes the explanation of the state as due to a mere revival of past impressions. Dreams are really more than revived impressions; they are new creations. A revival of the impressions left by previous experience is of course necessary for them, but it does not furnish their whole explanation. Dreams, so far as they are direct experience, should be placed on a par with waking; and it is accordingly assumed that objects are present then, apart from their knowledge. In memory on the other hand that is not the case, the reference in it to things as past being quite clear. The character of dream-objects, however, is held to be different from that of the objects of wakeful experience; but the explanation of this point we have to postpone till we reach the next section.

If the internal organ functions by itself in dreams unaided by the senses, that also becomes latent in sleep. Of the two elements that make up the jīva, one, viz. the antaḥ-karana, is lost in its cause Māyā or, to state it more definitely, in that part or aspect of it called avidyā which constitutes the adjunct of individual jīvas.[1] What endures then is the sākṣin *plus* avidyā which is known as the kāraṇa-śarīra or the 'radical adjunct' of the self as distinguished from its subtle body (liṅga-śarīra).[2] Consequently there is in sleep no subject at all as such and no states of consciousness as in dreams or waking. This makes the 'experience' of dreamless sleep quite unique, though occurring normally and almost universally. What we have in that condition is the sākṣin—not the jīva—associated with its own avidyā, in which the internal organ has provisionally merged. In this state also, we must remember, individuality persists; but the individuality then is due to the union of the sākṣin with avidyā and not with the internal organ. The avidyā operates in sleep only partially. It obscures the true character of reality, but does not split it up into a variety of 'names' and 'forms' as in dreams or in waking, since the discontinuous and mutually excluding vṛttis of the internal organ are absent there. The experience of sleep involves a reference to both these elements—continuance of personality and absence of all variety—as is shown by the later reminiscence[3] that one was asleep and did not know anything. Over and above these there is felt in sleep bliss which, according to a fundamental postulate of

[1] There is some divergence in the use of these terms—Māyā and avidyā. We confine them here respectively to Māyā in its cosmic character and in its 'incidence,' so to speak, on the individual.

[2] In place of the two adjuncts of the self as conceived in the Sāṇkhya-Yoga, we thus have three here: (1) kāraṇa-śarīra, (2) liṅga-śarīra and (3) sthūla-śarīra.

[3] The recollection by the jīva of what was experienced by the sākṣin is possible as the two are not really different. See SLS. pp. 155–6.

the system, is the very nature of the self and which, owing to the absence of all distractions then, becomes manifest. This unalloyed happiness survives even after waking, as shown by the state of repose that continues for a while; but it disappears as man lapses back into the vortex of common life—a belief which is Wordsworthian in its character.[1] 'All beings visit that Brahma-world day after day, but not one realizes it.'[2] None of these features of sleep, it must be noted, is 'known' at the time, for no knowledge, whether mediate or immediate, is possible in the absence of the internal organ. But they are nevertheless realized then as shown by the fact of their being recalled afterwards.

II

There seem to be strictly but two views in regard to the implication of knowledge—either to deny, like the Yogācāra school of Buddhism, that it ever points to an object outside or to admit that it does so always. To postulate the object where knowledge is true while denying it either directly or indirectly where knowledge is erroneous is self-contradictory. To Śaṁkara, all knowledge in the common acceptance of the term points to an object as it does to a subject, and there is no knowledge which does not involve this double implication. Where there is no object, there can be no knowledge.[3] The 'round square' and the 'barren woman's son' are unreal (asat) and there can consequently be no knowledge of them beyond a merely verbal one. But it may be asked how, if all knowledge alike points to an object, illusions occur. In answering the question it will be necessary to refer to the example given in the previous chapter to illustrate the pramāṇa known as arthāpatti which the Advaitin also recognizes. If Devadatta continues to be strong and healthy, though not eating by day, we do not at once modify or give up our belief about the need of food for living beings, but try to reconcile the observed fact with it, and in so doing we

[1] *Pañca-daśī*, xi. 74–5. [2] *Ch. Up.* VIII. iii. 2.
[3] See e.g. com. on VS. II. ii. 28.

assume that he must be eating by night. That is, when we are face to face with a fact which contradicts a well-tested view, we do not all at once revise that view, but endeavour to harmonize the new fact with it by means of a suitable hypothesis. In the present case, since it is inconceivable that knowledge should arise without an objective counterpart to it, the Advaitin assumes that there is an object even in the so-called illusion; and, in order to distinguish illusion from non-illusory knowledge, postulates a difference between the *types* of objects cognized in them. The distinction between illusion and ordinary knowledge is not accordingly due to the absence and presence respectively of an object outside corresponding to its content, but to the difference in the character of the object that is pointed to in either. Objects of illusion are not common to several or general, their presence not being vouched for by collective experience. The serpent (say) which a person sees in the dark where there is only a rope is special to him and may not be seen by others. It may therefore be described as 'private' or personal to him, while objects of common knowledge such as a real serpent are 'public,' for they are cognized by others as well. A second difference between the two types of objects is that while an object of illusion lasts only as long as its knowledge lasts—neither for a longer nor for a shorter period—that of ordinary knowledge is more enduring. The latter is already there before it comes to be apprehended and, generally speaking,[1] continues to be after its apprehension ceases, as is shown for instance by our recognition of it later[2]; the former on the other hand comes to exist *as* we apprehend it and ceases to be when our apprehension of it ceases. The one is described

[1] See *Gauḍapāda-kārika*, II. 14. An object may of course disappear and cease to be as we are apprehending it.

[2] It is possible to say that this feature characterizes illusion also, and that so far the distinction of the objects of ordinary knowledge from those of illusion vanishes. For example, the 'rope-serpent,' once seen, may be recognized after some time, if in the meanwhile the mistake has not been rectified. Such a position cannot be proved to be false; and there have been Advaitins who maintained it (Cf. SLS. pp. 105–6). But it lands us eventually in solipsism and is not the commonly accepted advaitic view.

as vyāvahārika or empirical; the other as prātibhāsika or apparent. Dream objects, to whose difference from those of the waking state we have already referred, are of the second type.

The objects which we have described as private, it is necessary to remember, are not mere ideas or purely subjective. If they were, the advaitic theory of knowledge would be the same as the Yogācāra one which Śaṁkara unreservedly criticizes,[1] viz. that there is no object apart from its knowledge and that the commonly recognized distinction between them is a fiction. No private object can indeed be conceived except as dependent upon a particular individual; the point to be noted is that it is not mental, but an object of mind. This is brought out clearly in the explanation given of the origin and nature of prātibhāsika things to which we shall soon refer. For the present we merely note that the foregoing account shows how mistaken is the common belief that Śaṁkara views the objects of everyday experience to be false or unreal. So far from doing this, he claims some kind of reality even for objects of illusion. To be perceived is for him *to be*, and his theory may therefore be described as an inversion of the one associated in western philosophy with the name of Berkeley. This explanation has one great merit. It accounts for illusion as it occurs. What we experience in it is that we *see* the serpent or silver; and this fact of knowing an object as present then and there is not explained, but is rather explained away in other theories of illusion.

In the light of this distinction among the objects of knowledge, we may explain error as arising when different types of things are related in a judgment.[2] In the example 'This is silver,' the 'this' (i.e. shell) is empirically real and 'silver' which is superposed upon it is only apparently so. In other words, error is 'illegitimate transference' or adhyāsa as Śaṁkara puts it in his celebrated Introduction to the *Vedānta-sūtra*. Though the empirical and the apparent

[1] VS. II. ii. 28–32.

[2] Cf. VP. p. 153. Satya-mithyā-vastu-tādātmyāvagāhitvena bhramatva-svīkārāt.

spheres are both objective, we, for the reasons assigned above, take that which is superposed as less real than that on which it is. The falsity of such knowledge is not realized until we become conscious of the disparity between the objects related in it. When a person is seeing silver where there is only shell, he certainly does not know it to be false. On the other hand, he then feels convinced that it is quite as valid as any other knowledge. But when he approaches the object, picks it up and discovers that it is too light to be silver, he at once realizes that he was in error. What leads to the discovery is therefore this other knowledge[1] whose object, because it is of the empirical kind, is not similarly sublated.[2] Now as regards the relation between the two terms involved in error: It cannot be identity, for things belonging to different levels of being cannot be identified. Nor can it be difference, for then the terms would not appear as subject and predicate in the same judgment as 'This is silver.' We cannot take it as identity-in-difference either, for that conception, as we shall see in the next section, is self-discrepant. The relation is therefore regarded as unique and is called tādātmya.[3] It is not real, because it obtains between terms that belong to two different orders of being. The water that is quaffed in a dream will not quench actual thirst. At the same time the relation is not unreal, for it is experienced. It is therefore like the lower of the two objects it relates, apparent, not empirical. We may further remark that the relation is such that negating the higher of the two relata necessarily negates the lower. But the reverse is not true. If the shell is denied, the silver *is not*; but the negation of the silver is quite conceivable with

[1] Parataḥ eva aprāmāṇyam: VP. p. 338.

[2] It should be noted in this connection that pain, pleasure and other modes of the antaḥ-karaṇa, though 'private,' are not thus sublated and are therefore not prātibhāsika. The same remark applies to the antaḥ-karaṇa also.

[3] Literally the word means 'identity' and is used in the Nyāya-Vaiśeṣika in the sense of the abstract identity of a term with itself. It is also used in the sense of 'identity-in-difference' by some like Kumārila. Here it has neither of these senses.

the affirmation of the shell.[1] This is what constitutes appearance. We accordingly describe the shell as the ground[2] of which the silver is an appearance.

It is necessary to eludicate further the idea of adhyāsa. From the fact that wherever there is adhyāsa, there is a confusion between two orders of being, we deduce that it presupposes ignorance. It is because we are oblivious of the shell that we see silver in its place. There are other causes also, such as the previous experience of silver, defective eye-sight, etc., to account for the mistake; but it will suffice for our purpose to confine our attention to the most important of them, viz. ignorance or avidyā. Now avidyā, which is only another word for ajñāna, implies, like jñāna, some person to whom it belongs (āśraya) and some object to which it refers (viṣaya). The notion of 'knowledge' is not complete until we mention the subject that knows and the object that is known. Similarly, in the case of avidyā, there must be someone whom it characterizes and an object which is misapprehended in it. In the present case, the person that mistakes the shell for silver is its āśraya, and the shell is its viṣaya. It is avidyā[3] thus determined that is described as the cause of silver[4]; and it operates in a double manner. It conceals the fact of shell and shows up silver in its place. To see silver where there is only shell, a necessary condition is the concealment of the shell. Suppression precedes substitution. These two aspects of it are respectively termed āvaraṇa or 'veiling' and vikṣepa or 'revealing.' As the avidyā does not put the shell entirely

[1] For this reason the silver is described as ananya with reference to the shell which Śaṁkara explains as 'not existing apart from.' Ananyatvam vyatirekeṇa abhāvaḥ. See com. on VS. II. i. 14.

[2] That is, the proximate ground. The ultimate ground is always spirit or caitanya.

[3] This avidyā should not be confounded with the one described above as the radical adjunct of the jīva. That is constitutive of the jīva; this is only a passing characteristic of it. The one continues till mokṣa is attained; the other disappears with the error it has occasioned.

[4] Avidyā is directly the cause of the illusion, but all knowledge has by hypothesis an object and that object, viz. 'silver,' here is ascribed to the same avidyā, not being traceable to any other source. See VP. p. 137.

out of sight, it is not lack of apprehension—a mere gap in thought—but misapprehension and is therefore described as positive (bhāva-rūpa). It is the contrary of vidyā, not its contradictory; and the condition for the resulting error to disappear is the removal of avidyā which happens when vidyā arises in the self-same person in regard to the self-same object. It is the reference to a particular individual and to a specific object which this avidyā involves that explains the uniqueness of the silver of which it is described as the source. Because it has a specific external object as its basis, the silver to which it gives rise appears out there—spatially determined—and is not a mere idea; and, because it has a particular person for its āśraya, the illusion which it occasions is special to him. It is this personal character that distinguishes private objects from the empirical ones which, as we shall see later, spring into being directly from Māyā and are 'public' or verifiable by others also. Though the objects we are now considering form an order by themselves, they are not altogether sundered from the other, for avidyā which occasions private objects is dependent upon the same source to which the common order of nature is due, viz. Māyā,[1] and is therefore described sometimes as tūlāvidyā or auxiliary avidyā.[2] It is owing to this sameness of the source that when Māyā is overcome in mokṣa both realms of objective being disappear alike. Otherwise though the common order of nature may cease to be then, the other might persist.

There is one important instance of adhyāsa which we must specially consider now—the ego or ahaṁ-padārtha. Systems like the Nyāya-Vaiśeṣika and the Mīmāṁsā regard it as a simple and ultimate entity. It is in fact synonymous with the self (ātman) in those doctrines. But the Advaitin denies the integrity of the self in this sense and takes it, we know, to be a complex of the sākṣin and the internal organ. His reasons in favour of this position are chiefly two: One is the fact of self-consciousness which by showing in the same self the contrary features of subject and object indicates its mixed character. The other is the uniqueness of sleep experience.

[1] SLS. p. 140. [2] VP. p. 168. Māyā is then termed mūlāvidyā.

If the ego or jīva were simple and endured throughout, all experience would alike involve a reference to it. But that is not the case, for sleep as interpreted here is without such reference. We are therefore compelled to explain it as consisting of two elements one of which, viz. the sākṣin alone, endures through the three states. The other, viz. the internal organ, is common only to waking and dream; and to it accordingly should be ascribed all the specific features of those states. 'Love, desire, pleasure, pain and so forth are experienced when the internal organ functions, but not in sleep; hence they must be of the internal organ.'[1] Now the Nyāya-Vaiśeṣika and the Mīmāṁsā, which hold that the ego is not analysable, maintain that it is distinct from the body, senses, etc. But there is ordinarily an implied identification of these distinct entities, as for instance when one says 'I am stout,' 'I am blind,' where 'stoutness' and 'blindness' which are respectively the characteristics of the body and the sense of sight are predicated of the self. These systems explain the identification as more or less consciously made, as for example when we describe a man as a 'giant' and as therefore having only a secondary or rhetorical significance (gauṇa)—supporting their position by reference to the equally familiar experience finding expression as 'my body,' etc., where the distinction appears explicitly. The Advaitin does not accept this explanation. He contends that the characteristic of gauṇa or secondary usage, viz. the consciousness at the time of the distinction between the objects identified, is lacking here and ascribes the identification to an unconscious confusion between the entities involved, viz. body, senses, etc., on the one hand, and the sākṣin on the other. It accordingly involves, in his view, ignorance of the true character of those entities and is a case of error or adhyāsa. There are indeed occasions, he admits, when we do distinguish between the two, as when we speak of 'our body,'

[1] Rāgecchā-sukha-duḥkhādi buddhau satyām pravartate:
Suṣuptau nāsti tannāśāt tasmāt buddhestu nātmanaḥ.

These are all vṛttis as inspired by the sākṣin and it is their vṛtti aspect alone that belongs to the antaḥ-karaṇa. The resemblance to the Sāṅkhya-Yoga here is clear.

but he explains them as only flashes of the truth which are soon veiled from us. This argument is applicable to the antaḥ-karaṇa also and when a person feels pain, for example, and says 'I am suffering,' he is illegitimately transferring to the true ātman what according to the previous reasoning belongs to the antaḥ-karaṇa.[1] If the ego is complex and is an instance of adhyāsa, the entities constituting it must belong to different orders of being. We get a hint here of a third kind of reality; for the internal organ, one of the two involved in it, is an empirical reality being an effect of Māyā and as such stands higher than appearances having avidyā for their source. The higher reality is the sākṣin or more strictly[2] sākṣi-svarūpa which is Brahman itself. It is designated true or pāramārthika reality.[3]

If error signifies that the objects related in it belong to different orders of being, truth by implication should consist in relating objects of the same order; but, for reasons to be explained presently, we shall take this definition as holding good only within the sphere of empirical things and not in the case of appearances which are contradicted when we judge them in relation to that sphere. A dream-judgment like 'This is an elephant' is not true although its two terms alike stand for realities of the prātibhāsika type, because both are set aside so soon as one awakes.[4] Pramāṇa we

[1] The Nyāya-Vaiśeṣika and the Mīmāṁsā also admit that the manas which corresponds to the Advaitin's antaḥ-karaṇa is different from the self; but they view pain, etc., as features directly characterizing the ātman. There is therefore nothing, according to those doctrines, that is out of the normal in the experience 'I am suffering' to need an explanation.

[2] The notion of the sākṣin, as already pointed out, is relative to an antaḥ-karaṇa and cannot therefore be regarded as ultimate. Sākṣi-svarūpa means the essence of the sākṣin.

[3] Some recognize only one kind of being. See VP. pp. 221–3. Some again do not make any distinction between vyāvahārika and prātibhāsika being. According to the latter, the reality of the waking state does not stand higher than that of the dream state—what is true according to either being sublated in the other. See Note 2 on p. 350.

[4] The ground of the adhyāsa here is taken to be spirit or caitanya, as indeed it is in the case of 'shell-silver' also eventually (VP. pp. 162–3). The only difference is that in the latter the illusion is mediated by an empirical object, viz. the shell, while in the former it is direct.

accordingly define as that which leads to knowledge whose content is not sublated (abādhita) as the result of later experience.[1] The silver seen where there is only a shell disappears the moment we scrutinize it, but the shell does not vanish in the same manner. The knowledge of the silver is therefore bhrama and that of the shell, pramā. True, even the latter may prove a delusion from a higher standpoint; but such a consideration may be excluded when we are contrasting empirical things with appearances. What is meant when we say that the knowledge of the shell is pramā is that, unlike that of the silver, it justifies its claim for truth throughout empirical life[2]—not that it is ultimately real. As regards the question whether novelty (anadhigatatva) should be regarded as a necessary element in truth (p. 313), the Advaitin is indifferent; but with his partiality for the Bhāṭṭa view, he would prefer to include it among the conditions of validity. In accordance with the orthodox view of revelation (p. 180), this condition is necessary in the case of śruti.[3]

The Advaita recognizes all the six pramāṇas mentioned in connection with the Kumārila school of Mīmāṁsā and generally agrees with it in matters of detail also.[4] Of the points of difference between the two, it will suffice to touch upon only the following here, all of them having reference to verbal testimony:—

(i) The Mīmāṁsā rejects the view that the Veda was ever composed by anybody (p. 312), and the Nyāya-Vaiśeṣika ascribes its authorship to Īśvara (p. 258). The position of Śaṁkara in regard to this point, like that of the other Vedāntins, is midway between the two. Like the Mīmāṁsaka, but unlike the Nyāya-Vaiśeṣika, he admits that the Veda is apauruṣeya; but he re-defines that word so as to make it signify not that the Veda has no author and is eternal, but that it is produced or, more properly, resuscitated at the beginning of each kalpa by one that cannot interfere either with its content or with the order of its words. In the case of works like the *Raghu-vaṁśa*, the author composes it just

[1] VP. pp. 19 ff. [2] VP. pp. 36–8. [3] VP. p. 298.

[4] Compare the saying: Vyavahāre Bhāṭṭa-nayaḥ.

as he likes. Here, on the other hand, the first promulgator of the Veda in every cycle who is God repeats it anew, but precisely as it was in earlier cycles. That is, the Veda is self-existent in this view also; only it is not the self-same Veda that always is, but a series of what may be described as re-issues of an eternal edition which goes back to beginningless time. This, it will be seen, is not in substance different from the Mīmāṁsā view, excepting that it finds a place for God in the doctrine.

(ii) Śaṁkara, following Kumārila, admits śabda to be a pramāṇa outside the Veda also; but he does not restrict its independent logical validity, within the Veda, to injunctive statements (p. 318). Assertive propositions found there may be equally valid, so that there is nothing in the nature of the Veda as verbal testimony to preclude it from treating directly of matters of fact (bhūta-vastu) like Brahman or the highest reality. Statements like Tat tvam asi which occur in the Upaniṣads thereby acquire independent logical value here; and there is no need to subordinate them in one way or another to ritualistic commands as in the Mīmāṁsā.

(iii) The truth revealed by the scriptures, contrary to what the Mīmāṁsaka thinks, is here the fundamental unity of Being. We shall see later in what sense this unity is to be understood in the Advaita, and may now consider the place in the scheme of pramāṇas of perception which seems to vouch for the truth of diversity and thus to come into conflict with the teaching of revelation that all is one. The primary aim of perception, like that of the other pramāṇas, is, according to Śaṁkara, to serve empirical purposes. It gives no guarantee for metaphysical validity,[1] so that what we commonly hold real may not be truly so. 'Common knowledge is true,' he says,[2] 'so long only as the identity of oneself with Brahman is not realized, as dreams are until one does not awake.' In other words, the transcendental ideality of the world does not exclude its empirical reality.[3] Such a view considerably modifies the notion of inherent validity (svataḥ-

[1] Cf. *Naiṣkarmya-siddhi,* ii. 5; iii. 44 and 83–6. [2] VS. II. i. 14.

[3] See Deussen: *System of the Vedānta*, p. 55. Cf. stanzas cited by Śaṁkara at the end of his com. on VS. I. i. 4.

prāmāṇya) which the Advaitin, like the Mīmāṁsaka (p. 307), accepts. That knowledge is true requires, according to the Advaita also, no explanation, for by its very nature it is so. This self-validity, however, for the reason just mentioned, is to be understood here as relative and not absolute as in the Mīmāṁsā. Even the validity of the Veda, generally speaking, is only such. When it teaches that svarga can be attained through the performance of a certain sacrifice, it is of course true; but the Veda does not thereby vouch for the *ultimate* reality of either the svarga or anything connected with it. The fact is that the Advaita recognizes a higher, viz. the absolute standpoint from which all pramāṇas alike, inclusive of the Veda, lose their relative validity. An exception is made only in the case of Upaniṣadic statements that teach the unity of all being. These statements are pramāṇa in the absolute sense, for the knowledge which they convey is never shown to be wrong. But it does not secure for the pramāṇa itself ultimate reality, for in mokṣa where nothing but Brahman remains, even that pramāṇa as such must disappear. It signifies that a false means may lead to a true end—a position which may appear untenable; but there are many instances in life where this happens. The image of a person as reflected in a mirror is not real, but it does not therefore fail to serve as the means of showing to him so many facts about his appearance. The roaring of a lion in a dream is not real, but it may wake the dreamer to actual life. It is necessary, however, to remember in thus admitting the utility of error that nothing here is absolutely unreal so that even a false means is not without a nucleus of truth.[1]

So much about vṛtti-jñāna or knowledge as it is commonly known to us. But according to the advaitic analysis of it, empirical knowledge is a complex consisting of a physical factor and a psychical one, neither of which by itself is adequate to explain experience as we are familiar with it. We have now to point out the full implication of this analysis on its psychical side. The sākṣin which is the psychical element is always present like an ever-luminous lamp, the enduring and changeless element in experience which does

[1] See Śaṁkara on VS. II. i. 14; *Naiṣkarmya-siddhi*, iii. 108–9.

not cease to be even in deep sleep. It is individual and determinate, being defined by reference to the particular internal organ with which for the time being it seems associated. It is accordingly termed jīva-sākṣin. What comes within the range of one sākṣin—through the medium of its own antaḥkaraṇa in the waking and dream states and through avidyā in deep sleep—is not necessarily within the experience of other sākṣins. But existent objects as a whole can be understood only as presented to some sākṣin, for consistently with the eventually idealistic position of the Advaita there can be no reality outside what either knows or is known. This line of reasoning leads to the postulating of a cosmic sākṣin or absolute consciousness (Īśvara-sākṣin) which sustains everything that is.[1] It is, in reality, the ground of the whole universe and is, as we shall see more fully in the next section, the Brahman of the Advaita. It is designated svarūpa-jñāna or pure consciousness. The vṛtti-jñāna draws its breath and substance from it, and the whole complex of empirical or finite knowledge would be nowhere without the light of this absolute or infinite consciousness.

To sum up: Our analysis of experience has led us, on the one hand, to an infinite consciousness or absolute spirit (anubhūti or caitanya); and, on the other, to two realms of objects which, however, have no being apart from that spirit. We may deduce this principle from the nature of the sākṣin as we have just done or from the nature of those realms of being. We may argue that just as the prātibhāsika reality points to a vyāvahārika one, the vyāvahārika in its turn does, to a pāramārthika reality. If an appearance lasts only as long as its jñāna lasts and the empirical persists ever afterwards, this higher reality is timeless. Thus we have altogether three orders of being of which two alone are related to time. The third, which is the same as the svarūpa-jñāna referred to above, is the Brahman of the Vedānta. The recognition of this higher reality reveals a new form of error. The one we have drawn attention to thus far is that in which a prātibhāsika object is superposed upon a vyāvahārika one. It is error as is familiarly known. But if error is illegitimate

[1] VP. pp. 102 ff.

transference, the superposition of an empirical 'what' on the highest Being also should be erroneous. This is not, however, error which occurs *within* the world of experience like the other, but lies at the root of it. It is involved in the very notion of the ego or the knowing subject (pramātā) because in it two incompatibles are, as we have seen, confounded with each other. It therefore vitiates all our knowledge at its source. The whole of the universe in the form in which it is experienced by us is due to this metaphysical error wherein the empirical is mistaken for the real, and is an abstraction apart from its ground, viz. Brahman.[1] That is, there is a higher standpoint from which even empirical things are only appearances. It is in this sense that the Advaita maintains that the world is not real (mithyā) and that Brahman is the sole truth. The conception of truth and error in the system thus becomes relative, and it is essentially wrong to speak of any knowledge as true or false without mentioning at the same time the sphere with reference to which it is adjudged. It was for this reason that we defined truth above relatively to a particular level of being, viz. the empirical. Really, however, even this 'truth' is an error. Only we should not forget that, according to the Advaita, all error is but partially so, for it contains a core of truth—the shell for instance in the case of silver and in the case of the shell itself when we regard it as not real, the higher reality of which it is an appearance.

III

The ontological position of the Advaita has already been indicated generally in dealing with its view of knowledge. We shall now restate the same, adding some details. Of the three types of being mentioned, we need treat only of two here, viz. the empirical and the true or the metaphysical. The former, we have already stated, is common to all and exists independently of individual consciousness. It also, as experienced by different individuals, is no doubt partly

[1] Contrast the Sāṅkhya-Yoga view where the elements constituting the empirical ego are independently real.

divergent, for each cognizes only so much of the world as is within the reach of his limited faculties and is in kinship with his particular temperament. To give the illustration of the *Pañca-daśī*,[1] a father may think that his son who has gone away from home to a distant place is alive while as a matter of fact he is no more. One and the same object again may occasion different and even opposite feelings in different persons. But these worlds as given in the experience of individuals are not entirely separate. They have, as indeed we ordinarily take for granted, a common basis unlike the dream-worlds, for instance, of two or more persons. That is the world as it is; and it is termed Īśvara-sṛṣṭa ('God-created'), while the same as it exists in the medium of one's individual consciousness is described as jīva-sṛṣṭa[2] ('jīva-created'). Such a view implies that we accept many selves. There is of course nothing preventing us from criticizing this position as a begging of the question, but the only alternative to it is solipsism, which, though as a theory it may be irrefutable, is repugnant to thought and really stultifies all effort at philosophizing. We shall accordingly take for granted the plurality of selves so far as our present discussion goes. These selves or jīvas differ from the common objects of experience in being coeval with time and not in it like them[3]—a belief which the Advaitin shares with the followers of the other orthodox systems. Thus each of the indefinite number of selves we have assumed has been there from the beginning of time or is anādi. The empirical world which is vouched for by collective experience presents both unity and diversity, there being a common and enduring element along with different and changing ones in it. It may be described as a systematic whole, for it exhibits a causal order. It also involves a purpose inasmuch as its creation, as explained in the chapter on the Upaniṣads (p. 79), rests upon a moral necessity. Such indications of physical and moral order in it, no doubt, are not altogether conclusive; but there is the significant fact

[1] iv. 20–35.
[2] It is the world as it exists for an individual that is the source of bondage to him, not the world as it is. See *Pañca-daśī*, iv. 32.
[3] Cf. Śaṁkara on VS. II. iii. 16 and 17.

that they become more numerous and clearer with the advance of knowledge and the growth of human institutions. When once the cosmic character of the world is admitted, we trace it back to a source which, though simple, accounts for all aspects of it. This source or the first cause is Māyā which symbolizes to us the unitary character of the physical world. Diversity is only implicit in it, while in the objective world that develops from it, it is quite explicit. There is, however, one important difference between Māyā and its products. The latter, as their very description as 'products' testifies, have all a beginning in time; but the former being the first cause can obviously have no such beginning. It also is therefore anādi like the jīvas alluded to above. Jīvas and Māyā thus form a new type of entities and differ from common objects which are all in time; but they are not, it should be added, altogether unrelated to time like Brahman or the ultimate reality.

It has been stated that the sphere of empirical objects is independent of individual consciousness. On the principle, however, to which we have already referred (p. 54) that whatever is, if not itself mind, must be for mind, it should depend upon some consciousness; for otherwise the statement that it *is* would be meaningless. Granting such an all-sustaining consciousness, it is easy to see what conditions it must satisfy. It should last as long as the world in its causal or effect form lasts. That is, it must be anādi. It cannot be any finite consciousness in the sense in which a jīva is, for it must know the contents of the entire universe. Not only this, whatever is known must also be correctly and directly known by it, for error and mediate knowledge which imply limitation of one kind or another are, by our hypothesis, excluded in the case of that consciousness. That is, its experience must be direct, complete and correct. This cosmic subject, as we may term it, to whom the whole of existence is related as an object, is the Īśvara of Advaita and it is the third of the entities coeternal with time along with Māyā and the jīvas. Here we find the triple factor forming the subject-matter of all philosophy and religion. To them we may add a fourth, viz. time itself to which we have all along been alluding but which cannot be brought under any of the other three heads.

We shall now briefly state the nature of these four entities which, though they are not distinct from the empirical universe, stand on a footing of their own:—

(1) *Jīva.*—This is the empirical self, the true nature of which has already been considered. It is manifold, each jīva having its own peculiar features, although agreeing with the rest of its class in many respects. It represents the spiritual element in the universe; but it is the spiritual element appearing not by itself, but invariably in association with physical adjuncts such as the antaḥ-karaṇa. Its essential associate, however, is avidyā, the individual's share of Māyā which is the adjunct of Īśvara. Just as the whole universe is the effect of Māyā, the portions of the universe which constitute the gross and subtle bodies of an individual self are conceived as the effects of that particular self's avidyā. In fact, the relation of Īśvara to the world is exactly parallel to that of the jīva to its own organism. Considered apart from these individual and cosmic accompaniments, the jīva and Īśvara are one or, more strictly, are not different. That is the significance of Tat tvam asi. The jīvas which we have assumed to be many are in consequence only empirically so; and the individuality characterizing each is due to its adjuncts such as the body and the senses. Intrinsically they are but one, for each is alike the supreme reality.

(2) *Māyā.*—This is the first cause of the physical universe and consequently corresponds to the prakṛti of the Sāṅkhya-Yoga; but there are important differences and metaphysically the two are poles asunder. From it spring into being not only organic bodies that house jīvas but also all inorganic nature. The things arising from Māyā we commonly regard as real; but truly they cannot be described as either sat or asat. They are known (dṛśya) and to that extent at any rate cannot be unreal, for the absolutely unreal, like 'the hare's horn,' is only words. Nor can they be regarded as real in their own right, for they are objective (jaḍa) and hence depend entirely upon spirit for their being. This characteristic of not being finally classifiable as either real or unreal (sadasadvilakṣaṇa)

constitutes the uniqueness of the things of experience and should naturally be found also in their cause, Māyā. They are neither something nor nothing, and are therefore termed mithyā. They are not unreal as commonly assumed by the critics of the doctrine; only they are not ultimate. Or, in other words, their reality is relative and they may be regarded as appearances when contrasted with the higher reality of Brahman. In giving rise to such things, Māyā resembles avidyā, the source of common illusions, and is therefore described as the principle of cosmic illusion. In this it differs from the prakṛti of the Sāṅkhya-Yoga which is real in the full sense of the term.

(3) *Īśvara.*—We described Māyā as the source of the physical universe. But this source, for reasons already assigned, being altogether dependent upon the cosmic sākṣin, cannot act by itself. In strictness, therefore, the two elements should together be reckoned as giving rise to the world. Here we find another point of difference from the Sāṅkhya-Yoga where prakṛti is supposed to be endowed with the spontaneity required for manifesting of itself the whole of the physical world. It is the cause of the world in this complex form or spirit together with Māyā that is the Īśvara of Advaita. Or as it is somewhat differently expressed, Māyā is the potency (śakti) inherent in Īśvara through which he manifests the objective world with all its diversity of names and forms.[1] But he at the same time sees through the diversity, so that he never misses its underlying unity as we do. Though the universe as emerging from Īśvara is not around but within him, the exercise of this potency gives rise to a sense of 'the other'; and Māyā may therefore be regarded as the principle of self-consciousness or self-determination. It interpolates a distinction where really there is none. In this sense, Māyā cannot be the source of the universe, but is a mere accessory to Īśvara in bringing it into existence out of himself. For reasons similar to those adduced in explaining the parallel conception of avidyā—the source of ordinary illusions, Māyā or the principle of cosmic illusion is conceived as more than a negation of

[1] See Śaṁkara on VS. I. iv. 3.

jñāna. The very fact that it serves as the cause of the visible universe shows that it should be so far positive. It is again, on the analogy of avidyā, described as having two powers—āvaraṇa and vikṣepa. In its vikṣepa phase it projects the aggregate of names and forms constituting the world. The function of āvaraṇa is to obscure the unity of Being; but since that unity is never concealed from Īśvara, Māyā in its āvaraṇa aspect is stated to be powerless over him. Nature does not veil spirit from him. This sets a vast gulf between the jīva and Īśvara. It, in fact, accounts for the bondage of the one and the freedom of the other. Owing to the power which the āvaraṇa phase of Māyā or avidyā wields over it, the jīva believes in the ultimacy of mere variety, and to this belief, as also to its fragmentary view of the world already mentioned, should be traced all the evil to which it is subject. It ordinarily identifies itself with the organism with which it is bound up and looks upon the rest of reality as wholly external. It develops likes and dislikes for a small part of it, and assumes an attitude of indifference towards the rest. In the case of Īśvara, on the contrary, such preferences and exclusions are impossible according to our hypothesis. He identifies himself with the whole world and the identification is not, as in the case of the jīva and its organism, due to any confusion (adhyāsa) between the self and the not-self, but is the outcome of a continual realization of the true nature of both. The ideal of morality as conceived in the Advaita, we may state in passing, is gradually to replace the narrow view held by the jīva by one like that of the cosmic self, whose interests coincide with those of the universe.[1] 'Considerations of "mine" and "thine" weigh only with the little-minded; to the large-hearted, on the other hand, the whole world is like a single household.'[2]

Such a conception naturally lends itself to a two-fold presentation, and that is why it is described not only as Īśvara or 'the Lord' but also as the saguṇa Brahman. The former being personal may be taken as the ideal of advaitic

[1] See Śaṁkara on *Ch. Up.* III. xiv. 1 and on VS. I. ii. 1–8.

[2] Ayam nijaḥ paro veti gaṇanā laghu-cetasām:
Udāra-caritānām tu vasudhaiva kuṭumbakam.

religion—standing for an all-knowing almighty God, the creator, preserver and destroyer of the world; the latter, not being so, as that of advaitic philosophy—standing for the Absolute which explains the world-system as it is. When we consider the universe in reference to this supreme subject, there is only one type of reality in place of the two found in the case of the jīva; and that is of the phenomenal or prātibhāsika type. For by hypothesis whatever is, is known to Īśvara and no part of it lasts longer than the time during which it is experienced. In this sense, Īśvara may be described as an eternal dreamer. But we must not think that he is deluded. That would be so if he did not realize the identity of the objective world with himself, or if any aspect of the truth about it remained unrevealed to him. What is meant by describing Īśvara's world as prātibhāsika is that its unity with himself being always realized, all variety *as such* is known to him to be a mere abstraction. It is just this distinction between the relation of the world to Īśvara on the one hand and to the jīva on the other that critics overlook when they say that according to Śaṁkara the objective world is unreal. It is no doubt an appearance to Īśvara, but not to us who have not realized its unity with ourselves. Till we are able to do so and make our life a mirror of our new convictions, we must view it as real whatever its ultimate nature may be.

(4) *Time.*—We have so far assumed an entity like time and taken it as lying outside the remaining three. It really represents the relation between spirit and Māyā.[1] Of these, the former alone is completely real and not Māyā also. Hence the relation between them, like that between the shell and silver, cannot be fully real. That is, time is phenomenal. In this connection it is necessary to point out the advaitic view of space. It is regarded as an offshoot of Māyā and the first object to be created,[2] so that the Advaitin does not place time and space on the same footing. Its conception presupposes the principle of causation already at work, but not so the conception of time. While all things born, excepting

[1] See *Vana mālā* on Śaṁkara's com. on *Tait. Up.*, p. 131 (Śrīrangam Edn.).

[2] *Tait. Up.* ii. 1.

space, are in time and space, space is in time only. Jīva, Īśvara and Māyā are neither in time nor in space.

These are the fundamental entities of the Advaita considered from the empirical standpoint. It is not necessary to enter here into cosmological details, for they are practically the same as those mentioned in the chapter on the Upaniṣads. These entities, it should be clear from their description given above, are not disparate. They are interrelated and together constitute a system which, as time is included in it, may be taken to be dynamic in its character. The question now to consider is whether such a conception is satisfactory enough to remain final. The conclusion of the Advaita is that it is not, whether we judge it from the standpoint of practical religion or from that of speculative philosophy:—

(1) Thus to view it as representing a theistic ideal: There is the well-known difficulty—to mention only one—of reconciling God's assumed goodness and power with the presence of physical and moral evil in the world.[1] Even supposing that evil exists only from our standpoint and not from that of God or Īśvara as defined above, the theistic position does not become fully comprehensible. We cannot, for instance, understand why God should have created the world. To ascribe a motive to him would be to admit that he has ends to attain; and that would be to question his perfection or all-sufficiency (paritṛptatvam). To deny a motive and ascribe the work of creation to his intrinsic nature or to some sudden impulse in him would be to reduce God to an automaton or attribute caprice to him; and either way his supposed omniscience is compromised.[2] There are solutions of such difficulties suggested in the Advaita as in theistic doctrines generally; and these attempts at justifying the ways of God to man are not without their appeal to the religious mind. But, as Saṁkara observes, they are not final because they 'have reference to the world of names and forms founded upon avidyā.'[3] In other words, such solutions, like the problems they solve, keep us tied to the realm of relativity and, as the essence of the relative is to point beyond

[1] VS. II. i. 34–6. [2] Ibid., 32–3.

[3] See com. on sūtra 33 *ad finem*. Cf. *Bhāmatī* on sūtra 34.

itself for its complete explanation, the theistic conception cannot be regarded as ultimate.

(2) The same conclusion is reached when we regard it as the philosophic Absolute. The relation for instance which appears to constitute its several elements into a system will on examination be seen to be not really intelligible. Let us consider first the place of the jīvas in it: Since, according to the doctrine, the jīvas do not originate and are anādi like the saguṇa Brahman itself, the relation between the two should be anādi. So much is certain. But what is the nature of this relation? It is not identity, for the saguṇa Brahman cannot be the same as any of the jīvas with its fragmentary experience. Nor can it be regarded as a collection of all of them, for that would give us only a collection of individual experiences and not, as required, an integral one which alone can serve as the ground and explanation of the whole universe. That is, we cannot identify the saguṇa Brahman with either any of the jīvas or with the totality of them. Equally impossible is it to think of it as altogether different from or outside them, for in that case there would not be that intimate connection between the two which is implied in the description of the whole as a system. A similar reasoning applies to the relation between the saguṇa Brahman and the physical universe emerging from it; only as the latter unlike the jīvas has a beginning, being produced, the relation is not anādi.[1] It cannot be identity, for an effect as such is not the same as its cause; nor is it difference, for then the two cannot be represented as cause and effect.

But it may appear to us that the relation in question is one of identity-in-difference. Such a conception itself, according to the Advaitin, is self-discrepant. This is a point which is discussed at great length in advaitic works.[2] It is not possible to enter here into all the details of the discussion; so we shall content ourselves with drawing attention to its main features.[3] Let M and N be two entities between

[1] If we take, instead of the visible universe, its source Māyā, the relation is anādi.

[2] See e.g. BUV. IV. iii, st. 1637–1787; *Bhāmatī*. I. i. 4.

[3] Cf. *Iṣṭa-siddhi* (Gaekwad's Oriental Series), pp. 18–22.

which the relation in question is supposed to exist. Now neither of them can *as such* be both identical with and different from the other. It would mean that M is both N and not-N and that N similarly is both M and not-M, which is a violation of the law of contradiction. When two things are distinct in fact, they cannot be the same. We cannot accept both sides of a contradiction to be true. But it may be said that this deficiency, if it be one, is vouched for by experience and that, since experience is our only guide, we must acquiesce in it (p. 161). Such an argument seems to the Advaitin like a refusal to think. He admits that we finally depend upon experience for determining the truth about things, but he does not therefore relinquish the right to re-examine the meaning of experience when it results in a palpable self-contradiction and seek for a new explanation of it, if possible. The data of experience, merely because they are such, put us under no constraint to accept them under all circumstances as logical verities. Further, it may be granted for the sake of argument that there is no valid ground for doubting the reality of the content of experience as it ordinarily occurs, when there is agreement among thinkers about it. But the point in question is not one about which we find any such agreement. Even the realist Naiyāyika, we know, postulates the new-fangled relation of samavāya in such cases with a view to avoid the necessity for admitting the real to be self-contradictory. Whatever view, therefore, we may hold about the verdict of experience in general, the present case at any rate is not one where it can be accepted without scrutiny. If M and N do not constitute an identity in difference directly, it may be thought that they do so mediately through features or elements in them—some of which are identical and others different. Thus we may say that M and N possess one or more common features which may be represented by *a* and, at the same time, exhibit differences represented by *x* and *y* respectively. According to this explanation, what is identical is quite distinct from what is different; yet the entities, viz. M and N, by virtue of such features, it may be said, are identical with and, at the same time, different from each other. Such an explanation may seem to solve the difficulty, but the solution is only apparent, for it merely shifts the difficulty to another set of things. It assumes that M and N are characterized by *a x* and *a y* respectively, and the assumption leaves us where we were, for we cannot satisfactorily explain the relation between a thing and its so-called characteristics. Now the relation between M and *a x*, to take only one of the entities, cannot be identity, for then the distinction between *a* amd *x* would vanish, both being identical with the same M; and with it also the relation of identity-in-difference between M and N. Nor can *a* and *x* be different from M, for then their character, whatever it may be, will cease to affect M and therefore also its relation to N. So we are driven to think of identity-in-difference as the only possible relation between these. That is, in explaining the relation in question between M and N, we presuppose the same relation within each of them; and pursuing the inquiry further will only lead to an infinite process.[1]

For such reasons the Advaitin views the relation between the saguṇa Brahman and its constitutive elements as unique or as tādātmya in the sense explained in the previous section—not to be characterized as identity or difference or identity-in-difference. Hence the conception of saguṇa Brahman involves adhyāsa, and like that of Īśvara cannot be regarded as ultimate. Or to state it differently, the saguṇa Brahman includes not merely reality but also appearance, which is something less than the real. The element of reality in it is the ultimate of Advaita. It should be carefully noted that this reality is not the mere unity underlying the diversity of the universe, for unity and diversity are relative to each other, and it is impossible to retain the one as real while rejecting the other as an appearance. Both of them are alike appearances and the advaitic Ultimate is what is beyond

[1] It does not alter the matter if M and N, instead of being two objects, are two moments in the history of one and the same object, say P. The argument would still be applicable to them, the only difference being that what are described as identical features are truly so in the latter, but are only similar and remain separate in the former.

them—their non-phenomenal ground (nirviśeṣa-vastu). It is for this reason that Śaṁkara describes his doctrine as advaita or 'non-duality,' and not as aikya or 'unity.' By discarding the notion of bhedābheda or, more specifically, by refusing to accept a changing Brahman as ultimate, Śaṁkara differentiates his doctrine from Brahma-pariṇāma-vāda advocated by other Vedāntins according to whom both the physical universe and the jīvas actually emerge from Brahman.[1] Brahman according to him does not evolve in this sense, but only gives rise to appearances which, though entirely depending upon it, affect it no more than the silver does the shell in which it appears. He thus enunciates a new view of causation which is different from both the pariṇāma-vāda and the ārambha-vāda with which we are familiar. According to it, the cause produces the effect without itself undergoing any change whatsoever. It is vivarta-vāda or the doctrine of *phenomenal* development. Viewed in the light of this theory, Brahman only appears as the world. It is the original of which the world, as it has been said,[2] may be regarded as 'a translation at the plane of space-time'; and Brahman depends as little for its being on the world as an original work does on its translation. This is what is otherwise known as the Māyā doctrine.[3] Though the doctrine as it appears here naturally shows considerable development in matters of detail, it has, as we have pointed out (p. 63), a definite basis in the Upaniṣads. The charge that it is alien to the Vedānta is therefore really without foundation. Again, by postulating a Reality behind the self-discrepant world of experience, Śaṁkara differentiates his doctrine from the śūnya-vāda of the Mādhyamika. The discrepancy characterizing the saguṇa Brahman or its relativity only degrades it to the level of appearance; it does not dismiss it altogether. If according to the Mādhyamika it is impossible for thought

[1] Some like Bhāskara take the universe alone as the parināma of Brahman and not the jīvas also.

[2] IP. vol. ii. 570.

[3] If the Advaitin sometimes uses terms implying belief in pariṇāma, he should be understood as speaking from the empirical standpoint. See Śaṁkara on VS. II. i. 14 and *Bhāmatī* on I. iv. 27.

to rest in the relative, it is equally impossible for it, according to Śaṁkara, to rest in absolute nothing. To use the terminology of the Upaniṣads, the Advaita denies only 'names' and 'forms' but not that which appears under their guise. Or, as an old writer has observed, while the Advaitin negates only distinction (bheda), the Mādhyamika negates it as well as the distincts (bhidyamāna).[1] That there is a Reality at the back of all empirical things again is not a mere assertion, for it is maintained here, as we know, that the thinking subject in us is not different from it so that its being becomes an immediate certainty. If we denied it, the very fact of denial would affirm it.[2] We may not know what it exactly is; but its presence itself, owing to the basic identity of ourselves with it, can never be doubted.

What is the nature of this Reality? As indicated in an earlier section, it may be represented on the one hand as the infinite Consciousness implied by empirical knowledge or as the infinite Being presupposed in all finite existence. But it is neither empirical knowledge nor phenomenal being, for each of them has appearance superadded to the real and so far fails to represent the latter in its purity. Such knowledge and being, though revealing the ultimate, do not represent it truly and the same is the case with all empirical things. While they are not apart from it, they cannot either singly or in combination stand for it. That is why Brahman as the ultimate is termed nirguṇa or 'indeterminate,' which does not amount to saying, as it is ordinarily assumed, that it is nothing, but only means that nothing which the mind can think of can actually belong to it. Whatever we think of is for that very reason objective (dṛśya) and it cannot therefore be an element in that which is never presented as an object (dṛk). The familiar categories of thought therefore are all inapplicable to it. Hence no direct description of it is possible. But we can indirectly point to it utilizing the appearances as aids; for an appearance, which can never be independent, necessarily signifies a reality beyond itself. In this sense every

[1] See SAS. iv. 20.

[2] Ya eva hi nirākartā tadeva tasya svarūpam: Śaṁkara on VS. II. iii. 7.

percept and every concept can be made to indicate the Absolute. The Upaniṣads prefer to direct our attention to it through terms like tvam or aham denoting the subject, for unlike other terms they, besides dispelling all doubt about its being, afford a better clue to its nature.[1] When such terms are combined with another like tat or Brahman in an assertive proposition like Tat tvam asi or Aham Brahma asmi, the reference to Reality becomes ensured. For the attributes which they respectively connote of the individual and of the cosmic subject—such as the bondage of the one and the freedom of the other—being mutually incompatible,[2] our mind abandons the explicit sense of the terms, and travels beyond those attributes to that in which they are grounded (nirviśeṣa-vastu) as constituting the true import of the proposition. The dropping of these attributes, we should add, signifies little because they are but illusive barriers erected by Māyā between the jīva and Īśvara. It should also be pointed out that we do not here identify the ground of one set of attributes with that of the other, for such identification would be meaningless without some difference equally real between them. To avoid this implication we merely deny the distinction between the two, so that what the proposition in strictness means is that the jīva is *not other* than Brahman.

The advaitic Absolute is not merely indefinable; we cannot know it either, for the moment it is made the object of thought it becomes related to a subject and therefore determinate. That is another important reason why the idea of Īśvara or saguṇa Brahman is rejected as inadequate to be the true goal of philosophy which the Advaita, like the other Indian doctrines, views as not merely arriving at a speculative notion or a conceptual formula of the ultimate reality, but to realize what it is in itself. The ideal of the determinate

[1] Cf. *Naiṣkarmya-siddhi*, iii. 100–3. All objects alike reveal being (sat) of some type or other. The subject which cognizes them reveals not only being but also thought (cit). Thus we may say that the Advaita recognizes kinds as well as degrees of reality.

[2] As other examples of distinction between the two, we may mention the following: The jiva's knowledge has many limitations, while God is all-knowing; God is mediately known, while the jīva is immediately realized.

Brahman has been elaborated in thought and it therefore remains a reality for thought. It is Brahman in 'an empiric dress'—the Absolute as it appears to us, and not as it is in itself. Its internal self-discrepancy to which we have drawn attention is in fact the result of its relation to thought. It is, as it is expressed, jñeya Brahman or Brahman that can be known. In itself, it excludes all relations (asaṁsṛṣṭa), including that between subject and object, and is therefore unknowable. But though it cannot be known it can, as we shall point out presently, be realized.

One should therefore be careful in understanding what exactly is meant when the Upaniṣads describe Brahman as nirguṇa and therefore as indefinable and unknowable. It is not in every sense beyond the reach of words. To suppose that it is so would be to deprive the Upaniṣads of the whole of their purpose. Even granting that the negative definition is the only possible one, it does not follow that the nirguṇa Brahman is a blank.[1] For all propositions directly or indirectly refer to reality and negation necessarily has its own positive implication. As a matter of fact, however, the Advaitins assign Upaniṣadic statements like neti neti—'Not this, nor that'—a secondary place while the primary place is given to those like Tat tvam asi, which point to the reality in us as the ultimate. That is, the negative statement is not to be understood in isolation, but along with positive ones like Tat tvam asi. Negation is only a preliminary to affirmation.[2] It means that the Absolute is not conceived here objectively—as merely inferred from outer phenomena; but as revealing itself within us.[3] This alters totally the significance of the negative description, for we are thereby constrained to admit not only its positive character but also its spiritual

[1] Being the Absolute in the true sense of the term, it may appear as 'nothing' to the dull-witted (manda-buddhi) as Śaṁkara says (see com. on *Ch. Up.* VIII. i. 1). Compare: 'I still insist that for thought what is not relative is nothing'—Bradley: *Appearance and Reality*, p. 30.

[2] See *Saṁkṣepa-śārīraka*, i. 250–6.

[3] If an objective reality be negatively described and all knowable features are abstracted from it, we may conclude that there is nothing of it left behind. The observation that 'pure being is pure nothing'

nature. It is not thus a bare or contentless being for which the Absolute stands here. Nor should the statement that Brahman is unknowable lead us to regard the doctrine as agnostic. It, no doubt, rules out all discursive thought as inapplicable to Reality; but it does not represent it as extra-empirical—as something wholly outside the world of experience. The nirguṇa Brahman is not the negation or the antithesis of the saguṇa, but is its very truth and is immanent in everything that goes to constitute it. Hence every aspect of experience, whether on the subject or object side, reveals it. Indeed irrepressibility (svayaṁ-prakāśatva) is its very essence and, like the sun behind a cloud, it shows itself in a sense even in being hidden. We seem to miss it ordinarily on account of the bewildering mass of appearances. But that is like not seeing the ocean for the waves. It is true that it cannot be grasped as an object of knowledge. But there may be other ways of 'experiencing' it; and the whole tenor of the advaitic theory of perception as well as its scheme of practical discipline, to which we shall refer in the next section, shows that there is such a form of experience and that we can 'know' Brahman by being it. This higher type of experience is not altogether unfamiliar to us. There are moments, though all too rare, when we transcend ourselves and when even the experience that is being lived through is not cognized. We pass in it not only beyond common consciousness in which the thought of self is implicit, but also beyond explicit self-consciousness to where thought merges in experience. It may be taken as a distant analogue of the attitude of the sage who, having through long discipline learnt to feel his identity with all that exists, at last succeeds in passing beyond even that state, and losing sight of the objective world and of himself as such, is straight away installed within Reality. That constitutes the consummation of Advaitic teaching.

Though the ideal of the saguṇa Brahman is thus inadequate

may accordingly apply to another form of Advaita which is named Sattādvaita, in contradistinction to the Ātmādvaita of Śaṁkara, and takes mere Being (sattā-sāmānya) to be the Absolute. See *Naiṣkarmya-siddhi*, iii. 101.

to be the ultimate of philosophy, it must not be regarded as useless. We have already seen how it furnishes an ethical ideal by following which the disciple can rise above his congenital limitations and acquire that moral fitness which is indispensable for success in achieving the advaitic goal. Even from the purely theoretic standpoint, it is not without its own value, as is shown for instance by the method followed in the Advaita. This method, we know, starts with the more or less diverse worlds as given in individual experience and discovers as their basis a common one. Systematizing the variety that is manifest in it, it then arrives at unity. And it is only afterwards, since this world of unity in diversity is itself an appearance on the reasoning adopted above, that the doctrine concludes to the spirit which lies beyond it as the sole reality. The contradictions and anomalies of ordinary experience have at first to be resolved at least in the seeming orderliness signified by the ideal of the saguṇa Brahman, if we are to reach the advaitic ultimate unerringly. Without the synthesis effected in it or, to express the same thing differently, without the jīva's avidyā being universalized as Māyā, we would land ourselves in subjectivism reducing the world to a mere private show, for there would then be no reason for postulating anything beyond what is present to individual consciousness. The Advaitin's criticism of the saguṇa Brahman should accordingly be understood as showing only the inadequacy of that conception to serve as the goal of philosophy and not as signifying that it is valueless.[1] But its value is restricted to the empirical sphere—a view which is entirely in consonance with the general advaitic position that practical utility need not rest on metaphysical validity. It is this distinction that has given rise to what are familiarly known as the 'two grades' of teaching in the Advaita—the higher one of the nirguṇa Brahman (para-vidyā) and the lower one of the saguna (apara-vidyā).

[1] See Śaṁkara on *Ch. Up.* viii. i. 1 and *Kalpa-taru*, I. i. 20.

IV

Since mokṣa, according to Śaṁkara, is not a state to be newly attained, but is the very nature of the self, we can hardly speak of a means in its ordinary sense for achieving it. It is realizing what has always been one's own innate character but happens for the time being to be forgotten. The Upaniṣadic statement is 'That thou art,' not 'That thou becomest.' The common illustration given here is that of a prince, brought up as a hunter from infancy, discovering afterwards that he is of royal blood.[1] It involves no becoming, for he has always been a prince and all that he has to do is to feel or realize that he is one. We might illustrate the point equally well by referring to the distinction between a solar and a lunar eclipse. In the latter, the light of the sun is actually cut off from the moon by the earth coming between it and the sun, so that the passing off of the eclipse signifies a real change in the condition of the moon, viz. the part that was enveloped in darkness becoming lit. In a solar eclipse, on the other hand, the luminary continues to be during the eclipse exactly as it was before or will be afterwards. It only appears to be eclipsed because the intervening moon prevents it from being seen as it really is. The re-emergence of the bright sun accordingly means no change whatsoever in it, but only a moving farther away of the moon or the removal of the obstacle preventing the sun from showing itself as it is. Similarly in the case of advaitic mokṣa, all that is needed is a removal of the obstacle that keeps the truth concealed from us and the discipline that is prescribed is solely with a view to bring about this result. It is therefore only in a negative or indirect sense that we can talk of attaining mokṣa here. Empirical life being entirely the consequence of an adhyāsa, the obstacle is ajñāna and it is removed through its contrary jñāna. The jñāna that is capable of effecting it should be, for the reasons mentioned more than once before, direct or intuitive (sākṣāt-kāra); and it should refer to one's own identity with Brahman, for it is the forgetting

[1] Śaṁkara on *Bṛ. Up.* II. i. 20.

of this identity that constitutes saṁsāra. Such knowledge is the sole means of liberation. Neither moral perfection nor religious acts are required as direct aids to it. The cultivation of the will and the purification of the affections are of course necessary, but they are only aids to jñāna,[1] not to mokṣa. It means that the morally impure will not seriously set about acquiring the saving knowledge. When once jñāna arises, it does of itself dispel ajñāna and the simultaneous revelation of spirit in all its innate splendour is mokṣa. To state the same in another way, ethical improvement and religious discipline are necessary for mokṣa but not enough. That is what is meant by karma-saṁnyāsa as advocated by Śaṁkara. The conception of jīvan-mukti is the logical result of such a view of the world and of escape from it. If knowledge is the sole means of release from bondage, freedom should result the moment it is gained; and there is nothing in the psychical or other equipment of the human being which renders its acquisition impossible here and now.[2]

The discipline is to be undergone in two stages—one, preliminary which qualifies for entering upon the serious study of the Advaita; and the other, Vedāntic training proper which directly aims at self-realization. Of these, the former is identical with karma-yoga as explained in the chapter on the Gītā and its aim is the cultivation of detachment. The latter consists of śravaṇa, manana and nididhyāsana. These have been already explained in the chapter on the Upaniṣads, but it is necessary to restate the position calling attention to what is peculiar to the Advaita. (1) *Śravaṇa*. This is study and discussion of the Upaniṣads with the assistance of a *guru*

[1] VS. III. iv. 26.

[2] The only other level of existence where the self can be realized according to the Upaniṣads is Brahma-loka or the world of Brahmā (*Kaṭha Up*. II. iii. 5), the mokṣa thus achieved being designated krama-mukti as stated in the chapter on the Upaniṣads (p. 74). It results, according to the Advaita, from the combination (samuccaya) of Vedic karma with meditation upon the saguṇa Brahman regarding it as the highest reality, either because the disciple does not know there is a higher one or because, knowing it, he feels himself unequal to the task of realizing it.

that has realized the truth they teach. The implication of this requirement is two-fold: First, it signifies that the ultimate philosophic truth is to be learnt through a study of the revealed texts. Secondly, it emphasizes the need for personal intercourse with a competent teacher, if the study is to be fruiful and shows that mere book-learning is not of much avail. (2) *Manana*. This is arguing within oneself, after knowing definitely what the Upaniṣads teach, how and why that teaching alone is true. The main object of this process is not to discover the final truth, for that has been learnt already through śravaṇa, but to remove the doubt (asaṁbhāvanā) that it may not after all be right. It is intended to transform what has been received on trust into one's own true conviction and brings out well the place assigned to reason in the Advaita. The recognition of the value of analytical reflection, we may note by the way, is rather a unique feature in a doctrine which finally aims at mystic experience. (3) *Nididhyāsana*. Manana secures intellectual conviction. But there may still be obstacles in the way of self-realization. For despite such conviction, there may be now and again an unconscious reassertion of old habits of thought (viparīta-bhāvanā) incompatible with what has since been learnt. Nididhyāsana is meant to overcome this kind of obstacle. It is meditation upon the identity between the individual self and Brahman—the central point of Vedāntic teaching. It should be continued till the desired intuitive knowledge arises and that identity becomes immediate (aparokṣa).[1] When it does, one becomes a jīvan-mukta. The ultimate philosophic fact is no doubt to be known through the testimony of the Upaniṣads; but if the knowledge conveyed by it is to bring real freedom, one should verify it by one's own living experience in the form 'I am Brahman' or Aham Brahma asmi.[2] It is this immediate experience or direct intuition of the Absolute, which is described as vidvadanu-

[1] VS. IV. i. 1–2.

[2] Cf. Kim tu śrutyādayo anubhavādayaśca yathā-saṁbhavam iha pramāṇam anubhavāvasānatvāt bhūta-vastu-viṣayatvācca brahma-jñānasya: Com. on VS. I. i. 2. See Dr. Belvalkar: *op. cit.*, p. 14.

bhava to distinguish it from lay experience, that accordingly becomes the final criterion of Truth here.[1]

The jīvan-mukta's life has two phases: It is either samādhi or mystic trance when he turns inwards and loses himself in Brahman; or the condition known as vyutthāna or reversion to common life when the spectacle of the world returns but does not delude him since he has once for all realized its metaphysical falsity. Diversity continues to appear then as the sun, we may say, continues to appear as moving even after we are convinced that it is stationary. A jīvan-mukta experiences pain and pleasure, but neither really matters to him. He does not necessarily give up all activity as is abundantly illustrated by the strenuous life which Śaṁkara himself led,[2] but it does not proceed from any selfish impulse or even from a sense of obligation to others. Blind love for the narrow self which ordinarily characterizes man and the consequent clinging to the mere particular are in his case replaced by enlightened and therefore equal love for all. The basis for this universal love is furnished by the Upaniṣadic teaching 'That thou art.' We should do unto others as we do to ourselves, because they are ourselves—a view which places the golden rule of morality on the surest of foundations. 'Who sees all beings in himself and himself in all beings—he will dislike none,' as the Upaniṣad[3] says; or as the Gītā puts it, 'He harms not self by self.'[4] The common laws of social morality and ritual which are significant only in reference to one that is striving for perfection are meaningless for him.[5] The jīvan-mukta, having transcended the stage of strife, is spontaneously virtuous. Impulse and desire become one in him. He is not then realizing virtue but is revealing it. 'In one that has awakened to a knowledge of the self, virtues

[1] Apart from the question of direct revelation, the Upaniṣads also should in the last resort be regarded as recording only such intuitional knowledge of ancient sages. See Note 4 on p. 182.

[2] Cf *Pañca-daśī*, vi. 270–8. It is interesting in this connection to refer to Śaṁkara's statement at the end of his com. on VS. IV. i. 15, which tradition views as an allusion to his own direct experience of the ultimate truth.

[3] *Īśa Up*. 6.

[4] xiii. 27.

[5] Cf. Śaṁkara on VS. II. iii. 48.

like kindness imply no conscious effort whatsoever. They are second nature with him.'[1] When at last he is dissociated from the physical accompaniments, he is not reborn, but remains as Brahman. That is videha-mukti.

[1] *Naiṣkarmya-siddhi*, iv. 69.

…ER XIV

…(*continued*)

…DVAITA

…ociated with the name of R… …ure is the attempt which it m… …ith the philosophy of the Ab… …th of which can be traced far… …re and in this lies the exp… …its appeal to the cultured as well… …on people. It resembles in this respect the teaching of the Gītā, though it naturally shows greater systematization both on the religious and on the philosophical side. Historically speaking, the elements of thought combined here are distinct. The first of them, viz. theism, is of the Bhāgavata type, inculcating belief in a personal and transcendent God who saves, out of mercy, such as are wholeheartedly devoted to him and are for that reason described as ekāntins ('single-minded'). The second element in the teaching is still older, being based upon the Upaniṣads. Of the two Upaniṣadic views to which we have alluded (p. 62), neither in its entirety proved acceptable to Rāmānuja, but his teaching is more like what is described as Brahma-pariṇāma-vāda[1] than Brahma-vivarta-vāda. The ideas of the unity of ultimate reality and of its immanence in the universe, as also the doctrine that jñāna[2] is the means of salvation, are derived from this source. As to the success with which the two teachings are synthesized here, we shall say a few words later; for the present, it will suffice to mention that the synthesis was not initiated by Rāmānuja, though that should not be understood as minimizing the value of his contribution to the final shaping of the doctrine. The attempt to bring together theism and the philosophy of the Absolute is very old and may be traced even in parts of Vedic literature

[1] See e.g. SB. I. iv. 27.

[2] This, as we shall see, is termed bhakti by Rāmānuja.

itself. We know that a similar synthesis is found in the Gītā where, as in the Viśiṣṭādvaita, it appears with the added feature that the theism is of the Bhāgavata type, not directly traceable to the Veda. The same also is found in one or other of its various phases of growth in the Mahābhārata, especially in the section known as the *Nārāyaṇīya* (p. 100) and in the Purāṇas such as the *Viṣṇu-purāṇa*. Only, in the time of Rāmānuja there was a fresh circumstance, viz. the reaction against the purely absolutist philosophy of Śaṁkara and its seeming negations calling for a new formulation of this old synthesis. There was, for instance, the advaitic identification of the jīva and Brahman which explains the Viśiṣṭādvaita assertion of the reality of the individual or its attempt to give the Hindus their souls back,[1] as Max Müller has put it. It was as a protest against views like these that the doctrine was given out in the South about 1000 A.D., and systematized somewhat later by Rāmānuja.

The sources of authority for the doctrine are two-fold, for which reason it is described as Ubhaya-vedānta; one, the Veda including the Upaniṣads and works like the Purāṇas which are for the most part based upon it; the other, the literature of the South found in Tamil which, though largely indebted to Vedic teaching, undoubtedly contains elements of non-Vedic thought. Of the immediate predecessors of Rāmānuja in this work of synthesis we may mention Nāthamuni (A.D. 1000), none of whose writings, however, has yet been discovered, and his grandson Ālavandār or Yāmunācārya (A.D. 1050), whose several works form splendid manuals of the essentials of the Viśiṣṭādvaita as they were understood before Rāmānuja took up the work of systematization. They are *Āgama-prāmāṇya*, *Mahāpuruṣa-nirṇaya* which is designed to show the supremacy of Viṣṇu as against Śiva, *Gītārtha-saṁgraha*, *Siddhi-traya* and two hymns—*Śrī-stuti* and *Viṣṇu-stuti*. Rāmānuja or the 'prince of ascetics' (yati-rāja), as he is described, is reputed to have been his pupil's pupil and his commentary on the *Vedānta-sūtra*, known as the *Śrī-bhāṣya*, that on the *Bhagavadgītā*[2] and his *Vedārtha-*

[1] SS. p. 189.

[2] The Upaniṣads were not explained by him separately and that work was left for a much later hand—Raṅgarāmānuja.

saṁgraha which gives an independent exposition of the creed, form the chief scriptures of the system. His other works are *Vedānta-sāra*, *Vedānta-dīpa*, *Nitya-grantha*, dealing with forms of worship, and *Gadya-traya*. Of those who came after him, we may note Sudarśana Sūri (A.D. 1300), the author of commentaries on the *Śrī-bhāṣya* and on the *Vedārtha-saṁgraha*. Then came Veṅkaṭanātha, better known as Vedānta Deśika (A.D. 1350), whose many-sided scholarship and long labours contributed much to establish the doctrine of Rāmānuja on a firm basis. First, he formulated even better than his predecessors had done the objections to the Advaita, taking into consideration the defence put up by its exponents since Rāmānuja's time. Not only did he thus render the doctrine stronger on its critical side; he also undertook the task of internal systematization and set aside once for all whatever departures from strict tradition had taken place by his time.[1] His is the second great figure in the history of Viśiṣṭādvaita and the early promise he gave of his future eminence is well indicated by the following blessing which Varadaguru, a famous teacher of the time, is said to have bestowed upon the boy when five years old: 'May you establish the Vedānta on a firm basis, vanquishing heterodox views; may you become the respected of the orthodox and the abode of abundant auspiciousness.'[2] His works are too numerous to mention here. Some of the chief among them are his *Tattva-ṭīkā*, an incomplete commentary on the *Śrī-bhāṣya*, *Tātparya-candrikā*, gloss on Rāmānuja's *Gītā-bhāṣya*, *Nyāya-siddhāñjana*, *Tattva-muktā-kalāpa* with his own commentary upon it called the *Sarvārtha-siddhi* and the *Śata-duṣaṇī* which is a vigorous attack on the Advaita. The *Yatīndra-mata-dīpikā* of Śrīnivāsācārya (A.D. 1700) is a short manual useful for beginners.

[1] Cf. *Adhikaraṇa-sārāvalī*. Introductory stanza, 25.

[2] Pratiṣṭhāpita-vedāntaḥ pratikṣipta-bahirmataḥ:
Bhūyāḥ traividya-mānyaḥ tvam bhūri-kalyāṇa-bhājanam.

I

While Rāmānuja holds in common with many others that knowledge implies both a subject and an object, he differs essentially from them in certain other respects. The most important of these is that discrimination is essential to all knowledge and that it is impossible for the mind to apprehend an undifferentiated object. What is known is necessarily known as characterized in some way, its generic feature being in any case apprehended along with it. The importance of this view we shall appreciate by comparing it for instance with the Nyāya-Vaiśeṣika one of nirvikalpaka according to which isolated reals are all that are apprehended at first (p. 250). According to Rāmānuja, such a stage in perception is a psychological myth and the savikalpaka of the Nyāya-Vaiśeṣika is itself primal. Any analysis of it into simpler elements is the result only of reflection and has nothing corresponding to it in the mental process as it actually takes place. This should not be taken to mean that Rāmānuja does not admit the distinction of savikalpaka and nirvikalpaka; only to him, the two alike involve a complex content. Perceptual experience is termed nirvikalpaka when the object is cognized for the first time. It is primary presentation that does not call up any previous impression of the same. A child sees a cow, let us say, for the first time; even then it sees the object as qualified in some way. When it sees a cow again, the sight of it is accompanied by a revival of the former impression and it is this second or subsequent apprehension[1]—the cognizing of the new in the light of the old—that is described as savikalpaka by Rāmānuja. While 'This is a cow' represents the form of perceptual experience at the nirvikalpaka level, 'This *also* is a cow' does the same at the savikalpaka. Accordingly the psychological development implied by 'determinate' perception is not from the

[1] It is pointed out that if at the second apprehension the former impression is not revived, the knowledge will be only nirvikalpaka and that it will continue to be so till such revival takes place. See VAS. p. 51 (com.).

simple to the complex as in the Nyāya-Vaiśeṣika; rather the complex itself, hitherto new, ceases to be so and becomes familiar through it. To put the same in another way, while according to the Nyāya-Vaiśeṣika only the savikalpaka involves judgment, the nirvikalpaka merely furnishing the material for it, according to the Viśiṣṭādvaita all perceptual experience alike involves it. The savikalpaka does not thereby become the same as recognition (pratyabhijñā): 'This is that Devadatta,' for the latter refers to one and the same object as perceived twice whereas the former arises when different objects of the same type are cognized. In both alike, no doubt, a present object is associated with the revival of a past impression: but while in the savikalpaka it is only the impression of the attributive element that revives, in recognition that of the particular individual (vyakti) also does. Further, though all perception equally entails judgment, recognition includes a specific reference to the distinctions of time and place in which the object is cognized on the two occasions. It is not only at the primal stage of perception that the unqualified object (nirviśeṣa-vastu) is not known; all jñāna, including that of the ultimate reality, is necessarily of an object as complex (saguṇa).[1] This constitutes a radical difference from Śaṁkara, who represents the Upaniṣadic ultimate as nirguṇa (p. 373). 'If the Upaniṣads describe Brahman as without qualities,' Rāmānuja says, 'all that the description can mean is that *some* qualities are denied while there are still others characterizing it.'[2]

To know the nature of jñāna, according to Rāmānuja, it is necessary to understand the classification of ultimate objects which is peculiar to his doctrine. To the well-known distinction between spirit and matter which are respectively termed cetana and jaḍa in Sanskrit, he adds another which is neither. Jñāna is of this intermediate type. It is unlike material entities in that it can unaided manifest itself and other objects neither of which is possible for them. But what it thus manifests is never *for itself* but always for another. That is, it can only show but cannot know. In this latter respect it is unlike spirit, which knows though it is unable,

[1] SB. pp. 70–5. [2] SB. p. 71.

according to the doctrine, to show anything but itself. To take an example from the physical sphere, jñāna is like light, which can reveal the presence of a jar (say) as well as of its own, but cannot itself know either, its revelation of things being always for another. It exists not for itself but for some-one else. Its teleology takes us beyond it. The classification of things here is accordingly not into jaḍa and cetana, but jaḍa ('matter') and ajaḍa[1] ('the immaterial'), where the second term stands for cetana and what is unlike it but is yet distinct from jaḍa. Jñāna pertains to one or other of the two kinds of spiritual entities recognized in the system, viz. jīvas and Īśvara. It is consequently described as dharma-bhūta-jñāna—literally 'subsidiary or attributive jñāna'[2]—which implies that there is substantive jñāna also. The various jīvas and Īśvara are jñāna in this higher sense. They are compared to the flame of a lamp to which belongs and from which proceeds their dharma-bhūta-jñāna like rays. This jñāna is supposed to be eternally associated with a subject—whether jīva or Īśvara—and constitutes its unique adjunct. When it 'flows out,' as it is expressed, from the subject to which it belongs and comes into contact with an object, it is able to manifest that object to it. Throughout mundane existence, it functions in a more or less restricted manner but it ever endures. Even in deep sleep it is; but it does not function then and does not therefore show itself, the theory being that jñāna is known only along with some object or not at all.[3] Then the jīva remains self-conscious along with the unrevealed presence of its dharma-bhūta-jñāna. In dreams, as will be seen in the next section, the actual presence is postulated of the objects dreamt of. Hence jñāna also is then known; but its action being much more impeded than during waking, the knowledge of dream-objects is dim and hazy. In mokṣa, on the other hand, entirely free action is

[1] *Yatīndra-mata-dīpikā* (Ānandāśrama Series), p. 51.

[2] Jñāna, though attributive to jīva or Īśvara, is in itself regarded as a 'substance,' as will become clear later.

[3] In the case of Īśvara the dharma-bhūta-jñāna, being all-pervasive, does not contract or expand; but yet it undergoes transformations. The consequent changes of form are what are meant by divine knowledge, divine grace, etc.

restored to it. It becomes all-pervasive, with the result that there is nothing then which falls outside its range. The liberated soul consequently knows everything. The analogy of the lamp and the rays may suggest that the dharma-bhūta-jñāna is of the same stuff as the jīva or Īśvara, but only appearing in an attenuated form. That, however, is not the view of Rāmānuja, who takes it as a distinct entity,[1] though always associated with and dependent upon another. It is, however, difficult to see the reason for postulating two kinds of jñāna, except it be the desire to make spirit in itself changeless and thus harmonize the doctrine with the teaching of the Upaniṣads whose whole weight, as Śaṁkara is never tired of insisting, is in favour of its constancy (avikriyatva).[2]

Jñāna operates through the manas alone or the manas as assisted by some organ of sense through which it streams out towards its objects which are supposed to be already there. Rāmānuja describes the process of knowing as starting from the soul, then reaching the manas and then, emerging through the senses, meeting the outside objects. When thus it comes into contact with an object, it is stated to assume the 'form' (ākāra) of that object and somehow reveal it to the subject in question. It is clear that the conception of dharma-bhūta-jñāna corresponds to that of the antaḥ-karaṇa in the Advaita, which also is supposed to go out similarly towards objects and assume their form before giving rise to knowledge (p. 345). But while the antaḥ-karaṇa in that doctrine is physical (jaḍa) and requires an extraneous aid, viz. the sākṣin, to transform it into jñāna, this is jñāna in itself. The aids it requires, like the manas and the indriyas, are only for determining its appearance in particular ways—as knowledge of colour, of sound, etc. It is not only knowledge that is regarded as a modification of dharma-bhūta-jñāna;

[1] According to the Nyāya-Vaiśeṣika, the flame comes into being first and the particles of tejas which constitute its rays are supposed to radiate from it afterwards. Cf. SV. pp. 842 f.

[2] That such is the aim will become clear when we consider the case of Īśvara, who by hypothesis is everywhere unlike the atomic jīva, and therefore does not stand in need of any such aid.

internal states like desire and anger are also its transformations, so that they are forms of knowing at the same time.

II

To turn now to the logical implication of knowledge.[1] We have just drawn attention in noticing Rāmānuja's description of the process of knowing to the fact that objects are viewed as existing before they are known. They are therefore to be reckoned as real; and, since they depend in no way upon the self or the knowledge which brings them into relation with it, their reality is not merely relative but absolute. Rāmānuja traces this realistic view to the old teaching of the Veda, using terms in doing so which are reminiscent of the description of knowledge given in the Prābhākara school.[2] In particular, his view is described as sat-khyāti which means that what exists (sat) is alone cognized and that knowledge in the absence of a real object corresponding to its content (yathārtha) is inconceivable. It is not enough for securing the correspondence here meant, if something or other exists outside to serve as a presentative basis. Consistently with Rāmānuja's view that a bare identity is a metaphysical fiction and cannot be known, the character of the object also should be as it is given in knowledge. In other words, the agreement implied in knowledge extends from the *that* (prakārin) to the *what* (prakāra) also of the object presented. While it is easy to understand this position so far as normal perception is concerned, the question will arise as to how it can be maintained in the case of illusions where we seem to have knowledge without corresponding things. Rāmānuja's explanation of them is two-fold:—

(1) In some cases the realistic position is maintained by him on the basis of the Vedāntic doctrine of quintuplication (pañcī-karaṇa) according to which objects of the visible world, which are all compounds, contain all the five bhūtas or elements though in varying proportions (p. 65). Thus in the case of the mirage, what is being looked at is a heated

[1] SB. pp. 183–8.
[2] Yathārtham sarva-vijñānam iti veda-vidām matam. Cf. PP. p. 32.

sandy waste which contains not only pṛthivī, the preponderating part of it, but also ap and the other elements however slight; and the apprehension of water there, we have to understand, is therefore only of what is actually presented to the eye. But such an explanation may do only in cases where the object of illusion, as in the example given, is one or other of the five bhūtas. Illusions, however, are by no means confined to such rare cases. We may mistake shell for silver where neither is itself a bhūta. To explain such cases, Rāmānuja resorts to an extension of the principle underlying pañcī-karaṇa. The illusion of shell-silver is due, among other causes, to the similarity between the two things, viz. their peculiar lustre. This similarity means to Rāmānuja the presence in the shell, though only to an extremely limited extent, of the very substance which constitutes silver. Likeness is to him another term for partial identity of material,[1] and so what is perceived even here is what is actually presented. That is, Rāmānuja justifies his view of sat-khyāti in such cases by pointing to what is a fundamental tenet of his system, viz. the unity of the physical world and the structural affinity that is discoverable among the things that belong to it.

(2) In other cases like the white conch seen yellow by a person with a jaundiced eye a different explanation becomes necessary, for as the yellowness is admitted by all to be there outside the knowing self, viz. in the eye-ball, the point requiring elucidation is not whether it is real but how it comes to be seen as characterizing the conch. The explanation of Rāmānuja, which is based upon the theory of vision current at the time, assumes that the yellowness found in the diseased eye-ball is actually transmitted from there to the conch along with the 'rays' of the organ of sight (nāyana-raśmi) as they travel to it in the process of seeing and that the new colour thus imposed upon the conch obscures the whiteness natural to it. The conch is accordingly supposed to become actually yellow, though only for the time being. Here also then knowledge is of what is given in respect not only of the relata but also of the relation between them. To

[1] Tadeva sadṛśam tasya yat taddravyaika-deśa-bhāk: SB. p. 184.

the objection that if the conch becomes actually yellow others also should find it so, the answer is given that the yellowness here is of too subtle a kind to be perceived by anyone who, unlike the person in question, has not followed it throughout its course of transmission.[1] The explanation is no doubt arbitrary and unconvincing; but what our present purpose requires us to note is the spirit of persistent realism that underlies it, not its scientific correctness. The question will readily occur as to how dreams are to be accounted for. There at least we seem to have experience without corresponding objects existing at the time. The explanation once again is arbitrary and it is stated, now on the authority of the Upaniṣads,[2] that objects like the elephant seen in a dream are not subjective but are present there at the time. 'They are created by the supreme Person (parama-puruṣa),' says Rāmānuja,[3] and adds that the reason for creating such unique things is the same as in the case of objects of the waking state, viz. the providing of *suitable* means for the individual to experience pain or pleasure according to his past karma. 'He creates these objects, which are special to each jīva and last only as long as they are experienced, in order that it may reap the fruits appropriate to the extremely minor deeds of virtue and vice it has done.'[4]

It is instructive to find out the significance of this twofold explanation. The yellow-conch and the dream-elephant are objects solely of individual experience; and though not unreal they last only as long as the illusion lasts and can, in the nature of the case, be testified to only by the person that sees them. The illusion of the mirage or the shell-silver also in a sense has reference to particular individuals; but the water and the silver perceived there by one, because they by hypothesis persist even after the illusion is over as actual parts of what is presented, are verifiable by all. This shows that Rāmānuja distinguishes two classes of objects—one which is cognized by all or many and may

[1] The analogy is here adduced of a small bird soaring in the sky which he, that has followed its course from the moment it began to fly, is able to spot easily but not others.

[2] *Bṛ. Up.* IV. iii. 10.

[3] SB. III. ii. 3.

[4] SB. III. ii. 5.

therefore be called 'public,' and the other, special to single persons and may therefore be termed 'private.' But it must be distinctly understood that such a classification does not mean that he admits different types of reality—an admission which would place his doctrine epistemologically on the same footing as Śaṁkara's Advaita (p. 350). In fact, it is in denying that there is such a distinction that he formulates the doctrine of sat-khyāti. In point of reality, private and public objects differ in no way. Both alike are outside and independent of knowledge, and both are absolutely real. A thing's being private does not take away from its reality. Our pains and pleasures are personal to each one of us, but they are not the less real on that account.

However diverse the explanation in the two cases and whatever we may think of its scientific value, it is clear that the aim of sat-khyāti is to show that jñāna, including the so-called illusion, never deviates from reality and that even in the case of objects whose existence can be vouched for only by individuals, there is no ideal or purely subjective element. If all knowledge be equally valid, it may be asked how the distinction between truth (pramā) and error (bhrama), which is universally recognized, is to be explained. It may appear to us from the examples cited above that error here is incomplete knowing. Thus in the case of the yellow conch, it is caused by our failure to comprehend its whiteness or, more strictly by our overlooking the fact that it is obscured. The omission and the consequent error are clearer still in the case of another example given[1]—the 'firebrand-circle' (alāta-cakra) where a point of light, owing to its rapid movement, is mistaken for its locus, because while the fact that it occupies every point on the circumference is apprehended, the other fact that the occupation takes place successively and not simultaneously is altogether lost sight of. But we must remember that there may be elements of omission, according to the doctrine, even in truth. When for instance we perceive shell as shell, there is by hypothesis present in it silver, but it is ignored quite as much as the shell aspect is when the same object is mistaken for silver.

[1] SB. p. 187.

Similarly in the case of the desert when we cognize it as such, our mind lets slip the element of ap supposed to be contained in it. The fact is that while sat-khyāti postulates that only what is given is known, it does not admit that all that is given is known. Knowledge, no doubt, is always of the given and of nothing but the given; but it need not be of the *whole* of what is given.[1] It would not, therefore, be right to conclude that error in general is incomplete knowing. Since completeness like validity fails to differentiate truth from error, Rāmānuja enunciates a new principle, viz. that for knowledge to be true in its commonly accepted sense it should, in addition to agreeing with outside reality, be serviceable in life. When the mirage and the shell-silver are described as false, what we have to understand is not that water and silver are not present there, for in that case we could not have become conscious of them at all, but that they are not such as can be put to practical use. The distinction between truth and error comes thus to be significant only from the practical standpoint; from the theoretical one, it does not exist. All knowledge without exception is valid and necessarily so, but such validity need not guarantee that what is known is adequate to satisfy a practical need. A geologist may correctly adjudge a piece of ore as golden; but it does not mean that a bracelet (say) can be made out of the metal in it. This is the significance of including in the definition of truth not only yathārtha or 'agreeing with outside reality,' but also vyavahārānuguṇa or 'adapted to the practical interests of life.'[2] If knowledge should conform to vyavahāra, it should satisfy two conditions. It must, in the first place, refer to objects of common or collective experience. It is deficiency in this respect that makes the yellow-conch and the dream-elephant false. Because their being private to a particular individual is overlooked at the time, they

[1] The peculiar view upheld in sat-khyāti, however, makes one thing certain. There can be no errors of commission. Here is a point of agreement between Rāmānuja's sat-khyāti and Prabhākara's akhyāti. The two are not, however, identical. Compare Vedānta Deśika's description of the former as akhyāti-saṁvalita-yathārtha-khyāti in SAS. pp. 403–7.

[2] *Yatīndra-mata-dīpikā*, p. 3.

are confounded with the corresponding objects of the waking state; and this deficiency when discovered exposes their falsity. In the second place, it should comprehend the preponderating element in the object presented. The object we call shell may contain silver, but the shell part predominates in it; and it is this predominance that explains its being put to use as the one and not as the other. The silver, though certainly present, does not count practically on account of its slightness (alpatva); and this feature when discovered reveals the erroneous character of the knowledge in question. Pramā not only apprehends rightly so far as it goes, but also goes far enough to be of service in life. Bhrama also is right so far as it goes; but it does not go far enough and therefore fails to help us in the manner in which we expect it to do. So when erroneous knowledge disappears and truth comes to be known, as Rāmānuja's commentator says, the object (artha) is not negated but only activity (pravṛtti) is arrested.[1] The discovery of error, as we said in connection with Prabhākara's view (p. 317), affects the reactive side of consciousness, not its receptive side.

Two important corollaries follow from such a view. The practical activities of life do not require a complete knowledge of our surroundings. It is enough if we know them approximately fully. In other words, purposive thought is selective, not exhaustive; and partial or imperfect knowledge is not necessarily a hindrance to the attainment of the common ends of life. The doctrine also recognizes a social or inter-subjective side to knowledge. So far as theoretic certainty is concerned, there is no need to appeal from the individual to common consciousness; for, as we have more than once remarked, it is in the very nature of knowledge without reference to its being peculiar to one or common to many to point to reality; but its serviceability depends upon the general though tacit testimony of society—upon the 'common' sense of mankind. These observations are sure to suggest a likeness between the doctrine of sat-khyāti and what is now known as Pragmatism. Both recognize the instrumental character of knowledge and adopt practical

[1] Jñāna-phala-bhūta-pravṛtti-bādhyatvam: SB. (com.) p. 185.

utility as the criterion of truth. But there is one important difference. Rāmānuja admits the cognitive value of knowledge apart from the practical, whereas Pragmatism in its familiar form makes no such distinction. Even in error, there is some revelation of reality so that in adopting the pragmatic attitude he does not relinquish the logical. In fact, knowledge according to him has not one but two functions to perform—to reveal reality and to serve the purposes of practical life. Both are equally important; and if either is to be emphasized more than the other, it would undoubtedly be the former. In other words, Rāmānuja, unlike the pragmatist, is interested in truth for its own sake and values knowledge 'more for the light it brings than for the fruits it bears.'

The theory which we have so far sketched very much alters the nature of the epistemological problem. The question to be decided about knowledge is not whether it is logically valid or not—for by deficiency in this respect knowledge would lose its very title to that name—but whether it has or has not a bearing upon practical life. In other words, it is not quality that varies in knowledge but relevancy. If we take this along with what was stated above, viz. that even truth commonly reveals reality only incompletely, we see that the sat-khyāti doctrine contains the suggestion of an ideal form of knowledge which is not only valid and has practical value but is also complete or all-comprehensive. This ideal of perfect knowledge, which we may deduce from the premises of sat-khyāti, is actually recognized by Rāmānuja as characterizing the jīva in mokṣa. Throughout saṁsāra, jñāna operates under limitations for defects of one kind or another interfere with its free activity. Consequently common knowledge, including pramā or truth, only half reveals reality. Its full revelation is possible only in mokṣa when all deficiencies are overcome and all possibility of 'error' is removed. Man's vision then becomes extended to the maximum. 'It blossoms to the full,' enabling the liberated to know everything fully and as it is.[1]

As regards pramāṇas, Rāmānuja recognizes only three:

[1] Compare the kevala-jñāna of Jainism (p. 159).

perception, inference and verbal testimony. His conception of the first from the psychological as well as the logical standpoint has already been explained, and there is nothing of importance to be noted about the second. In regard to verbal testimony, Rāmānuja follows the Mīmāṁsakas in general and holds that its subject-matter is special to it—what never falls within the range of the other two pramāṇas. In agreement with the other Vedāntins he also maintains logical validity for assertive equally with injunctive propositions. Though resembling Śaṁkara in his views so far, he differs from him in other respects. It will suffice to refer to two of them here. The Veda, we know, is in two sections, which seem to contradict each other in what they teach; and, since both alike are looked upon as revealed, it becomes necessary for every school of Vedānta to explain their mutual relation in some manner. According to Śaṁkara, the two are really antithetical, and he gets over the antithesis between them by assuming that they are addressed to different classes of persons (adhikārin). The karma-kāṇḍa is intended for one who is still under the spell of avidyā and the jñāna-kāṇḍa, for one that has seen the hollowness of the activities it commends and is striving to transcend them. What is desirable and true from a lower standpoint is thus undesirable and not altogether true from the higher. Such a gradation of the teaching is permissible according to the Advaita with its belief in the relativity of prāmāṇya (p. 359). Rāmānuja does not admit any such antithesis, and maintains that the two portions of the Veda together form but a single teaching intended for the same class of persons. They are complementary to each other in the sense that the uttara-kāṇḍa dwells upon the nature of God and the pūrva-kāṇḍa upon the modes of worshipping him.[1] But such a co-ordination of the two sections, it must be added, presupposes that the pūrva-kāṇḍa is to be understood in the spirit of the Gītā teaching and that the various karmas taught in it are to be performed not for obtaining their respective fruits but for securing God's grace.[2] In thus attaching equal logical value to the two sections of the Veda, he differs not only from

[1] *Yatīndra-mata-dīpikā*, p. 27. [2] See Note 2 on p. 332.

Śaṁkara but also from the Mīmāṁsaka who subordinates (p. 299) the Upaniṣads to the Brāhmaṇa portions (karma-kaṇḍa) of the Veda. The exact bearing of this view on the practical discipline prescribed in the Viśiṣṭādvaita for the attainment of mokṣa, we shall consider later. The second point of difference is that Rāmānuja reckons not only the Veda as revealed but also the Pāñcarātrāgama[1] regarding the whole of it, unlike Saṁkara, as eventually going back to a Vedic or some equally untainted[2] source. The āgamas deal, generally speaking, with the worship of idols, particularly in temples; and the Pāñcarātrāgama, as distinguished from the Śaivāgama, is devoted to establishing the supremacy of Viṣṇu.[3]

III

Rāmānuja recognizes as ultimate and real the three factors (tattva-traya) of matter (acit), soul (cit) and God (Īśvara). Though equally ultimate, the first two are absolutely dependent upon the last, the dependence being conceived as that of the body upon the soul. Whatever is, is thus the body of God and he is the soul not only of inorganic nature but also of souls or jīvas.[4] It is in this connection that Rāmānuja formulates the relation,[5] so important in his system, of apṛthak-siddhi or 'inseparability' which obtains between

[1] To all appearance, Bādarāyaṇa is against āgama. Compare Śaṁkara on VS. II. ii. 42–5.

[2] This is known as the Ekāyana-śākhā. See SB. (com.) p. 559 (Madras Edn.).

[3] The Vaikhānasāgama, which also upholds the supremacy of Viṣṇu, seems to exhibit closer kinship with the Veda.

[4] Since according to Rāmānuja inorganic matter also is ensouled, God is its self only mediately through the jīva (see VAS. pp. 30–1). Yet he is sometimes spoken of as being so directly. Cf. *Rahasya-traya-sāra*, iii. pp. 121–2 (Bangalore Edn.).

[5] The Nyāya-Vaiśeṣika postulates the relation of samavāya between things that are inseparable. The Viśiṣṭādvaita discards this relation as superfluous and views inseparability itself, which it regards as the nature (svarūpa) of the two relata, as apṛthak-siddhi. Strictly it is not therefore a relation (see SB. II. ii. 12); but it is still sometimes spoken of as a saṁbandha. (Cf. SAS. p. 590.)

substance and attribute and may be found between one substance and another. It may be described as the pivot on which his whole philosophy turns. It is parallel to, but not identical with, the Nyāya-Vaiśeṣika samavāya. The two agree in so far as the relata which they bring together are regarded as quite distinct and real; but while samavāya (p. 235) is an external relation, the conception of apṛthak-siddhi is that of an internal one. The example given in illustration of it, viz. the relation between body and soul, brings out clearly its intimate character. The body is defined by Rāmānuja as that which a soul controls, supports and utilizes for its own ends.[1] Matter and souls, being the body of God, are to be regarded as directed and sustained by him and as existing entirely for him. The inseparable unity of matter, souls and God—the first two being entirely subject to the restraint of the third in all their forms—is the Brahman or Absolute of Rāmānuja. Since Rāmānuja identifies the relation here involved with that between the body and the soul, his conception of the Absolute may be described as that of an organic unity in which, as in a living organism, one element predominates over and controls the rest. The subordinate elements are termed viśeṣaṇas and the predominant one, viśeṣya. Because the viśeṣaṇas cannot by hypothesis exist by themselves or separately, the complex whole (viśiṣṭa)[2] in which they are included is described as a unity. Hence the name 'Viśiṣṭādvaita.'

This conception of unity may be illustrated by taking a common example like a 'blue lotus.' Here the blueness is quite distinct from the lotus, for a quality cannot be the same as a substance. But at the same time the blueness as a quality depends for its very being upon a substance—the lotus here, and cannot therefore be regarded as external to it. The complex whole of the flower in question is, in this sense of *necessarily* including within itself the quality of blueness, spoken of as a unity. It will help us to understand this view well if we contrast it with those of some other

[1] SB. II. i. 9. This intimacy of relation is expressed thus—niyamena ādheyatvam, niyamena vidheyatvam, niyamena śeṣatvam.

[2] Cf. SB. p. 132 (com.): Viśiṣṭāntarbhāva eva aikyam.

schools. Rāmānuja recognizes a real distinction between the quality of blueness and the substance of lotus. Hence his view differs from the Advaita for which all distinctions are alike only apparent. It differs likewise from the Nyāya-Vaiśeṣika though maintaining a real distinction between the two entities, because it regards that they are not external to each other. But this should not lead us to think that Rāmānuja, like Kumārila (p. 323), advocates the bhedābheda view for he does not admit identity of any kind whatsoever between the entities supposed to be distinct, the unity affirmed being only of the complex whole.[1] The term 'Viśiṣṭādvaita' is more usually explained in a somewhat different manner—especially in interpreting verbal statements affirming unity like Tat tvam asi. But the idea underlying it is the same. If we take the proposition 'The lotus is blue,' the quality of 'blueness' according to this explanation, because of its attributive character, points necessarily to some substance to which it belongs. This blue substance is a complex whole. The lotus also may similarly be looked upon as a complex whole, comprising the attributive element of 'lotus-ness' and a substance which it characterizes. The identity that is expressed by the proposition is of these two complexes.[2] Or, in other words, the two terms—'blue' and 'lotus'—have distinct meanings but refer to the same substance (prakāryadvaita). What is signified is not therefore a bare identity which excludes the viśeṣaṇas. It includes them and it is their difference that calls for an affirmation of identity in the above sense. Otherwise we may be misled into thinking that the two complexes are distinct. In the example that we have taken, there is only one viśeṣaṇa. There may be several, which again may be co-existent or may appear in the viśeṣya successively. When for instance we think of a youth whom we knew as a child, the two viśeṣaṇas due to distinction of age appear one after the other; but they do not lie outside the unity of the individual in question. Such identity is found not only in the case of substance and its attributes as the above examples may suggest but also in that of substance and its modes, e.g. clay and jar. In fact, it obtains wherever we

[1] Cf. SB. pp. 75, 204–5; VAS. pp. 50, 97–8.

[2] SB. p. 132.

have inseparable correlatives. Of two such entities, the major member is designated prakārin; and the minor, prakāra.

The central point of the teaching of the Upaniṣads, according to Rāmānuja, is the unity of Brahman in this sense; and he, like Śaṁkara, cites in support of his view the two kinds of co-ordinate propositions that occur in them—one, affirming the identity of the soul and Brahman, and the other, that of Brahman and the material world. But he differs totally from him in their interpretation. Before stating his explanation of them, we must briefly refer to another aspect of the doctrine. According to Rāmānuja all things that are, are eventually forms or modes (prakāra) of God. Similarly all names are his names,[1] so that every word becomes a symbol of God and finally points to him. This deeper significance of words, described as vedānta-vyutpatti, is what only the enlightened comprehend. According to it no word ceases to signify after denoting its usual meaning, but extends its function till it reaches the Supreme.[2] In fact, it is only the latter that is conceived as the essential significance of a word. Now let us select for illustrating Rāmānuja's interpretation the well-known Upaniṣadic maxim—Tat tvam asi. The term tvam in it which commonly stands for the jīva really points to God who is the jīva's inner self (antaryāmin) and of whom the jīva and, through it, its physical body are alike modes. What the term tat means in it is also the same, but viewed in a different aspect, viz. God as the cause of the universe, as shown by the context in which it occurs in the *Chāndogya Upaniṣad*. The identity meant by Tat tvam asi, according to the explanation of the term viśiṣṭādvaita given above, is of these two complexes—God as the indweller of the jīva and God as the source of the world. The final import of the statement is that though the world and the individual souls are real and distinct, the Absolute in which they are included is one.[3] 'They are eternal with God but are not external to him.' In the advaitic interpretation of the same, the distinction due to the viśe-

[1] Some exceptions are made. See SB. pp. 205–7.
[2] Aparyavasāna-vṛttiḥ śabda-vyāpārah. Cf. VAS. p. 36.
[3] SB. pp. 198–9.

ṣaṇa elements is rejected as but an appearance though, as we have tried to show, no identity as such is taken to be implied by it (p. 374). Here the distinction is not denied; and, at the same time, the organic unity of the whole is affirmed.

This is only a general account of the Viśiṣṭādvaita view of Reality. To state the same now more in detail: Rāmānuja recognizes, as it is clear by now, the distinction between substance and attribute; but the attributes are not further distinguished, as in the Nyāya-Vaiśeṣika, into guṇa, karma, jāti, etc.[1] and are comprehensively termed adravya or 'what is other than substance.' There are thus only two main categories of which the second, adravya, is always and necessarily dependent upon the first, dravya, although neither, in consequence of the unique relation that obtains between them, can be or be thought of apart from the other.[2] The adravyas are reckoned as ten. Five of them are the qualities of the five bhūtas—sound, etc.—and the next three are the guṇas in the special sense of sattva, rajas and tamas, which are the characteristics of matter (ạcit) or prakṛti. Three of the adravyas are thus general; and five, specific. Of the remaining two, śakti or 'potency' is that property of a causal substance by virtue of which it produces the effect, e.g. plasticity in clay, attractive power in a magnet, burning capacity in fire. The tenth adravya is saṁyoga, by which is meant as in the Nyāya-Vaiśeṣika an external relation like that between the floor and a jar.

Not only is adravya distinct from dravya in this system; the dravyas themselves are to be distinguished from one another. But what is a dravya?[3] According to the Viśiṣṭādvaita conception, whatever serves as the substratum of change is a dravya. It means that Rāmānuja accepts the pariṇāma-vāda or sat-kārya-vāda. But it is the attributive elements (viśeṣaṇa) alone that change, for which reason the

[1] Karma or action is explained as mere disjunction and conjunction and therefore as expressible in terms of saṁyoga and its opposite, vibhāga. Jāti, as in Jainism or in the Sāṅkhya-Yoga, is only a certain disposition of the several parts constituting the thing. Abhāva is conceived positively as in the Prābhākara school.

[2] Pṛthak-pratipatti—sthityanarha: SB. p. 205.

[3] SAS. p. 590.

complex whole (viśiṣṭa) is also spoken of as undergoing modifications. The substantive element (viśeṣya) in itself is changeless. God viewed as the viśeṣya is changeless and the soul also is so,[1] but the dharma-bhūta-jñāna which belongs to them changes. Matter, which is entirely a viśeṣaṇa, itself changes.[2] The relation between it and its transformations, say, clay and jar is, as already pointed out, apṛthak-siddhi. But if we consider a lump of clay (piṇḍa) which, and not mere clay (mṛt), is regarded here as the material cause of the jar, the relation between them is stated to be identity (ananyatva, literally, 'non-difference'). Whatever difference there is between the two is explained away as the material is the very same, though the disposition of its constituent parts in them may differ.[3] There are six dravyas answering to this description; and they are divided into two classes—jaḍa and ajaḍa, as already explained. The jaḍa includes prakṛti and time (kāla); and the ajaḍa—dharma-bhūta-jñāna, nitya-vibhūti or śuddha-sattva, jīva and Īśvara. We shall now add a few words of explanation regarding each of these:—

(1) *Prakṛti*.—This is the dwelling-place of the soul and, through it, of God himself. Nature is thus alive with God. 'Earth's crammed with heaven, and every common bush afire with God.' We shall best understand its character as conceived in this system by contrasting it with the Sāṅkhya view of it with which it has much in common. The chief differences are: (i) The three guṇas—sattva, rajas and tamas—are supposed in the Sāṅkhya to be its constituent factors, and prakṛti is merely the complex of them all. Here, on the other hand, the guṇas are conceived as characterizing it so that they are distinct although inseparable from it. (ii) The prakṛti of the Sāṅkhya is infinite, but here it is taken to be limited in one direction, viz. above, by the nitya-vibhūti of which we shall speak presently. (iii) in the Sāṅkhya, prakṛti is theoretically independent of the puruṣa, but here it is entirely under the control of spirit, i.e. jīva or Īśvara. The relation between them is apṛthak-siddhi so that neither

[1] Not all viśeṣaṇas therefore change, though whatever changes is necessarily a viśeṣaṇa. [2] SB. III. ii. 21. [3] SB. II. i. 15.

admits of separation from the other. Owing to this difference, Rāmānuja's conception of prakṛti is much superior to the Sāṅkhya one. The entities evolved out of prakṛti and the order of their evolution are exactly as stated under the Sāṅkhya.

(2) *Kāla.*—Time is viewed here as real; but it is not outside the sole reality recognized, viz. Brahman or the Absolute, though it does not merge in it. So it does not subsist by itself, as it does according to the Nyāya-Vaiśeṣika (p. 229). Nor is it but a phase of prakṛti as in the Sāṅkhya-Yoga (p. 270). Time also, like prakṛti of which it is the companion, so to speak, admits of change or undergoes pariṇāma; and moments, days, etc., are represented as its evolutes. Unlike time, space is derived from prakṛti and is included only through it in the highest reality. Of prakṛti and time, neither can be said to be prior to the other; but the same cannot be said of space, for prakṛti is prior to it.

(3) *Dharma-bhūta-jñāna.*—As we have already dealt with this, only a few words need be added now. It characterizes jīvas or Īśvara and is always, as its name indicates, secondary to them, the relation between them being inseparable. It is conceived as both a dravya and a guṇa[1]—a dravya inasmuch as it, through contraction and expansion,[2] is the substrate of change; a guṇa inasmuch as it is necessarily dependent upon a dravya, viz. jīva or Īśvara and cannot be by itself. It is knowable as in the Nyāya-Vaiśeṣika, but by itself and not through another jñāna (p. 251), for it is self-luminous and shows itself though it cannot become self-conscious.

(4) *Nitya-vibhūti.*—We have seen that prakṛti is characterized by the three guṇas. If of these we leave out rajas and tamas and conceive of it as characterized only by sattva, we get an idea of nitya-vibhūti and see why it is called śuddha or unalloyed sattva. On account of this peculiar character, it ceases to be material (jaḍa) and becomes 'immaterial' (ajaḍa) in the sense already explained. It is sublimated prakṛti, a sort of super-nature. Since, however, the three guṇas are represented here as constant attributes or qualities

[1] The term guṇa here means 'secondary' and does not bear the significance which it does in the Nyāya-Vaiśeṣika.

[2] SB. p. 83.

of prakṛti and not as its constituent factors as in the Sāṅkhya, it becomes hard to imagine how any *one* of them can alone be conceived of as a characteristic when the contrast of the other two is removed. Further, according to the explanation given, prakṛti and nitya-vibhūti possess a common feature, viz. sattva, and therefore prakṛti also to that extent should be non-material. In that case its entire separation from the ajaḍa category would not be quite accurate. These discrepancies are in all probability to be explained as due to the system being eclectic in its details, and have led the later Viśiṣṭādvaitin to differentiate between the two sattvas and declare that they are altogether distinct (vilakṣaṇa).[1] Except in this important respect, nitya-vibhūti is similar to prakṛti. Briefly it is the material out of which the things of the ideal world, and the bodies of God and of the liberated souls are made. It is 'matter without its mutability' and has been described as a fit means to the fulfilment of divine experience.[2] The domain of nitya-vibhūti is limited below by prakṛti but is infinite above. Vaikuṇṭha, the city of God, is supposed to occupy a part of it. Though a sharp demarcation is made between prakṛti and nitya-vibhūti, the latter, it is stated, is found within the region of the former as for instance in the holy idols worshipped in sacred places like Śrīraṅgam, those idols being viewed as permeated through and through by this material. The reverse cannot happen and prakṛti does not encroach upon the region of nitya-vibhūti.

(5) *Jīva.*—In dealing with dharma-bhūta-jñāna, we have already referred to the nature of the jīva. It is of the essence of spirit and has dharma-bhūta-jñāna always associated with it. In these respects consists its essential affinity with God. The jīva is not here, as in the Advaita, merely the assumed unity of individual experience, but an eternal reality. In its natural condition of mokṣa, its jñāna expands to the maximum, reaching the ends of space, and there is nothing then which it fails to comprehend. In saṁsāra as a whole the jñāna is more or less contracted, but never absent,

[1] See Vedānta Deśika: *Rahasya-traya-sāra.*

[2] Prof. P. N. Srinivasachari. *Rāmānuja's Idea of the Finite Self* (Longmans), p. 62.

not even in deep sleep where it only ceases to function and does not therefore reveal objects. The jīva itself, apart from its jñāna, is viewed as of atomic size—a mere point of spiritual light, and its functioning in places where it is not, as for example in seeing distant things, is rendered possible by the expansion and contraction of its dharma-bhūta-jñāna. 'Though monadic in substance it is infinite in intelligence.'[1] The jīva is not merely sentience; it is also of the essence of bliss. This aspect of the jīva's nature again will remain more or less obscured in saṁsāra, becoming fully manifest only when liberation is achieved. The diminution in its capacity to know or to enjoy is temporary; when released, it is restored to its omniscience and eternal happiness. The jīva with its physical body derived from prakṛti and with God for its indweller is the meeting-point, so to speak, of the material and the divine which explains the gulf which often separates man's ideal aspirations from his actual life. The jīvas are infinite in number, and in addition to those that are on their trial here (baddha) or have already achieved their salvation (mukta), the doctrine recognizes what are described as nitya which have never been in bondage. They are beings like Viṣvaksena who have from all time been attending upon God. Each jīva is in reality both a kartā and a bhoktā, i.e. an active and purposeful being. It is also free and God, who is its 'inner ruler immortal,' must be supposed to control it without interfering with the freedom that belongs to it.[2]

(6) *Īśvara.*—The conception of God also in the system has by this time become clear, rendering it unnecessary to say much about it now. Īśvara too is of the nature of spirit or intelligence and is of the essence of unsurpassed bliss.[3] Like the jīva, he also possesses dharma-bhūta-jñāna whose transformations constitute his several psychical states. Owing however, to his omnipresence, there is really no need for such an aid in his case; and its postulation is intended solely to secure constancy to spirit in itself. The term Īśvara is used in a double sense. First, it stands for the entire universe

[1] Prof. P. N. Srinivasachari: *op. cit.*, p. 26.
[2] VAS. pp. 139–42.
[3] VAS. p. 249.

with all its spiritual and material elements included in it. In this sense, Īśvara may be thought of in two stages—as cause and as effect. In dissolution (pralaya) he subsists as the cause with the whole of the universe latent in him; in creation (sṛṣṭi), what is latent becomes manifest. Subtle matter becomes gross; and souls, expanding their dharma-bhūta-jñāna, enter into relation with physical bodies appropriate to their past karma. The causal form includes within itself everything that is required for the development signified by creation, so that Īśvara is the whole and sole cause of it. In other words, God is self-determining and the universe develops from within unassisted by any external agency (p. 82). It is because he *grows* into this cosmic variety that he is called 'Brahman' (p. 54). That would ascribe change to God which is against the prevalent teaching of the Upaniṣads; but Rāmānuja tries to explain the difficulty away by holding that the change is only to be secondarily understood—as sa-dvāraka. God does not suffer change in himself, but only through the entities comprehended in the whole of which he is the inspiring principle. But it is not easy to see how he can be said to remain changeless when his inseparable attributes are changing. This Īśvara in himself, regarded as the unchanging centre of the changing universe, is the other meaning of the term. Such an Īśvara of course does not exist isolated by himself, but it is still legitimate to make the distinction because the viśeṣya element in the Absolute, like the viśeṣaṇas, is real and ultimate. In the former sense, Īśvara is the Absolute of Rāmānuja; in the latter, he is the antar-yāmin and dwells within whatever is —whether soul or matter.

This absolutist view which is chiefly based upon the Upaniṣads is intertwined in the system with the details of a theistic creed which, historically speaking, goes back to a different source. In that phase, God is conceived as completely personal. He is looked upon as having pity for erring man and as actuated by a desire to show mercy to him. Benevolence, indeed, is one of his essential features. He is known as Nārāyaṇa or Vāsudeva, and the latter designation is a sign of the presence in the doctrine of elements drawn from the

Bhāgavata religion. He is also known as Para or the Supreme. In this form he dwells in his own citadel Vaikuṇṭha which, as we said, occupies a corner in the domain of nitya-vibhūti. He manifests himself in various ways to help his devotees: One of the most important is known as vyūha. It is fourfold: Vāsudeva—a differentiation within Para Vāsudeva and therefore to be distinguished from him—Saṁkarṣaṇa, Pradyumna and Aniruddha. They are all incomplete manifestations, and God appears in them in different garbs. Another way in which the Supreme manifests himself is as avatārs (p. 98) which are well known. They are classed together as vibhava. Still another manifestation is known as the antaryāmin whose presence within is common to all the jīvas and who guides them like a friend.[1] It is God incorporate—possessing a rūpa—and should be distinguished from the one referred to above which bears the same name and which, as taught in the *Bṛhadāraṇyaka Upaniṣad*,[2] is the essence (svarūpa) of God.[3] The last of the manifestations, called arcāvatāra, is as holy idols worshipped in sacred places like Śrīraṅgam.

Now as regards the success with which the two teachings have been assimilated here: The attempt, so far as it aims at identifying the ultimate of philosophy with the ultimate of religion, has its undoubted excellences. But it is one thing to think of the two as the same and quite another to try combining a particular philosophic doctrine with a particular religious creed. The theistic creed that finds place in the present synthesis had, as the result of its long history, developed a host of concrete details, not all of which for lack of adequate rational support could fuse with philosophy. The philosophic doctrine included in it was, on the other hand, the result of one of the most daring speculations in the whole field of thought; and its conception of Reality was the least personal. Hence there are some discrepancies in the doctrine resulting from the synthesis, such as those we had occasion to mention in speaking of the notions of antaryāmin and nitya-vibhūti. Another instance of the

[1] *Yatīndra-mata-dīpikā*, p. 88.
[2] II. vii.
[3] See *Rahasya-traya-sāra*, v. pp. 283–4.

same disaccord is found in what we shall point out in the next section, viz. the retention in the doctrine of the 'esoteric restriction' of the saving knowledge of bhakti by the side of the popular pathway to release of prapatti. The fact is that the Vaiṣṇava religion was there in all its completeness in the time of Rāmānuja. As a practical creed, it had indeed served human needs in an excellent manner and given rise within its fold to more than one saint of pre-eminent mystical power. But it lacked support from the Upaniṣads and this lack of support should have become the more conspicuous after Śaṁkara had expounded them in a specific manner. The attempt made in the Viśiṣṭādvaita was to secure for Vaiṣṇavism the needed support. It was thus practical exigency rather than any organic connection between the two teachings that led to their synthesis. We may illustrate best the resulting discrepancy by reference to the conception of the Absolute in the system. Rāmānuja admits several ultimate entities, but holds at the same time that there is only one Being—that of the viśeṣya, all the attributive elements deriving their being from it.[1] If all these entities are existentially one, it is difficult to see how the distinction between them can be ultimate. It is just this lack of independent being that the Advaitin means when he denies reality to elements of diversity in the Absolute.[2] If to avoid the above difficulty we assume that each viśeṣaṇa has its own *separate* being, the absoluteness of the Absolute vanishes and it will be hard to think of it as a unity except in a secondary or figurative sense. The only other alternative is to define the relation between the several entities constituting the Absolute as bhedābheda, thus predicating both identity and difference of them. But such an explanation, even supposing it is logically sound, is, as already pointed out, totally unacceptable to Rāmānuja. The notion of apṛthak-siddhi on which the conception is based is as imperfect as that of the Nyāya-Vaiśeṣika samavāya which it is intended to replace. The only difference is that while samavāya tries

[1] Cf. SB. II. ii. 31. See also the discussion of this point by Raṅgarāmānuja in his com. on *Muṇḍaka Up.* I. i. 3.

[2] See Note 1 on p. 353.

to unite what are supposed to be distinct, apṛthak-siddhi tries to separate what is supposed to be one. Both alike represent efforts to seek what it is not possible to have, viz. a half-way house between inclusion and exclusion. The system, so far as it is based on Vaiśṇavism, endeavours to secure ultimate reality for the souls as well as matter; but loyalty to the Upaniṣads drives it to modify it, thus rendering the result logically unsatisfactory.

IV

As in the Advaita, the practical discipline here also begins with karma-yoga in the Gītā sense, which purifies the heart and fits a person for knowing the truth; but it is quite different in what follows. The training that is distinctive of the Viśiṣṭādvaita is two-fold:—

(1) *Jñāna-yoga.*—This means meditation upon the jīva after knowing its true character through śravaṇa or study of the scriptures under a proper *guru.* Those only that have achieved success in karma-yoga can enter upon it. Its object is to realize how the self is different from its several accompaniments like the body, senses and so forth with which man usually identifies it and how attachment to them impedes spiritual progress. When this yoga is carried to fruition, the discipline does not terminate, for according to Rāmānuja, the jīva though an ultimate fact is not the Ultimate. The disciple may have succeeded in realizing his nature in relation to the physical environment; but there yet remains the task of discovering the same in relation to God, the highest fact of the universe. Man cannot, according to Rāmānuja, know himself truly until he knows God. The means prescribed for such knowledge is termed bhakti-yoga.

(2) *Bhakti-yoga.*—This marks the culminating stage of the discipline. It presupposes a reasoned conviction regarding the nature of God as taught in the Viśiṣṭādvaita, and those alone that have successfully pursued jñāna-yoga in the sense just explained can begin it. Bhakti here is equated with dhyāna and may therefore be taken as upāsana or meditation taught in the Upaniṣads, provided we remember that it

implies also love. It is not a mere austere concentration of the mind on Reality, but a loving contemplation of a personal God.[1] There is also another implication in it which is equally the result of the conception of the jīva characteristic of the doctrine, viz. the feeling of one's absolute dependence (śeṣatva) upon God as the sole power in the universe. Bhakti-yoga also thus consists in meditation like jñāna-yoga; but it is meditation that is suffused with feelings of love and dependence. Success in this part of the discipline results in the attainment of what may be described as divine vision, actual mokṣa resulting when the soul is severed from the probation of flesh. This is in accordance with the ancient ideal of finding release in a life hereafter, and no jīvan-mukti as such (p. 19) is recognized here as in Śaṁkara's Advaita.

Another important difference from the Advaita is that the obligation to perform karma is not a feature of the preparatory stage only. It continues even when one enters upon bhakti-yoga, so that the ideal of karma-saṁnyāsa as known to the Advaita (p. 339) is rejected here. Man should never abandon karma of the nitya variety or unconditional duties, for he will then become sinful and miss salvation on account of neglecting what is enjoined in the Veda. So far Rāmānuja agrees with Kumārila. But there is here the positive purpose that bhakti, which has been described as 'salvation in becoming,'[2] might grow through karma and ripen into intuition. Adherence to karma in this stage is not therefore for subjective purification as in the earlier one, but for advancing further and further in the life of the spirit. And karma, with its purpose thus transformed, will continue till the very end, for the immediate experience of God is not believed to arise until the moment before departing this life. The discipline for mokṣa thus consists of both jñāna and karma; yet it is the former alone that is regarded as the *direct* cause of release, the latter being taken to be only an accessory and not a co-ordinate aid. Hence, though insisting upon the performance of karma throughout life, the Viśiṣṭādvaita like

[1] Cf. Sneha-pūrvam anudhyānam bhaktiḥ. Quoted in SB. p. 35 (com.).

[2] IP. vol. ii. p. 705.

the Advaita (p. 379) does not advocate what is known as samuccaya-vāda.[1] Before we close this topic we must draw attention to the widening in its scope which karma undergoes in the system. It includes not only whatever is prescribed in the Veda but also prayer and devotional worship as understood in Vaiṣṇavism (kriyā-yoga).[2]

As in the other Indian systems, mokṣa is conceived here also as freedom from mundane existence. But over and above this is the idea here of reaching a supra-mundane sphere and there enjoying in the presence of God the highest bliss. The imperfect prākṛtic body of the jīva is then replaced by a perfect one, so that release does not mean here a disembodied state as it does in many another doctrine. It is this ideal world—'the Highlands of the blest'—that is constituted out of śuddha-sattva. Picturesque descriptions are given of the place. There God is seated on his white throne and is served by his consort Lakṣmī—interceding on behalf of man—and by all the souls of the nitya and mukta variety. It is a place of absolute peace and perfection, and the joy of all there lies in following the will of the Supreme. When a bound soul is liberated, it is led to this region and, welcomed by all there, it is at last received by God as his very own. An account of the triumphal progress of the spiritual pilgrim till he arrives at the throne of the Lord is given in the first chapter of the *Kauṣītakī Upaniṣad*.

This is the normal or regular means to release. But a person, to follow it, must belong to one or another of the three higher castes of Hindu society; for it is only such that are qualified to receive instruction in the Veda and the Upaniṣads. So the course described heretofore becomes considerably narrowed in its usefulness. The Viśiṣṭādvaita therefore recognizes along with it another pathway to God which any one, irrespective of caste or rank, may follow. That is known as prapatti.[3] The word is derived from *pra-pad*, meaning 'to take refuge with' or 'to piously resign,' and points to a belief that salvation is obtained through free grace. It is described as śaraṇāgati or flinging oneself on God's compassion. It consists in absolute self-surrender,

[1] SB. III. iv. 26. [2] Cf. VAS. p. 5. [3] See *Gadya-traya*, iii.

and signifies a resolve 'to follow the will of God, not to cross his purposes, to believe that he will save, to seek help from him and him alone and to yield up one's spirit to him in all meekness.'[1] In one of its forms described as 'resignation in extreme distress' (ārta-prapatti), it is believed to bring deliverance immediately. A single moment of seriousness and sincerity is considered enough; and this also testifies, in the eyes of the Viśiṣṭādvaitin, to its superiority over bhakti which means a long and laborious process of training. The inclusion by Rāmānuja in his doctrine of a means to salvation which is accessible to all, explains the wide popularity it has always commanded; and the social uplift of the lower classes to which it has led is of great value in the history of India. But it is outside our purpose to dwell upon that aspect of the Viśiṣṭādvaita at any length. Rāmānuja attaches so much importance to prapatti that he makes it essential to bhakti also in its final stages.[2] He maintains that it represents a form of knowledge and is not therefore in conflict with the Upaniṣadic view that jñāna alone is the means of release—an explanation rendered necessary by prapatti being the distinctive characteristic of Vaiṣṇavism rather than of the Vedānta. The prominent place given to it in the teaching shows the need for absolute self-suppression whatever course of discipline a person may follow. Though zealously upholding the persistence of personality, Rāmānuja commends the cultivation of an attitude which makes one feel and act *as if* that personality did not exist. He means thereby that it is not belief in a permanent self but selfishness which is the enemy of true life.

[1] Ānukūlyasya saṁkalpaḥ prātikūlyasya varjanam:
Rakṣiṣyatīti viśvāsaḥ goptṛtva-varaṇam tathā:
Ātma-nikṣepa-kārpaṇye ṣaḍvidhā śaraṇāgatiḥ.

[2] See com. on BG. xviii. 66.

INDEX